DUTCH IMMIGRANT WOMEN
IN THE UNITED STATES,
1880–1920

Dutch Immigrant Women in the United States, 1880–1920

SUZANNE M. SINKE

UNIVERSITY OF ILLINOIS PRESS
URBANA AND CHICAGO

Publication of this book was supported by a grant from
the Statue of Liberty–Ellis Island Foundation
© 2002 by the Board of Trustees
of the University of Illinois
All rights reserved
Manufactured in the United States of America
C 5 4 3 2 1
∞ This book is printed on acid-free paper.

Library of Congress Cataloging-in-Publication Data
Sinke, Suzanne M.
Dutch immigrant women in the United States, 1880–1920 /
Suzanne M. Sinke.
p.   cm. — (Statue of Liberty-Ellis Island Centennial series)
Includes bibliographical references and index.
ISBN 0-252-02731-0 (cloth : alk. paper)
1. Dutch American women—Social conditions—19th century.
2. Dutch American women—Social conditions—20th century.
3. Immigrants—United States—Social conditions—19th century.
4. Immigrants—United States—Social conditions—20th century.
5. Protestant women—United States—Social conditions—19th century.
6. Protestant women—United States—Social conditions—20th century.
7. Sex role—United States—History—19th century.
8. Sex role—United States—History—20th century.
9. United States—Emigration and immigration—Social aspects.
10. Netherlands—Emigration and immigration—Social aspects.
I. Title. II. Series.
E184.D9S56   2002
305.48'83931073'09034—dc21   2001006007

CONTENTS

ACKNOWLEDGMENTS

Academic work is based on debts. For me the first debt is to my parents, for standing by me through the process of finishing this work. My second debt is to my partner for his ongoing good nature and willingness to share housework and child care. On the academic side I have many to thank. Two fellowships from the U.S. Department of Education for Foreign Language and Area Studies, along with one fellowship from the Dutch Ministry of Education, made it possible for me to learn Dutch. The Dutch language faculty at the University of Minnesota assisted me well beyond that. My special thanks go to Hinke van Kampen, who made sure my Dutch improved in Amsterdam as well as in Minneapolis, and Klaas van der Sanden, who made me a better translator of nineteenth-century texts. A McMillan Fellowship from the University of Minnesota allowed me to spend a year doing research in the Netherlands. Henriëtte Schatz and Caroline Smits at the P. J. Meertens Institute in Amsterdam both assisted me greatly in working with the materials there and in interpreting language shift. The staff of the International Institute and Archive for the Women's Movement in Amsterdam put up with my protracted presence with equanimity. Annemieke Galema extended hospitality and did joint research with me in Leeuwarden. Robert P. Swierenga, my mentor from my master's degree, offered encouragement and advice at various points in the process. And at the University of Minnesota Rudolph Vecoli, director of the Immigration History Research Center, provided a stimulating atmosphere and ongoing opportunities to discuss immigration issues generally as well as insightful comments on my own work. Several colleagues at the Social Science History Computer Lab at the University of Minnesota, Stephen Gross, Matt Sobek, Cathy Fitch, and Jim Brown, assisted me with census abstracting and calculations. Terry Meinke provided pictures and lots of family information. Janet Sjaarda Sheeres offered invaluable raw data on women from Groningen as well as genealogical tips. Linda Kerber helped in tracking down Iowa laws, as well as piquing my interest in legal differences. The staff at Heritage Hall, Calvin College, helped me in various ways. In particular I wish to thank Herbert J. Brinks and Zwanet Janssens for their extraordinary efforts. Larry Wagenaar and other staff at the Joint Archives of Holland offered a nice atmosphere as well as some hints on sources in their collections. Various individuals read and commented on parts of the manuscript or on conference papers which then made their way into this text. Of those, I want to give special thanks to Donna Gabaccia, Robert P. Swierenga, Hartmut Keil, Hasia Diner, David Gerber, Sara Evans, Kathryn Kish Sklar, Mary Jo Maynes, Ann Waltner, Caroline Smits, Walter Kamphoefner, Conrad Bult, and Herb Brinks. What remains, warts and all, is still mine, but it is a better product for their assistance.

* * *

Unless otherwise specified, all translations in the text and the notes are my own.

DUTCH IMMIGRANT WOMEN
IN THE UNITED STATES,
1880–1920

INTRODUCTION

Perspectives on Migration

"The Dutch expect a lot of their women." With these words my grandmother warned my mother about what she could expect if she carried through her plan to marry a second-/fourth-generation Dutch American. There was more than a bit of truth in those words and this book helps explain why. This is a story, a history if you will, of Dutch Protestant immigrant women in the United States in the period from 1880 to 1920. It is a story told in large part through the words of those involved. For while there are many histories of the Dutch in America, few pay much attention to women. Yet the story goes beyond the boundaries of this group or this period. It is also an instructive tale of gender, and what happens to it in the process of migration. One of the basic laws of migration, one which people have not noticed often, is that it rearranges gender roles.[1] To describe how people put those roles back together, sometimes replicating, sometimes revising, sometimes totally reformulating their ideas of what women and men should do, I use the term *social reproduction*.

The parameters of the study developed over a period of years. I originally chose to study the Dutch because of my own ethnic roots, and then I branched into women's history when I found that no one had studied women within this group. The religious division replicated much of the historiography on the Dutch, and with good reason. The predominant form of Dutch American ethnicity that developed in the United States, and particularly the variety of patriarchy it entailed, came out of the Dutch Calvinist tradition. In many ways the experience of Catholic Dutch immigrants replicated that of these Protestants, but in important ones such as relations to other ethnic groups it did not. Non-Christian Dutch immigrants were few and their experiences quite different. So I kept the focus on Protestants. Within the Protestant designation there were still variations, and the differences between the (Dutch) Reformed and Christian Reformed denominations, the two major Dutch American churches, provided a spectrum on which to make comparisons between competing traditions and forms of adaptation.[2]

The chronological focus on the turn of the century I chose for several reasons. Dutch migration to the area of the United States divided into three distinct periods. The first, beginning in 1609 and continuing through the colonial period, was important in gaining an American foothold for the Dutch (making Dutchness seem American) and later in the efforts of the descendants of the colonial Dutch to assist a second wave of migration which began in the late 1840s and extended up to World War I. Otherwise, there was little continuity between these two movements. The two in turn had a similar relation to a third wave in the post–World War II period.[3] My chronological focus fell in the second wave. Within that I chose the post-1880 era, which coincided with some of the heaviest migration and which occurred during a time when a series of women's issues appeared in political and personal debates. I ended with 1920, when the second wave of Dutch (as well as other European) immigration to the United States was coming to a close with changes in the international economic scene and (in the following four years) with restrictive legislation, and when women in both the Netherlands and the United States had just succeeded in attaining the vote on a national level—the peak of a woman's movement in both countries. With this time frame and group focus, then, I sought to explore women's adjustment from one location to another.

Gender roles interweave into extended familial networks, communities, and entire societies, hence they could not migrate intact. The closest people came to replicating them was in mass communal migration, such as several Dutch Seceder congregations undertook in the mid-1800s, where entire congregations moved across the Atlantic and settled together in a new location. Yet even for them, new circumstances required men and women to do things differently than in the past. For those who came as individuals and families later in the century, the shifts were more pronounced. Much of the everyday activity done by Dutch immigrant women a century ago sought to replicate, adjust, rearrange, and sometimes totally recast the kinds of activities they had learned to do as women. The same could be said for men, though we know much more about the kinds of remunerated work men took on and about quite a number of their communal and societal roles.[4] For that reason I chose to focus on women. Within a generation or two gender roles could settle back into something akin to normal fluctuations and shifts. The changes would subsequently come from within the culture. For the first generation and a half at least, however, immigrants paid more conscious attention to trying to re-create their roles. Sometimes they chose to reconfigure them. Sometimes they had no choice. Studies of both the parameters and the choices form the bulk of this work.

For many Dutch immigrant women, and other immigrant women I would argue, migration meant a greater variation in roles than they would have experienced had they remained in their homeland. It also meant challenges to their ideas of proper gender behavior. Women reacted along a spectrum, with some embracing new opportunities and others working valiantly to maintain older traditions, often with great success. Because these migrants entered the United States in a period in which educational and employment opportunities for women were expanding rapidly, and in which they tended to see some of these changes in the United States rather than in the Netherlands (where such changes were taking place as well), their perception of the "new world" included a notable gender component. Based on a number of other studies of immigrant women in the period, I would argue that for young women, most notably those who migrated alone but also those who came as the generation and a half (daughters of migrating parents), the turn of the century, with its economic opportunities, skewed demographics, and cultural constructs, offered a particularly fluid screen on which to play out new gender roles.[5] Immigrant women of other groups, most often in cities, were the forerunners in these areas. Still, the Dutch had some representatives among the ranks of those who embraced new causes and careers.

The majority of Dutch immigrant women, however, came at a stage in their lives where many opportunities applied to their children only. Married, children in tow: these were more often characteristics of the migrants in this group. The women went about their daily lives in new circumstances. The Dutch were one of the most rural of immigrant groups in this period, moving more often than most in rural to rural tangents.[6] They concentrated in ethnic enclaves in various areas of the Midwest and beyond. This clustering made some aspects of re-creating community life easier. Yet it still took time and energy to reestablish bonds.

To create a picture of Dutch immigrant women's lives I adopt a strategy of concentric circles, examining first women's lives at home: family ties and the necessities of life (food, clothing, shelter).[7] Someone who utilized terminology from Friedrich Engels might call these biological reproduction. I find that a useful term, though the activities I describe in those chapters go beyond the basics of keeping people alive. A further circle entails activities which clearly tied the home with realms outside its boundaries: work for wages and unremunerated work to avoid spending, and informal and eventually formal health care issues. A larger circle of life in the community encompasses two more chapters: education and worldview, and finally the role of churches in women's lives. To describe many of these activities, and to explain the elaborations of the earlier chapters, I use a term which some sociologists use: social reproduction. It combines a number of other concepts, including kinship work, housework, status enhancement, and the work of caring and integration.[8] None of the activities were automatically limited to women, though in Western societies women have tended to do many of them more often than men. Without those activities there would be no families, communities, churches, and most everything else in society. Most importantly, I uncover how women's work patterns compared before and after migration. For each chapter I include the story of one woman in somewhat greater depth, illustrating some of the key issues for that section. Most were unusual in some way, if only that they left sufficient records to create a brief life sketch.

While each individual could tell her own story, there were also larger patterns of what happened to women's roles for this ethnic group in this time period, which also offer suggestions about what we know about immigrant women's roles generally. Historians know a great deal more about immigrant women now than when I began doing research on Dutch Protestants in the early 1980s. At that time, scholars looked at women within families, and were just beginning to look beyond the bounds of women's roles as wives and mothers. In the intervening years the focus shifted more outside the home, and then to integrated works such as this one. Several issues came out of that literature which I incorporated into my research.

One was the debate over how conservative immigrant women are, because so much of the material on some groups, Germans in particular, indicated women were the arch-conservators of tradition. Were they traditionalists "contented among strangers," to use the title of one work, or was this the "land of freedom" where women no longer had to shovel manure?[9] It was obvious that the answer was both, depending on the individual and her circumstances. The hard part came in determining who would choose which path and what factors made that possible. On average I could describe Dutch women as relatively conservative in adjusting gender roles, but not if they came as single young women. This also corresponded with the second image of immigrant women from this time period, as innovators, working-class pioneers in leisure, dress, and work organization. Scholars sometimes refer to this as generational difference. I suggest we need to look much more closely at the point in the life cycle at which a woman emigrated. This was the first of five factors I found most instructive in charting women's adaptation to a new culture. The second was the degree of ethnic clustering in their new home, particularly of her extended family members. This was a defining feature of whether women could re-create many familial and social networks, and of the degree of control which the ethnic group could place upon its young adults. Third, proximity to urban areas largely dictated the degree to which women were exposed to "dominant" American roles and various opportunities. Fourth, class made a major difference in perceptions and opportunities. It translated into education for girls and certain leisure activities for women. Adult women who were already part of a bourgeois life in the Netherlands generally did not like migrating, while young women from this background were the ones most likely to take advantage of American educational and career opportunities. Women's place in the ethnic/racial hierarchy of America, the fifth factor, was often invisible, yet it was a stiking determinant of opportunities from the ability to migrate at all to marriage options to job possibilities. There were other factors as well, time period, rank in sibling order, personality, etc., which also factored in, but I found these five (age and marital status at migration, family and ethnic clustering, rural/urban location, class, and race) most pertinent.[10]

In making these suggestions about what influenced women's adjustment I imply that at the least one of them, age and marital status, was more important for women than for men, though I will not try to prove both sides of the gender question in this book. Instead I will pay a fair amount of attention to what researchers sometimes call the generation and a half, that is, those children who migrated with their parents but who still had memories of the old world, and to the second generation. It was among these daughters (more so than sons) that the generational gap was most strongly also a cultural one surrounding gender roles. Here, the familial and communal values of European roots conflicted with more individualistic American ones.[11]

Sources and Methods

To find out anything about Dutch Protestant immigrant women I needed sources not simply about them but by them. In this I was fortunate, for the Dutch were a literate people by the end of the nineteenth century. They wrote letters and sometimes diaries, and family members and archives saved some of them.[12] The best of these collections offered an extra boon, for at Calvin College the collections included the correspondence of entire families, which sometimes went in both directions across the Atlantic.[13] I examined those where women were prominent correspondents in the turn of the century period, but I did not limit my research to women's letters. Instead I used the family collections, which allowed me to find out more about events and activities from different perspectives.[14] Sometimes the differences in perceptions even between husband and wife were considerable.[15] In addition I picked up a few family histories, papers, articles, and other writings which also contained letters, and gleaned stories out of them.

Further, a group of Dutch dialectologists out to find the remnants of nineteenth-century speech traveled the United States in the 1960s, recording interviews with Dutch Americans as they went.[16] While their purpose was not historical research as such, they asked open-ended questions about how people lived, what they did, and how they coped with various shifts in setting and language. I had full access to those interviews at the P. J. Meertens Institute in Amsterdam. In some ways using someone else's oral history collection infuriated me, for there were so many unasked follow-up questions, so many other things I would have liked to know. But that collection opened up the words of nearly three hundred Dutch Americans, many in their eighties or nineties in 1966, whom I could no longer meet. Through the eyes of age they described a world they remembered, sometimes vaguely, sometimes well. In particular, they described what they knew about language and language shifts.

For additional information, and to verify certain patterns, I sought out other types of sources. The church consistory records were nearly as difficult to access as they were rich in information which rarely made its way into other sources. The reports of church discipline cases offered another side of life in a patriarchal world that continued to set its beat to another drummer than the American legal system, one much more akin to early colonial New England.[17] Newspapers from the Dutch community added insight into reading and advertising patterns, as well as providing a Dutch counterpart to American prescriptive literature. Records of church groups and other women's organizations brought in ideas of women's organizational lives. Finally, I sought out the U.S. Census Public Use Sample from 1910 and other published quantitative sources, to see if what I read in letters, which was "real" in the perceptions of those involved, was also borne out in numbers.

To find out what difference immigration made in Dutch Protestant women's lives I also needed to know about the world from whence they came. In the Netherlands that meant looking into conditions in the countryside, particularly of the areas of highest emigration. And it required special attention to the history of women in those areas. In the United States it required examining research both on Dutch Americans and on women. Like the literature on many immigrant groups, that on the Dutch generally ignored women, while the literature on women ignored migrant women for the most part until recently.[18]

In order to place these women's experiences in focus, I chose to utilize the theoretical concept of social reproduction. Sociologists have used the term with somewhat differing definitions. It developed out of economically based models, challenging them to include nonwaged activities. Yet I was not interested in developing an "economic woman" to complement "economic man," both making their decisions in life based on the bottom line. Rather, I wanted a framework to describe a variety of roles in re-creating families, networks, and communities. The closest description I found to what I wanted to include under this rubric was by Dutch feminist Anja Meulenbelt, in what she termed *de koesterende funktie. Koesteren* translates variously as 'to nourish', 'to care', 'to nurse', and 'to cherish'.[19] Thus my definition went beyond the basics of biological reproduction and activities necessary for the reproduction of people, to the way in which people carried out activities from child socialization to cooking to household work arrangements. Beyond that, I incorporated what anthropologists have called kinship work, that is, the creation and maintenance of ties to family members.[20] And then I went one step further, to the creation and maintenance of ties to friends and to community building. These together constituted what I term social reproduction.

Placing this in the context of international migration meant creating an ethnographic portrait.[21] It also meant including the variables of change of place and change over time into that portrait—no easy task. I sought in doing this to keep in mind that social reproduction was only a label for the activities, not a program which stated that conservative values would dominate. This deserves stress: social reproduction as I use it does not simply mean reproducing what people had known. In order to understand what a woman might reproduce, one must know the background as well as the new setting. Hence I provide only a quick overview of the situation in the Netherlands and of Dutch migration in the following section. In each of the subsequent chapters I describe both the before and after of migration related to particular themes. The transatlantic approach is hardly new, but it is imperative in uncovering social reproduction.[22]

The Netherlands and Migration

At the turn of the twentieth century the Netherlands was caught up in a major political organizational shift which would eventually result in pillarization [*verzuiling*]. Just as the Dutch-descended in South Africa helped put *apartheid* in place along racial lines, those in the Netherlands used religious divisions to separate society, and in the process to brand organizations working for class solidarity as evil. Under pillarization, society divided into Catholic and Protestant (later subdivided) and eventually nonconfessional "pillars." In this system of vertical segregation, which lasted into the 1950s, schools, hospitals, unions, newspapers, political parties, and in general much of daily life divided according to pillar. The Netherlands was unusual in the degree to which these divisions be-

The provinces of the Netherlands, 1900

came part of the political landscape. Abraham Kuyper, a theologian and head of the (orthodox Protestant) Anti-Revolutionary party became prime minister at the turn of the century, and his party became and remained a major political force in this period, pushing for such divisions. Emigrants were often followers of Kuyper and his movement.

Between 1880 and 1920 several measures broadened the electorate in the Netherlands, and the government generally took a more active role in family life. The confessional (Catholic and Protestant) parties managed what historian Siep Stuurman called a "moralization" of Dutch society. They were not always successful in their stress on family rights, nor did the leadership's adamant antifeminism prohibit the burgeoning of women's organizations both within and outside church ranks in this period.[23] But the parties did codify a variety of measures which broadened the reach of what was "political": laws concerning school attendance and support, child labor, women's wage labor, and bans on abortion and on distributing information concerning contraception. They also obtained state support for institutions run by religious organizations.

Many problems facing society had their roots in the economic transformation taking place in this period, whereby factory work and large-scale, mechanized agriculture overtook home production and family farming.[24] Even the elite slowly realized that for many, wages as seamstresses, washerwomen, or in factories were insufficient for survival. Vincent van Gogh, who portrayed life on the land in gloomy yet poignant canvases, wrote his brother in 1883: "a woman, no matter how good and noble she is by nature, if she is without means and is not protected by her family, is in the great and immediate danger, in my opinion, in today's society, of sinking into the maelstrom of prostitution."[25] Economic developments differed regionally, particularly according to the soil type, but in general the mechanization of agriculture and the consolidation of holdings to increase efficiency in the late nineteenth century sparked a major exodus of people from the countryside to the cities of the Netherlands, and in some cases to the shores of America.

The Dutch had international migration rates below most of their European neighbors, since the Netherlands had served as a country of immigration for much of the nineteenth century.[26] The changing economic structure late in that century created unease for a significant proportion of the Dutch population which ranked in the middle class and had its base in business and trade. Middle-class organizations formed to assist, pacify, and control a growing (and threatening) working class. Middle-class women's groups set out to fight what they recognized as ills of a stratified society which practiced a double standard: prostitution and the ban on paternity suits by single mothers.[27] Prior to 1880 many young women in the cities (specifically domestics) either had been born in the city or had immigrated from other countries (notably, France and Germany); after 1880, the number of young women from the Dutch countryside coming to the cities rose rapidly.[28] It was partly to avoid such a shift from rural to urban life that some rural families sought the relatively better agricultural opportunities of the United States. They came into a Dutch American world already well established.

The histories of nineteenth-century Dutch immigration to America usually begin in the late 1840s with Albertus van Raalte, the dominie (minister) who brought his congregation of Seceders to the "wilds" of western Michigan and founded Holland. Dominie Hendrik P. Scholte led his congregation to the prairie where they founded Pella, Iowa, at about the same time. Several other Seceder congregations followed and settled around these hubs, making them the seats of two major colonies of Dutch America. The Seceders were followers of the pietistic revival in the (quasi-state) Reformed Church. They suffered harassment and sometimes official persecution in the Netherlands up through the 1830s, and faced a social stigma thereafter. Their dream of founding a new order—another version of the "city on the hill"—combined with deteriorating economic conditions to spur emigration.[29] In these cases, the financial resources of the group, the rural orientation of the migration, and the desire to move en masse to found colonies meant a relatively high proportion of women at the early stages of migration. These founding mothers had to improvise in new physical surroundings, but the basic hierarchy of the social world remained intact. If anything, the church's role increased, partly by design but partly because little else existed.

The immigrants who came in increasing numbers after 1880 arrived in a Dutch American Calvinist world that allowed them to replicate a way of life that was under severe stress in the Netherlands—stress from industrialization, from population pressure, from forces of change. These immigrants were part of a larger migration of people, mainly "economic migrants" but also some political and religious refugees, escapees from the draft and from arranged marriages, part of much larger migrations that flowed back and forth across borders if they could. Patterns of migration in the Netherlands were changing around the turn of the century, with increasing numbers of urban migrants and increasing numbers of singles. Yet these individuals tended to migrate to the Dutch colonies, or within Europe, while the migration to the United States remained heavily familial and much more strongly rural in origin.[30] Economic grounds were rarely the only ones sparking emigration, for neighboring communities facing similar circumstances saw distinctly different migration patterns. Chains of migration brought people from one specific locale to another.[31] Dutch emigration records listed about 128,000 persons headed for the United States between 1880 and 1920. U.S. figures listed over 172,000 immigrants from the Netherlands at the same time. The Dutch records certainly missed many, and the U.S. officials probably did not catch everyone either, especially early in the period.[32] Return migration rates were relatively low, estimated at 15 to 18 percent.[33]

Once in the United States the Dutch faced the same economic conditions that many others did: economic cycles of boom and bust, agricultural shifts toward larger size and greater technology, increasing opportunities for women in the paid workforce. Many opportunities were available to the Dutch partly on the basis of their status in the developing notions of race and eugenics. Accepted from the outset as white, and with the further advantage of a Dutch tradition dating in the United States to colonial times, the group could parlay their inherited genes into various preferential options.[34] When the Dillingham Commission published its massive studies of immigrants in 1911, the Dutch were among those they considered the good, of "old" stock, despite their otherwise similar backgrounds to many "new" immigrants of the time.

The Dutch differed from other groups in certain ways. Unlike women from Sweden, Finland, or Ireland, few Dutch women migrated alone to the United States to seek domestic or other work positions.[35] Rather, if they went, they generally remained in the familial context. Migration took place with parents, or at the very least siblings and other relatives. A majority of all Dutch migrants in this period came with at least one other family member. Even at the peak of single migration during World War I, 60 percent of migrants were still coming with families. Among single migrants, there were only about 25 percent women most years.[36] In this the Dutch resembled Norwegian immigrants and some other rural-to-rural migrants.[37] They rarely followed the pattern of groups, such as the Chinese, Indians, or Italians, of men migrating alone and women remaining behind within communal settings and familial systems.[38] Other Dutch migrants, those headed for colonial settings in Asia, South Africa, or South America, had a different demographic profile. But for the Dutch Protestants who continued to come to the United States, nuclear family separation meant a severe breakdown in daily gender role divisions and hierarchies which would have upset the world much more than the challenge to extended family roles posed by migration. The form Dutch Protestant ethnicity took in the United States relied on this background, beginning with the stress on forming stable nuclear families. Hence I begin by looking at women and their relationships within families.

CHAPTER 1

Family Matters

The Dutch language distinguished between the nuclear family, *het gezin,* and the extended family, *de familie.* All relatives from aunts and uncles through nieces and nephews through cousins and second cousins, every person related by blood or marriage, was *familie.* As a child I would hear relatives complaining about *familie ziekte,* literally family sickness but in practice an overdose of extended family members. It usually referred to a relative who took up residence in one's home for several days if not weeks, a person who upset the normal schedule and demanded special treatment in a variety of ways, or to a half-dozen surprise visits from relatives within a short period, requiring at some point a mad rush to the grocery store to buy extra food.

Familie ziekte struck turn-of-the-century immigrants in different ways, for they had to reconstruct families disrupted by migration. The hard-won gains of assisting another nephew, a brother and his family, an elderly parent, or the family's younger children to join earlier arrivals in the United States and the subsequent struggle to establish them financially underscored their interest in familial solidarity. The cultural imperative to care for extended family changed when it crossed the Atlantic, for logistical barriers got in the way. Once in the new world the immigrants could maintain "normal" family ties with others who lived near them, but the geographic barriers of the ocean, and sometimes of distances within the United States, made some tasks impossible, and led to shifts in form. Further, though the Dutch migrated as families to a large extent, the sex ratios of who in the family migrated still favored men over women, leaving a demographic imbalance on both sides of the Atlantic.

The social and biological reproduction of the family would continue, but for many Dutch Protestant women immigrants families in America took a somewhat different form, one in which a woman had to rely more heavily on the nuclear family and on extended family gained through marriage. It was a world where women had greater independence in choosing their spouses and better marriage opportunities than in the Netherlands. It was also a familial landscape where never-married older women, "spinsters," almost completely disappeared and where never-married older men were also rare. In this sense it was very different from the Netherlands of the same era. Consequently, the roles such older single people otherwise might have filled either in the family or in society remained largely empty for a generation of immigrants, and the community had to adjust.

The family was the most important institution in turn-of-the-century Dutch America, even more important than the church. The family functioned as an economic and emotional base for every immigrant I studied, even the most rebellious.[1] It was the bedrock of the realm of social reproduction; it provided the setting and the personnel for much of immigrant life. A significant amount of information in women immigrants' letters concerned family. Many of the roles women associated with family underwent some change because of migration, yet the migrants generally tried to preserve rather than restructure the form of family they knew. In this process, women had only limited power to make the decisions.

In essence, for most ethnic women, family was a matter of survival. In the nineteenth century few could earn a sufficient income on their own, at least not enough to support children, nor could they manage in old age without the contributions of children, either in the form of work or of wages. Early studies of immigration sometimes romanticized women's familial roles, and ignored workplace and wage-earning activities.[2] Yet until recently immigration historians also have written little about the role that many ethnic women, through a long span of American history, have considered their primary adult occupation, as housewife, mother, and participant in familial economic endeavors, whether paid or unpaid.[3] For Dutch immigrants as opposed to some other groups this was particularly important—first, because of the absence in the migration stream of many single women who might have had access to money to assist other women to migrate, as was the case among the Irish, and second, because of the general lack of women's organized networks, which contributed to the low level of influence married women had on migration patterns, in contrast to groups such as recent migrants from Mexico.[4] Dutch Protestant women did have input in migration decisions, but only at very specific points in their lives could they actually make the decision to migrate on their own or to bring over other kin.

Legally the Dutch community did not face many restrictions on family reunification, as did the Chinese of the same period, for example. Nor did they face an ambiguous racial status or miscegenation laws targeted against their unions. And while the Dutch emigrant population rarely possessed considerable means, neither were they impoverished, as were the Irish famine emigrants of the mid-nineteenth century. The rural nature of the Dutch migration to America supported the "need" for couples to run farms, and for children who would then serve as farm labor, though the family remained central to urban Dutch America as well. A family economy in which all members contributed to the good of the whole, sometimes to the detriment of their individual needs, was typical. There could have been other ways to organize life and labor, but this was the arrangement to which most Dutch migrants were accustomed, and for the most part it made the transatlantic passage with them. A very tiny minority, however, used the geographic move to escape a world in which remaining single was difficult in both economic and social terms. They restructured their world, finding substitutes for or foregoing some of the activities which normally surrounded family. They also tended to leave behind Dutch American community organizations and contacts. The stories of Cornelia De Bey and Cornelia De Groot in later chapters highlight how American opportunities allowed them to do this. The American setting, in which individual rights (including for women) tended to be more developed at an earlier date than in the Dutch case, assisted in this process.

I could best describe social reproduction as it concerned family, then, as a spectrum on which individuals on one end attempted to maintain family ties as they existed in the Netherlands in every way, while those on the other end tried to escape from them. Most fell toward the conservative end of the spectrum. In any case, migration required individuals to make some changes in family organization. Among the Dutch, the degree to which many were successful in keeping such organization intact and in adjusting to new geographic realities illustrates that for many of them, family mattered. Such was the case for Jantje Modderman Negen.

Jantje Modderman Negen

Most Dutch immigrant women lived and died without leaving much of any record. One such person was Jantje Modderman Negen, who migrated from a rural area of northeastern Groningen to the United States around the turn of the twentieth century. Generations later a family genealogist reconstructed basic elements of her life out of Dutch parish records, ship passenger lists, U.S. census schedules, cemetery entries, and other such documents.[5] While there were no interviews, no letters, no diaries, no written records of her thoughts, there were still many things which one could surmise out of the data available. Moreover, many aspects of her life illustrated patterns that were common for women like her. Jantjen Modderman, as her name was listed on her birth record, was born in Ekamp, Groningen, in 1839. She was the daughter of farm laborers who spent their lives in nearby Oostwold, a small town near the German border.[6] In 1862, at age twenty-four, Jantjen Modderman married Jakob Negen, age twenty-

eight, also of Oostwold and a laborer. Both were slightly below the average age
of first marriage for the Netherlands as a whole, but closer to average for the
laboring population in their region. This group had little incentive to wait to
marry, and probably were earning some of the highest wages they could anticipate.[7] The following year their first son was born. In 1875 husband Jakob died,
leaving Modderman Negen to raise her three surviving sons, ages twelve, nine,
and six, on her own. Only the oldest was eligible for general work outside of
agriculture, but it would have been typical for even the youngest to assist seasonally if there was farmwork available.[8] The fact that she and her sons were
listed as able to read and write in the U.S. census schedules years later indicates
that both she and the children had at least a basic education. The combination
of Modderman Negen's low economic status, the presence of children, and age
(late thirties) at the time her husband died meant her chances of remarriage were
almost nonexistent. Widowers sometimes remarried in this period, but they
tended to marry previously never-married women.[9]

Modderman Negen somehow managed to keep the family going, a daunting
task given their economic status. What made it worse was an agricultural crisis
in the 1880s, which hit especially hard in sea clay regions such as theirs along the
North Sea coast. Perhaps relatives or friends assisted. Having three sons as opposed to daughters meant the earning potential was greater, at least if jobs were
available, because male workers at any age received higher wages than their female peers. Further, Dutch law gave Modderman Negen, as head of the household, the right to her children's earnings until they reached majority, which was
set at age twenty-five or at marriage. Yet this was the time period of a "mass exodus of excess farm hands" in the region, as farms shifted from labor-intensive
to capital-intensive agriculture. When the youngest son, Jurjen, was about twenty-
three he joined this exodus to the United States in hopes of a better economic
future, specifically a farm. He did so when the percentage of single migrants from
the Netherlands to the United States was rising rapidly.[10] He settled on a farm in
Iowa, beginning as a farmhand. By 1900 he was a U.S. citizen and a partner on a
farm, living with another family, and ready to start a family of his own.

After a decade in Iowa Jurjen Negen returned to help his mother and other
relatives emigrate—and to find a spouse. It was a common pattern among Dutch
immigrants for a young man to go to America and then return after a few years
to find a wife. The demographics of the young adult population were complementary on each side of the Atlantic. Jurjen Negen was part of the reason that
an entire generation of Dutch women had fewer available marriage partners
than their male counterparts because of sex-skewed migration. In the Netherlands, as opposed to in the United States, there was an abundance of unmarried women. Hence many Dutch women became immigrants shortly after
marrying a visiting Dutch American man. In some cases the couples had an
"understanding" to marry before he emigrated. According to family lore Jurjen Negen had such an agreement, but his original intended married someone

else in the intervening years. In any case, once back in the Netherlands Jurjen married Aafke Schipper, who was fifteen years his junior, after a whirlwind court-ship. Perhaps Jantje Modderman Negen or another Dutch relative suggested Schipper as a potential spouse. The Schippers lived just a few miles away, and as laborers they faced similar bleak economic and marital prospects, especially for women.[11] Or it might simply be that he chose the daughter of a family al-ready intent on going to the United States, making for a greater circle of family connections in the new world. The fact that one of her brothers was already in the Midwest and that others in her family joined the migration hints at that possibility.[12] In any case, Jantje Modderman Negen gained a new daughter-in-law shortly before they both emigrated.

Modderman Negen left the Netherlands in 1902, when she was over sixty and had been a widow for over twenty-five years. As a widow she had the option of making the decision to go on her own, at least if she had the funds or someone who would provide them. Whether any other option was economically feasi-ble, or palatable, is another question. In her case, however, the migration party insured that she would have an extensive extended family in the United States from the outset. When she boarded the SS *Haverford* in Antwerp she was in the company of not only her son who had come back and successfully found a spouse but also another son and his spouse with their children. Modderman Negen herself was on the passenger list next to the parents of her new daugh-ter-in-law, Aafke Schipper Negen, and several of Aafke's siblings, all from the same vicinity in Groningen. According to a church history, Jantje Modderman Negen was sick most of the trip, unable to come on deck and plagued by the lack of water and crowded conditions.[13] Had she not been with the group, she might have encountered difficulties at Ellis Island, but with them there was no concern she might become a public charge. The entire group, plus another Dutch family traveling with them, listed their destination as Morrison, Grundy County, Iowa. Two years later Jantje Modderman Negen's brother Helmer Modderman arrived with his spouse and children, including his daughter Anna Modderman.[14] Within a year Anna married Martin Schipper (brother of Jan-tje's daughter-in-law), linking the families yet again. Family connections con-tinued to operate in Iowa in other ways as well. Jantje Modderman Negen was listed as "attending physician or midwife" on the birth certificate of her grand-child Helmer (son of Jurjen and Aafke) in 1905. At that point she was living in Dike, Iowa. Her sons and other relatives rented farms in the area.

In 1912 Reina Otten Negen, wife of Jantje's older son, died, leaving behind at least five children ages two to thirteen. Jantje Modderman Negen, who was now over seventy, moved into her son Hindrik's home to assist with housekeeping and child rearing. It would have been difficult for him to have kept on farming with-out such help or immediate remarriage, and finding a woman willing to take on a family of five young children would not have been easy. A few years later all the Negens and some of the Moddermans and Schippers moved to Crooks Town-

Jantje Modderman Negen
on the family farm in Minnesota. Photo courtesy of
Terry Meinke.

ship, near Renville, Minnesota, where all bought farms.[15] They were part of a larger group of Dutch and East Frisian settlers from Iowa who moved to the Renville area. A Dutch Protestant settlement had formed in a three-county area there in the 1880s under the auspices of a Dutch real estate promoter with a base in Groningen who advertised in Dutch American newspapers.[16] The census of 1900 listed 141 persons of Dutch birth in Renville County, with another 153 in neighboring Chippewa and 207 in Kandiyohi County, the base of *"de kolonie."*[17] The Christian Reformed Church which the Negens joined had begun services in 1890.[18] Though it was a lengthy process before the families were all settled together on land they owned, the possibility that people who came from their background could eventually have farms in the United States was one of the most potent enticements to migration possible. The fact that the families had gone through more than one move together before settling somewhat more permanently in one locale was a typical pattern among successful Dutch immigrants of this era, and a characteristic of the Renville settlement generally.[19] While this was a good move economically, the families arrived in Renville at an inopportune time in terms of international events. As World War I broke out the more established Ameri-can population had trouble distinguishing Dutch from "Deutsch" (German), and this was even more the case in settlements like theirs, which mixed Dutch and German members.[20] The community sought to divert suspicion, especially after the United States entered the war. The Ladies Aid group at Modderman Negen's church was active sewing and knitting for the Red Cross, while one of her grandchildren (one born in the Netherlands) served as a soldier. He returned safely, and by 1920 was farming in the area, as was his brother.[21]

So at the close of her life, Jantje "Jennie" Modderman Negen lived with her son and the grandchildren she had mothered (some of whom were farming on their own), near her other son and daughter-in-law and their ten surviving children, and near her former shipmate and the mother-in-law of her son, who lived with Jantje's niece and surviving family.[22] She also lived in the same township as at least two other families from Oostwold, Groningen. Though she did not speak English according to the census of 1920, her sons did, and she could have gone to church and carried out other tasks in the Dutch American settlement in Dutch.[23] Jantje Modderman Negen died in 1925 at the age of eighty-six and was buried in the Emden Cemetery north of Renville, Minnesota, where many of her relatives were also buried.[24] The interconnections of her family with other migrants and their extended links between generations helped the families through otherwise difficult times. Hers was one of the more successful family reconstitution stories which I encountered. Though many married women migrated with several young adult children, and thus created extended families quite rapidly, few had the connections that she did. At the same time, it is unclear whether Modderman Negen wanted to come to America originally, or whether she simply was caught up in the family move. Had the others gone and left her behind, she would have lost regular contact with many of her closest kin. Making the trip across the ocean, settling in a new country, all after age sixty, could not have been easy. As the church history stated, "It was especially difficult for the women, who missed the 'gezeligheid' [*sic*] (coziness) of their life in Holland or Germany."[25] Yet the situation she faced at the end of her life in Minnesota was much better than that she could have anticipated had she stayed in the Netherlands. Modderman Negen's story was unusual in that few women of her age migrated, and even fewer migrated with such a large group of kin. But several of the other elements of the family story, such as her son Jurjen's return to the Netherlands to find a wife, were much more typical.

International Marriage Market

Within a setting of international migration, marriage choices and opportunities changed dramatically. Migration might mean a new life with the economic wherewithal to marry, a more favorable sex ratio, or additional options for life outside marriage. Just as there was an international labor market, by which workers from one country made their way to job opportunities in another, so too was there an international marriage market. The two functioned similarly for the Dutch. Persons could look at job or marital opportunities in the area, but if these were not "good" in their subjective viewpoint, they might consider what the possibilities were elsewhere. In making the decisions about where to go the individuals frequently received information from others. This news could take a general form, indicating good opportunities for paid employment or marriage, or a specific form, with the offer of a job or a marital proposal. Letters, visits by prospective spouses, word of mouth, personal ads—all could impart information on marriage possibilities. Opportunities for marriage changed on both sides of the Atlantic due to migration. If the interviews and letters I studied are any indication, then a significant proportion of young men migrated at least in part in order to earn enough money to marry, while a substantial number of young women came as newlyweds, as fiancées joining their intendeds, or as individuals who knew their chances on the marriage market were greater in the United States.

In the Netherlands during this period, a major segment of the female population remained single. From 1880 to 1920 the rate in the Netherlands did not vary a great deal, running around 20 percent never married for women aged thirty to forty-nine.[26] Sex ratios remained relatively equal, though with a slightly higher number of women than men, a condition attributed to migration.[27] In the United States the situation was quite different. Dutch men consistently outnumbered Dutch women among the ranks of the population: 132 to 100 in 1910, 134 to 100 in 1920.[28] The consequences of different sex ratios and economic opportunities for marriage appeared clearly in Dutch American marriage rates. In the 1910 Public Use Sample of the U.S. census only 6 percent of the men remained never married at age forty-five or above, well below the Dutch average.[29] But the figures for never-married women in the over-forty-five group were even more striking—only 1 percent of these women had never married. Virtually *every* Dutch immigrant woman married and the category of "spinster" nearly ceased to exist for that generation in the United States.

While most immigrants may have been unaware of the exact demographic situation which prevailed on each side of the Atlantic, they recognized the consequences very clearly on a personal level. Lubbigje Schaapman, a young woman who immigrated with her family to California, wrote long letters to her bosom friend Willamientje Beltman. In one letter not long after arriving she described all the new arrivals and those planning to migrate there: "So Mientje, you can well see that the boys continue to come, but no girls. Here there are 10 Dutch boys but only 2 Dutch girls."[30] In a later letter she put the options in more concrete terms: "You wrote in your letter, Mientje, that you would go into domestic service around Zwolle in May. But I think you should come here. . . . In May if not before the two Dutch boys who came over with us are going back to Holland, the one [will stay] . . . and the other, with whom I went out for a while, will come back he says, but if he is going to bring a wife, I don't know, see, that way you could come along."[31] Schaapman assumed her former beau would seek a wife while in the Netherlands, and since she assumed he had no one in mind, why not her closest friend? Schaapman did not fail to mention job opportunities as well, but marriage looked like a good way for her friend to get to the United States as far as she was concerned. In this letter, as in others, she remained nonjudgmental if not non-nonchalant about describing the young man in question.

The Dutch, like other immigrants, relied at times on correspondence both formal and informal to find spouses.[32] Widows in the Netherlands, at least those who did not qualify as elderly, received reports of significantly better chances for remarriage in the United States. R. H. Brinks wrote a letter highlighting two examples. First, he acknowledged getting news of his sister's widowhood, then he offered some advice. If her children were "good" then she should come to join him in rural Iowa. Then, at least, she could live off their wages, if not find a husband who needed the farm labor as well as a wife. Second, he noted his brother Jan had married a widow with four children: "a good woman and some money to boot and from a good family."[33] Dutch American widowers, on the other hand, were some of the most likely candidates to rely on letters to find a spouse, not a surprising fact considering the small numbers of unmarried older women in most Dutch American communities and the pressing need to have female gender roles filled. After Jan Brouwer, an immigrant to northwestern Iowa from Friesland, lost his wife, he wrote back to the Netherlands arranging to marry another "Fries." Brouwer's bride Grietje did not have a chance to catch her breath (or change her mind) once she arrived in Orange City. The couple went straight to the courthouse and to the church to wed officially. Jan Brouwer described it: "I came home with my wife without her knowing what that home was. I was really happy that we were married because I had a real need for a wife. It was too much work for mother at my place."[34]

A "letter bride" in Dutch practice was not exactly a mail-order phenomenon, though in some cases it sounded like that. Rather, the correspondence served as a solution to a problem posed by distance and demographics, and satisfied a cultural desire to marry one of one's own kind. In this pattern a man would write back to a female acquaintance, asking if she would like to marry him, or ask a third party, via correspondence, to look for someone and then put him in touch with her. The two would then agree by letter to marry. The man also (at least legally) had to attain the permission of the woman's family if she had not reached majority, which was one of the reasons this process was easier for men seeking slightly older women or widows. Parental consent, which many felt was a social or moral imperative in addition to a legal one, could be impossible in some cases.[35] If all agreed, she would depart, generally in the company of another group of migrants. In some cases the potential groom would pay her passage. In other cases the money for passage was part of her dowry, a factor which made her a more attractive prospect on the marriage market. While correspondence was a practical approach, it contained many pitfalls beyond the usual questions of whether this was a person one actually wanted to marry, and it also tended to lengthen the period of negotiations compared to face-to-face contact.

Among Dutch Protestant immigrants in this period I found few letter brides, and then most often in cases such as the Brouwers, where the man was a widower. On the other hand I encountered many cases where a male immigrant left "his girl" behind with an understanding that he would write and send for her later. This kind of separation was fraught with uncertainty for all involved. Even in the best of scenarios, once he emigrated there would be only sporadic contact until the two could marry. A letter every two or three months was the most a transatlantic couple could anticipate, and a letter every six months was more common. Sometimes other migrants going back and forth would bring news, but most of the time it was a waiting game.

Even if the understanding continued, the two could grow apart in the intervening years. Aafje de Vries's letter to a female friend in the United States expressed the heartbreak of such a situation. De Vries, of Appelscha, Groningen, had received news of the marriage of her former beau. Though she made vari-

Jurjen Negen and Aafke Schipper at the time of their wedding. Negen returned to the Netherlands briefly to find a wife and to bring over other members of his family. Photo courtesy of Terry Meinke.

ous comments on how the situation would have to be for the best, she was understandably bitter: "No, I would never have thought that it would turn out this way. . . . My folks didn't want me to go to America and he did not want to come here, . . . but if I had known from the start, then we would never have gotten involved, because I gave up my entire youth to this. I never went anywhere."[36] Perhaps the greatest irony for De Vries was that her former beau returned to marry another Dutch woman and then remained in the Netherlands.

That the parents of these women had something to fear was evident from various sources. In a church discipline case from western Michigan in 1880, church elders sought to rectify the situation of a young woman who immigrated to join her fiancé as they had agreed, only to have him marry someone else shortly after her arrival. The church demanded he pay the "jilted" woman the monetary equivalent of all costs to get back to the Netherlands plus a little more for her trouble, which she could use however she wished.[37] For those who were part of transatlantic chains of migration from one village to another such social control was still possible, but not everyone was. According to Lini Moerkerk de Vries's autobiography, her mother's fiancé came to the United States to earn some money and then to send for his intended. This he did, but shortly after she arrived he married another woman "for her dowry."[38] Lini Moerkerk de Vries's mother in turn married someone else out of "spite," and more importantly because she was already pregnant by her original fiancé. It is likely that the marriage was not one she otherwise would have undertaken, since her spouse was well below her in social class and from a different religious background.

The real danger of prenuptial pregnancy added to a more general concern with prostitution. The white slavery scare, which flooded the papers on both sides of the Atlantic, warned about the hazards of migration for single women. Immigration authorities, for this reason, set impediments to entry into the United States for a young woman migrating alone around the turn of the century, with the justification that they were easy prey for unscrupulous characters seeking prostitutes.[39] With chain migration and proper documents many Dutch women bypassed this barrier,[40] but it was one more reason why some young women preferred for a potential spouse to come back to the Netherlands in order to marry, or for the couple to marry and migrate together, even if did mean having a smaller financial base with which to begin life together in the United States.[41]

Each potential spouse's role in the social reproduction of the family was different, leading to distinctly gendered perspectives on whether to migrate or not and under what conditions. Financially, the best solution as far as many men were concerned was for a young woman to migrate herself and work for wages on her own for a few months or more in order to make the basis for a farm, home, and family more secure. Because men were particularly concerned with providing the financial base for the family, this often steered their considerations. Women (and their parents) on the other hand, while not oblivious to financial concerns, wanted to make sure family formation actually took place, and that social controls on sexual behavior (i.e., the opportunity to force marriage if necessary) were in place, which would protect young women from disgrace and abandonment or even from damaging their opportunities for marriage. Likewise parents had different perspectives on the migration of sons or daughters, just as young adults had different perspectives on the permanency of their moves. Estimates of remigration vary from 15 to 18 percent, but all indications are that these figures applied almost exclusively to men.[42] Men might work for a few years and then return to marry and stay in the Netherlands. Women rarely returned, and the migration of a daughter to get married was almost inevitably permanent.

While some Dutch immigrant men sought spouses through letters to their family and friends in the Netherlands, others resorted to a more impersonal means to get this correspondence started, classified ads. Such was the case of Sjuk Bergsma, who migrated to Renton, Washington, in 1911, with the understanding that his girlfriend/fiancée, Jeltje Scholten, would join him. According to family tradition she was in no hurry to marry and kept putting off her departure. By 1913 he was tired of waiting so he placed a classified ad for a Frisian woman in *Hepkema's Courant,* in the Netherlands. By chance Scholten read the ad and decided she had better leave to join him soon.[43]

Such ads also existed in Dutch American papers. *De Hollandsche Amerikaan,* for example, published out of Kalamazoo, Michigan, sporadically included personal ads for marriage or acquaintance—mixed in with ads for celery workers, land, music lessons, or goat stud service. Sometimes these were combination ads: "WANTED: A middle-aged woman to work as a housekeeper; or later, on mutual agreement, to get married."[44] From 1919 through 1920 twelve marriage ads appeared. Of these, seven were placed by men over thirty, four of whom identified themselves as widowers, and three were by young men.[45] Personal ads of this sort were part of many Dutch American newspapers I consulted, at least for a period of time when the paper also ran other kinds of classified advertisements. The high proportion of widowers/older men in my sample from *De Hollandsche Amerikaan* reinforces my findings from letters, indicating a general problem in finding suitable spouses for this group of men, for whom the need for a spouse was pressing but was not likely to be solved by the normal channels of social life.

A second group of men also resorted to classified ads on occasion. Dutch immigrant men, unlike those of some other nationalities, would rarely consider farming without wives. Hence the decision to begin farming for a single man almost always coincided with marriage. The personal ads in *Pella's Weekblad* around the turn of the century included notices from men in newer western settlements where sex ratios were particularly skewed, and more generally for those ready to begin farming: "*Marriage* A young man who wants to buy a 320 acre farm in Ransom County, North Dakota from [land agent in Pella], wants to meet a girl or young widow who is willing to share joy and sorrow with him in that lovely land of the north. Letter and picture [to the paper] Discretion assured."[46] The one ad I located written by a woman indicated she had similar expectations: "*Marriage Proposal* A young lady of 22, good looking, would like by this means to come in contact with a young man, preferably one with his own farm, in order after getting acquainted to get married. This advertisement is honorably meant. Secrecy requested and assured."[47] The interest of a young woman in advertising for a mate herself must have sounded rather audacious to Dutch-born ears. I found personal ads in *Pella's Weekblad* occasionally around 1900, but they were rare to nonexistent by the 1910s.[48] On the other hand *De Volksvriend*, a paper out of Orange City, Iowa, with a wider circulation, carried marriage ads very frequently in the 1910s. Most of these were placed by somewhat younger single men, often farmers. On 30 January 1919, for example, one man advertised for a "Christian girl" of twenty-five to thirty-five and an "Iowa farmer" of thirty sought a "Dutch girl" of the same age. Both were mixed in with other classified ads and carried the title "MARRIAGE PROPOSAL" in Dutch.[49] While personal ads were extant in parts of Europe for more than a century, it seems they became more common in both the United States and Europe as migration and literacy rates increased. People generally sought those of like background. Groups with a third-party matchmaking tradition, such as German Jews, appear to have utilized such ads more frequently than those such as the Dutch who did not have this cultural background.[50]

Within the older Dutch American communities of the United States, the resort to letters or ads generally was not necessary, and courtship patterns replicated Dutch counterparts to a large extent. As in the Netherlands, young couples often met in particular social settings. The workplace (whether farm or factory), church services or activities, or the local fair all proved good opportunities. Weddings themselves allowed young adults to meet, since a couple might celebrate with people from their church congregation and extended family members. The Dutch *slenteravond* (strolling evening), which was common means of pairing for young people at the turn of the century in rural areas and working-class neighborhoods in the Netherlands, also existed in parts of the United States.[51] Amry Vandenbosch, though he did not note the old world counterpart, described one in Chicago in a book published in 1927: "The young people meet each other at the Sunday evening church services or at the mid-week meetings. In the Ashland avenue community there is an interesting institution called the 'market.' After the Sunday evening services the girls walk back and forth between Roosevelt road and Hastings street and Ashland avenue. The young men from all the Dutch communities congregate here and pick out the girl they want. The girls continue their promenade until the young man of their choice comes along."[52]

Courtship in the United States, according to most immigrant letters, continued to take place to a large extent in group settings, with opportunities for couples to go off on their own at some point. To what extent they could engage in physical intimacy at that point was ambiguous. A humorous exchange of "love letters" written in dialect and printed in *Pella's Weekblad,* included the plea of a young man: "in another week there is a fair [*kermis*] and I would really like to have a girlfriend," to which his correspondent replied "that would be possible but you must not do what my former beau did, who after the fair left me on my own; if you will keep your word and continue the relationship with me after the fair then I will go out [*vrijen*] with you."[53] *Vrijen* was the term used to discuss young people who were courting, and while it did not necessarily connote a sexual relationship it could also refer to cuddling or love-making.

Courting patterns for the well-to-do took other, more formal forms both in the Netherlands and the United States. A farmers' daughter in the province of Groningen, for example, could expect a young man to invite her by letter to a dance. He would then pick her up, dance with her the entire evening, and then bring her home and the two could enjoy coffee together. After coffee they could make another date. "Coffee" might include a late night supper and the couple might spend most of the night together.[54] Parents sanctioned physical intimacy, thus, within controlled surroundings. Patterns among the farmworkers were less formal of necessity—there was no parlor in which to meet.[55] The acceptance of opportunities for intimacy, though, was similar in the early part of the period. For both groups, however, by the turn of the century, a change was underway. The social acceptance of prenuptial pregnancy, one consequence of this type of courting, dropped.

Respectability in courtship related to class standing in the Netherlands, but it also related to religious conviction. The neo-Calvinist followers of the *Doleantie,* in the forefront of the emigration movement, sought stricter control on young adults and their sexuality. Thus in Dutch America premarital sex became a prime concern for communities trying to enforce religious purity *and* to be accepted into the middle class of the new land. Both required a campaign against this "peasant" or "old world" sin. Fear of strict church sanctions operated as a deterrent among young people. Coupled with this was the desire to join a bourgeois world, one which tried to embrace virginity until marriage, at least for women. But the rising consciousness of sexuality and the freedoms young people began to see, particularly in urban areas, acted as a counterweight and made control of premarital sexuality more difficult. Courtship patterns, in this sense, were quite similar on both sides of the Atlantic. Control over young adult sexuality, however, could be more difficult to maintain if family connections were lost with migration.

One of the big differences in courting which came with migration was the variety of persons available and the sense of who was a "suitable spouse." Many migrants sought spouses from the same region, if not village, from which they emigrated. It was easier to talk to someone who understood the same dialect, and there was a certain security in choosing someone known to various friends and relatives. The exacting nature of chain migration among the Dutch, exemplified in the story of Jantje Modderman Negen and painstakingly traced by Robert Swierenga, meant these local links continued.[56] Considering the sex ratios of initial migration, in which women were nearly always underrepresented, marriage to a "local" person was more likely for women than for men. Yet even for women, the possibilities of meeting and marrying someone "Dutch" but not of the same provincial or local background were considerably higher in the United States than they were in the Netherlands. The trend was pronounced in older settlements where the chains of migration came from a variety of regions. Immigrants blended their regional identities over time and generations. By the 1960s, in interviews women would simply report: "I married a Dutchman and *all* of my sisters married Dutch men."[57] Even in early years letters indicated that the immigrants recognized that the surrounding population could not distinguish between provincial backgrounds, let alone local ones. In the face of others, there was a more unified "Dutch America." Yet within the Dutch American community the regional backgrounds remained strong at first.

A further step of remove, seen extensively in the second generation or in settlements with imbalanced sex ratios, was to simply identify people as Dutch, which could as easily mean of Dutch descent. Lubbigje Schaapman, for example, reported: "Where Stevens went, near Sacramento, there are more Dutch girls there. Actually they are American of Dutch descent."[58] The demographic data also identified second-generation Dutch as the most common group for "intermarriage" among the new immigrants. Writers differed as to whether these types were proper spouses or not. Aart Plaisier, writing from a heavily Dutch area of western Michigan in 1915, reported: "I think that I will go back to the Netherlands to look before I marry, maybe I can turn up a helpmate. It is sad here regarding the females."[59] His brother Gerrit seconded the opinion: "Now they say that there are no girls in America, but I can tell you that there are more girls than boys here in Grand Rapids, but they don't want to speak Dutch and they have a lot of say in things.[60] . . . the girls are nice enough, but they are the boss."[61] Complaints by first-generation men about second-generation women or about women who migrated young enough to have adopted "American" ways were common in men's letters.

Intermarriage, according to some theorists of ethnic identity, signified the end of ethnicity, or at least an important point of decline.[62] I found some cases where that was true, generally among people who wanted to stop being Dutch. For others however, there were few changes after marriage to someone outside the group. If anything some Dutch men and women used out-marriage as a means to fulfill one of the primary goals coming from their ethnic background. The term *intermarriage* could apply as easily to a Frisian-Zeelands immigrant marriage as it could to a first- and second-generation Dutch immigrant marriage, to the marriage of someone from Coevorden with a Bentheimer (Dutch-speaking Germans who lived across the border), or to a Catholic-Protestant Dutch match. Migration increased the opportunities for some of these matches, while decreasing others. Statistics, however, could never tell whether the individuals considered what was going on intermarriage, nor whether it meant a change in ethnic identity for them.[63] The most important factor for those who married persons not of Dutch descent was urban residence. In Grand Rapids, Michigan, or Paterson, New Jersey, but most especially in Chicago, Dutch immigrants sometimes found mates of other backgrounds. Intermarriage across national lines may have been rare, but when it occurred it followed certain patterns. Beyond Dutch and Dutch-descended, "Yankees" of English or Scottish descent proved the most common spouses, with Germans following a close second.

In addition to national and regional identity of spouses, another aspect of marriage choice which changed with migration was the importance of a dowry. A turn-of-the-century Dutch woman generally expected to possess a dowry in the form of goods, some money, and various skills necessary in running a household. The dowry by the end of the nineteenth century was informal for the majority of the Dutch, but it included a trousseau replete with gold or silver jewelry. The biggest investment (for those who could afford it) was frequently the *oorijzer* (special headwear).[64] Better wages for women in the United States meant the chance to gather the dowry more quickly, not to mention dropping the need for the *oorijzer* in most cases. Moreover, in the United States, some could manage to marry without a dowry. The desire for a good mate combined with better wages led some men to finance the trip of a fiancée or to marry a local woman without means simply because women were scarce. Perhaps the most typical stance on a dowry was that of a widower who advertised for a spouse: "Some means desired, but not required."[65]

While a dowry took on less importance in America, the need for a man to earn enough or have saved enough to support a family did not change, or if anything it intensified. This also led to the pattern of men living and working in the United States for years, then returning to marry and live in the Netherlands on the money they had saved. Such was the case with D. Riemersma, who returned to Friesland after many years in Iowa. Riemersma used his savings to buy an inn, and at age forty-three he married a woman aged twenty-three. He was quite satisfied with the situation: "you wrote concerning my getting married, if that was a bit of a disappointment, oh no! not at all! I waited a long time and I was strongly against it at times, but luckily I can say that it didn't come too late. Even though the difference in ages is large, we get along with each other well."[66] Whether he considered marrying in the United States was unclear. The chances of his finding a young Frisian woman there willing to marry someone twenty years her senior, however, were slight.

Age acted as an important factor in marital decisions, and some records indicate that age patterns of marriage in Dutch immigrant communities varied according to the age of the community, which in turn reflected the sex ratio of the population.[67] Newcomers in frontier areas wanted mates from the same ethnic background just as did later settlers, but the lack of women at this early stage meant that young women were in higher demand. Even women with no financial resources of their own could anticipate proposals from older local men with considerable financial worth. The age difference might put them at a disadvantage in terms of power relationships within the marriage, but the chances were that the wife would outlive the husband and either run her own household or perhaps marry again. By 1910 the Dutch in the United States overall followed age patterns not unlike those in the Netherlands. Women tended to marry in their early twenties (by about age twenty-four), while men generally waited a few years beyond that, until their late twenties.[68] The difference was thus not in age so much as in the percentage who married.

To what extent could women choose their mates? Perhaps the best way to imagine the marriage market for women is to note that the better the chances that women could support themselves economically, and the better the chances for marriage generally, the better their ability to turn down proposals without worrying that it was the only opportunity to marry or to survive. I did not encounter any cases where a woman reported that she chose her future husband in terms of making an overture toward marriage, with the exception of personal ads, which did not exactly qualify as marriage proposals. A woman could express interest in a man, but it remained his decision whether to ask her to marry him. Several examples also illustrated that a woman had little chance to regain a lost beau if she once spurned him.[69]

Both in the Netherlands and in the United States individuals could make up their own minds about potential spouses, but men had greater cultural currency to make choices. Third parties entered the picture only in an informal way, suggesting possible mates. Parents, however, could exercise considerable sway and even veto power in advising about spouses, at least if they lived in the area. Here again migration altered patterns of social reproduction significantly. Young adults in America had greater leeway in making their own choices. Anna Kuijt exemplified this pattern, as well as the extremes of the marriage market. Kuijt, according to her sister Jeanette Goedhart, writing in 1909, was destined to stay single and impoverished. Kuijt arrived in the United States with no special training other than a smattering of English and a little experience as a domestic, and further, she had a chronic leg condition that, when it flared up, incapacitated her from work, meaning she lost her job with regularity. The doctors in Chicago, after one of these bouts, recommended she not continue working as a domestic. Kuijt's sister worried about what would happen: "We just don't know what Anna can do instead of domestic service. She never learned anything else and she isn't so young any more, and a girl can barely earn her keep at anything else."[70] Goedhart suggested sending Kuijt back to the Netherlands for the rest of her siblings to care for her. The somewhat obstinate (according to her relatives) Kuijt managed to stay in Chicago, and ten years later she married a "Yankee" after a brief courtship.[71] For a sickly woman of thirtysomething without much of a dowry, to marry at all was almost a miracle. Kuijt broke the Dutch pattern in terms of age, physical condition, lack of familial influence, and in terms of spouse from another ethnic background.

Anna Kuijt had not even informed her relatives she was courting when she sprang the news: "You must have looked at that rather strangely eh? that suddenly I was married. Well thus far I don't have any complaints and no regrets even though it all happened quite quickly."[72] It was standard for a young man or woman to at least report they were going to get married, allow a little time to lapse, and then send news of the wedding. This not only allowed family members to register their reservations but also left time for money and presents to make their way across the ocean, making the beginnings of a life together a little easier. Anna Kuijt Bates could justify her "short" courtship, five months of sporadic contact from first meeting to wedding, by the fact that her new husband was financially secure, the only son of a woman who owned a house.

Kuijt's case also highlighted a casual attitude toward a wedding and hinted at the ease with which one could marry in the United States, both points which astonished Dutch migrants. To Dutch immigrant eyes the bureaucracy and regulations surrounding a marriage were surprisingly lax. "Sjoerd is married and that is really easy here."[73] Unimpeded by miscegenation laws or cultural customs which seriously challenged the American legal standard (such as child marriage or proxy marriage), Dutch immigrants could and did marry to suit their schedules. One farmworker wrote in 1898: "Our plan is to marry next week, but I don't know which day. I still have to arrange the paperwork . . . people don't have big weddings here, but we like it that way."[74] Compared to the Netherlands, where the couple had to post banns in advance and the celebration often took place on two consecutive weekends, this casual attitude was revolutionary. Likewise, Jan Brouwer wrote that he opted for an "American wedding" with no fuss: "Thus everything was over in two hours."[75] Dutch immigrants frequently commented on the ease of marriage, either as a boon or as an open invitation to abuse. An article in *Pella's Weekblad* entitled "American style" described a young man who chose a partner in five minutes based on looks only and was married fifteen minutes later, to which the editor commented "For how long?"[76]

Others continued the tradition of a large celebration, but chose to do it American style. Pieterdina Smit, who lived in Chicago with several siblings until her marriage, threw a party: "We had a good wedding celebration at Griet and Frits' place. We had Negro musicians. The blacks here are outstanding in terms of music. . . . I had a blue silk dress with a white veil which reached to the ground."[77] Smit's celebration outdid most, as she was the only one I encountered who mentioned hiring musicians. Some Calvinists opposed music other than psalms, and many had moral qualms about dancing.[78] Smit's clothing color combination also reflected a trend among Dutch Americans. Wedding dresses for the not so well-to-do in the Netherlands generally were black. Part of the reason was practical, because they could not afford a dress only for this occasion, and so it had to serve as a woman's one good dress after the wedding. Dark colors showed less soil than light ones, and furthermore, in the Netherlands in the nineteenth century, dark colors were considered the appropriate attire for married women. Affluent women shifted to white and other light colors earlier, but among the emigrant group, exposure to white wedding dresses for "average" people generally came in the United States. Most commented on this as something new and different. Rarely, however, would they go so far as to wear white themselves. Some of the more adventurous, like Smit, might wear a dark color with a white veil.[79]

Gezina van der Haar Visscher wrote entries in her diary for all the weddings she attended, but more about her daughter Sena's wedding than most. She did not mention anything about clothing or decorations. Rather, as was her custom, she recorded which dominie performed the ceremony, which dominie (a family member) gave the benediction, and which Dutch psalm the group sang at the end of the ceremony. The description went on: "we lined up to wish them happiness as husband and wife. They received many fine presents, also silverware. After that the refreshments were passed around and there was a great plenty for everyone. There were four preachers and three professors present and more speeches were made. We all had a good time and the party broke up about eleven o'clock."[80] In describing another child's wedding, she noted that as was the custom, the dominie congratulated the newlyweds first and that the refreshments consisted of "fine food, coffee and chocolate milk."[81] What she meant by fine food remains a mystery. Listening to speeches by dominies and professors was a far cry from dancing into the night. The Smit and Visscher weddings reflected two different and competing traditions within the Dutch American community, one more secular and the other religious. Neither group relied on several wedding traditions from the Netherlands, traditions based on different geographic settlement patterns and a different legal system.

In the Netherlands a wedding of a prominent couple might be "announced" by decorating the wings of one of the large local windmills, as well as through flying flags in the village. All marriages required the reading of banns from the courthouse. Cornelia De Groot described wedding festivities in Friesland thus: In the weeks before the wedding, the parents of the bride decorated their home with greens and flowers and invited friends and relatives for tea, "boerejongens" (raisins stored in rum with sugar), and cake. Later in the evening the parents would provide coffee and a buffet of bread, meat, cheese, and rusk if they could afford it. The following week the parents of the groom put on the same kind of festivities, again with singing, dancing, games, and "comical recitations." The men smoked pipes at these gatherings, the groom a special yardlong Gouda clay pipe decorated with artificial flowers, a pipe which would thereafter serve as a memento of the celebration. The wedding took place on a weekday at the town hall, with the mayor conducting the ceremony. Sometimes, especially in small towns, couples had a "benediction" by a minister the following Sunday, but religious authorities could not legally marry the individuals.[82]

Several factors interfered with replicating these conditions, even if people wanted to do so. The lack of concentrated rural settlement patterns, that is, most farms within sight of the local town, and the absence of large windmills eliminated the visual signs in the landscape. Posting engagement notices in the paper, sometimes in the Netherlands as well as the United States, and making such announcements at church took a more important role. Extended families and friends were less likely to be close enough together to celebrate several weekends in a row, and many immigrants wanted to avoid this expense. One major gathering related to the wedding became a more common pattern. In some cases, probably more often for the second and later generations, wedding showers hosted by various friends or female relatives took the place of the long afternoon celebrations at each set of parents' homes. *Pella's Weekblad* included many notices of wedding showers by the 1910s. These, at least from the accounts, appeared to be aimed primarily at women, in contrast to the social gatherings surrounding a wedding in the Netherlands.[83] According to the Dutch American newspaper reports, weddings generally took place in the bride's home, or if she had none, in the home of a friend or at the parsonage. A minister often officiated.

Increasingly bourgeois status also allowed Dutch Americans to adopt certain rituals around engagement and weddings which existed but were not always financially possible in the Netherlands. Engagement pictures were a must for the well-to-do and those who looked to American trends. "You wrote that the little pictures already told too much, right? . . . This summer we will pose together—not one of those small things. . . . Should we also send official news about the engagement while Eisse is here? . . . I have already thought of placing an announcement in a couple of papers like the *Groninger* and *Standaard,* then everyone would know at the same time."[84] Many working-class Dutch, whether domestics or industrial workers, however, did not (and in many cases could not) opt for this kind of extravagance. Dutch American papers would post the names of all individuals married in Dutch American communities whether or not the couple paid for an additional notice. A formal wedding picture, one which could be sent across the ocean, however, was standard.

For a tiny, and I mean tiny, minority of women, the United States allowed a reasonable life for a woman who remained single. Both Cornelia De Groot and Cornelia De Bey, whose stories are in later chapters, made careers in the United States and never married. The United States in general had a large number of possibilities for them, but as part of the 1 percent never married of their generation among Dutch immigrants, they found less tolerance in Dutch American circles. An article in a 1910 edition of the Dutch American paper *The Banner* made the case clear in recommending a book with the subtitle *Thoughts about Marriage*: "[T]he unmarried state of adults is contrary to God's will and frequently caused by wrong motives."[85] The category of unmarried woman above about age twenty-five remained suspect among the immigrant generation. Just as single women found greater acceptance in the Netherlands, they lost their place among the U.S. Dutch. That women like De Groot and De Bey fought for educational opportunities for women, and for suffrage, only intensified the association of the women's movement with those who challenged family in Dutch immigrant eyes.

Overall, the function of marriage in the migration process represented a significant gender difference among the Dutch migrants of this period. Women came to marry; men returned to marry. Women practically never returned to marry, though they might return with a spouse. Men rarely migrated to marry someone specific, whereas they often sent for wives. The United States represented a better chance at marriage for both men and women, and the ideal of heterosexual couples reigned as the epitome of Protestant Dutch American family life. The women I studied did not label the process of finding a mate a "marriage market," but some political activists and journalists, especially those in the woman's movement (both in the United States and in the Netherlands), did.[86]

Het Gezin

Marriage was by far the most socially sanctioned role for an adult Protestant woman (or man) in both the United States and the Netherlands. Letters going in both directions across the Atlantic continually asked the marital status of young adults. If a daughter reached her mid-twenties, or a son his late twenties, parents would begin to explain why that individual was not married yet. Dutch Protestant children either in the Netherlands or in America grew up surrounded by the expectation that at some point they would get married and have children, starting their own *gezin* (nuclear family). Still, the ubiquity of the pattern, and thus the pressure to marry, was stronger on the U.S. side. "Spinsters" were unfortunate or even "unnatural" women who for whatever reason had been unable to attract a husband, aberrations from the norm, rather than a normal phenomenon which regularly applied to a minority of women and a positive choice for some.

Marital status was probably as important as any other factor in Dutch immigrant women's identity. Closely related was motherhood. Relatives and friends automatically assumed a couple would have children, and that these children would then grow up and marry, carrying on the cycle of life. The fact that there were always exceptions, those who did not have children, did not deter the rest from assuming this was the standard and expecting it of all. One of the major shifts underway on both sides of the Atlantic was an emotionalizing of familial relationships. In this, "love" became a more important factor in choosing mates and describing marital relations. Further, the psychological distance between parents and children narrowed, placing more emphasis on affective relations between parents and their offspring. The concepts of motherhood and fatherhood changed dramatically in this context. Most immigrants, however, did not take part in these changes extensively. Rural life and working-class standing insulated them from the shifts prior to migration, and the ethnic subculture of Dutch America generally tried to control the direction of familial roles in the United States. As with many other aspects of change in the period, immigrants often associated primary stress on the mother's role (as opposed to the father's) in the home and child rearing as an "American" pattern. The challenge, then, entailed moving into a bourgeois lifestyle without losing the form of patriarchy in the family which many Dutch Americans felt was their cultural heritage and religious duty.

Married Dutch immigrant women, at least until the end of this period, rarely discussed the quality of the relationships they had with their husbands in their letters. If they did it was in sweepingly general terms. Most often, women simply wrote that they had "good" husbands. "Bad" appeared in conjunction with reports of such things as physical abuse, drunkenness, lack of monetary support. Jantze Buist Schoemakers, a Seceder who was exceedingly pious in her remembrances, recalled that her second marriage, though to a believer, had its flaws: "We could live in peace. As for the rest, there was much to be desired. I was not always satisfied, and one who is dissatisfied is not always grateful."[87] Women wrote reports about their marriages most frequently in the first few months after getting married, or shortly after a husband's death. Either they did not write often about their relationships or such letters did not survive. Women did however write about other people's marital problems if conditions were extreme.[88] Rarely would they provide information about someone else's marriage much beyond the first year unless it was bad. "Love" became primary in the vocabulary surrounding marriage for a minority during this time, though interviewees, looking back on the turn of the century through the perspective of old age in the 1960s in a country obsessed by love, discussed marriage in romantic terms.[89]

After marriage came childbearing, at least according to expectations. P. Jonker, writing an article in De Gereformeerde Amerikaan, preached: "But we must keep in mind that a childless marriage is abnormal, is unusual, and should be written off to the destructive influence of sin. Unless what is natural is suppressed by the overriding influence of sin in man or woman, then a childless marriage is more or less a scourge for life to those involved."[90] Exactly how soon after marriage the children arrived could be a problem, but beyond nine months Dutch families, neighbors, and friends anticipated new additions. There was, however, something going on in terms of birthrates in the Netherlands at the turn of the century, something called birth control.[91] It appeared formally in 1881, with the appearance of the Nieuw Malthusiaanse Bond (New Malthusian Society), which followed the example of a similar English group. It rapidly became so closely associated with limiting births, that "new-malthusian" in Dutch connoted both abortion and birth control. In an 1884 report the society provided information on several forms of contraception—coitus interruptus, sponge and douche, pessary, condom.[92] The steady drop in the Dutch birthrate from the 1870s to the 1920s attested to the success of birth control efforts.[93] According to several studies, however, such information made its way to rural areas and the working class in the Netherlands slowly.[94]

Prospective immigrants did hear about the existence of the new-malthusians and about the "sinfulness" of birth control. Abraham Kuyper, in a widely publicized speech of 1891 on moral improvement, "Het sociale vraagstuk en de christelijke religie [The social question and Christian religion]," spoke out strongly against contraception and against abortion. This became an important part of his campaign to connect law to morality. In 1911, the Christian parties succeeded in banning not only all forms of abortion, including the generally accepted "medical abortion" to save the life of the mother, but also to put a gag rule on information concerning contraception. The business went underground.[95] Kuyper, like his opponents the new-malthusians, recognized overpopulation as a problem in the Netherlands, but his solution was emigration and colonization. Many of his followers ended up in the United States.[96]

Contraception and abortion thus came into the focus of public debate around the turn of the century as part of the larger civilizing campaign. Another element of the campaign was to stigmatize prenuptial pregnancy. By 1910 the Netherlands had the lowest per capita rate of illegitimate births in western Europe, and the percentage of forced marriages, that is, where the prospective bride was pregnant, at least according to some records, was also comparatively low.[97] Still, governmental officials found major regional differences. Workers from Friesland generally garnered praise, whereas those in the neighboring province of Groningen appeared as among the worst.[98] Both provinces had some of the highest emigration rates, and these were concentrated among the workers who were the focus of governmental concern. Thus, in the Netherlands the turn of the century witnessed both an increasing use of birth control and decreasing legal access to contraception and abortion.

Coming from this background, Dutch immigrants to the United States in general found few major differences, most notably the decentralized (state or municipality based) form of much lawmaking concerning morals. In the United States campaigns were underway to criminalize prostitution, the Comstock law forbade distribution of information on contraception, and abortion was both illegal and extant in most states.[99] But whereas "new-malthusian" was synonymous with contraception in the Netherlands, in the United States the key phrase of the late Victorian era was "voluntary motherhood," and it entailed abstinence. This bourgeois ideology, which lacked the strongly anti-religious connotations associated with new-malthusianism, might have appealed to a minority of Dutch Protestants had they been aware of it, or had they wanted smaller families, such appears to have been the case among the second generation.

Among the immigrant generation fertility was high, high enough to indicate the absence of birth control for many. Amry Vandenbosch was not off base when he reported that Dutch immigrants in Chicago frequently had families of eight to ten children.[100] The 1910 Public Use Sample included eighty Dutch-born women in the over-forty age group, and they averaged just over seven children ever born.[101] In rural settings children helped to provide the farm labor which was otherwise unavailable or expensive. Even within rural areas, however, women sometimes had mixed feelings about a "large" family. Geertje de Jong Schuiling provided a rare reference to family size: "[She] must already have her ninth child. The fun doesn't seem to be over for Jentje, because that soul is really getting her hands full. I shudder to think of it."[102] Schuiling herself had four children when she wrote this, at least two not yet toilet trained.

Dutch American religious leaders frequently stressed the need for large families and decried the trend toward limiting births. The English-language *Banner* made the connection to birth control explicit in a 1910 article: "Not all barrenness is involuntary, some of it is self-imposed. With former generations nature had its course, and therefore there were usually big families. Among some of the second and third generation of the Dutch in this country big families are the exception, and so one can not help but think . . . that some are following the devices of many of their neighbors. . . . I would say to all: remember God sees you and you are responsible to Him, and also that you have a duty in this world to the human race."[103]

The Helmer and Lupke Modderman family around the turn of the century. Having eight children was typical of the immigrant generation. Photo courtesy of Jane Eppinga.

Dutch immigrants expected to have children once they got married, and people would talk if they did not, but pregnancy, like sexuality, was not a subject to discuss in print. Letters often gained a label according to the most important news they conveyed, so there were many letters "about the birth of" someone. But the "child" existed in their letters for the most part after birth. Before that time if the expectant parents wrote anything, and many did not, they generally avoided the term pregnant, using pseudonyms instead. Once the child arrived a letter was in order, as with this example from 1893: "I can report to you that we are all healthy and that Grietje had a son. Mother and child were both quick. Before the birth it was difficult because of the extreme heat. We had a hot summer, around a hundred [degrees]."[104] Correspondence indicated that families did not share intergenerational knowledge about pregnancy transatlantically. The same lack of reporting was generally true of nursing.[105] Regarding bodily processes and many basics of child care, thus, women without extended family nearby either went without any information or relied on other local sources.

With the arrival of children, men and women took on parental roles, roles which presented class-based contradictions in this period. The process of emotionalizing family life, which elevated motherhood and child rearing, had already begun in the middle class during the nineteenth century in the Netherlands, and was slowly moving into the working class after the turn of the century.[106] Still, working class families in the Netherlands, according to many sources, paid little attention to the individuality of children until after World War I. They, in comparison with more middle-class families, relied on their offspring for specific roles, notably economic contributions to the family budget. Government reports from the period illustrated the monetary bind of many farmworkers' wives, who actually were co-workers with their mates, who took jobs which paid at rates which made child care impossible, requiring them to leave infants with children or very elderly women, or to bring them to the fields where they lay largely unattended.[107] This contrasted the middle-class ideal of the mother in the home concentrating on child socialization.[108]

The publication of *Pedagogische beginselen* in 1904 (and its appearance in several further editions) heralded a more serious interest in child development, particularly for school-age children, among more orthodox Protestants in the Netherlands, including many of the farm-laboring class. For this group the stress continued to be on breaking the will of the "sinful child," which required corporal punishment. This went against the dominant strain of Protestant thought of the time, which advocated a somewhat closer relationship between parents and children, with more persuasion than coercion. The more orthodox view prevailed among many who migrated. A second aspect of this orthodox view was the clear positioning of father as head of child socialization, even if the mother carried out much of it. Less orthodox Protestant prescriptive literature gave the mother a bit more leeway to make decisions in the home about child rearing, but not much. When Abraham Kuyper, leader of the Doleantie, described the relations between parents, he indicated that the father must set the standard and govern clearly. The mother was only to follow his instructions, and because of her weaker nature, the father should supervise her work with the children carefully to make sure she stuck to his plan.[109] Dutch law made it clear that men were the heads of the household and had full control of all that took place within it.[110]

This was the vision of family arrangements many Dutch immigrants brought with them. Migration may have sped the move into the middle class for some, but it did not necessarily mean a shift toward maternal power in the household, which after migration could appear as an "American" pattern. The version of paternal authority to which many migrants ascribed had various manifestations: "Meal time father always asked a blessing; after eating, a chapter was read from the Bible and Grandpa returned thanks to the Giver of all. This was always kept up, no matter how busy they were."[111] Men leading devotions, reading one chapter of a book of the Bible each night, was a common pattern. Unlike dominant American society, where men were slowing moving away from Bible reading and prayer by the turn of the century, many Dutch American families stuck strictly to familial prayer and Bible reading at which all members of the family were present.[112] The father led the discussion in such cases, though any member of the family might be called upon to do the reading. Prescriptive articles set forth the husband as leader of family conversation as well.[113]

The imperative for fathers/husbands to head their families also had an impact on migration patterns. In the case of the Koert family, who moved to Lynden, Washington, father and son arrived first with the intention of getting settled (and earning some money) before sending for the rest of the family in the Netherlands. Back in Rotterdam Peternella Koert and her other four children were in the process of selling the family business while two children worked and one went through teachers' training. Because the Koerts had started out with the idea of homesteading in Alberta, the separation had already lasted a few months when the father and son arrived in Lynden. This arrangement did not suit the leaders of the church the Koerts sought to join. The local history quoted the pastor around 1912: "This man can not remain here without his family."[114] The consistory of the church agreed and they co-signed a loan for the fare so the remaining family could come immediately. Likewise, church consistories on either side of the Atlantic would excommunicate a woman who refused to follow her husband if he chose to migrate.

Information on a mother's role and how it coordinated with that of her spouse was less prevalent in Dutch American sources than one might expect. There were tributes to motherhood generally, and to specific mothers. As in the letters, people assumed women took care of small children.[115] They also trained daughters in household tasks as they got older. Beyond that, mothers promoted religious training, and other basic education, though exactly what that included differed from family to family. But this came in addition to other household tasks, and other duties often took precedence. Just as was the case for the rural German-speaking women studied by Linda Schelbitzki Pickle, combining women's tasks with child care was particularly difficult on farms, where women were active in the barns, gardens, and fields.[116] For those without extended family there was often a stage in the life cycle where there were small children and no help to care for them. When Elizabeth Menkens Schreurs's toddler daughter wandered outside "unnoticed," found a scythe, and nearly severed her toe, it was a comment on the difficulty of keeping track of toddlers, and a hint at the other jobs within the home which took precedence over that supervision.[117] Mothering, while important, often had to wait for other activities. As interest in mothering increased in the dominant culture at the turn of the century, Dutch American culture picked up on part of it but then translated it in such a way as to undergird a particular vision of patriarchy.

How Dutch immigrant women related to their children was often evident in their letters. To some extent the amount of information related to the time period—the later, the greater. But it also had to do with the woman's evaluation of childhood, and with a woman's normal outlet for sharing information about children, so that mothers and sisters generally learned more than others. Maaike Huigen consistently included the number, names, and ages of children, with few embellishments, in her sporadic letters to the Netherlands. Sometimes she just made a list with ages, and sometimes she tried to give a bit more detail. For example, in 1881 she wrote a letter from Pella, Iowa, in which she mentioned sending a picture of her family to her father and siblings. "Antje is a strapping gal of thirteen and a half and she helps me a lot since she is very handy. Then Geert and Jacob a pair of strong boys ages 11 and 9; then Neeltje and Maria ages 7 and 4; then Cornelia a nice girl with red cheeks and black eyes, 2 years old: so that is already a big household."[118] This was a world apart from Klaaske Noorda Heller, an immigrant to Washington who brought "life" into her descriptions of her children. Writing to her mother and other family in the 1890s, she portrayed a household scene: "Malenus walks to us and brings me a little [piece of] wood and then he says stump. Mommy, he makes a song of everything. If he looks at his little hand then he takes it by the fingers and then he sings as loud as he can finger after finger . . . he is sitting by me here now in the chair and he plays with his box of blocks which we brought along from Ulrum."[119] By 1920 most of the immigrant women I studied discussed their children in more detailed terms. Lengthy descriptions like Noorda Heller's went hand in hand with more emotional relationships.

Perhaps the most striking feature of motherhood for many Dutch American women, in comparison to the dominant culture, was the lack of control of child rearing which many indicated. Prescriptive articles in church-related publications drew frequently on the theme of fatherhood and a father's role at home, chiding American society for abandoning the proper roles: "If child-rearing is to take on its true form, then the father is the one doing the raising. . . . God set forth this rule and it remains so."[120] Within the Dutch American community this meant first of all a denial of the idealized motherhood of the dominant society, and second an attack on materialism, because of which men found it necessary to work outside the home so much and put their energies elsewhere. "The greatest occupation in the world is the raising of children" stated one editorial in 1910, aimed at men and women equally.[121]

Often Dutch American publications stressed God as the role model for fathers.[122] In this schema fathers ruled their wives and children. Few questioned this ideal, except in unusual circumstances. One of the father's tasks, particularly in more conservative Protestant circles, was handling discipline. As Amry Vandenbosch, writing about Dutch American communities in Chicago, succinctly stated: "Family discipline is often rigid."[123] Drawing the line between appropriate corporal punishment and child abuse was one of the tasks which sometimes fell to a church consistory, but it could also become a legal issue.[124]

The same applied to relations between spouses. A very negative interpretation of a husband's power appeared in Cobie de Lespinasse's novel of Dutch American life, *The Bells of Helmus,* modeled on her own youth at the turn of the century in Orange City, Iowa. In one part of the story the dominie's wife talked to a man who tried to control the religious practice of his wife:

> "*Juffrouw,* you mean well and I honor you for it. But the wife must obey the man. He is the head of the house and she must obey. The Bible teaches this."
> "And if Lena will not obey, Kees?"
> "Then I shall strap her. The man is the head and the wife must obey."[125]

While wife beating was not common in my sources, in practice a wife did have to follow her husband's lead or face serious consequences. An unusual but still illustrative case was that of Lena Goemaat Versteeg, who faced off with her spouse in *De Volksvriend* over her right to buy and sell goods. Cornelis Versteeg wrote "Everyone is warned hereby not to buy anything from my wife or to sell anything to her without my orders." Her reply, printed directly below it, accused him of doing this because she had sold two bushels of potatoes in order to buy fuel, to which he had agreed. She then went on to a long list of complaints: "[H]e cannot live with any woman . . . he does not know how to best irritate [me] because I acted appropriately."[126]

Under the version of marital property rights which Cornelis Versteeg utilized, a wife had no rights to buy or sell anything, even what she raised or made on her own. This form of subordinate status in terms of property existed until the mid-twentieth century for women in the Netherlands, while in the United States, it began disappearing on a state by state basis in the 1840s.[127] Iowa was typical of the Midwest in this sense. Women began receiving separate marital property rights in 1846, and as of 1870 both spouses could make contracts independently of one another and a woman's property and earnings were her own. Custom often included butter and egg money, and by implication garden produce, as a woman's, though in court it still belonged to the husband.[128] While in practice the differences were not great, this did represent one of the areas where the legal status of women challenged patriarchal power in the United States more than in the Netherlands. Patriarchal power in the United States was enshrined in many other ways, for example, by laws which stated that a woman must reside with her husband, statutes which made it mandatory in a legal sense for a woman to follow her husband if he decided to migrate from place to place.[129]

The vision of patriarchal power also applied to religious belief, though the state did not enforce this. When Klaas Schuiling decided to change religious denominations, his sister in the Netherlands was more than a little upset, not least of all for the problems it could cause his wife and children: "Does Geertje think the same way about this or differently? . . . Does Geertje agree that the children should go to another school, or did you just force that because you think that is it better?"[130] For persons with a religious worldview which stressed the husband as leader of family worship, it was difficult if not impossible for a woman to maintain a different denominational affiliation. In my sources it was only when the husband was irreligious, a fairly uncommon phenomenon, that this might succeed.

One way that churches promoted a familial ideal was to stress that families should attend church together. In some churches in the Netherlands in the nineteenth century men, women, boys, and girls sat separately from one another. Some churches in the United States continued this practice, as did the one Jantje Modderman Negen attended in Renville, Minnesota.[131] But even more switched to the "American" custom of families sitting together. This was one more way of stressing nuclear families in the new setting. Likewise many churches in the Netherlands still utilized the pew rent system which helped maintain spatial differences between classes. Dutch American prescriptive literature argued this was wrong. Pew rents, according to one article, were "contrary to the spirit of democratic America."[132] In any case I did not find evidence that pew rents were common in the United States. The consistory notes, however, did indicate that young people continued to sit separately from their parents, by choice, often to the dismay of the elders in charge of keeping down noise during services. Elders preferred for parents to have primary responsibility, including for young adult children.

There was one instance in which nearly all commentators referred to parenthood: death of one parent. "Motherless children" or "fatherless children" were common currency in the exchange of Dutch American writers. None expected a widower to keep the children for long unless there was a woman to "help" or if one of the daughters was old enough to take over her mother's role. The most common job advertisement aimed at women in *De Volksvriend,* one of the largest Dutch American papers, published out of Orange City, Iowa, and circulated widely in Dutch American communities elsewhere, was for a housekeeper for a family without an adult woman. Sometimes the ads placed by such individuals bordered on desperation: "Housekeeper needed for a family with four children. If I do not find one soon I will have to give up the children."[133] The threat here was real. Infant care, cooking, and housekeeping were women's roles in Dutch America. Without immediate remarriage, extended family as in the case of Jantje Modderman Negen, a housekeeper, or older daughter, men did resort to placing their children out. Widows fared somewhat better. Most adult women had experience in field work and in many of the tasks generally assigned to men, but not vice versa. The heaviest tasks most associated with men, like ploughing, could be done by male friends/co-religionists, though even on this women sometimes literally took the reins.

A premise of collective responsibility beyond parental roles underlay prescriptive articles in De Gereformeerde Amerikaan and The Banner: parents were responsible for their children, but it was also the duty of the church, in the congregational as well as denominational sense, to ensure that they promoted a society good for children and to protect "their" children from bad influences. In one article on the "Morals of Holland Young Men," the author mused: "Could the church do more than she is doing to keep her children in line? Are the agencies of the church sufficient for American conditions? Would associations and clubs outside of the church, but under good Christian control, be advisable? Are some congregations too large for the church officers to look after?"[134] The final question referred to the practice of deacons or elders from the church patrolling urban areas to make sure the teenagers were not going to inappropriate settings, whether theaters, dance halls, or "houses of ill-fame." Similar sentiment spurred a plethora of Dutch American–supported blue laws to make sure that on Sundays, when these moral police were at church, others could not get into at least certain kinds of "mischief." For young people who got caught, discipline took the form of physical punishment. The biblical injunction by which immigrants equated sparing the rod with spoiling the child found its way into many sermons.

Only certain elements of children's lives made their way into letters and interviews. As with other subjects, the absence of information could be just as important as its presence. Two Dutch celebrations for children, the feastdays of St. Martin and St. Nicholas, were part of Cornelia De Groot's description of her Dutch girlhood.[135] They were not practiced overall in the Netherlands, and were more prominent in Catholic than in Protestant areas, though by no means confined to them. St. Nicholas Eve, the fifth of December, was the time for children to receive presents, as opposed to Christmas, which was set aside for religious services. In the United States, it appears that families rapidly shifted to the Christmas gift-giving standard. Ytje Schuiling wrote in 1900 that her little brother Thijs did not get anything for St. Nicholas because people did not celebrate it where they lived (Manhattan, Montana). Rather he got a toy ship for Christmas.[136] Dutch American newspapers confirmed this pattern. While in the 1910s neither De Volksvriend nor De Hollandsche Amerikaan carried regular advertisements for St. Nicholas celebrations, with the exception of traditional baked goods, both carried many ads for Christmas presents, including dolls, trains, and rolling horses. These papers, and *Pella's Weekblad* in addition, used an American-style Santa Claus as the illustration for such ads and added a child looking a stocking or a Christmas tree with lighted candles. The bulk of the ads appeared in December, but after St. Nicholas Day.[137]

Another aspect of familial life which did not appear in letters was sex education. Other sources, however, indicated that it was absent in many homes despite the promptings of many. *The Banner,* for example, sought to find ways for families to address this touchy subject. In 1909 an editorial encouraged families to use Dr. Stahl's "Self and Sex Series," indicating that "our boys and girls have had untold injury done to their souls and bodies by having the mysteries of our origin and sexual life unfolded to them by polluted lips of godless boys and girls, or of still more ungodly adults."[138] A similar editorial appeared the following year, and two years thereafter the newspaper recommended another sex education manual, this time one in Dutch.[139] To what extent families actually used these books or provided this education, however, is unclear. One Dutch immigrant who grew up in the province of Noord Holland before moving to western Michigan reported that as a child, people told her storks brought babies. "I was the youngest and I had never had any sisters. And I wanted a sister so badly. So when I saw one flying I would say, oh man, please stop at our place."[140] Other sources indicated that individuals did at least receive a modicum of information just prior to marriage, either from a dominie or from a book.[141]

One of the most candid accounts of sexuality I encountered was that of Lini Moerkerk de Vries, who was exceptional in many ways. Moerkerk de Vries was the daughter of Dutch immigrants and raised in the Reformed Church. In her autobiography she reported being sexually abused at about age six by a missionary who was supposedly giving her Bible training. In her account she was not exactly sure what was happening other than it didn't seem right, so she told her mother of the incident. This was one of several occasions when her mother accused her of leading the man on and being a "whore."[142] Moerkerk de Vries described her confusion when her mother warned that her "belly would swell" long before she understood what this meant. At puberty, her parents offered no additional information. Rather, she learned about the facts of life from some of her non-Dutch contacts. During this period she worked at several textile mills in the Paterson area, and she described how the owners and more senior men assumed a young woman worker was fair game for sexual conquest and how she managed to fight sexual harassment on the job successfully with the assistance of other workers. Moerkerk de Vries's knowledge of human sexuality gained a scientific basis when she went to nurses training. Later after having a child herself and then becoming a widow, she joined the birth control movement, working for a time in New York for Margaret Sanger in her pioneer family planning clinic.[143] Moerkerk de Vries's life went well beyond the period of my study, and several aspects of her life were much more typical of the second generation, which she represented, than the first. She did, however, provide insight into some elements of Dutch American life. The lack of sexual education which she chronicled vividly was one hinted at by many others.

The prudishness that some lamented was not the only tradition brought from the Netherlands. A second, countervailing tradition accompanied some immigrants, a folklore of bawdy jokes and songs which did not make its way into print as often. While public sexual expression was frowned upon in most sections of the Netherlands, there were plenty of individuals who knew the little sea ditties or farmer's wife stories. One interviewee from Iowa recited a few poems he learned from his grandmother: "The farmer's wife went for a walk / wearing pants without buttons."[144] Another ditty passed down in the family of Winterswijk emigrants began: "The king of Egypt / Had a thing that bounced [alternative meaning: *vulg.* screwed], / Between the legs and under the fanny [alternative meaning: down it goes]"[145] This kind of information appeared more often in interviews, song collections, or "Yankee Dutch" books, not in letters. But both men and women knew of and would recite such information, though generally it was men who did so more often. That may have been due in part to the gendered nature of joke telling, particularly dirty joke telling, in the twentieth century. Still, the stories illustrated another side to Dutch American Protestant life. Where young people learned such jokes, however, was not clear.

Such were the roles and the idealization of roles within Dutch American nuclear families. Migration did little to change these relations for any except the young, particularly young women, who had a chance to live "American" before marriage. Unlike the dominant population, Dutch American Protestants for the most part did not adopt an idealized motherhood, though they clearly had to fight to keep fatherhood in its "proper" place. Some churches changed their seating practices to emphasize nuclear families and lack of class divisions. Parents adjusted holidays and some activities for children. Shifts toward more attention to child socialization and toward more emotional relationships within marriage took place roughly simultaneously on both sides of the Atlantic, though some may have seen them as "American" and used this as a reason to avoid them. Nuclear families, if anything, gained more importance with migration. What changed more dramatically was the relationship of the nuclear family to the extended family.

De Familie

The realm of extended family ties, *de familie,* underwent some of the most wrenching changes in the process of migration. Those women who could reassemble these networks in the United States were generally the most satisfied with the move. But there were a variety of ways in which women could maintain family ties. The most obvious way was for the entire group to migrate, as with

Jantje Modderman Negen. Chain migration operated similarly. Thus Lubbigje Schaapman came to America with her parents and younger siblings in 1911. They joined one of her cousins, Gertie van Konynenburg, and her husband, who helped arrange a farm rental for the Schaapmans. Two of the Schaapman children, both sons of working age, had preceded the rest of the family by a year, and both had wage-earning positions as farmhands to assist the family budget.[146] The Schaapmans had a somewhat better financial base than other immigrants, but many others followed the pattern of waiting for family members who preceded them to gain a foothold. They also followed a pattern typical of those who wanted a better life for their children.[147] The Schaapman parents could have lived out their days comfortably on their farm in the Netherlands, but it would not have sustained their children for many years beyond. Emigrating allowed them to continue an agricultural way of life into the next generation.

How a family arranged the migration chain varied. Widows frequently migrated with all their children at one time. Working-age children might emigrate with relatives and friends first, and their wages, as in the example of the Schaapman family, supported the rest of the family. In other cases the working children paid for the passage of their siblings, or elderly parents stayed behind. Young adults might migrate in groups, often of siblings, but sometimes as couples directly after marriage. Uncles, aunts, and cousins often had a role in assisting migration as well. One woman, who was twenty-two when she migrated with her parents in 1907, recalled that when they arrived in Minnesota she already had three uncles with farms in the vicinity of their destination who helped them get established.[148] Friends and congregation members could play an important role in spurring migration as well, especially in offering advice and perhaps a place to stay on arrival. But generally it was family members who supported one another financially, who sent tickets, who made arrangements for the newcomers.

Even with the best of planning, however, things could interfere with the prospective emigration. Changes in economic conditions, whether land fraud in Colorado, a period of labor unrest in Paterson, New Jersey, or a series of bad harvests in Iowa, could result in warnings to wait in immigrant letters. But other factors could enter in as well, factors on both sides of the Atlantic. Marie van Huis recalled that her father promised her mother they would return to the Netherlands after two and a half years. World War I began in the meantime, and they had to wait until ocean travel was safer. The extra few years was enough to convince some of the children to remain in the new world.[149]

For the majority of Dutch immigrant women, one of the most important ways to evaluate the United States was in terms of how many family members were there. As one woman from Pella, Iowa, reminisced, moving to a staunchly Dutch American community, even to a settlement from the same village, in this case the Herwijnen neighborhood, was not always enough: "Mother? [pause] . . . oh, she missed Holland heaps at first, oh yes. She had one brother here, that was all, and my father had more brothers and sisters. That helped, but it was still like she could not break away from her house, from her family as easily."[150] Likewise, Geertje de Jong Schuiling, living in Montana, wrote about an upcoming wedding, that at least one hundred Dutch people would be attending. Child care was a problem for them all, she noted, since there were no domestics and no extended family members around. Her frustration came through clearly: "I wish that I had just one family member here or J. and her girls."[151] Those outside the Dutch community complained most about the distance, the homesickness, the lack of family.

The demographics of migration, which even though family-oriented for the group as a whole still favored males somewhat, meant that women had potentially fewer female extended family relations within the United States after migration. Basically brothers were more likely to recruit other brothers and nephews, and male cousins and friends than to successfully recruit sisters or other female kin. A woman had only a small window in her life course at which she could independently decide to migrate if encouraged, either as an unmarried young adult or as a widow. In both cases she also had to have the means to migrate, and given unequal wages she was less likely to be able to do this without support than were her male kin. Men's greater leverage in making decisions about migration meant that married women, while not without influence, could not unilaterally decide to go with their consanguine kin.[152] Married men also needed to convince spouses, but the evidence from letters and family histories indicates they could force this decision quite effectively. For women, these patterns

This Kok family gathering took place at the home of Teunis and Rolina Kok DeValois in Lynden, Washington, ca. 1906. Photo courtesy of Archives, Calvin College.

meant a significant number who had more in-laws than consanguine kin, particularly in terms of female relatives, in the new location. This helps explain the reluctance of many women to eagerly support their spouses' decisions to migrate.

The case of the Ten Hoor family is illustrative of this pattern. Foppe ten Hoor and Leentje Melles Veenboer ten Hoor lived in Haule, in the province of Friesland, and had eleven children. The first to migrate was their ninth child and sixth son, Willem ten Hoor, who left with his spouse Hendrikje Houtman ten Hoor and their two children in 1883. Willem's little brother Gerhardus followed, and he eventually married a Dutch woman who had migrated with her parents. Three nephews of Willem, all sons of different brothers, also migrated around the turn of the century. Two were already married and had children, the third married a Dutch American woman in the United States. Though they migrated at different times, the male relatives all settled close to one another in western Michigan. There were many sisters and nieces in the Ten Hoor family, but none of them joined this migration according to the detailed family genealogy.[153]

Trying to settle family members together was a common phenomenon. One woman in Sibley, Iowa, noted that her daughter Ana "lives close to us, her property and ours lie next to one another."[154] In cases such as this, family visiting could take place on a day-to-day basis, for coffee. Frequently this was the strategy of the family farm, not only in order to have joint farming ventures but to increase the size of the farm for the coming generation. In urban areas the pattern differed somewhat. There, young adults were more likely to share housing with siblings, either a group of siblings living together or a single sibling joining a married sibling and family.[155] Such residential patterns were primarily ways to save money, but they also allowed family members to share household tasks and to have company.

What exactly did it mean to have a relative living in close proximity? Gezina van der Haar Visscher provided a hint in her diary. She and her brother Arend lived in the Holland, Michigan, area. Both were married and had several children, but they still shared important segments of their lives. They attended the same church much of the time and frequently met for dinner or coffee along with religious discussion. When Gezina's horse died, Arend lent her one so she could get from the farm into town. After her husband died, Arend drove her around at times, and his children would stop by to visit her. The two families celebrated birthdays, anniversaries, and high school graduations together. Besides presents for such occasions, Arend also gave his sister and her family a stove. When his child was seriously ill, she assisted with nursing. When a mutual friend died, he broke the news. When Holland put on a fiftieth anniversary celebration, she wrote a historical sketch which he then read aloud at one of the large prayer meetings.[156] In short, they were part of one another's lives in major and minor ways on a weekly if not daily basis.

Van der Haar Visscher was also involved in the lives of her adult children. For example, in 1895 she gained two grandchildren.[157] While she did not record the pregnancies in her diary, just the births, reading back over the previous months one could find clues that she was assisting in particular ways. There were more joint sewing sessions than normal and in one case she paid an extended visit to one daughter in the latter months of the pregnancy when the daughter's husband went on a trip. These were things which came in addition to regular visits, assistance with housecleaning, shared meals, and celebrations. These were things which women without older female relatives nearby missed, and for which they had to find substitutes.

The letters of Dutch immigrant women were usually a part of this substitution process. A woman could write at least some of the things she in many cases would have shared in person. Beyond that the letters contained reams of material on the everyday fare of extended family relations, much of it couched in terms of "I wish I could . . ." In some cases writers may have been observing a polite convention, especially when it came to sending money to relatives. In other cases the consistency with which an author presented the desire to see a new baby, have coffee with an aunt, or stroll with a brother along a canal they knew from childhood indicated both a kind of homesickness and the irreplaceable loss of one segment of their social and familial world. Such feelings, however, were not confined to the immigrants but also affected those left behind.

"How are your two little kids? Are they growing? I wish I could see you all again. . . . Give little sis and brother a kiss from me."[158] "I would like to send a pretty hat to your little Mettje, that won't work so give her a kiss for me."[159] With only these quotes it would be impossible to tell which letter came from the United States and which from the Netherlands. The family news people shared often had this quality. Certain conventions crept into the letter writing, just as common patterns for what to send and when to write became entrenched. People wrote to acknowledge birthdays, to give reports of births or deaths, to wish the recipients a happy new year, and to answer the letters of their relatives.

The desire to demonstrate to the relatives that the children were learning to write, either in English or in Dutch, was a common phenomenon. If the children started writing at an early age they could "meet" their Dutch relatives in print. The information that they shared, which frequently replicated what their parents wrote, was less important than the act of sharing it. The parents already knew that writing could be an emotional bridge across the Atlantic, and they sought to strengthen that bridge by adding another generation. The Schuiling children, Thijs, Sietske, and Ytje, each wrote a note to put in the envelope for their Aunt Klaaske in August 1912. Thijs mentioned that they had suffered a hailstorm and that soon they would renovate the kitchen with running water. Sietske noted the new kitchen as well, and added that a young friend was learning to ride a horse. Finally, Ytje reported about school vacation, the lack of a schoolmaster at the moment, and how she helped her mother with washing and ironing. Their father, whose letter was last in the bundle, noted that the children were playing together in the attic since it was a rainy day.[160] Weather, play, holidays, helping with household tasks, changes in the home, school activities, horseback riding, and local friends—these were also themes in the letters of other young Dutch American correspondents. The penmanship, spelling, and vocabulary illustrated that the children were doing the writing.

Literacy in a common language, in the Dutch and Dutch American context, was crucial to maintaining close transatlantic ties. News could travel in many ways, and the sense of responsibility to family could overcome many obstacles, but in the turn-of-the-century setting, writing was the most common way to share transatlantic news. For many families, such a form of communication was a novelty. Migration to America in this period made it impossible to share news on a frequent basis in any other way. Several of the women I studied were reasonably well educated and could write in fluid prose. The majority, however, possessed what most would consider basic literacy. They could write to convey news and a sense of caring, but had difficulty in writing at times, as attested by the unconventional spelling, dialect, and grammar in many letters, and by passages which were ambiguous at best. Over time the difficulties of correspondence could worsen, particularly for correspondents who began to function more and more in English or for the elderly as they faced physical impairments which made writing more difficult if not impossible over time. For the minority who could not write, migration meant having to rely on others to transmit news to and from the family. Either other people did the reading and writing for the individual, with all the pitfalls of having someone else "translate" one's ideas onto paper, or the individual had to wait for other migrants to carry news personally from one location to another. In the Huigen Annyas family, Maaike Huigen served as a translator, both in terms of language and literacy. She wrote letters which sometimes included news from her husband, who never learned to write, and she translated the notes from her daughter Nellie, who wrote in English.[161] On the other hand, those who wrote to farm laborers in the Netherlands often had to depend on the *boer* or *boerin* (farm owners) to relay the news, either by reading it to someone or by physically turning over the letter.[162]

Person-to-person gossip, the mainstay of village and farm news transmission, could also take place on the transatlantic scale. News in that case, however, had to rely on someone making the crossing and delivering the message. Ethnic newspaper notices indicating who would be going to the Netherlands in the near future helped people identify possible messengers. A person headed in either direction could expect many of the local residents with friends or relatives in the other locale to ask the traveler to deliver verbal messages, often a barrage of them. Yet the senders did not always trust these messengers. Likewise, much news could not wait for the next international traveler. Because travelers were more often men than women, the news they shared was less likely to include much about women's gendered activities.

It was all too easy for people to lose contact. A correspondent frequently noted how she did not get around to writing as often as she felt proper. "It has been quite a long time since I last wrote you."[163] Some tried to deflect criticism by anticipating the disapproving comments of the recipients: "You will probably say well finally a letter from America. Yes uncle I admit that we should have let you hear from us sooner."[164] But the criticism could go the other direction as well, as when Maaike Huigen's relatives did not write her of her father's death.[165] A family quarrel could end contact. It was one thing for two sisters living in the same village to quarrel; it was quite another for two living on opposite sides of the Atlantic. The potential in the latter case for total loss of contact was considerably greater.

After coming to the United States Dutch immigrants all expanded their definitions of "far." Bridging distances personally was important to many of them, hence they tried to visit extended family members at times. Hannah Bruins Vander Velde noted that two of her mother's brothers and their wives came to visit for the winter holidays.[166] For crop farmers without many animals, winter was the best time to visit, despite the chances for bad weather. Elderly family members could travel year round, though summer weather conditions made this the most common time for visiting. And for the rare and treasured return visit to the Netherlands, which many correspondents discussed and few managed, late spring to early fall was the only reasonable time. Dina Oggel wrote her sister in 1895 about two visits, one she made to Michigan and one her brother made to this sister in the Netherlands: "We got a letter from brother Kus from Holland, Mich. in which he wrote quite a lot about your people . . . [they] really had a good time with you. It is enough to make one get jealous. I can well understand that it was difficult to leave your people from both sides. Parting is always so difficult. I went through that this summer myself, when I was in Michigan and met Jan and Dirk and Marien whom I had not seen in 19 years. And we had a wonderful time together."[167] If the distance was great, a "visit" often lasted several weeks. This was the case either for families spread out across the United States, or for those living around the world. Anje Nieveen Mulder expressed a common resignation when she reported "our family is spread out into three states and it is impossible to say if we will ever be together again."[168] She went on to note that she had been to visit her parents on a recent trip, and that her younger sister Aaltje was coming to stay for the winter. She, like many others, could expand her vision of distance for daily and weekly activities, but the days of traveling and the cost involved in going to see relatives in another state made this an expensive and infrequent possibility.

A brief look through the local news and correspondents' sections of Dutch American newspapers added weight to this impression. For example, in *Pella's Weekblad* in 1916 each issue carried more than a hundred short reports of visits, illnesses, and accidents, and generally news of several small (and scattered) Dutch American communities. Men alone were more commonly listed as traveling from place to place, sometimes visiting both family and friends, than were women alone. Much of this mobility, however, was related to business, as in the case of the Iowa man who stopped in Holland, Michigan, after having sold his produce in Chicago. But lone men were also more likely than lone women to appear as Sunday visitors, the most common day for being sociable (according to the paper) among those who lived in visiting range. Married couples, sometimes with children, appeared very frequently in news reports as visiting kin. Lone women, either single or married, or even groups of women, did not show up as visitors as often, though women did appear to visit for longer periods of time than did men on average in my small sample. "Mrs. Marinus and Mrs. John de Zwart went . . . to Kilburn, Iowa, to visit their sister Mrs. Leydens for a week."[169] A married woman might go to her parents' home for a week or two, or a young woman might go to stay with relatives for the summer. At least according to this paper, women in these mainly rural communities were less involved in day-to-day visiting that spanned much of any distance.[170] Even if a woman did have relatives nearby, her ongoing daily tasks may have prevented much visiting, especially if the kin was not immediately adjacent to her own residence. Other Dutch newspapers such as *De Volksvriend* and the Sioux Center *Nieuwsblad* also carried visiting reports.[171] Whether word of the married woman going from Lynden, Washington, to Grand Rapids, Michigan, to visit a sibling, or of the couple from Ripon, California, visiting relatives and friends in Pella, Iowa, or of the young woman in Edgerton, Minnesota, who just returned from a visit with her aunt and uncle in Chicago, the local news and correspondents' reports included this information.

A few families organized more general means of bringing extended family together. Jacob van Hinte, who traveled the United States in the 1920s, pointed out the stress placed on family reunions. Such reunions, he noted, were also a custom in the Netherlands, though not nearly as important there. Van Hinte cited the example of the Ton family, which set a record with its 1920 family reunion in Roseland, Illinois, of over seven hundred members. The Tons all descended from two farmhands and their families who immigrated around 1850. By 1920 the family members were spread out all over the country, a common problem after several generations: "The fact that families are separated by such great distances evidently accounts for these reunions. Family members do not meet often enough, if at all, in their day-to-day routine. Parents, too, seldom see their children all together. Therefore they schedule definite dates for reunions and hold them on those days even after the parents have died. . . . [it] can only be surmised to what degree there is a need for family solidarity, for a sense of belonging."[172] The family reunion exemplified a changing reality of Dutch life in America. One had to plan to get together with relatives who, in many cases, did not live around the corner. The extended family became something one had to work to preserve, rather than something one could take for granted.

In studying Dutch American families I came to a recognition of the importance of family ties in the ethnic group's economic success and in women's well-being in many situations, yet I could hardly overlook the strict prescriptions on gender roles and the pain and anguish suffered by women who could or would not adhere to them. The vast majority of the letter writers had at least one extended family member nearby, and most tried to build extended family connections through children who married and started their own families. It was the group who wanted to maintain family ties but could not who had the most difficult time with migration. These were the most uprooted, the women who fought emigration, who complained in letter after letter of homesickness, and who tried desperately to find substitutes, most often in the church, for the extended family they left behind. In general these were married women, and I encountered them more frequently on the plains than in the cities. Some women enjoyed the freedom of seemingly endless space and new opportunities, but others saw mainly the difficulties of trying to fulfill their various family roles in a setting which made many of them impossible.

Family and State Ideologies

Lack of extended family, distances between relatives, and loss of family bonds were not simply a matter for individuals and their families. The Dutch Calvinist view of the world in this period was a corporatist one in which family and community intervened between state and individual. The Dutch shared this characteristic with other immigrants, particularly from Germany and Scandinavia.[173] One of the factors which contributed to problems of adjustment was the rapidly shifting nature of laws regarding families in this period, and the competing national visions of family, enshrined in different political systems. Dutch immigrants could try to maintain the patriarchal power of the husband as head of household over wife and children as they understood it, but in the American setting the newcomers, as a relatively small ethnic group, would have little impact on the national political stage.

The Netherlands was in the midst of a civilization or moralization campaign which led to pillarization, the form of vertical segregation I described in the introduction.[174] Leaders of the moralization campaign, who came from the confessional parties, successfully ingrained in the public discourse an association of women's rights with liberalism and socialism. In other words, arguments based on science and societal advancement, which were a mainstay of the American Progressive movement of this period, automatically ran up against two of the major (and sometimes ruling) political parties in the Netherlands. Spokespersons from the women's movement in this context often stressed women's special nature and the shift of formerly private tasks into the public realm. They did this to an even greater extent than their American counterparts.[175]

One of the ways in which women's rights questions, albeit in a rarefied form, came to general public awareness in the Netherlands was through the crowning of Wilhelmina as queen in 1898 and her subsequent marriage to Hendrik of Mecklenburg in 1901. A few commentators, particularly from among the orthodox Protestants, claimed no woman should rule. Others sought to make special exceptions to Dutch law in order to make it possible to carry on the royal family line of Oranje. One of the questions they faced was how to handle her citizenship, which according to Dutch law would automatically become his at marriage. This they solved by having him change his citizenship first. They also forged an agreement that the children would be "Oranje" first in the line of family names, the position usually reserved for the husband's primary surname. He received no right to her income, nor an income of his own, both typical characteristics of a woman at marriage in the Netherlands. As to his "marital power" over her, it was enshrined in law and ignored in public.[176] The debates illustrated women's status in marriage, but because they applied to royalty, who were always an exception to the rules, the general population could not expect similar treatment. Given the interest in things royal among part of the working population, including many potential migrants and those already in the United States, at least some of the issues may have resonated with people's own situations.[177]

The question of citizenship was one which also had a great deal of importance to women who migrated. In this area American law reversed its course from most developments concerning women in this period, by stressing familial bonds more emphatically. According to the naturalization law of 1855 a woman's citizenship was automatically that of her husband, as long as she would otherwise be eligible for citizenship (i.e., not a prostitute or a member of an inadmissible race). It did not matter whether she protested or agreed—if he became an American citizen so did she. He, but not she, would receive a certificate of citizenship. Neither could a married woman initiate citizenship proceedings.[178] The Expatriation Act of 1907 elaborated on this, and brought U.S. law closer to its Dutch counterpart. Under this act, if an American woman married a foreigner, she forfeited her right to remain a citizen. So a second-generation Dutch American literally became Dutch if she married a new immigrant from the Netherlands. There were significant dangers involved should something happen to the husband. While under the 1907 law a widow of an alien who had made a declaration of intent to naturalize could still become a citizen without filing her own petition, such was not the case for others. A widow whose spouse had not filed first papers, regardless of her own place of birth, could be deported if she requested public aid. Thus widows' and mothers' pensions, which were developing in several states, were unavailable. Likewise if the male U.S. citizen went back to the Netherlands to marry but then died on the way back, the spouse had no U.S. citizenship rights. Not until the Cable Act of 1922 did women have the option of determining their nationality (applying for naturalization, maintaining citizenship) on their own. That came on the heels of quota legislation, by which once the country's quota was filled, women arriving as spouses could come in only under a special parole status, as visiting aliens. This made it much more difficult for them to petition for naturalization.[179]

In U.S. law the prerogatives of patriarchy clashed with those of race at times.

With the 1875 Page Law, targeted at Asian "coolie" labor and prostitutes, U.S. government officials made it difficult if not impossible for Chinese women to join husbands in the United States. This was strengthened with the Chinese Exclusion Acts beginning in 1882, which forbade the migration of wives of laboring men.[180] The Japanese government, facing similar stereotypes, stopped male migration under the Gentlemen's Agreement of 1907, but men could still send for spouses, whom they could also marry in absentia. The resulting "picture brides" helped fuel the agitation for a total ban on Asian migration.[181] For Asian women generally, naturalization was not possible because they were not "white," and according to the doctrine of an 1868 Supreme Court decision, women automatically became citizens on marriage to an American *except* in cases of racial ineligibility. Agitation through the early 1900s against wives entering who could be excluded on other grounds (medical condition or immorality) added to this mix.

Such was the situation facing Bertha Gendering, a Dutch woman who married an immigrant who acquired U.S. citizenship. According to the immigration case files, the couple lived together for seven years, and then the husband deserted her before his naturalization was finalized. Two years later she sued for divorce, but in the meantime she had met and begun living with another man. When this new couple made a trip to Europe, they were denied reentry to the United States on the grounds of immoral conduct (unlawful cohabitation). But according to Dutch law Gendering had forfeited her citizenship with her first marriage, hence the judge ruled that she was an American and could not be excluded on these grounds. The immigration files mentioned in passing that Gendering had married by proxy when she was in Amsterdam and her husband was in New York. This was not a typical Dutch marriage pattern.[182] In the same time period immigration inspectors repeatedly tried to exclude Japanese women on exactly those grounds, though consular officials noted that this was perfectly legitimate (and not unusual) in Japan.[183] Gendering's case was one of several which formed the grounds for revising U.S. laws about marital citizenship in the 1920s, making race (in the form of ethnic/national group) a discriminatory category for European immigrants. Up to 1920 however, Dutch women rarely faced challenges to acquiring U.S. citizenship through marriage. Moreover, in the halls of Ellis Island, Dutch women migrating to join husbands generally got the benefit of the doubt.[184] The relatively unproblematic entry of Dutch women into the United States throughout the period was directly related to their "whiteness" in the pre-1920 legal racial hierarchy. In Dutch immigrant letters about the trip, the absence of stories about women being detained and questioned intensely (a commonplace for Asian women) was telling.

Dutch Protestant immigrants rarely wrote about women and the law. When they did find differences, though, the laws generally were more favorable to women in the United States. Aart Plaisier wrote the following commentary in Grand Rapids, Michigan, in 1912: "Now, there are plenty of lovely girls [here], but you have to be careful. If you try to say something to a girl on the street (hello, sis), she will call an officer and you go into the slammer or it costs 18 dollars. Yes, the stinkers do have such a law here."[185] Plaisier probably learned of the law from his brother Gerrit, who also reported it and explained that being in jail was "not very pleasant."[186] The other major source of comment on women's legal rights dealt with divorce. Letta van 't Sant, writing from Grinnell, Iowa, in 1910, included the story of a neighbor couple that separated after only nine months of marriage. "He dragged her out of the house by the hair and then she demanded a third of everything, and he gave it to her."[187] In general, U.S. divorce laws tended to be more open that Dutch ones in this period, a topic I deal with in greater depth in chapter 6. Immigrants tended to learn about legal measures dealing with women piecemeal, often by their own experience or that of someone close to them. Adding to a lack of legal expertise was the rapidly shifting nature of legislation about women.

Positions concerning women's rights came to head in debates concerning woman suffrage, which became law on a national level at roughly the same time (1919–20) in both the Netherlands and the United States. The ideology of roles within the nuclear family surrounded the campaigns for women's rights in both countries. There was, however, a difference between the two. In the Netherlands one could try to brand individual rights as a foreign ideology introduced by the French Revolution, but many adherents to these lines of thought were indisputably Dutch. In the United States the theorists of individual rights generally came from outside Dutch Protestant ethnic boundaries.[188] Thus it was much easier to play upon ethnic solidarity and decry individualism under the banner of socialism, since Dutch socialists rarely migrated.[189] As *The Banner*, a Dutch American publication, stated in a 1912 article challenging woman suffrage: "According to the Bible church, state, and society are composed not of individuals, but of the family as a unit. Now the family is not merely a loose aggregation of individuals, but a unit of which the father is the head and public representative."[190] Klaas Schooland of Calvin College wrote in a similar vein for the *Grand Rapids Press*, arguing that individualism as a basis for society fit in well with "socialistic-democratic communism."[191]

A related strand of opposition to suffrage rests on the idea of women as subordinate to men generally and unfit for political participation. As *De Gereformeerde Amerikaan* reported in 1908: "To make woman the equal of man is to break God's ordained order."[192] Likewise the Christian Reformed and Republican *De Hollandsche Amerikaan* made its opposition to women in politics clear. In August 1920 when a Republican woman was running in a special election for a state congressional seat, the paper carried her ad but put "Adv" at the bottom of the short piece. I encountered only one other piece out of thousands labeled as an advertisement in the period 1919–20 in this paper, and it also was of a woman running for office. In both cases the editor wanted to make sure the readers did not confuse carrying the advertisement with support, since similar articles often were written by the editor. In the first case the paper carried a very similar article the following week which was an endorsement for the male candidate: "Let us Support Our Candidate." The text read in part: "There is a female opposing candidate, and for that reason he specifically asks all those who vote, to put a check by **his** name. . . . Let every Dutchman in Kalamazoo vote for **Elton R. Eaton**" (bold in original).[193] While the woman candidate had used a typical American strategy of saying she had the instincts of a housekeeper and felt that women should take those instincts into government, there was no support for this position from the paper, which opposed a woman voting, let alone running for office.

A variation on the argument that women were unsuited for politics was that based on separate spheres. Dutch politician and theologian Abraham Kuyper published a collection of his articles from *De Standaard* in 1914 as *De eerepositie der vrouw* (The Honored Position of the Woman/Wife). In this he used as his primary metaphor the division of life into public and private spheres, arguing, as did many in the United States, that women did not belong in the public arena.[194] The ideal of separate spheres had not carried much currency in the Dutch immigrant context, though it did make some inroads among later generations. Debates on suffrage helped to promote selective elements of the ideology. One of the authors in *De Gereformeerde Amerikaan*, based out of western Michigan, in 1916 discussed the "natural" differences of women. The author, arguing in much more formal language than that of most such articles, explained that women had less "passion" (*hartstocht*) but rather greater calm and self-control. A woman was closer to nature in his view, and her role as the "weaker" one came from nature. Still, he admitted: "[A]s soon as she would understand that she would not be the prettier [*schooner*] one, then she would no longer be the weaker one."[195]

Pella's Weekblad, a less conservative, Democratic paper with a circulation of about two thousand in the early 1920s, took a more moderate stance, though in some ways a similar one. Just before the 1916 election on woman suffrage in Iowa the paper carried a long article explaining why the editor was against the idea. First, the paper noted that women worked in all fields of endeavor, hence the idea of a woman "belonging in the home" did not have much meaning. Further, it noted that much of the opposition to woman suffrage was from saloonkeepers, whom it identified as not having the most laudable reasons for opposition. Then it went on to indicate that woman suffrage would take place at some point. Finally, however, the editor explained that "Woman is the showpiece of God's creation. We would not like to see her fall from that pedestal, where she receives the rightful honor of all right-thinking men."[196] It was an argument widely in use in "Yankee" circles as well. Whatever their reasons, the voters in the largely Dutch American townships around Pella voted heavily, 459 to 167, against woman suffrage.[197]

When women began to get suffrage this put conservative Calvinists on both sides of the Atlantic in a difficult position. Leaders of the Anti-Revolutionary Party (Orthodox Protestant) in the Netherlands were an important political force, and as such they did not want to lose their influence, yet neither did they want to take a position against their beliefs. It was in this context that the party went through a long series of debates on whether woman suffrage was biblical, with one faction finding it not just allowed but a duty. *De Hollandsche Amerikaan,* a conservative Republican paper in Kalamazoo, Michigan, followed the debates closely, and stood fast through 1919 and 1920 on its position that for most women voting was against the Bible. It further chided the religious leaders in the Netherlands for taking a pragmatic stance to maintain political power rather than standing on principle.[198] The issue turned pragmatic for them in 1924 when an attempt to outlaw private schools in Michigan set up a difficult choice for orthodox Calvinists, who were supporters of Christian schools. Many had suggested that women should not vote even after they gained the right nationally in 1920. Yet opposition to private schools was strong, even among some Dutch Americans, who felt it was counterproductive of making the public schools fit the appropriate model. Under these circumstances some of the Christian Reformed engaged in a "get out the vote" campaign aimed at women.[199]

Woman suffrage was not just an issue for secular political life, it also had its counterpart within churches. The Dutch American churches took different paths concerning voting rights within the church congregations. In the Netherlands the Hervormde Kerk gave voting rights to women in 1899, and the Reformed Church in America, its U.S. counterpart, left the decision up to the congregations, so that by the 1910s women had full suffrage in some churches. Others allowed confirmed women members to vote on certain issues but not on others. I found no indication that any Christian Reformed Churches opened regular suffrage to women prior to 1920, though there was a range of opinion among ministers on this. Gradually the resistance to suffrage lessened, but the antagonism toward visions of equality remained strong.

* * *

The social reproduction of the family in the United States took different forms for the Dutch than it did for some other groups. Immigrants from the Netherlands benefited from U.S. immigration policies, for officials looked with favor upon exactly the kind of enterprise which many Dutch were interested in pursuing in this period—familial settlement of rural areas by "whites." What did it matter if farming was a declining segment of the U.S. economy by the turn of the century? People like the Dutch could serve as positive examples to deride other ethnic groups: those who came alone because industrial wages would only support individuals, leaving the social reproduction of their world in other lands; those who came alone because the government prohibited the immigration of family; those who came alone because their cultural traditions stressed role patterns which did not encourage the migration of nuclear families. Dutch Protestants, to the Dillingham Commission which surveyed immigrant groups in 1911, were "good" people, not because they were just what America needed but because they were closer culturally to the policy makers themselves.[200] The advantages of being Dutch in this hierarchy of immigrant groups were great, but for the Dutch involved in the migration, people coming out of a background of farm labor or small farms just like many other immigrants, the advantages were less a matter of consciousness and more a boon that assisted in ways both mundane and innumerable. The acceptance by the U.S. government of the kinds of marriage patterns preferred by the Dutch was one of these ways.

Ideas about marriage and women's roles in the family were in tremendous flux at the turn of the century. Many of the migrants missed out on the changes in the homeland before migration, and in some cases their rural residence in the United States insulated them from experiencing such changes prior to the end of my study period. Birth control, more emotional relationships between parents and children, and more interest in romance were part of these general trends. But migration itself made for changes. Changing mores surrounding sexuality related to economic status, and the Atlantic crossing frequently led to upward economic mobility. Marriage chances changed when one stepped on the boat, if not before.

The international marriage market in which Dutch women participated, whether they wanted to or not, was one of the biggest shifts in women's opportunities related to migration. Migration made marriage possible for many, and vice versa. Marriage opened up the primary role available to adult Dutch Protestant women, as wife and mother. The familial nature of the migration created the potential for many Dutch immigrant women to maintain patterns of family life, especially for the nuclear family, though in some cases also for the extended family. Among those who crossed the Atlantic there were divergent ways to reproduce the world of the family. On the one end of the spectrum were the rebels, a minority of women who used the move to America consciously to challenge extended family and community norms and to adopt a more individualistic view of the world, one more common in U.S. rhetoric, as well as in U.S. legal practice. At the other end of the spectrum were those immigrants who came en masse. Uncles, aunts, grandparents, children: chain migrants like the Jantje Modderman Negen family who supported one another in a variety of ways. On average women had less power to determine migration patterns than men and hence were usually not in control of the chains. The dismay of those who could not put together extended family, especially for those times when they would normally have been crucial, makes it clear why women were sometimes hesitant to move without other kin.

CHAPTER 2

The Bare Necessities
and Their Elaborations

Both Dutch and Dutch American women, in their adult years, generally had responsibility for the functioning of their household: preparing food, arranging and cleaning household goods and the living quarters themselves, doing the wash, a wide variety of home production, obtaining items for home consumption, and managing the assistance of children in these tasks. Work in the home, not for wages but necessary for the sustenance of the family, filled a significant part of the days of most women. Even for women engaged in wage labor outside the home, and for those busy with farm chores, these household activities remained their responsibility. From the money-saving darning to the money-earning egg sales, women's contributions to the household economy were irreplaceable.[1] The standard refrain that a household could continue after the death of a husband but that it could not function if the wife died illustrated the worth immigrants placed on women's contributions to the functioning of a household. Basically, adult married women took on the task of making a house a home. For most, the United States offered the economic conditions to make this task easier, even if the move entailed a number of sacrifices.

As Andrew Heinze noted, consumption could serve as a "bridge between cultures."[2] What people ate, what they wore, their household furnishings, all served to illustrate their degree of adaptation to a new setting. In the realm of social reproduction these were some of the areas over which women had the most control, and yet in comparison to the Jewish families Heinze described, Dutch immigrant women typically had much less power within the household. In this they were much more akin to rural German-speaking women of the Midwest.[3] In rural areas, where most Dutch immigrant women of this period settled, farming was a family venture. Women's productive activities in the garden, barn, and home, not to mention their assistance in the fields, had a direct impact on how much would be available to eat, wear, and use or display. Yet women did not have ultimate power over purchases, particularly large ones.

In urban areas the family economy still prevailed, though the imprint of consumption was easier to see, as was the generational difference. Just as the Italian and Jewish young women of New York adopted American clothing, so too did young Dutch immigrant women of Chicago or Grand Rapids.[4] Becoming "American" frequently meant adopting middle-class consumption patterns. Further, the Dutch, like other northwestern European immigrants, could look "American" (i.e., white and not foreign) simply by wearing clothing from the United States.[5]

The cry of the immigrants was not bread and roses but meat and a new dress. Potential migrants wanted to know wages in relation to prices, what could they buy in terms of food, clothing, and other things a family used daily.[6] A family's living standard depended on how the woman in charge of housekeeping managed the finances. It was her job to "stretch" the funds and opportunities available to their fullest, so that the family lived as comfortably as possible as cheaply as possible. What that usually meant was that a woman "stretched" herself: her work hours lengthened, and her physical burden increased. In this chapter I will touch on how women accomplished a variety of household tasks, and how this differed in America from the Netherlands. Because a large proportion of these women and their families came from and settled in rural areas, and because household and other tasks in these settings were inextricably intertwined, I will also examine women's roles in farm and garden work. The next chapter will then take up in greater detail how women stretched family budgets. To understand what immigration could mean in material terms, let us begin with the life of Elizabeth Menkens Schreurs.

Elizabeth Menkens Schreurs

In September of 1849, when the eyes of many people around the world were on the United States because of the gold rush and when the major Dutch American settlements of the nineteenth century were just getting started in the Midwest, Elizabeth "Betje" Menkens was born in the Netherlands. Her father was a master cabinetmaker in Enschede, a city close to the German border in the province of Overijssel. After the death of her mother when Menkens was about fourteen, she took over much of the gendered role of housekeeping for her father and four siblings. In 1874, at age twenty-five, she headed for the United States to join her beau, Gerrit Schreurs, in Iowa. She traveled alone, steerage class, on the *Minnesota* out of Liverpool.[7] As her daughter later reported: "Betje wouldn't consent to an immediate marriage—if she was to live in Amerika she wanted to know American cooking and American house-wifery."[8] One would not have guessed that from her first job, as housekeeper for Rev. Henry Kleinsorge, the

German pastor of the Deutche Evangelische Kirche (German Evangelical Church) in Cedar Falls and a recent widower. Menkens learned to speak German in her first year in America and joined this church. When Kleinsorge remarried, Menkens went into domestic service with the Knapp family, this time with the assurance that she would learn "American" housekeeping.[9]

At the Knapps, "Betje" became "Bette." She surprised her employers through her frugality, choosing to do her own washing instead of spending part of her weekly $2.50 for the services of the laundress. Menkens's daughter described the general relationship between employer and servant in this case as "democratic and courteous." Menkens ate with the family at lunch, which was typical of American patterns, but not at suppertime when the father was present. Just as in the Netherlands, when Menkens became too ill to work she had to quit her job and move in with friends, who helped arrange a quick wedding. In February 1876 she and Gerrit Schreurs married and promptly moved into a home of their own in Cedar Falls. The two had saved enough to buy a $600 home outright. It was "a small house and smaller barn, standing in a half-block of land" on Normal Street, named for the Iowa State Normal School, which was about a mile south.[10]

While owning a home pushed the family toward middle-class status, her husband was still a laborer, and he was often caught in the vicissitudes of the economy. Work was scarce the following winter, so Menkens Schreurs watched week after week as her husband left town to chop wood several miles from Cedar Falls. She probably prepared the food which he took with him, food that had to last the week each time. Without adequate clothing or shelter, he suffered from frostbite. She, meanwhile, was in the late stages of pregnancy and used her time, among other things, to put together two woolen quilts out of scraps supplied by the laundress she had gotten to know at the Knapps. One quilt was her own, and the other was for the laundress. Menkens Schreurs may have used hers that winter, but at least in later years it was more for decoration than utility. The fact that she made pieced quilts at all showed how well she had already adapted to American conditions, for they were not typical in the Netherlands. Menkens Schreurs also did the housework in her home, sharing household equipment such as flat irons and probably conversation with her next-door neighbor Mrs. Wild, whose husband, a German immigrant, was off cutting wood with her husband.[11]

In March 1877, a little over a year after her marriage, Menkens Schreurs gave birth to her first child. Her husband stayed home with her through the agonizing five days of labor, and Mrs. Wild assisted as she could. Probably the length of the confinement led them to call a doctor, who still could do nothing. Wild handled the washing and other household tasks to ease the burden after the baby finally made her appearance. Menkens Schreurs would reciprocate not long afterward, when Wild gave birth. Though money was still tight the following year, the Schreurs bought a cow, according to the family history, "to provide an ample supply of fresh milk for the baby."[12] More than likely they also hoped to sell or trade part of the milk or milk products. Given that Gerrit Schreurs was working long hours on the railroad at that point, Menkens Schreurs probably had to do the milking at least part of the time. Yet she clearly aspired to a middle-class lifestyle, one to which she had already become accustomed from her years in housekeeping and service in others' homes. If she followed that vision, she would have limited her tasks to those within the house as much as possible.

The following year Menkens Schreurs was pregnant again. Childbirth went so fast the second time around, in November of 1879, that the baby arrived before Gerrit returned from fetching Mrs. Wild. As their daughter reported, "[t]he months that followed were really hard—pork was around a dollar per hundred pounds, but they didn't have money to buy a hog to kill."[13] Like many other accounts, this one equated economic status with ability to buy meat. Conditions had not improved much when the census-taker came through in 1880, for Gerrit Schreurs listed himself as a having been unemployed for four months during that year. Menkens Schreurs (as she was listed literally on the census schedule) was "keeping house" and caring for her two children, ages three and one.[14] Making ends meet must have been difficult, and the cow had died in the meantime, eliminating that source of regular nourishment. They still owned their home, but beyond that poor economic conditions for laborers meant meager meals.

When Gerrit Schreurs began working at a more steady position for the owner of a local flour mill, G. N. Miner, he moved the family closer to his job and into one of the houses also owned by Miner.[15] At the new house and lot on Fourth Street, Betje Menkens Schreurs had a better variety of foodstuffs close at hand. Their daughter later wrote that "Gerrit maintained a garden," though it is more likely Menkens Schreurs was doing much of the work. In addition they had access to apple trees and currant bushes, a chicken yard, pigs, a cow, and leftovers from the mill in the form of cobs and cockle seed for fuel. "Thus with fuel, vegetables, fresh and home-canned fruit, a share of the eggs, milk and meat, three barrels of apples and a keg of sorghum put down cellar for winter, the family was well provided for, though the income in money was only about forty dollars a month."[16] The account indicated that Menkens Schreurs was canning, collecting eggs, storing vegetables and fruit, and processing several kinds of meat. Sorghum was a common sweetener for baking, and given that they were working for the owner of a flour mill, the chances were good that she also did her share of baking. She probably would have been the one stoking the fire most of the day with cobs and cockle seeds, which was not the easiest fuel to use. Though funds were still rather limited, the family hired a woman to do the wash.

Menkens Schreurs gave birth to her third and last child in 1883, when she was about thirty-four. The relatively small family hints at birth control at work, a characteristic of middle-class ideals, though there may have been a medical problem.[17] Gerrit Schreurs, according to his daughter, worked ten hours a day, six days a week at the mill, which left little time to do things with the children or in the home. Family outings came on Sundays, including a yearly jaunt up the Cedar River to pick wild grapes. Menkens Schreurs made jelly, while her husband made wine. The family moved rapidly into a middle-class lifestyle in the next few years. They bought a coal burner, sewing machine, "parlor" carpet, and hand-operated washing machine. The mill owner gave their oldest daughter a "Western Cottage" organ and the family found local men to give her lessons. The children had good shoes and plenty to read, whether from the local library or the papers to which their parents subscribed.[18]

In 1890 this stability ended abruptly. Gerrit Schreurs, who was known for his quick temper, quit his job after an argument with one of the bosses. His daughter reported that "the shocked amazement in Bette's face made him angrier still." Elizabeth Menkens Schreurs's life changed drastically as a result of his decision. Though she had been a lifelong city dweller, now over age forty she was to go into farming. The family, or more specifically Gerrit, bought an eighty-acre farm in nearby Butler County. Of the $2,300 price, they had to mortgage $1,800. Friends and neighbors helped the family move seven wagons full of furniture, with some of the books getting damaged from rain before they could be safely stored. Even their young daughter knew from the start that paying the mortgage would be difficult. "[T]he main plank in the Schreurs platform of household economy for most of the next decade was to be, 'Make it do, or do without.'"[19]

The farm took priority in purchasing as they got the operation underway, with cows being one of the first big investments. They added pigs and raised corn to feed the livestock. Gerrit switched back to wearing wooden shoes for a time, as a way to cope with the muddy yard, on the example of the men at the local creamery. After falling down trying to catch a pig, he gave it up again. The family history did not include many details of which tasks went to which parent in the barn and garden. At the very least Menkens Schreurs was preserving and preparing much of the food, including animals they butchered. If she was like many Dutch immigrant women, she also assisted in the dairy, perhaps washing equipment if not milking. In the fall the children picked apples, and Menkens Schreurs dried enough to fill a sack to use in baking pies during the winter.[20] Apple pie attested to American eating habits as well.

When harvest time arrived, the two older children joined their father in the fields. "[W]hat good food mother prepared! That and the endless patching of husking gloves were her contribution to the corn harvest." Twice a day between meals she sent the youngest daughter out to deliver cookies and something to drink to the workers. That daughter too joined the work, gleaning the areas they had already covered. The daughters also assisted in work in the home, such as cleaning the soft-pine kitchen floor. "On Saturday night . . . mother and I scrubbed that floor with broom and hot, sudsy lye water—too much lye made it red, though. We swept the dirty water out through the open door, rinsed with more hot water, swept that out, then mopped the floor dry. . . . Mother scorned a mid-week mopping that would eventually make the boards grimy, which, Dutch-born housewife that she was, she could not endure."[21] What this meant was that the floor, even with carpet strips, was filthy by Saturday. To solve the dilemma Menkens Schreurs convinced her husband to put in a hardwood floor which could be mopped more regularly.

Town was three miles away, too far for a regular walk.[22] Peddlers sometimes came through offering their wares, and if the money was there Menkens Schreurs bought household items: a tin dipper, unbleached Irish-linen tablecloths with additional lace for trimming. By 1893 her daughter reported "an epidemic of agents had hit the country, organ agents, book agents, sewing machine agents, orchard agents."[23] Attending church was probably the main time Menkens Schreurs got off the farm in the early years, and even that did not always work since it was six miles including a river crossing to the Evangelical church they had joined, and they only owned one open two-seated buggy. When a Congregational church opened in Parkersburg, somewhat closer, the family switched. Menkens Schreurs took part in women's activities there, making biscuits for the ice cream socials and watching the young women raise money and sometimes do some courting through box socials. Such fund-raisers based on women's activities, particularly selling baking and crafts, were not something typical of a Dutch background, though many Dutch American women's groups would eventually adopt them.

The Schreurs lived on a farm, but the family still knew of what was happening elsewhere and wanted to take part in a bourgeois lifestyle. They had hopes to visit the Chicago World's Fair in 1893, but finances prevented it; prices were low for hogs and drought made the situation worse. Still, they sent their oldest daughter to normal school in Cedar Falls that year for the training she would need to prepare for a job. When the Iowa census-taker came through in 1895 Elizabeth Menkens Schreurs was still listed as "keeping house," though that probably meant something different in terms of her work than the last time she had that census designation. On the other hand, she had the assistance of her three children—Rosa, who at age seventeen had already been teaching for a year, Henry (sixteen), and Lizzie (eleven). Her husband was enumerated as being able to vote, indicating that she too was now an American citizen. Several of their neighbors were from the Netherlands.[24] There was a schoolhouse on the corner of their lot, which at least the younger daughter could attend.

By the turn of the century, when Elizabeth Menkens Schreurs was fifty years old, she was listed on the federal census as reading, writing, and speaking English. Her daughter described what that meant: "Bette never mastered spoken English, though she read avidly, English, German, and Dutch. Her spoken English always remained a source of embarrassment to Gerrit who very soon spoke it . . . without accent."[25] The census also revealed that the family was still paying off the mortgage on the farm, and that Menkens Schreurs's only son no longer lived there, leaving the two daughters to help.[26] Ten years later both daughters were gone, but so was the mortgage. Elizabeth Menkens Schreurs had to do her own housework and farm tasks once again, though the census listed her occupation as "none."[27] There was still no electricity on the farm, though it had come to Cedar Falls more than twenty years earlier, just before the family moved out of town.[28]

Sometime in the next few years the couple moved to neighboring New Hartford, in part probably because Menkens Schreurs became an invalid. Her husband had to take over much of the housework. Gerrit Schreurs turned the farm over to his youngest daughter and her spouse before his death from a stroke in 1919. Elizabeth Menkens Schreurs lived another ten years, dying of influenza at the age of seventy-nine in January of 1929.[29] Where she spent those years was not clear in the family history, though it most likely was with one of the daughters. In any case she was buried in Oak Hill Cemetery, near New Hartford, the same location as her husband.[30]

Were it not for her accent, Elizabeth Menkens Schreurs probably could have passed for an old-stock American by the time she reached middle age. She certainly tried to operate her home that way. The things her daughter identified as Dutch—frugality and cleanliness—were stereotypical and did not necessarily fit the patterns of consumption and cleaning in the stories. Still, Menkens Schreurs, like so many other immigrant women, evaluated life in part on the basis of the food she could put on the table, the clothing and household furnishings the family possessed. And like many families, economic ups and downs meant that these varied from year to year. Also typical was that after having spent some time in an American household, Menkens Schreurs adopted some of these patterns and did not want to go back to older ways.

Food

> In this rich land of wheat, corn, oats, barley and so many other things food is cheap and the standard of living higher than anywhere else. Three hot meals a day with meat (beef as well as pork) is the custom here and in the summer often a couple of snacks as well. Many a day laborer on a farm in Zeeland stuffs himself with a pile of potatoes and a bit of bread with bacon fat and has to do his work on this.[31]

In the last five hundred years of European history few things have spurred women to radical action as consistently as food.[32] Whether to riot for potatoes or to cross the Atlantic, providing good food for the family served as a potent incentive for women, and immigration promoters, such as the socialist writer above, played on this theme. Dutch women, whether in the Netherlands or in America, held responsibility for acquiring and preparing food. By the late nineteenth century, the differences between regions and classes in the Netherlands in terms of what kind of food families could expect, including type and price of bread, were significant.[33] In rural areas, the primary sources of emigration, conditions differed according to crop and soil type. Farmworkers' families complained bitterly of the poor wages and long hours which meant meager meals, even when they had their own gardens. "[My mother would] weed the wheat and oats in the Netherlands, and that was all done by hand. . . . mornings around ten, she always took the coffee pot along, then she stoked a coal fire on the ground and put the coffee on and then she had to fix something to eat . . . and when she came home, she had to fix dinner of course, a hot meal . . . the gravy they used with the potatoes, she said, was nothing more than some water with a few droplets of fat in it."[34] What this immigrant woman described of her mother's life as a farmworker in the Netherlands appeared also in official reports from the turn of the century.[35] On average, 51 percent of a working family's cash income went for food in 1890. In overall terms the amount of food and the number of calories workers consumed rose from 1870 to 1911, but the trend did not apply across the board.[36]

Day laborers on the large farms of Groningen, Friesland, and Zeeland generally fared poorly according to most indices. For both day workers and those with more permanent positions, farmers with much acreage generally hired families, that is, a married couple and their older children, as a unit or hired the husband for field work and the wife for barn and domestic work.[37] Field work divided to some extent according to gender, but servants who normally worked in the household, as well as women who normally did not work for wages, often took to the fields seasonally. In the fen communities of Groningen, for example, the shift to more market-oriented agriculture just before the turn of the century meant intensified soil use and the need for fertilizer. To produce fertilizer farmers changed the layout inside their barns, tying the cows in small stalls and keeping them in more often so that their wastes would not scatter. Collecting and spreading the manure was women's work.[38]

On large farms the farmer's wife, the *boerin*,[39] assumed a critical economic role, and a privileged one. The larger the farm, the less she did directly and the more she organized, but her responsibilities included (1) tending to the slaughter of pigs (and sometimes cows) and the subsequent preparation of smoked meat and sausages, (2) churning milk from the cows (and sometimes sheep) and sale of butter, (3) daily care and feeding of chickens, pigs, and calves, (4) storing of vegetables and fruit, especially large quantities of potatoes, green beans, and cabbage, (5) preparing meals for family and staff, and (6) tending the garden.[40] The *boerin* rarely emigrated, but her help did. That former agricultural workers could themselves oversee these tasks in America, albeit without the employees to help, was a badge of success.

For those coming from sandy soil regions, however, the pattern differed. In these areas farms were smaller and more heterogeneous. Women in these areas generally still had responsibility for small livestock (pigs, goats, calves, chickens), vegetable and flower gardens, and to some extent milking and the subsequent manufacture of dairy products (butter and cheese) if there was a surplus, and cleaning of the milking apparatus. Help for these tasks came primarily from the children if there were any, with perhaps one young female domestic to assist at times. In addition, wives took the place of hired hands in assisting with field work. Over time factories took over the processing of milk, though women tended to retain cheesemaking in the home.[41]

On medium-sized farms, where two or three generations sometimes shared the house at one point in their life cycle, the oldest woman (usually the younger woman's mother-in-law) was in charge of cooking. According to a study of Winterswijk around 1900, meals for a typical day consisted of tea before milking, pap or bread just after milking, coffee with bread at about 10 A.M., stew at noon (consisting of carrots, cabbage, or brown beans with a little bacon and potatoes), pancakes at 4 P.M., and pap at 9 in the evening.[42] Women brought the coffee and pancakes to the fields. The women also had to prepare the slop for the animals, usually a cooked mixture of root vegetables with cut cabbage, flour, and buttermilk. At slaughtering time they made various sausages and salted, dried, pickled, and otherwise preserved the meat.[43]

With the agricultural depression of the 1880s and later in an increasingly international grain market, many small farmers had to supplement their income with other wage work. This usually meant that the wife would engage in or continue agricultural work with the help of the children (if they were old enough) while the husband sought work elsewhere. Studies of workers' budgets uncovered many such cases. One family from Deventer, consisting of a man (a sawmill hand), his wife, and two small children, for example, rented a piece of land where his wife grew vegetables for the family. The wife also tended goats there and would divide the milk so that her family had some and the rest she could sell. The woman noted that the family usually ate rye bread and potatoes, used butter sparingly, and that she made over adult clothing for the children. The government reporters, while complaining that the family still spent money for alcohol, nonetheless noted that the husband respected his wife's ability to maintain and supplement the family budget.[44]

In the United States, women's work on the farm continued along old patterns, but eating habits underwent a change. Perhaps the family did not earn a fortune, but the food was better: "Bacon and eggs are everyday fare, potatoes, apples, onions, cabbage, and all the vegetables you can imagine are here too . . . there is a surplus of butter and milk."[45] Such reports served as a potent stimulus to emigration among the agricultural laboring class, those who assumed this kind of consumption was only for wealthy farmers. Immigrants sometimes termed their letters *spekbrieven,* literally bacon letters, because little could convey their success as well as reports of eating lots of fat pork.[46] For others the term *spekbrief* implied that the immigrant letter contained money, the "fat" from one's abundance.

Over time the family eating patterns changed. Anna van Beek Peters's description of cooking for the harvesting crew illustrated some of the encroaching American patterns. Not only did the women have to prepare a large roast for the threshers, they also baked pies and potatoes and cooked vegetables and other things separately on the stove.[47] The baked goods, as well as the size of the portions of meat and the separate vegetable dishes, were uncommon in the Netherlands. The pattern of women working in the fields until the children were old enough to help, or the family well enough off to hire help, continued. Older children, however, also meant more mouths to feed. One woman from northwestern Iowa figured that she averaged eight people for meals for the year, but had twenty to twenty-five people to cook for during threshing. She also had to clean up after them, not a pleasant task for someone who hated doing dishes.[48]

Even in the midst of poor harvests and economic downturns, most Dutch immigrant women indicated that they managed to subsist quite well with their large gardens and small livestock. In immigrant letters, assuring relatives that the family had enough food, and describing exactly what they ate, often fell to women. "We have a good deal to eat for the winter: a cow, 1 sturgeon of 125 pounds, a halibut of 80 pounds, a few salmon at 12 pounds each, and a half tub full of flounders . . . as for potatoes, cabbage, carrots, turnips, and such things, we also have enough."[49] In this family's case the Groningers (people from Groningen) of their area contributed to their food stocks, giving away the "garbage" fish they brought in with each catch. Seafood formed an important part of the diet of certain coastal areas of the Netherlands, but those on farms of the interior rarely could afford it. In the United States proximity to the ocean or to inland fishing areas also made the difference in whether an individual or a family could expect such fare on the table. Klaaske Noorda Heller, quoted above, writing from a coastal area of Washington, could serve fish regularly. Oysters were a holiday specialty which appeared in the grocery stores ads of several Dutch American communities. Likewise herring was standard fare at some Dutch celebrations, and it made its way to places like Iowa as well.[50]

The reports of Lubbigje Schaapman in California illustrated how drastically eating patterns could change: "It sure is different here than in Holland. Cooking a meal, in the morning, and at noon, and at night. There is no rye bread here. But there is canned fruit, peaches, apricots, pears, berries. Everything is first cooked, then put in bottles or jars and then you have to tighten the lids. . . . [We have] Oranges, syrup, butter, eggs, meat, coffee every day."[51] The selection of foodstuffs in her area was more extensive than elsewhere, but the refrain of three warm meals a day, usually with meat, stood in stark contrast to the diet of many Dutch workers. As late as into the twentieth century, butter, sugar, and meat all fell in the category of rationed luxuries for the class of families who normally emigrated. Schaapman's description, from 1911, also illustrated another "American" pattern. With relatively low sugar prices and the introduction of standardized glass jars at the turn of the century, women in the United States began to do their own canning, allowing them to put more variation into their winter diet and to use their gardens more extensively.[52] Elizabeth Menkens Schreurs had been ahead of many other Dutch immigrants in this.

Dutch American women had an easier task than those from some other ethnic groups, because most standard products for Dutch "cuisine" were readily available in the United States. Rarely did they complain about a lack of specific foods. An early account of Pella, Iowa, indicated that nearly every house in town had a vegetable garden, and that everything grew well "except cauliflower." The Dutch settlers there planted asparagus beds "and they look as good as what is expected in Holland in the best tilled beds after two years."[53] Only at holiday time did Dutch American women consistently note the absence of specialty foods or the people who normally prepared them: oliebollen (a sort of spice doughnut usually eaten for New Year's), waffles from street vendors, poffertjes (another sort of doughnut), or local delicacies.[54] But even many of these kinds of specialties found their way into the bakeries of Dutch American communities. At the beginning of December stores in Pella and in Orange City advertised St. Nicholas letters and cookies, sometimes banket (a filled pastry) and other holiday baked goods.[55]

Certain entrepreneurs imported items from the Netherlands, particularly those for which women had already developed brand-name loyalty or goods which were standard equipment in the "old world." Others manufactured "Dutch" goods on American soil. Many of these found their way into a Dutch American periodical, *De Boodschapper*, published by Rev. R. L. Haan out of Grand Rapids, Michigan, until *De Huisvriend* absorbed it around 1920.[56] *Boodschapper* had two meanings in Dutch: shopper or messenger (as of the good news—gospel). The paper mixed advertisements for Droste Cocoa and Holland Rusk with Dutch American sermons and religious writings. The paper was meant in part to be a pamphlet available free as part of a proselytizing campaign, but it was sold as a subscription magazine as well. The audience in the latter case was the growing group of Dutch Americans in western Michigan who had

Cocoa was one of the most commonly advertised imported products in Dutch American publications. Note that the woman in traditional dress is serving the one in modern attire.

gained a financial base to afford various products but who still had to be convinced to spend their money.[57] Many of the advertisers provided services to Dutch Americans, but Holland Importing was one of the few which regularly featured food products.[58] *De Huisvriend* (friend of the home), though it began with no advertisements in the 1890s, began introducing them just after the turn of the century, and by 1905 it also featured ads with long lists of imported items: cocoa, cheese, (Dutch style) peas and beans, herring, cod liver oil, rapeseed oil. Most Dutch American newspapers I consulted at least carried ads for Dutch tea and cocoa.[59]

One other way food regularly appeared in newspapers was as an advertising gimmick. Auctions announced in either *Pella's Weekblad* or *De Volksvriend* sometimes offered free lunch as part of the day's activities.[60] Others also offered free food as an incentive to come. A particularly interesting example appeared in *Pella's Weekblad* in 1916. The Van Zante brothers placed a large ad for their "Big Factory Stove Sale." Everything in the ad was in English except one line: "During the demonstration donuts and coffee will be served free."[61] Playing on people's frugality and love of coffee could combine with trying to sell.

According to letters, women adopted relatively few "American" items into their daily diet at first. Neither pumpkins nor squash appear in their extensive lists of food, though most Dutch immigrants lived in areas where these vegetables grew readily. Many women simply equated good food with what they already knew and avoided new tastes. Aukjen Pruiksma explained how her relatives gave her family a nice reception after arrival in New Jersey in 1895: "Last evening [we gathered around the table] . . . partaking of a delicious meal, consisting of potatoes, meat, green beans and plum pudding. Aboard the ship we could get enough to eat, but it was all so foreign."[62] The lack of interest in "foreign" foods continued for quite some time. Writing in 1927, Amry Vandenbosch described the eating habits of the Dutch in Chicago: "The first and second generations stick to the foods to which they were accustomed in the old country. Their food is inclined to be heavy, some of their most common foods being Dutch cheese, gray and green peas, and brown beans."[63] But to eat these things one still had to buy them. For those who lived in less ethnically homogeneous areas, shopping could be a challenge. The DeValk family of Chicago resided in a mixed ethnic neighborhood, one where Germans and Italians predominated: "When mother went to the store, she had to save a few coffee beans and hold up two fingers for two pounds, and the same with rice."[64]

If financial conditions made it necessary, or products were unavailable, immigrant women had to find substitutes. Thus Jeanette van Rooyen described the food used by her grandparents when they first moved onto a homestead around Hospers, Iowa. Cornbread was one of the staples because corn grew well there, as did potatoes. Roasted peas took the place of coffee, which was neither readily available nor cheap. Prairie tea, which grew wild in the area, served as another beverage. Wild onions and ground cherries, also native to the area, filled out their meals.[65] As with so many other items, the time period and degree of set-tlement in the area made for significantly different chances for consumption. Even in Hospers, a much more extensive array of items was available through mail order by the turn of the century.

Friends and family could play a significant role in introducing newcomers to American varieties of known foods, as illustrated by the Woudenberg family papers. According to these letters, when the family arrived in Paterson, New Jersey, in 1910, "One of the uncles handed his newly arrived brother a fair-sized red, red fruit, and told Willem these were American apples, a little softer in tex-ture than the European kind but equally as delicious. So Dad Woudenberg, being eager to sample a superior product, opened his mouth wide to take a good, healthy bite. Imagine his surprise when the inside was soft and very juicy. . . . That was Dad's introduction to the American tomato."[66] The fruits and vege-tables known in the Netherlands were also on the tables of America with a few exceptions. While corn grew in certain sections of the Netherlands, not all mi-grants had access to it prior to migration. Thus immigrants in the Midwest, who often raised corn for their livestock and for sale, would mention introducing cornbread or cornmeal mush to their diets. Their letters made it clear they had to explain that people, not just animals, could eat corn.

One new pattern was the celebration of Thanksgiving, complete with turkey. In 1880 the only indication of the holiday in *De Volksvriend* was a translation of the president's Thanksgiving address. Twenty years later, advertisers in Dutch American papers sought to promote this celebration as an occasion for special sales, and they wished their readers "*smaakelijk eten,*" the Dutch version of *bon appetit.*[67] In 1919 one Dutch American store in Kalamazoo, Michigan, included a poem about buying chicken, duck, goose, or turkey in its Thanksgiving ad in 1919, which it rimmed with a border filled with turkeys. That the ad used the word "turkey" in English but listed the other poultry in Dutch indicated that some people were probably unfamiliar with the Dutch equivalent, since turkey was not common in the Netherlands.[68] The use of a poem written for the occa-sion, however, was typical of Dutch celebrations. Another ad in the same edi-tion also included cranberries, oysters, and good coffee along with turkey (this time in Dutch). Of these, oysters and good coffee could have represented a lux-urious meal in the Netherlands, but cranberries were more typically American.

Orchards and berry patches, if the climate allowed, added not only to the diet but also to the pocketbook. Again, those varieties most well known in the Neth-erlands tended to be most popular with immigrants. Even oranges, an infrequent treat on Dutch American tables (outside California or Florida), were a holiday treat in the Netherlands. One advertiser sought to play up that image and in so doing to entice people to come to Florida to pick strawberries and other items: "*Guests requested—Hollanders!!!*" The text listed the foods people would "eat and pick" around Christmas, including head lettuce, green beans, cauliflower, new potatoes, oranges, grapefruit, pineapple, tangerines, and bananas.[69] American holiday specialties found only limited acceptance, and then most often among women who worked as domestics or who came at a young age. More common was the case of Klaaske Noorda Heller, who wrote in 1897 that Americans celebrated their birthdays by having a party with cake, but then added "I do not know much about the customs here or at least I do not go along with them much."[70] Many Dutch American women, in retrospect, characterized a "typically Dutch" cuisine as meat and potatoes, with a few vegetables.

Pork, and pork mixed with beef, remained the preferred meat, with chicken on occasion, often when a hen stopped laying. Accounts of the earliest Dutch pioneers of the mid-nineteenth century sometimes mentioned food generated by hunting, particularly rabbits.[71] By the turn of the century references to hunting and fishing (other than commercial) or to the products they generated were more sporadic and came primarily from the newer settlements on the plains, indicating that most Dutch immigrants grew or bought the crops they ate.[72] Railroad connections in the countryside and expanded food distribution systems in urban areas made this a viable option.[73]

Still, the garden was the primary source of food for many: "Our beans froze in the garden last week so now I have to replant. I have a little bit of everything in: green onions, radishes, lettuce, cabbage, carrots, yellow and green peas."[74] Such crops sometimes became the mainstays of economic opportunities as some Dutch immigrants turned to truck gardening. Dutch settlements produced vegetables, especially onions and celery, to be sold in large cities, operating as produce suppliers to cities such as Chicago, Milwaukee, Grand Rapids, and Kalamazoo.[75] Men generally ran larger truck gardening farms, though women in some cases took on this work as well, and as in the Netherlands, those who rented to farmers often specified they wanted a married couple or entire family for agricultural work.[76]

While the relative abundance of foodstuffs generally gave women a sense of pride in providing good meals for their families, it also often meant more work. There were more items to preserve, whether at butchering time, or during the harvest, or (for city dwellers) when things were in season.[77] There were more things to prepare and put on the table. Rather than making do with hot mush or serving bread with a bit of lard for breakfast or "coffee," housewives more often served meals with two or three warm dishes. Also, women added something to drink to the menu. The excess of milk products meant that a family had fresh milk or buttermilk to accompany the main meal, whereas many families in the Netherlands went without.[78] In the Netherlands water generally came from cisterns, whereas in the American Midwest wells became more common because of the less reliable rainfall conditions.[79] Women's letters and reminiscences said little about whether or how much women (or men) drank beer or *jenever* (Dutch gin). Church disciplinary records included occasional reprimands for drunkenness. Traditionally men drank more alcohol than women, often as part of gender-specific activities outside the home. Alcohol was one of the items which remained expensive in America, even more so than in the Netherlands. Active temperance campaigns in both the Netherlands and the United States added to the incentive to drink less, as did the association of public drunkenness with disreputable working-class people.[80]

Aside from the addition of meat to people's diets, the most important culinary change was the introduction of baked goods from the home oven. Whereas bread-making was generally the task of a baker in the Netherlands, in the United States women generally baked their own bread, and other items as well: "I bake bread and cake and pie, so that does not cost too much."[81] The number of women who commented on this indicates that it was one of the most significant alterations in daily patterns. Several factors contributed to the trend toward homemade bread. First, rural women often lived too far from the nearest baker to bring their preshaped loaves for baking (a common practice on small farms in the Netherlands). Second, baker's bread had the reputation of the food of the working class in the United States, with the consequence that domestics learned the middle-class notion that you should bake your own. Third, it was cheaper to bake one's own bread, and frugality was the watchword of many Dutch housewives. In this changeover the gender divisions of baking shifted. While a baker was often a man in the Netherlands, home baking became a craft for women in the United States.

By the late nineteenth century a cast-iron stove including an oven was commonplace in American households, and such stoves appear as one of the early purchases among Dutch immigrants.[82] Baking, however, required practice. White bread became the love of the masses, regardless of how many times reformers explained that it had less food value than other products. In the Netherlands families in certain regions ate rye bread as a staple, viewing white bread as the privilege of the well-to-do.[83] In those cases the changeover to wheat flour involved a significant alteration in tastes. Justifying it as a step up the social ladder made the change more palatable.

Just as the amount and variety of food increased, so did the standards for baking. Women reported not just who could bake but who baked well. Thus Heintje Oggel van Bruggen wrote in 1888: "[Neeltje] can bake a tasty fruitcake and doughnuts too."[84] In more Americanized church congregations such as that of Elizabeth Menkens Schreurs, "pie suppers" and ice cream socials gave opportunities for comparison. Even if Dutch immigrant women did not take part in these at first, their prevalence in reports about women's activities in papers such as *De Hope* and *Pella's Weekblad* helped introduce them to the next generation. As congregations organized their own women's mission groups, baking and other crafts became an acceptable way for women to raise funds publicly.

A "good housewife" needed to have baked goods on hand for coffee or tea time. Sunday afternoons were the most common time for visiting, but "having the coffee pot on" meant an open door to guests, whether the coffee was actually ready or not.[85] The afternoon beverage sometimes was tea rather than coffee, but the ability to provide "real" coffee (not a substitute or a watered-down version) or quality tea along with some baked goods exemplified a household's prosperity as well as hospitality; so too did the presence (or absence) of cream and sugar, the type and number of coffee spoons, the cups, the room in which it was served, the tablecloth, and a variety of other things.[86] When Elizabeth Menkens Schreurs bought Irish linen tablecloths with lace, even though the family still had a big mortgage to pay, she probably had just such occasions in mind.

For the first generation, the "coffee" was one of the few social activities for both men and women which was not associated with the church. As one historian noted, on farms it was common to serve coffee five times a day, and any snack between meals might be called "coffee time."[87] The Dutch Protestant immigrants I studied took at least one extended coffee break every day, generally another lunch.

LUNS TIME

When moeder hallers, "Luns is klaar"
Dan komen wij op high
En zitten pleasant by elkaar
Met coffee, cake en pie.[88]

[When mother hollers, "Lunch is ready"
Then we come running
And sit down pleasantly with one another
With coffee, cake, and pie.]

Coffee times with guests occurred less frequently, but immigrants normally organized their schedules to take part at least once a week and looked forward to unexpected visitors at other times. Though children sometimes joined the gathering, immigrants generally considered coffee a beverage for adults and coffee time as an opportunity for adults' conversation. Indulgent grandparents might offer the little ones a cup of "coffee," mainly milk and sugar with a brown tint, at an early age so they would feel more a part of the festivities.[89]

Coffee or tea time allowed the family to offer hospitality without the work of overnight accommodations or large meals. Failing to offer or join coffee time could engender disapproval. In Anna Brown's reminiscences she noted that her mother, an Englishwoman, remained aloof from her Dutch mother-in-law's coffee gatherings, but her father went to his mother's nearly every day to have coffee and chat in Dutch.[90] Coffee was often a part of a social network of food exchange for extended families, an exchange which could take on much more extensive proportions during holidays.[91] Coffee time was a ritual of sociability, one which slowly disappeared as wage work set forth a more rigid system of time management. With this change coffee time took on another, less positive connotation; it became the koffie klets, a gossip session associated primarily with women.[92] The gendered nature of such visits was clear in a 1916 advertisement for Hamstra's Dutch Java Tea: "The desire for a second cup is often the reason that a visit with the neighbor woman or female friend turns into a most enjoyable [*allergezelligste*] tea time."[93]

Meals, on the other hand, retained a familial character. According to letters and reminiscences, Dutch Protestant immigrant women cooked and organized their meals so that everyone could sit down at once to eat together. Domestic servants, hired hands, visitors, non-nuclear family members: all ate at the family table, and everyone ate the same food. This stood in stark contrast to large farms in parts of the Netherlands, where staff often ate separately (usually in the kitchen) and, moreover, were not allowed to eat the variety and quantity that stood on the table in the next room.[94] While the patterns were not absolute, the shift overall was evident.

The family meal, where Reformed fathers underscored the religio-cultural patriarchal tradition by praying as the head of the family and where children learned such dogmas as speak when you are spoken to, operated as one of the relatively few uninterrupted opportunities for family interaction. Immigrant reminiscences portrayed starkly varying pictures of these gatherings. Some expounded on the positive value of shared time and conversation, while others abhorred the stern parental control and silent atmosphere. In any case, the housewife had a distinct role in preparation of food, usually with the assistance of her children. She made sure everything was on the table, and that everyone got enough, sometimes eating less herself in order to assure it for the others. Reprimands to the greedy could also be part of this. Anna Rebertus Rutgers, known in her family for many Dutch sayings, would scold her children if they spread their butter too thick: "Not double thick, you don't have to eat it all up today, even if it is good. Tomorrow is another day."[95] Children (except nursing babies) ate the same food as their parents. Thus Geertje de Jong Schuiling reported in 1901: "[Thijs, 2 years old] is quite healthy . . . he always finishes his bacon and lard first."[96]

The gender division related to cooking was strict. Even when women worked side by side with their male kin in the fields, they alone were responsible for meals without the assistance of men (and often not of boys). Dutch immigrants frequently assumed men did not know how to cook. When Anna Kuijt heard her Dutch relatives took a trip to Germany, she wrote "who cooked the meals for Uncle?"[97] Not surprisingly, single male Dutch immigrants tended to board with friends or relatives rather than care for a household themselves. But others noted that in America, at least if the circumstances required, men might manage. Lubbigje Schaapman, for example, cooked occasionally for her brother, who was still single but already had a farm. Still she reported he could wash and clean and can, at least if he wasn't too busy with farmwork. "There are many men here who can fend for themselves, who can bake and fry everything, but that doesn't mean they like it!"[98] Women took charge not only of meal preparation but also of clean up. After the meal the housewife cleared the table and did the dishes, or she allocated these chores to her children, especially older daughters. Dutch immigrants considered nearly anything dealing with food preparation a woman's domain. Only in the realm of purchase did men sometimes intrude, and that seems to have differed from family to family.

For the most part, immigrants indicated foodstuffs were cheaper and more readily available in the United States. Did reasonable prices and more variety actually lead to better nutrition? As Dutch Protestants moved into the middle class they picked up on a growing concern with nutrition. The home economics movement, which some American women learned about from women's magazines such as *Ladies' Home Journal*, long edited by Dutch American Edward Bok, or in women's columns in various newspapers, slowly garnered attention in the Dutch American community.[99] As nutrition became part of the school curricula in states such as Iowa, by late in the 1910s, some Dutch Americans became exposed to it in that setting.[100] Prescriptive literature addressed issues of eating habits and household organization, but the approach among orthodox Dutch Americans was quite different than that of the home economics movement. Rather than promoting science in the form of "proper nutrition," at least part of the Dutch American prescriptive press took on the issue of proper eating habits in the form of a critique of the sin of gluttony and a call for frugality. "In regard to food there are two ways of wasting: first by throwing away food, and second by overfeeding. . . . It is surprising what quantities of rich food some consume, with many it is twice as much as the body needs. This is a waste, and for the gluttonous person it is actually a detriment. . . . People are digging their graves with their teeth. . . . Our abundance of sugar and grease is weakening and killing." The author, interestingly, sought to subvert criticism of price fixing by trusts, a practice under investigation at the time, and put the blame for high prices (specifically in Chicago) on "the extravagance of the American people."[101] At this point the ideal had come full circle. Abundance was good, but too much abundance was bad. In this way, eating less for good health could be the banner of those food producers (including some Dutch American ones) who raised their prices. Dutch immigrant women, at least according to their letters and reminiscences, were not convinced by American ideals about "proper nutrition."[102] Grease and sugar tasted too good.

When Genevieve Gough described the Dutch in Iowa in 1923 she wrote: "The genuine, hard-working Hollander is often a man of domestic tastes, closely attached to his home with its simple comforts, and a housewife's excellent cooking affords him the best treat. Dutch dishes are of well cooked and wholesome food. It is needless to say that the Dutch eat heartily."[103] Though stereotypical, she illustrated two key points about the social reproduction of foodways: first, one of the key benefits of migration in the eyes of many immigrants was the ability to provide ample food; and second, tastes in food did not change much in the first generation.

Clothing

While Dutch immigrant women largely continued old world patterns of food consumption, some turned rapidly to new styles and types of clothing. Younger women adapted their clothing styles most quickly, but older women also sought to vary patterns and make use of new yard goods. Part of the adjustment had to do with differing climates or the availability of particular fabrics and patterns, but much of it simply was a longing for light colors and prints, the luxury of a hat and leather shoes, and the convenience of store-bought underclothes. Making clothing, from buying yarn, thread, buttons, and fabric to sewing by hand or with a machine, crocheting, or knitting, remained a gender-specific task within the family, a task for a woman. Even buying ready-made clothing items often fell to women. Women also cared for the clothing, whether washing, ironing, putting away, darning, patching, or making over hand-me-downs. Immigration coincided with the spread of sewing machines and the growth of the ready-made industry in the United States, making the manufacture and procurement of clothing much easier over time. Though the same phenomenon had occurred in the Netherlands, many immigrants had been unable to afford the new items. Thus their memories were of a Netherlands where coarse wool hand-me-downs abounded. The new prosperity in the United States which allowed more and better clothing also entailed the need to wash more clothing and to wash it more often as standards of cleanliness rose.

In the Netherlands at the turn of the century, a woman's dress signified her status in society. If food consumption was a matter of prosperity, then clothing was even more a matter of class. As a standard nineteenth-century saying proclaimed: "Man should dress according to his *stand*."[104] Beginning around 1850, the slow proliferation of machine-made cloth and sewing machines offered women of the bourgeoisie in the Netherlands a chance to dress as only the most privileged had up to that time. It was not bourgeois women who ran these machines, however, but their seamstresses.[105] The sweatshop industry grew to major proportions in Dutch cities as economic conditions allowed this bourgeois group the chance to buy more and better clothing. Printed fabric like calico and high fashion styles frequently came from another country, the import costs making them entirely the domain of the well-to-do. Yet the affluent of the Netherlands also distinguished themselves from the "lower classes" by buying machine-made clothing. Whereas the bourgeoisie could abandon spinning, weaving, dying, and the production of some clothing, poorer women still frequently carried out these tasks themselves.[106]

Young women in the Netherlands did the piece work, ran the machines, and did the finishing, working for "hunger salaries" as the National Exhibition of Women's Work in 1898 described them. Just as in the United States, these low wages allowed for significant profit for the manufacturer but meant that the women who made the clothes could not buy them.[107] Most female factory workers and domestics could not afford clothing above their social station—nor could they be seen in public in such clothing.[108] Low wages and high prices for items such as hats, high-heeled shoes, and tailored dresses upheld class differences. In the circles from which emigrants came, this difference became visible in the late nineteenth century when wealthy farmer's wives increasingly tried to dress like urban "ladies." At first they sported such attire on Sundays or holidays only, but increasingly the phenomenon of dressing as a proper lady related to a degree of wealth that allowed women to supervise more help and thus withdraw from field and garden work on the farm.[109]

The issues concerning clothing for well-to-do Dutch women at the turn of the century centered around conspicuous consumption and for some around the reform movement, which sought to do away with the corset.[110] Women in the countryside took longer to adapt to these patterns. Even the *boerin* on a medium-sized farm would wear practical clothing on workdays. Wooden shoes, worn with several pair of heavy woolen socks, operated as standard footwear for outdoor work. Inside, people wore heavy woolen socks and sometimes slippers. Increasingly, the bourgeoisie viewed wooden shoes, standard footwear for the working class and farming families, as a badge of poverty.[111]

Cornelia De Groot, a farmer's daughter, described the other layers which kept out the cold in poorly heated (and generally damp) surroundings: "our many pieces of loose and heavy underclothing made us appear very round and fat and clumsy. We wore a flannel shirt without any shape, next a loose chemise of muslin, then a knitted 'borstrok' or breast-skirt of worsted or cotton yarn according to the season; on top of this a 'lyfje' or underwaist, next something resembling a corset-cover made of either woolen or cotton material. . . . Our dresses were made of durable woolen goods, usually dark-colored."[112] In the next passage De Groot reminisced as if she had few clothes, but her three or four dresses, one for "best," one for Sunday, one for school, and one for play, as well as her many underclothes, were much more than the average farm laborer's daughter could afford.

Strict gender divisions in clothing were rising in importance for the middle class in the Netherlands from the mid-nineteenth century onwards, and this also had an impact on the workers. Long skirts were impractical for work in the often-muddy fields, yet they were standard. Even the pantlike waders worn by women oyster gatherers, who worked in knee- to thigh-high water, included a large space at the top for the women to tuck their skirts in, so technically they were still wearing dresses.[113]

By the turn of the century the "civilization" campaign going on in the Netherlands focused attention on proper clothing, noting the lack of underclothes among the poor and unemployed. A circular from a domestic servant placement bureau in 1903 stated: "You would be astonished if you knew how many girls employed as day workers are running around, girls who are hindered only by a lack of underclothes from going into a regular domestic service job."[114] Parents cited lack of clothing, especially shoes and underclothes, as a reason children could not attend school. A letter written in the name of an illiterate widower to a relative in the United States illustrated the theme, exacerbated by the absence of a woman: "Your brother Gerrit Jan cannot earn enough to provide all the children with what they need. . . . The children run around nearly naked, oh!"[115] Most emigrants fell between the extremes, neither totally lacking in underclothes nor possessing more than a couple of outfits.

A second major trend was the move from traditional clothing to a more "modern" style.[116] In the countryside throughout the Netherlands in the nineteenth century people displayed regional background, age, and wealth concurrently in the *klederdracht* (traditional dress), reserved for Sundays or holidays. The hats, scarves, aprons, patterns, and prints of these dresses, which dated back over a century, illustrated heritage. Many of the formal pictures immigrants took to send to relatives or to save for posterity, at least earlier in the period, featured women in such traditional dress. One of the most important parts of this costume was an *oorijzer,* or special headpiece, which showed the age and wealth of the woman. Women who wanted to dress more modestly or in a more modern style, would switch to black dresses, but might continue to wear the *oorijzer* and starched white cap. Cornelia De Groot described this headwear in Friesland as

> a helmet made of the purest, softest gold, and beneath it a white muslin cap . . . and over this . . . one of black silk. . . . mother covered this helmet with a beautiful cap of old lace that had a border of rounded folds standing straight from the neck at an angle of about forty-five degrees. . . . Near the ears . . . ornaments resembling miniature shields or large buttons. Some of the farmers' wives also had fastened on their foreheads silver plates studded with diamonds. . . . The caps of the wives of the day-laborers were made of silver and their clothes were very simple and of coarse, cheap material.[117]

If the family could afford it, girls received a modest version of the headgear at about age twelve. At sixteen, or at marriage, a woman would have her formal gold helmet. In most villages throughout the Netherlands women wore some sort of lace cap with stiffly starched angles, augmented by gold or silver ornaments and various sorts of jewelry illustrating familial wealth.

The conservative rural population held to these styles long after they had disappeared from the urban scene. As ready-made clothing and "fashionable" hats began to reach the masses it heralded the demise of this kind of finery (and the headaches they entailed). The patterns all converged around the turn of the century. Migration speeded the process for many. In some cases it literally caused the shift, since a woman's *oorijzer* could be sold in order to put together money for passage.[118] Though in Dutch American communities people beyond the first generation sometimes wore the outermost lace cap and ornaments on special occasions, as attested to by the picture of Hendrik Scholte's granddaughters in Pella, Iowa in 1907, for most, traditional clothes faded within

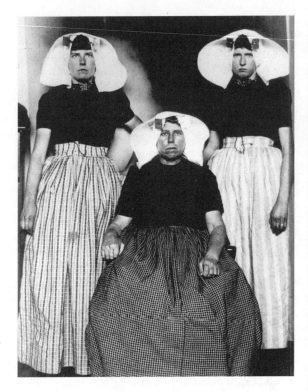

The headgear of these women, photographed at Ellis Island, indicate they are from the province of Zeeland. "Immigration and Refugee Services of America Records," box 491, folder 18, Immigration History Research Center, University of Minnesota. Photo courtesy of IHRC.

a generation.[119] In urban areas, or in non-Dutch settlements, the shift was often more rapid, for clothing could identify one as foreign on sight, and many did not want that notoriety. "In Sacramento . . . People stared at us, especially at mother's cap. And then they put our picture in the paper."[120] Others made the change before they came but found that the stereotypes continued: "I hadn't been here very long when a few ladies came and asked if they could borrow my clothes for a party [she showed them her best dress]. . . . No, they wanted my funny clothes. . . . They meant my Dutch clothes. They thought that I arrived looking like a Volendammer. My husband said, well, her wooden shoes stand on the coast of New York."[121]

Immigrants had differing views of the practicability of *klompen* (wooden shoes). Women in Yankee settlements became sensitized to the foreignness of their footwear in "American" surroundings, but in Dutch American settlements they were a common sight. Nearly every medium-sized Dutch settlement had a *klompen* maker in the nineteenth century, making it possible to purchase them, yet by the 1920s several had gone out of business.[122] Newspapers such as *De Hollandsche Amerikaan* and *Pella's Weekblad* regularly featured the latest styles in women's shoes, but not *klompen* by the 1910s. In the 1910s *De Boodschapper* only carried ads for novelty wooden shoes.[123] Young women generally expressed a preference for more fashionable leather shoes and looked down upon those who wore wood.

Urban residents often associated *klompen* with poverty and a rural (or working-class) mentality. Farm wives, however, sometimes preferred wooden shoes, especially for work in the garden and barns, because family members could easily slip in and out of them before entering or leaving the house. Another advantage was their strength, especially if one got stepped on by a cow during milking. Many families had both wood and leather, and wore *klompen* for work and other shoes according to the occasion. What astonished most women in terms of footwear was its absence in summer: "Children go around barefoot most of the time in the summer, even dominies'."[124] In the Netherlands lack of footwear was a sign of poverty. Immigrant women justified their (to Dutch eyes) unconventional lack of footwear by noting the hot climate and local customs, but several also added that going barefoot offered a kind of freedom, and it was comfortable.

Another change involved raising hemlines. The women's dresses and hats featured in advertisements in *De Hollandsche Amerikaan* of Kalamazoo in the 1910s were typical "Yankee" fare, well above the ankle and slim in styling. Such was also the case in *De Volksvriend* and *Pella's Weekblad*. The bourgeois emphasis was evident even in the words they used to describe themselves. The Bogaard Modiste Zaak (Bogaard Fashion Store) of Pella informed its customers in 1917 that it had recently sent the head of its ladies department to St. Louis to learn about the latest hat styles.[125] "La Mode" clothing store in Kalamazoo took out large ads in *De Hollandsche Amerikaan* in 1920. A similar move was underway in the Netherlands, and it had its basis in the common link to a French ideal. While the ultimate fashion statement came from Paris, in Dutch American communities it was more likely the nearest big city which set the standard, even if that meant Des Moines, Iowa. In any case the stress on "newest" and "latest" fashions was well ingrained in Dutch American papers by the turn of the century. Whether people followed these fashions was another question. Genevieve Gough, a native of Pella writing about "Iowa's Hollanders" in 1923, explained: "the gaudiness and latest models from the world's fashion centers are not paraded where the Dutch live."[126]

Still, letters indicated that young women tended to adopt American fashions rapidly. Jeannette Goedhart gave her sister a piece of advice prior to migration: "Don't buy any new clothes because when you are here you will have go along with the fashion here, and in California it is warm."[127] Most women did not need any coercing to follow American styles, just enough money to buy them. Trijntje Stormzand wrote proudly of her daughter: "Jekje works in a brush factory for $2.50 a week. . . . She would not take a back seat to any farmer's daughter in the Netherlands in the way she dresses."[128] I cannot stress enough the social mobility involved in a farmworker's daughter dressing as well as a farmer's daughter.

The most startling aspect of "Yankee" clothing for many was the presence of bright colors, not just for the apron but for the entire outfit. Trijntje Kooiman, working on a farm in Hawarden, Iowa, wrote to another domestic in the Netherlands: "In the summer maids like me run around in white dresses or skirts. That is pretty unpractical but as long as it is in fashion nobody cares."[129] In the United States young women could enjoy much more in the way of fashionable clothing, though in many cases it became a point of contention for some that daughters, especially those in urban areas, spent their money outfitting themselves rather than saving it or supporting the family.[130] They discussed buying hats, dresses, coats, and shoes, not necessarily in bright colors but certainly stylish.

For the older generation and some of the more conservative, especially early in the period, simple, dark-colored outfits remained classics. Pictures in the Dutch American collections of west Michigan and in church histories generally showed older women in dark colors, with trim.[131] By the 1910s there were exceptions, but many continued to wear what would have passed as stylish bourgeois clothing in the Netherlands in the latter nineteenth century. This esthetic also went with Dutch American missionaries. When the Rehoboth Mission to the Navajos opened it advertised its success in 1912 by picturing a young Navajo woman, a convert, in a standard dark-colored dress with small ruffles on the breast and the ubiquitous emphasis on the waistline.[132] Other pictures from the mission emphasized the same theme. What the Dutch American community cast off, but considered appropriate, became the "new" clothing of the mission. Civilization came in the form of a long dark skirt, a shirtwaist with trim, and a corset.

Corsets were the target of simultaneous campaigns in the Netherlands and the United States to reform women's clothing. Those campaigns also found their way into the Dutch American community, as in *The Banner*: "The women of old Holland must do more and harder work than most women here, and since this is a good part work in the open air, they keep in better trim through it."[133] The author could thus combine his argument about corsets being bad for the health of women with a condemnation of women taking "male" jobs, that is, jobs outside the home and farm. This attack on corsets was less successful than the fashion trend of the 1910s toward a slimmer, less curved line. Still, many Dutch immigrants did not prefer this ideal, even if they adopted the styles. Weight was a sign of prosperity and hence sometimes a badge of success. "Mientje you wrote that I had changed so much, and that I was so fat and had a double chin. . . . Well maybe that has to do with the pictures. In any case neither of us will be slim, and that is not a bad sign."[134] Others wrote of letting out their clothes or buying new things because the old ones were too small. All wrote in fairly positive terms.

By the 1910s a few immigrants were raising hemlines to show ankles, though the major shift upwards came after the study period. Dirk Nieland, in his 1920s Yankee Dutch spoof "Sonnieschoel Pikkenik" (Sunday school picnic), described this. The protagonist's wife won the "fat women's race" because "Mrs. Molenpaard is somewhat behind the times, you know, and still wears awful long skirts." Molenpaard fell over her hemline, revealing legs so bowed that "a good sized pig" could run through them.[135] An even more traumatic change for some was the shift to pants. Dingena Tannetje van Beek Berkhout, who arrived in Grand Rapids, Michigan, in 1908 at the age of fifteen, reminisced that when she was young a friend wanted to go skiing and asked her mother, "Can I wear pants? [The mother] answered, "I hope that you never put them on in my lifetime. . . . That would make me so unhappy."[136]

De Gereformeerde Amerikaan, unlike much of the Dutch American press which relied on clothing advertisements, took a negative view of most clothing changes in its articles. In 1904 it took on "mannish women" who adopted "male" clothing styles, whether hat, overcoat, tie, shirt, or vest.[137] A few years later it attacked women's fashion as much too expensive and women's hats in particular as a sign of "worldly splendor," which contradicted the Reformed marriage vows.[138] "With the remnants of dead birds and worms [our lady] seeks to advance her attractiveness and elevate the praise of her admirers."[139] At the same time, the English-language publication *The Banner* also took up the campaign. *The Banner* used stories such as "How Debby's Mission Money Put Her Mistress to Shame" to illustrate that philanthropy was a better goal than clothing. Still, the story illustrated that the author knew what was on the mind of a young domestic: "[Debby] had never had any pretty clothes, and she was trying hard now to buy a new dress. . . . She wanted a blue one, dark blue, with velvet on the collar and cuffs."[140] How effective these articles were, however, is less evident.

One of the big differences in women's fashions was the move away from clothing one made to ready-made. Men's clothing made this move first. In 1880 a shop in Orange City, Iowa, advertised its "Summer Fashions," by which it meant a series of new pictures of recent styles which a dressmaker could then replicate.[141] By the turn of the century, however, the competition was beginning. An ad in *Pella's Weekblad* in 1902 made this clear: "Ladies, the only way to get a 'dress' [in English] that fits well and looks good on you is to have it fitted and made by male tailors. Average store dresses are made to fit everyone 'somewhat,' but they are never very precise."[142] Ads for cloth and patterns as well as sewing machines were also present. But one store included a large number of ready-made items for men and children along with a long list of materials for women's dresses in its 1902 ad.[143] Dutch American newspapers by the 1910s regularly carried advertisements for clothing stores which featured items for the entire family.

Letters indicated that Dutch American women could increasingly rely on (and afford) certain ready-made items, notably menswear, socks, and underclothes. Even in the countryside the booming mail-order catalog business along with the expansion of the Rural Free Delivery system meant that by 1900 women nearly anywhere could obtain ready-made clothing as well as other items per post.[144] The Schuiling family, writing from Manhattan, Montana, in 1912, mentioned not only that the entire family went through the mail-order catalog before sending in orders but also that their local country store carried most items: "There isn't too much sewing these days, it is just as cheap to buy finished goods as by the yard. In the store you can find everything from a silk dress to match-es."[145] Schuiling may well have been alluding to a popular Dutch song: "In Sinkel's store you can buy everything, hats and caps and ladies' corsets."[146]

To what extent Dutch American women took advantage of ready-made goods depended on several factors: their financial situation, the time period, how old they were at migration, and how long they had been in the country. The older they were at migration, the more likely they were to make more of the clothing for the family. Part of this age difference related to educational practice. In the Netherlands school for girls frequently included extensive training in sewing and other handwork, a practice less common in America.[147] "Klaaske you wrote ask-ing if the girls learn sewing or knitting here. They do nothing like that at school here, just a little handwork, for example embroidering a handkerchief or doing something on paper. Nothing really useful. So we have to teach sewing our-selves. . . . You can get patterns in the stores for 10 or 15 cents . . . every month there is a new fashion print. . . . People don't wear much knitted clothing here and then it is much better to buy it because the yarn here isn't worth any-thing."[148] Immigrants also had to make due without the services of an in-house or door-to-door seamstress, a common phenomenon in the Netherlands but a rarity in rural areas of America where immigrants lived.[149]

Migrants often lost the assistance of certain female relatives and friends who traditionally helped with sewing chores. Women immigrants generally wrote about clothing matters to other women, often to women who might otherwise have had something to do with outfitting the family. Sending scraps of cloth back and forth across the Atlantic, requesting patterns, yarn, and thread were com-mon. But shipping costs prohibited the extended family and friends from pass-ing on hand-me-downs or making over an old piece of clothing for someone in America on a regular basis.[150] If the immigrants kept up these patterns, it was among the friends and relatives in the area. Gaatske, a domestic servant, exem-plified the overarching pattern. She wrote a letter thanking her former employer for a second-hand brown skirt, and in the same letter she mentioned going to town with another immigrant domestic to buy a new dress.[151] After the turn of the century prosperity and the mass market increasingly made purchase rather than home production the means to acquire clothing. Still, sewing clothing for women and children remained the task of most Dutch American housewives for much of the period.

For most Dutch American women, the process of sewing in the United States differed little from in the Netherlands with the exception of the absence of cer-tain yard goods, either the type of material or the pattern, to which they were accustomed. Likewise, finding the appropriate yarn or thread for darning was not always possible. But, in keeping with the refrain of frugal consumption, many women noted going to great lengths in order to repair their families' cloth-ing. For farming families, major sewing took place in the winter, when garden and field work let up. Repairing clothing, however had to go on year round.

Elizabeth Menkens Schreurs was not alone in darning husking gloves over and over. In an article comparing American and Dutch maids, Cornelia De Groot noted that American women had "done away with many domestic duties the Dutch housewife and her daughters still stick to such as knitting stockings and mending every hole and tear."[152] According to immigrant letters, darning and mending occupied a significant part of women's "spare" time. Klaaske Noorda Heller voiced a common complaint when she wrote: "there is much more waiting for me to do than I can do with the sewing and all."[153] Some had sewing machines (which despite the installment payment plan remained a rather expensive item) to help with the work.[154] A common pattern was that those who had sewing machines in the Netherlands either brought them along or bought machines to use in the United States. When three siblings contemplated emigrating, Jeannette Goedhart suggested they just bring one machine along, since they could share it. In her next letter, when it appeared that only her sister would come, she elaborated: "Concerning your sewing machine, I think you can bring it along, but if you can sell it for a good price then that is all right too. . . . They don't use hand driven machines here; they use pedal machines . . . [they] cost 35 to 40 dollars and then you have a top notch sewing machine."[155] Advertisements for sewing machines were a regular feature of *De Volksvriend*. In 1880 the local distributors of "New Home" sewing machines in Orange City, Iowa, provided the names of sixteen individuals who had bought their product. Among them were several leading families in town.[156] Further, in the 1910s, the Grand Rapids Furniture company, based out of Grand Rapids, Michigan, but with stores in various places in the Midwest, used the offer of a free sewing machine with a $150 purchase to lure customers.[157]

A few immigrant women would make a living with their sewing machines, though the dressmaking trade was dying out in this period. The lack of extensive school training for girls along these lines, combined with increased school attendance and the availability of ready-made wear, resulted in a loss of skills over a generation. Immigrant domestics and second generation women frequently noted they could not knit, crochet, or sew complex patterns. By the end of the period, sewing was at least partially a social activity for women who had time to get together with others, and had changed in meaning. Sewing circles, as well as women's and girls' groups in the church, reported their activities to the Dutch American press: "The Sherman St. Ladies' Aid Society will have an Apron Sale, (also some fancy work and quilts), Thursday."[158] Having the time to do "fancy work" was a sign of leisure and of middle-class status generally.

If women had time for such activities, perhaps they could do something else, thus the same paper carried a much larger article printed in bold from the League of Christian Reformed Churches for the Welfare of the Soldiers, asking ladies' aids and girls' societies to knit wristlets, sweater-vests, and sweaters for "the boys."[159] World War I generally heightened the association of women's work and public service. Reports from Dutch American communities around the country attested to the formation of Red Cross chapters which engaged in a "knitting mania."[160] To make sure no one would be left out, *Pella's Weekblad* published knitting directions for items like wristlets in Dutch, adding suggestions for which size needles and yarn colors.[161] By January of 1918 the Pella chapter of the Red Cross had produced 165 pairs of socks, 59 wristlets, 67 sweaters, and various other items.[162] At a time when the Dutch generally were under suspicion for disloyalty, knitting for the troops became an important way to show one's patriotism. Likewise, articles in the Dutch American press called on women to cut back on use of meat and sugar in particular. Whether people on farms followed these instructions was more questionable. In terms of other consumption patterns, however, the war meant that prices for various kinds of goods rose. The patterns of material betterment, as in other times of hardship, were slowed. Yet the papers also reported that conditions in the Netherlands were much worse.

The United States symbolized not just material betterment but technological advance as well throughout the period around the turn of the century. Again the change was one also taking place in the Netherlands, albeit more slowly.[163] While immigrants raved about the new farm machinery, the biggest technological shifts for some Dutch immigrant women late in this period were the introduction of a washing machine and (especially in urban areas) indoor plumbing. Not everyone had either, and certainly it was more common in 1920 to have both than it had been in 1880, but the trend began during this period. The clothing many immigrant women could now afford needed care, especially regular washing.[164]

Early washing machines required nearly constant attention, and saved little time, but they released women from the long periods of hands immersed in soapy water, and from at least part of the normal scrubbing routine.[165] In the 1890s Klaaske Noorda Heller wrote her mother: "I got a washing machine. It cost $50. They are the best things you can have. I wash every load clean in 10 minutes and then I cook it once more. I cannot wash it all at the same time, it has to be done in loads."[166] Noorda did not mention whether her machine included a hand-cranked wringer as well.

The first washing "machines" worked on woman power. Neither electricity nor gas engines made much of an appearance prior to 1920, so the energy came from elbow grease. To women reminiscing about the turn of the century, washing, even with some mechanical aid, held few pleasures. Viewed from the perspective of the electric washing machines of the 1960s, there was little modern or technological about their early washing apparatus: "We had a washboiler . . . a big kettle that went on top of the stove. Then we put about five pails of water in it, and when the water was warm, then we put lye in, and then the hard stuff from the water came to the top and you had to skim it off, and when you had skimmed it off then we put the soap in. But that soap, you could hardly put enough in. . . . When we were first married then we had to crank the washing machine by hand."[167] Reading between the lines, it appears that "good husbands" sometimes "helped" with washing, as in hauling some of the water, but it remained a woman's responsibility to care for the clothes.

After washing and line-drying came ironing. As one woman reported, ironing took a good deal of time because you had to iron everything—from clothing to sheets—and many items needed starching as well.[168] Of the letters and interviews I consulted, few noted a technological advance in ironing. When Anna Kuijt worked as a domestic for a non-Dutch family in Chicago in 1911, she wrote that she was "putting the socks and underclothes through an ironing machine now."[169] Another woman recalled that her mother got an electric iron shortly after Zeeland, Michigan, got electricity around 1902: "My father took care that she had good things to work with."[170] Most immigrants probably used the standard technique of heating irons on the stove, using several irons so one could reheat while another was in use. Electricity, and thus electric irons, did not make their way into most rural Dutch American households prior to 1920.

According to Susan Strasser's history of housework, if women had discretionary money to help with household work, their first expenditure was for laundry. As she stated: "[E]ven women of limited means sought relief in the form of washerwomen, commercial laundries, and mechanical aids."[171] That was the case with Elizabeth Menkens Schreurs after she had experience in American housekeeping for a period, but not when she first arrived—and turned down the offer of laundry services. In general it appears that Dutch American women used mechanical aids as available and affordable, but their sense of frugality (and the household budget) often kept them from sending out the laundry or hiring a domestic servant to do it. In lists of household goods which people acquired, washing machines were one of the top priorities, but often behind a couple of stoves and a cream separator (not to mention most of the farm machinery). That they turned to washing machines so quickly was probably part of an American pattern of adopting technology, for indications were that in the Netherlands this came somewhat later.[172]

I found conflicting information on whether Dutch immigrant women were more or less particular than their American counterparts in terms of cleaning clothing. A few wrote that Americans were more particular about clothes in general. Jantje Enserink van der Vliet, writing from Minnesota in 1909, stated: "Most [Americans] don't do much in terms of housekeeping. They make a great to do about clothing on the other hand."[173] Having more outfits usually made cleanliness a bit easier, though washing might take place at the same intervals. Others writers contrasted the cleanliness of Dutch dress to American standards: "the same work clothes had to be worn several days in a row before a clean batch was ready. Dad must have thought many a time what a far cry this was from the white jacket and apron in his tidy and clean meat market in Holland."[174] In any case the technological changes in some homes, washing machines, soap powders, and running water, made cleaning clothes considerably easier. As in the Netherlands, that led to higher standards. Immigrants who saw these changes taking place in the United States, even if they heard of them going on in the Netherlands later, still associated them with "America."

Shelter

As with food and clothing, Dutch American women held primary responsibility for the care and maintenance of their abode. Unlike the first two necessities, however, women were less involved in production. Instead they were in charge of keeping things clean, in order, running smoothly. Men held primary responsibility for providing a house or apartment, women for making that house a home. *Gezelligheid,* a term which does not translate well, epitomized the ideal of this process.[175] To make the physical surroundings livable, a place where people felt comfortable and where hospitality reigned: women undertook these challenges in the name of *gezelligheid.* For the less affluent, the crucial term, though they rarely used it, was *huisbeleid*—household management.

On a practical level, women allotted tasks around the dwelling according to gender and age. When young they sometimes worked as domestics and in any case generally learned household skills; when older they sometimes tried to find domestics, at least if they could afford them, to help with the chores. Everyone in the household had certain things which he or she could contribute to household order. As the family grew the woman could delegate more tasks, but the ultimate responsibility for a functioning (and perhaps even *gezellig*) house, remained with her. In the parlance of the home economics movement, women had to be good managers. In the parlance of Dutch immigrants, women had to be good housewives.

What exactly did Dutch immigrant women expect in terms of living quarters? Few of them described their living quarters in detail prior to emigration, and those who did tended to be unusually affluent. According to various reports, the Netherlands experienced a significant shortage of housing around the turn of the century. Much of this shortage had to do with rising standards, but by any measure many dwellings were cramped, damp, and dreary. The government blamed private builders and landlords for the problems in the cities, and took its first step toward public housing projects in 1901 with the Wet op Volkshuisvesting (law on housing for the people). The law, which allowed inspectors to condemn houses, did little to alleviate conditions in the country. "In the countryside the barest necessities are absent [as in the cities], and moreover the apartments are generally smaller, the families larger than in the city. The limited resources of the inhabitants leads to the use of sod huts, sheds, and houseboats, and unacceptable cohabitation occurs frequently."[176] At the upper end of the economic spectrum, technological changes like indoor plumbing and electricity began taking hold around the turn of the century. Concurrently the affluent decorated their parlors and dining rooms with rugs, knickknacks, heavy overstuffed furniture, pictures, porcelain tea sets, and starched linen or lace tablecloths. The well-to-do in the countryside could not compare to the urban elite, but both stood in contrast to the stark surroundings of workers' quarters. Lace, linen, or crocheted curtains graced the homes of those who had the time or money to make or buy them. As one report stated, in the champagne years for large farmers in Groningen, 1850 to 1880, families invested in "luxury": expensive furniture and other household goods. A piano served as the ultimate status symbol.[177] In the lean years thereafter, farming families had to struggle to maintain this status. Rural families involved in putting out work around 1900 generally had a stove, perhaps wallpaper and a few pictures.[178]

Ideas about proper living combined with economic improvement in other areas to spur families to renovate their living quarters. Winterswijk typified this pattern. There, families began putting up a separating wall between the living and working quarters in the farmhouse. Next they might add a regular kitchen or a side kitchen, and finally an indoor toilet.[179] In the process the family might also increase the number of bedsteads, each provided with a straw mattress, so that fewer children had to share beds.

Cornelia De Groot described her family home in Friesland in detail in her autobiography. Several aspects of her description implied the family status as well-to-do: a large brick house, china on the mantelpiece, a parlor separate from the regular living quarters, several rugs, paneling as well as wallpaper, a mahogany table, various copper kettles, and "quite a collection of dainty cups and saucers, teapots, creamers, sugar-bowls and such things."[180] Like many Dutch houses, her parental home was divided into a front section for living and a back section which served as a barn. But unlike small farmers, the De Groots also had several other barns, putting distance between themselves and the animals and also between themselves and the servants. Farmworkers frequently lived in separate quarters from the *boer*'s family, whether a sod hut, barn, or cottage.

Friesland boasted a relatively favorable reputation in comparison with other provinces for its treatment of workers. The other extreme came in the neighboring province of Groningen. In a section of Groningen characterized by high emigration rates, domestics generally lived in the stalls next to the animals. There was no heat, nor a place to dry clothing, a significant logistical problem for those with only one outfit. Had the farmer's family lived under similar circumstances domestics might not have complained, but this occurred at a time when the *boerin*'s house generally consisted of a living room, parlor, bedroom, and kitchen.[181] Wealthy farmers generally retained several servants, including at least two domestics.

Another affluent woman emigrant, from Amsterdam, hinted at this kind of physical distance between the bourgeoisie and their servants. In an interview she mentioned she had never been in the kitchen prior to migration, so at age twenty-one she neither knew how to do dishes nor how to bake. Her parents employed two maids and two scrub women who did all the household tasks, from polishing the children's shoes to cleaning the copper utensils.[182] The kitchen door thus became the barrier between two worlds.

The other group of women who discussed housing, most often in negative terms, were those who moved from urban areas to relatively unsettled ones. Janet Huyser complained bitterly about nearly everywhere the family lived in the United States. In Chicago the family moved into a relatively large house but without an inside toilet (which the family had in Barendrecht before migrating in 1911). Next they moved to Winnie, Texas: "Our abode was an old, wooden, unpainted house, if you could call it that . . . [it] had two rooms, a large room which served for a bedroom and a smaller kitchen . . . what a contrast to our palatial home in Holland."[183] The family did not do well economically, and eventually sold the house and land along with an oak linen closet, the only piece of furniture they had brought from the Netherlands, in order to leave that location quickly. Letters and information from families such as this helped dissuade potential migrants with more affluent backgrounds. Just as the Dutch East India colonies attracted the wealthy with their opportunities to enhance class privilege with racial overtones, so the United States became the mecca for those seeking to break out of the Dutch class system.[184]

The majority of Dutch immigrant women came from rural areas and more modest economic circumstances. Thus their expectations for housing were different. The Schaapman family moved from a brick farmhouse/barn in Overijssel to a two-story wooden frame house with a large front porch and separate American-style barns in California. Earlier immigrants prepared the way for the Schaapmans, who came as a family, so when they arrived their new home was under construction. Lubbigje Schaapman reported: "Our house is not ready yet. We have four rooms, 2 upstairs and 2 downstairs. Upstairs there are 4 bedsteads where I and the boys sleep, and mother and father sleep downstairs. We have a stove that cost 40 dollars, that is pretty expensive, but it is large and pretty . . . we also have a wind mill that pumps the water through pipes to the barn and to the house . . . in the house you only have to turn the faucet and you get water."[185] The biggest differences in rural areas, clear from pictures but less frequently mentioned in immigrant women's letters, were the separation of house and barns and the use of wood instead of brick as building material.

Previous immigrants generally organized housing for their relatives and friends, either buying or renting accommodations ahead of time. One couple newly arrived in Roseland, just outside of Chicago, in 1882 described the procedure there. "Building cannot proceed fast enough to accommodate the people, and then one must pay 8 or 10 dollars rent per month for the new houses . . . a poor hollander cannot do that hence often two families move in together and have coffee and meals together."[186] They then offered to share their own home with another couple that was thinking of emigrating. Twenty-eight years later the refrain was still the same: "school teachers can hardly find a boarding place, so if you come here you could easily keep boarders. . . . there is also a place where you can buy land."[187]

According to their letters, Dutch immigrants often shared houses with their relatives for at least a short time during their lives. Most frequently it was an

The Onne and Antje Noteboom Eppinga family in front of their frame home near Hull, Iowa, ca. 1912. The furnishings, from lace curtains to buggy style, indicate a reasonable economic status. Photo courtesy of Jane Eppinga.

elderly parent or parents, but young adult siblings shared housing in their first months or years in the United States as well. Family formed one of the most secure means of surviving economically. H. Schoonbeek wrote in 1894 that thousands of people were out of work in the Grand Rapids area. "I live with my wife's father and mother, both elderly people. They had their own home and now they rent that house, so you can well understand that I am not sorry about that."[188]

A common theme in immigrant letters was the desire for a house, and if the family had one, for a better one. Not all succeeded. Cornelia Smit's dream of using her inheritance money to build a combination house and shoemaker's shop never materialized. Instead, seventeen years after her marriage, she and her husband could only rent a plot of land outside Grand Rapids where she did the farming while her husband worked in a machine shop.[189]

The mobility that brought a family or individual to the United States did not necessarily stop once on American shores. Social mobility frequently tied into geographic mobility, a trend that worried some Dutch Americans. An article in *De Gereformeerde Amerikaan* tried to convince middle-class Dutch Americans who came from less than affluent backgrounds that they should heed the example of Dutch farms where the houses bore the family name and the descendants lived in them for generations.[190] In other words, they should quit moving around so much.

Most if not all women whose letters I read reported at least one and sometimes several moves connected with a search for better economic opportunities. Anje Nieveen Mulder noted that her extended family moved out of Nebraska because of rising land prices; the parents and their married children could better afford to buy acreage in Kansas. "[W]e have rented a farm for this year. R and his brother J are now working together to build a house on our land."[191] While a few immigrants reported living in sod houses on the plains until they could afford something better, the typical American house in rural areas was constructed of wood.[192] Even primitive houses by the turn of the century usually consisted of two rooms, often with bedrooms as well. In urban areas the conditions were sometimes better. Aukjen Pruiksma wrote from Paterson, New Jersey, in 1895: "[Jetze and Manne] have a good sized house; four rooms including two bedrooms and a basement. In the basement they have a stove where they do the cooking."[193] Genevieve Gough described the homes of Pella and Orange City in 1923 as "very modern and up to date" one- and two-story frame buildings, mixed with a few brick homes. Only the green and yellow shutters hinted at the Dutch background of the inhabitants.[194]

When immigrants sent pictures to their relatives, they generally were of family members. In some cases however, they also included the family home. The pictures Jacob van Hinte collected during his 1920s journey through Dutch America also attest to the wooden frame houses, often with front porch, of working-class Dutch immigrants. In Grand Rapids, the least well off had to make do with trees but not much space between the house and the street. Those with more money could afford the enclosed brick porches and green setback of areas like Worden Street.[195] Unlike in the Netherlands, the Dutch in the United States generally encountered the characteristic midwestern American checkerboard of square lots and roads which met at right angles. Though builders and planners had to adjust to rivers, lakes, and grain elevators, most of the settlement followed a grid. In the cities right angles and straight lines contrasted with the typical Dutch pattern of curving, narrow streets which spoked out from a central square that functioned as a hub.

The Dillingham Commission study of 1911 reported on conditions among various immigrant groups, all of them living in the poor neighborhoods in New York, Philadelphia, Chicago, Boston, Cleveland, Buffalo, and Milwaukee. According to this, the Dutch families, 144 of the 15,127 in the study group, lived well in comparison to most other groups. The average family of five had a five-room dwelling, and the average number of persons per bedroom was two.[196]

What home furnishings a family brought with them or bought depended on their financial status and the generosity of their relatives. A woman from Nijverdal noted that when they arrived in Iowa they had little. She and her husband bought six chairs from their brother-in-law, and got a table and a stove. A neighbor made a "dresser" out of an old chest, and the family bought a rug for the floor. New furniture had to wait until they moved into a new home because "the men had to have everything for the farm first. They had to have machinery, otherwise they couldn't do anything."[197] Rag rugs, flour sacks stuffed with straw for mattresses, improvised furniture: immigrant families that put their money into getting started farming frequently could not afford much more at first, but most reported buying additional household goods over time.[198] For those in the western Michigan area, the Dutch presence in the furniture industry spurred further purchases.[199] Many immigrants noted a big shopping expedition just prior to moving into a home and perhaps some smaller purchases over time. Not long after Klaaske Noorda Heller arrived in the United States in 1891, she described the family home:

> About our furniture—we have a table with turned legs. A person can pull it open and lay a board in the middle of it just like the table top. We have nine comfortable chairs made of wood with cushions—good looking chairs with curved arms. We have a dresser with a mirror and a hanging lamp. We have a large cookstove with a large tin wash boiler with copper handles. The stove has a copper water reservoir in back. The stove has four openings in the front and a large oven. Everything is made of cast iron. Two pots, one for roasting, are commonly used here. . . . We forgot to take our kettle along.[200]

Ads for household goods, particularly furniture, were a staple of the Dutch American press. As one ad stated "Men want work-saving machines—Why not women?"[201] In this case the store was selling kitchen cabinets. A large cabinet designed to hold several common kitchen needs and provide some counter space was a typical feature in other papers as well. In *De Hollandsche Amerikaan* this was the one item which consistently had a woman in traditional Dutch dress next to it in the ads, though all other housewares featured women in the latest styles, or in domestic servant uniforms by the late 1910s.[202] Other items of furniture, from living room to bedroom to dining room suites, were also common in the press by that time. One of the ubiquitous images was that of a rocking chair, an American piece of furniture with much cultural importance. Whether the immigrants bought these very often, however, was not clear. Some photographs indicated at least a few did, though generally those with more affluent homes.

As in the Netherlands, the prize possession was often a piano or an organ. Even in 1880, *De Volksvriend* of Orange City carried regular ads for pianos and organs. *De Boodschapper* and other Dutch American publications also carried advertisements for these instruments, though the prices ranged well beyond the means of many. Pianos and organs were a part of many Dutch immigrant homes, as were other instruments. Elizabeth Menkens Schreurs was not alone in acquiring an organ and getting music lessons for her daughter. All the Dutch American communities which contained colleges boasted many concerts and musicians who then trained the next generation. Musical instruments were one of the badges of middle-class status to which people aspired. An organ or piano was one of the last big items a family might buy, and thus a measure of having truly made it.

On the one hand, Dutch American merchants tried to entice potential cus-

The Ensink family of western Michigan in the 1880s illustrated economic prosperity both through their home and clothing. Note the rocking chairs on the porch. Photo courtesy of Archives, Calvin College.

tomers. On the other hand, some writers felt such luxury might be sinful, and looked back wistfully at the old days in rose-colored remembrances of poverty-stricken happiness. A series of articles in *De Gereformeerde Amerikaan* in 1898 reported: "Whenever women think they have to have a piano, even though no one in the household can play or is taking lessons, and have a sofa that is always covered, on which no one may sit, then things have reached a bad state."[203] Note that in both these cases it was the women who wanted the items. Many women had fond memories of the Netherlands or wanted to return, yet none of the sources I consulted indicated that anyone wanted to return to a one-room house with no running water. Those who were most affluent in the Netherlands had greater difficulty adjusting because they often faced a step down the material as well as social ladder, at least at the outset. Those who began with little could bring all their worldly belongings with them; those with much had to pick and choose and pay extra luggage costs.

Advice to future immigrants on what to bring constituted a staple of immigrant letters. Anna Kuijt, a domestic servant in Chicago, wrote about smuggling cigars through customs, and how she managed not to pay anything on her teapot. She also wrote that a family accompanying her had to pay a fortune to bring an organ, and had various goods besides, from a milk can to a tray for drinking glasses. "I would suggest to you not to bring too much, namely no wash basin, for the apartments all have bathrooms here and there is a sink in there. They do not have much furniture here, a few chairs and a bookcase, that is all."[204] Transatlantic mobility generally meant that old armoires and other heavy furniture the family might possess, even many an heirloom, never made the journey. Likewise mobility within the United States often meant selling off some of what one had in one place and buying new items in another location. *Pella's Weekblad* often had notices for moving sales. Sometimes families rented a train car for transport, while in other cases such as that of the Schreurs they managed to put their belongings in wagons and move the distance. Mobility cut back on what people could haul. On the other hand, the Schreurs and others also acquired more over time as prosperity allowed more purchases. In Dutch American communities some stores catered to bourgeois tastes. "A true paradise for the female sex" declared one ad, which featured fine china and glassware, from Haviland and Delft to Dresden and Limoges.[205] Even in rural northwestern Iowa, porcelain sales went on from an early date.[206] Yet from most immigrant accounts, more basic items were standard.

Housekeeping, in particular cleaning, depended on a variety of factors. Because domestic help was cheap and exploitable in the Netherlands, Dutch families, even small farmers, could often afford at least a general maid. The standards the housewife set for herself and for her help in terms of cleanliness differed dramatically according to how much help she had, either from servants or family members, and from place to place. *De Volksvriend,* which circulated nationally among Dutch Americans, reported in 1921 on a women's committee in Orange City, Iowa, which would clean the street and alley around a dirty neighbor's house and then send a bill for their services.[207] The urban bourgeois had more to clean, and more people to clean it. That did not stop the Dutch farm wives from setting high standards, whether in terms of scrubbing the street or washing the windows. Housewives who worked ten-hour days in home industry, or who took an active role in farmwork, rarely could maintain the same standards as the bourgeois. But the stereotype, and the reality of much of Dutch society, was an attachment to cleanliness that differed dramatically from American standards.

"You don't have all that work here that goes on in Holland every week. First no street scrubbing, no scouring and polishing and no dusting; that makes a huge difference, right?"[208] Geertje de Jong Schuiling, whose other letters indicated she did scrub the floor occasionally, did not mean she never cleaned, only that she no longer felt she had to do these jobs as often. And furthermore she had given up trying to keep the floor clean all the time. As for street scrubbing, or even scrubbing of the front porch steps and sidewalk adjoining the house, a ubiquitous practice in the Netherlands, there was no need because they were all dirt. In the countryside there were no steps and no sidewalk. The cities had a different kind of architecture from Dutch cityscapes, one less conducive to street scrubbing, and fewer neighbors who scrubbed. Many women attributed their diminished standards of cleanliness to the unavailability and price of domestic help. Even if they could find domestics, they could not expect servants to work as in the Netherlands—there were too many employers, especially Americans, who offered better wages and working conditions.

Cleaning, with or without domestics or daughters, included a once- or twice-yearly ritual of absolution. Few women looked forward to spring cleaning, nor to its fall counterpart, yet the evidence indicates that most everyone did it. "May 27. We have been busy with housecleaning but are nearly finished."[209] Women in the Netherlands did it as well.[210] Thus, when Klaaske in the Dutch province of Friesland wanted to entice her sister-in-law to write she included this as one of the topics: "Geertje why don't you send along a letter too. I think you can always write something about housekeeping. . . . We started the big cleaning this week, cupboards and clothing and so forth."[211] What exactly the big cleaning entailed, most writers left somewhat vague. Some of the tasks included restuffing and cleaning straw mattresses, taking up carpeting, washing walls, cleaning ovens and lamps, and washing windows. Of note, the tasks Susan Strasser listed as part of spring cleaning included a number of activities which Dutch domestics reported doing at least once a week.[212] American advertisers picked up on to the stereotype of cleanliness and named a leading national cleaning product Dutch Cleanser. At the same time, the image on the package, with its wooden shoes, old-style hat, and short stick to beat away dirt, was a bit of an ethnic slur, like other images of domestic servants who were "foreign" in some way from the American standard. I did not encounter any advertisements for Dutch Cleanser in Dutch American newspapers.

Spring cleaning time was a major theme in Dutch American advertising. "It is Cleaning Time!! Do you have good equipment?"; "Dutch Housewives! Things needed for spring cleaning"; "House cleaning time is here. Do you need a Rug, Carpet Sweeper or Draperies?"[213] Various kinds of brushes, chamois cloths, and rag cloths for mopping were part of the list of items provided by importers.[214] Others used this as a time to sell carpet, curtains, wallpaper, and paint, and even to try to introduce home improvements. Large purchases invariably required a husband's approval. While there were some such as Gerrit Schreurs who would go along with such expenditures, there were also others like Harry Saving, of Lynden, Washington, who liked to say "A woman wants many things and when she gets it [sic] she wants something more. Don't you know!"[215]

* * *

An article on the domestic life of Dutch Americans in 1898 exemplified some of the shifts in the social reproduction of basic necessities. The author argued that parents needed to watch out that the children did not succumb to eating too many sweets, a problem of the American setting. He went on to note that parents should try to follow the American custom of more commodious sleeping accommodations for the children, so that older children did not share the same bed, a common practice in the Netherlands for the group that emigrated.[216] This was part of the moralization campaign in the Netherlands as well. As in most settings, "American" stood for the changes of industrialization and mass consumption, and most importantly of embourgeoisement. Larger homes with more beds and fewer persons sharing them were a part of that process. So too was more and cleaner clothing. Conspicuous consumption in the form of food, clothing, and shelter became ingrained in Dutch American minds, and through immigrant contacts back into the Netherlands, a vision came into being of America as relatively classless and a land of abundance.

When Dutch immigrant women changed their cleaning habits, they related the change to the cost and availability of domestics and to the differing standards in the United States. When they changed their food and housing it had to do with the family's financial position. In all the basic necessities, American conditions forced some changes. In several areas women embraced those shifts as one of the main benefits of migration. By the late nineteenth century even the most self-sufficient of farms was tied into the money economy, so that food, clothing, and shelter became contingent, at least partially, on money. Women, regardless of marital status, number of children, or age, needed to operate in this setting. Money thus gradually became the primary way to acquire basic necessities, rather than just their elaborations.

CHAPTER 3

Making Ends Meet

Among Dutch immigrants production for wages remained primarily in the hands of men, but women also had economic roles, ones which undergirded the social reproduction of gender relations within families and contributed to family economies. Most immigrants came from a class of people who assumed women worked hard, whether or not what they did was formally called work or given monetary compensation. After migration Dutch Protestant women, at least in most cases, continued their roles as contributors to the family economy, sometimes by a mixture of home production and frugal consumption, sometimes by part-time service jobs, sometimes by full-time employment. At the turn of the century, women had fewer opportunities than men to earn a living in a paid position, either in the Netherlands or in the United States. But the opportunities for wage work and the remuneration were better in the United States. Moreover, the distinction between paid and unpaid work had less significance in farming settings or in family enterprises. To further complicate the picture, governmental statistics on both sides of the Atlantic during this period frequently assumed married women should be listed as housewives, ignoring part-time or seasonal paid work.[1] Women applauded many of the new job opportunities, but these jobs generally went to the second generation, or at least the generation and a half—those who migrated with their parents. This chapter is about various kinds of work: gendered opportunities for paid work and many of the tasks directly related to household production which allowed a family to avoid spending money. These were places where social reproduction often blended into production with no clear boundaries.

In the Netherlands employers and sometimes entire industries excluded women from most jobs during this period.[2] Women's wages, on farms, in factories, and elsewhere, remained well below those of men. Yet for the lower middle and working class, economic survival depended on the "contributions" of women to the family budget. A government survey of workers' budgets from 1891 showed that in urban areas a man's wages might be sufficient for a family, but in the countryside there were almost always at least two wage-earners, either husband and wife or husband and child[ren].[3] In shops and on farms where women worked together with husbands, brothers, and fathers, one should speak of a family economy and family wages.[4] Often, they were literally family wages, paid or turned over to the head of household. Even in the most common occupation for single women, domestic service, wages generally went at least partially if not entirely into a family pot. Married women frequently combined housekeeping with part-time work, taking in laundry, keeping boarders, sewing, making cheese or butter. Working and saving formed the complementary activities of women, sometimes with others in the family and sometimes alone, sometimes for wages and sometimes to spare them.

Dutch immigrants generally came from a social background where people assumed women worked, either for wages or for the family farm or business. How much a woman worked depended on the family finances and on the stage in the family life cycle.[5] It was a badge of financial success for a farmer to say his wife did not work in the fields, because it meant he could afford enough hired hands, both men and women, that his wife rose to the status of manager. She in turn had a heavier workload in the house, arranging meals for these workers and maintaining a lifestyle appropriate to their status. Around the turn of the century, politicians, concerned with the impact on the family of late but rapid industrialization in the Netherlands, sought to protect women and children with a variety of laws. In the process the legislators shifted their concern from women in general to married women in particular.[6] Yet agricultural work and domestic service, the two fields in which most immigrant women worked prior to migration, remained outside the purview of these measures. For many, the difference between the categories was minimal, because domestic servants in the countryside frequently worked at least as much in the barns and at certain (often gender-specific) tasks in the fields as they did in the house.[7] In Janet Sjaarda Sheeres's compilation of occupational titles for women migrating on their own from the province of Groningen between 1881 and 1901, for example, about half (392) listed their occupation as domestic service, but of these close to 90 percent had job titles which indicated work in a rural area or specifically on a farm. Another 26 percent (205) were just "workers."[8] In the Netherlands wages for women agricultural workers tended to be low, though they differed regionally.[9] The evaluation of this work was also changing, and over time it became less common for young women to go into domestic work in rural areas, especially in Friesland, where the bourgeois ideals of womanhood began to have more influence. Overall there was an exodus of young women from the countryside to the cities, where domestic service, while still onerous by some standards, was much less so than in rural areas. Rural jobs generally began to disappear with mechanization, and more opportunities in factory and service work appeared, notably after the turn of the century. For most women, however, such jobs were tied to one stage in the life cycle.

The Earning Years

In the period from 1880 to 1920 both the Netherlands and the United States waged successful campaigns to curtail child labor. Both passed legislation which limited working hours and required longer school attendance. In both cases, however, children, unless they had affluent parents, finished schooling about the time they reached adolescence. Further, children engaged in agricultural work generally escaped the law, if not with formal exemptions, then in praxis.[10] For the group that emigrated, children's paid or unpaid work for the family, especially during their teenage years, was a part of the standard life course. This was the time when the family could gain economically on its "investment," the economic drain of raising the child up to that point. As one man who immigrated with his parents reported: "My mother . . . was nothing but a slave. She worked for well-to-do farmers since she was ten years old—the first five years for twenty-five guldens per year to help in the kitchen, feed the other help, tend to the chickens, and keep the house clean. And they mean clean in Holland. That meant twenty-five guldens for her parents, and they had one less mouth to feed."[11] I do not wish to make it sound as though families only wanted children for money. But a Dutch American family, like its Dutch counterpart from the same economic background, expected the children to play an economic role. One woman in New Jersey in 1895 wrote: "The men earn good wages and it does not look too bad for us either. When the children get a job we will be able to make a 'go' of it and have a good living."[12] Another woman, living in Pella, Iowa, in 1882, explained: "Dirk and Cornelia have big children. Such people can really get ahead here."[13] The assumption in these cases was that children would do farmwork for free or hand over their wages to the parents, as was the Dutch custom. Over time young people challenged this assumption.[14]

   Dutch American mothers expected that they could turn over an increasing amount of their daily routine to their children. Because of the rural nature of Dutch migration in the period, much of children's work was unpaid, assisting on the farm and in the household. Nor did the authorities enforce restrictions on children's work on the farm and at home as long as the youngsters showed up in school most of the time. Dutch women reported their relief at turning over tasks to their daughters, while daughters sometimes complained about how much they had to "help." Both sons and daughters would help with household tasks, though daughters were more likely to handle many cleaning and cooking duties. In the American world where domestics were generally too expensive for Dutch American families to afford, at least for any length of time, daughters took over this role. Daughters reported handling most household tasks, but most particularly child care, washing, and cleaning. Work in the barn, especially milking, went to both sons and daughters, as did several aspects of field work.[15]

In urban areas both daughters and sons would work for wages in a variety of settings, but the daughters continued to be responsible to a much greater extent than sons for assistance in household tasks. Having wage-earning children often meant that a mother could retire from or did not need to enter the labor market herself: "Trijntje is also very happy that she is here [Roseland, Ill.]. Her three children work for wages every day . . . she no longer works for someone else."[16] The length of time a child had to assist in family activities and in the family economy varied, but normally it was until marriage.

One common migration strategy was to wait until the family had several teenage children before setting off for America, assuring chances for wage earning, as well as for the basics of home care from nursing to housework. Daughters thus could take on the role of unpaid domestic help or of wage-earners, or switch between the two as needed. This constituted a problem for some "children." One Dutch American woman reported that her mother's parents insisted that she, then age twenty-four, migrate with them to the United States because they needed her to care for her younger siblings.[17] Likewise, Wilhelmina Woudenberg, age seventeen, had just found a good job as a domestic in a fashionable home in Amersfoort when her parents decided to emigrate. As her brother stated, "[She had] no mind to go to America, but was reproved by Father that as a child of the family she had no voice in the matter."[18] Woudenberg's case illustrates a typical pattern. She entered the labor market shortly after arrival in Paterson, New Jersey. When her mother became seriously ill in 1913, she left her job and came home to handle the nursing. Several other children continued to work to provide for the family.

Even when Dutch American daughters assumed much of the household work, the terminology was still that they "helped." As one woman wrote: "Mother also dispensed with a maid, so I had to help in the home, and my school days were over."[19] What she meant was that she took on a full-time unpaid job. Likewise daughters as well as sons served as unpaid hired hands in the barn and fields. With farm chores, as with domestic work, children might do the same activity for a wage if the family needed the money more than the extra hands. Thus Oono and Klaaske Noorda Heller wrote: "The boys are going out to cut wood again, and we can pay the interest on our loan from that. We also hope to have more land cleared."[20] Seasonal work in truck gardening or in the canning factories were common in the areas surrounding Holland, Michigan, and on the southern fringe of Chicago, both large Dutch American settlements.

Until the parents officially turned over the farm or house to one of the (married) children, the mother held responsibility for organizing the tasks and for making sure they got done. A child generally did not move out of the parental home until marriage except, if female, to work as a domestic, or, if male, to take

Daughters in the Ensing
family showing off the
corn crop before they pick
it, Hudsonville, Michigan,
1912. Photo courtesy of
Archives, Calvin College.

a job in a location that was too far removed to commute. Thus Gezina van der
Haar Visscher's adopted son Dick lived with her for at least thirteen years, during which time he worked sporadically at a factory in Holland, Michigan. Only
when repeated health problems made it clear that he could no longer continue
his job did the family decide Dick could move elsewhere. And like many children of immigrants the next choice for Dick was a place near a sibling.[21]

For girls, unlike boys, the jobs they began shortly after finishing school were
often the only wage-earning positions they would hold. Wage work was a part
of the normal life course for women but not a continuous activity. They might
return to it if widowed, and they often supplemented family wages in various
ways. The kinds of positions they took generally fell into a few categories. In 1919
De Hollandsche Amerikaan of Kalamazoo, Michigan, a small city with a rural
hinterland, carried classified ads of openings which matched the overall categories of work available for Dutch American women in many parts of the United
States. Domestic service in a variety of designations led the list with twenty ads;
factory work, including several openings at a local furniture factory, in bookbinding, and at baking companies came next; sales followed with only three
offerings for the year; and finally there was one job advertised for office work.[22]
Each of these areas deserves closer attention, particularly since immigrants compared what they saw in the United States against their experiences in the old
world.

Domestic Service

For many young women in the Netherlands, domestic service was a rite of passage in the years between school and marriage. Supposedly this would operate
as an apprenticeship in housekeeping for a young woman before she started her
own family, though for many in rural areas work in the fields, gardens, or barns

was just as prominent. These were earning years for her parents, when the daughter switched from requiring support to providing it. Few women continued as domestics after marriage, because day positions were uncommon and live-in work difficult to combine with one's own family life. For others, however, domestic service remained a lifelong occupation. Rising through the ranks of domestic jobs, that is, occupational upward mobility, was possible to some extent and might culminate in a position as a cook or housekeeper working for a wealthy urban employer. Such women received considerably better pay and better conditions than the beginning "all-around maid." Sometimes women chose to stay in domestic service. At other times it was the only option available.

By the turn of the century, factory jobs with better wages and more free time began to draw part of the potential domestic population elsewhere. The Dienstboden-Congres of 1898, a national conference on domestic service, highlighted this trend. The bourgeois organizers of the conference used it as a forum to complain about "the domestic problem," that is, the lack of qualified help. Even they admitted that the conditions of service for domestics resembled those of serfs from the Middle Ages, and that without free time, coordination of household work to prevent unnecessary tasks, introduction of household appliances where possible, and in general better treatment, few "qualified" types would consider this profession.[23] The kind of training these employers envisioned was extensive to say the least, but an apprenticeship relationship, by which a domestic learned about household care and maintenance from her employer, did not enter into the ideal in these primarily urban settings.[24] Instead, employers expected their personnel to possess the necessary knowledge. While the bourgeois women debated qualifications, domestics discussed labor organizations and how to promote them.[25]

Organizations operating as employment agencies as well as protection agencies for young women began opening in the 1880s in major cities in the Netherlands, responding to a growing number of incoming single women, often rural residents seeking work. A brochure from one such employment agency for domestics in Amsterdam (Bemiddelingsbureau tot Plaatsing van Dienstboden), dated April 1903, pointed out two major shifts in the character of domestic work. First, the domestics came from the proletariat rather than the middle class. Second, the employers now included the petty bourgeoisie, those who could not really afford someone but who had to have at least a day servant in order to maintain status.[26]

Low wages for domestics in the Netherlands made their employment possible for families of meager means. In Groningen in 1896 domestics aged 13–14 earned 30–40 guilders, at age 15–17 it was ƒ50–100, and above age 17 they earned ƒ110–50, all in wages per year, in addition to room and board.[27] That same year a domestic in Friesland might earn up to ƒ180, at least if she could milk well.[28] It was also the year that the government changed the laws to drop the "domestic tax" on persons who lived with the family but did not primarily do household work.[29] The distinction of working in the home only as opposed to also taking part in outside tasks was largely one of urban versus rural settings, though there were domestics in rural areas who concentrated on tasks in the home. In a study from 1913 the average wages reported for domestics were a bit higher, but the figures were not divided between urban and rural settings. Thus an all-around maid received per year ƒ100–200; a second maid ƒ90–160; a kitchen maid ƒ130–300.[30] The General Federation of Household Workers, after carrying out a similar study of wages in 1914, reported that wages differed tremendously according to location, sometimes within the same city. Still, wages in the countryside and in small cities tended to be low, as in Assen, where kitchen maids earned ƒ50–110 and second maids ƒ30–85 per year.[31] A children's maid, whose main task was child care, might earn ƒ10 per year.[32] Live-in domestics received room, board, and often money to pay for the wash (which had to be done separately from the family wash) in addition to wages, though the quality of housing and food and the amount of wash money could differ.

Most of the developments around the "professionalization" of domestic service went unnoticed among the group of people most likely to emigrate, yet one aspect of this phenomenon did play a role. Farmers as well as those in small towns increasingly saw a domestic not only as a worker but also as a status symbol. Being able to afford to hire someone to do the wash, a bit of sewing, or help with a major farm task lay within the means of some potential emigrants. At least at some point in the family life cycle, they might be able to have some help. A government report on the province of Groningen stated "[The boerin] has changed from working farmer's wife to lady who assumes more and more the clothing and manners of urban culture. At the end of the nineteenth century she became ma'am [juffrouw], in the twentieth century, my lady [mevrouw]."[33] Women from this background were most likely to complain about the lack of servants in America.

My lady generally did not emigrate, but often her domestics did, and they remembered what kind of treatment they received at the boerin's hands. Not only could domestic servants give detailed information about care of the household, including cleaning and care of the dwelling, they also could describe the atmosphere in which they worked. Gé Constens reported that "mevrouw," who came from "not a bit better background than I did," first insisted that she eat in the kitchen, as did most domestics in urban areas. Then the mevrouw asked Gé to dry the dishes while she washed. "Naturally I put my plate and silverware next to the dishes. And then I saw suddenly that she took my plate away from the rest of the dishes and put it in a corner. . . . And after everything was done, the pots and pans, everything . . . [then she] washed it. . . . [So I asked her] Why do you do my plate and silver in the last [dirty] water? I said: At home we do the cat's dishes in the last water."[34]

The treatment of domestics as little better than animals was a common complaint.[35] While some domestics had more amiable employers, sometimes even employers who treated them as family, the standard refrain was one of long hours, hard work, poor pay, being on call twenty-four hours a day, and a cold and bare attic or basement room. On large farms in parts of Groningen the domestics slept in the animal stalls. Such households employed, on average, two domestics. The *grote meid* helped with milking, churning, cooking meals, and in the winter with spinning and sewing. The *lutje meid* or *kleine meid* helped in the barns, scrubbed the pots and pans, peeled potatoes, and handled a variety of other tasks.[36]

If women in the Netherlands complained of a servant "problem" as it became more difficult to get help around the turn of the century, those in the United States had, in comparison, a crisis. Simply finding a domestic could be difficult, as seen in this report from 1882: "Young people can go where they like. There is a major shortage of domestic servants both girls and boys."[37] For most, however, the problem was wages. Geertje de Jong Schuiling wrote in 1918: "It was a lot easier in Holland! Help is so expensive here . . . a maid earns 15, 20 or 25 dollars a month, and that isn't small change."[38] At the 1918 exchange rate, that was ƒ37.5 to ƒ62.5 per month.[39] Thus one month's wages for domestics in that area were equal to a half-year's wages in parts of the Netherlands, and nearly triple even the best monthly wages for domestics in the Netherlands. All letters that mentioned domestics reinforced this pattern, though not necessarily to this extent.

Those who advertised to try to employ domestic servants also followed this pattern. *De Volksvriend* in 1920 included many classifieds. Typical were one seeking a "girl" to do housework, "no washing"; an advertisement for a *dienstbode* (domestic servant) on a farm for a family of five "no small children or invalids. Salary $10/week"; family seeking a "girl" to work in the home with opportunity to attend high school at the same time.[40] Throughout Dutch American papers, most notably in the 1910s but also in earlier editions, ads for domestics had to entice, either with good working conditions or with special benefits. As in the Netherlands, one of the shifts was away from farm jobs, hence "only housework" was a common element either for those trying to attract young women, as well as for those placing ads trying to find employment.

Young women who had worked as domestics in the Netherlands and then went to work in the United States almost unanimously raved about how much better conditions were. Typical was the story of Clare de Jong, who got a job on a farm in Minnesota: "I am not coming back to Holland to work any time soon. They don't make much of the work here. I have been here nearly six weeks and I have yet to wash a window. The same holds true for the rooms too. I just sweep the floor and mop, and that's it. . . . When I first went to mop the floor the missus gave me a long stick with old rags on it, but it works, I promise you."[41] Compared to washing the windows every week and scrubbing the floor on one's hands and knees, this sounded like paradise.[42] Only cooking and cleaning, no milking, no manure spreading, nothing difficult, you get paid well for your work: with these and similar comments about domestic service immigrants tried to entice young female relatives and friends to the United States. Some had hopes of getting help themselves; others simply saw better opportunities for these young women. When one man wrote "A domestic has the same status as a daughter,"[43] he was exaggerating only slightly. Not only did domestics join the household, so too did hired hands, which meant in principle a host of boarders for Dutch American housewives. Even seasonal workers like those in the harvest crew often slept and ate in the house with the family.[44]

Dutch Protestant immigrants expected their daughters to help with various chores, cleaning, and child care, either in the parental home or as domestics earning money for the family. Generally they looked favorably on domestic work (though by the end of the period some young women opted for other jobs). None of the letters I consulted indicated that anyone felt it improper to work in this capacity in someone else's home. Quite the contrary, most considered it a good opportunity to earn money while still working at household tasks. Other sources, however, affirmed the aversion of a minority of affluent immigrants to sending their daughters into service.[45] Elizabeth Menkens Schreurs fit that pattern, coming from a master craftsman's home. Her first job was as a housekeeper, which was considered more appropriate for someone with middle-class status or pretensions. Once educational opportunities expanded, more immigrants, like the Schreurs family, steered their daughters along these lines. Less affluent families continued to expect daughters to work in their years between finishing basic education and marriage. There were, however, different categories of service, some of which the Dutch rejected. William Goedhart, for example, cautioned his sister-in-law: "Concerning maid service in a hotel I will tell you straight, such girls are generally not well thought of."[46] Service in a private home in an urban area, and in particular that of a professional family (though not a wealthy one), was the goal of many Dutch immigrant women. Unlike Irish, Swedish, or Finnish immigrant women, few opted for a longer career of domestic service with the possibility for rising in status along the way.

While some American literature in this period played up the danger of sexual harassment from employers, both letters and articles in the Dutch American press stressed that the greatest danger in domestic service was not immoral employers but the lack of parental supervision.[47] Fears of illegitimacy or prenuptial pregnancy weighed on parental minds. Young women sometimes played on those fears. One woman living in the province of Zeeland tried to convince her brother in Sheboygan, Wisconsin, to borrow the money for her passage, threatening otherwise that a relationship the family considered improper would continue: "If I get a domestic position in Middelburg then I'll have nearly every evening free and if I see him then I will go with him."[48] Because of the age range involved, many young women met and dated their future husbands while in domestic service; the danger was prenuptial pregnancy. While some Dutch American newspapers carried articles on domestic service leading to white slavery, they generally were translations of English-language publications. They served primarily as a warning that young women should not migrate alone, which rarely occurred anyway, and to inform immigrants of assistance groups in New York.[49]

When the financial position of a family was bleak, relatives could be rather convincing about the positive value of domestic service. Jacoba [Kootje] Akkerman knew her nieces did not have passage money for America but suggested that they come anyway. "The village of Roseland lies before me, but rising above it you can see the tall magnificent buildings [of Chicago] where the big money is earned. Oh sis, they don't demand you work really hard as long as it is good and neat." Akkerman went on, asking that her niece write directly to her, and then closed: "Grietje, advise your children, even if you don't want to see it while you are still living, to go to America later."[50] Akkerman, like thousands of others, equated good wages with a better future. She also reinforced the impression that domestic servants did not work nearly as hard in the United States. The number of people who commented on this pattern was striking. In 1911 Lubbigje Schaapman wrote a friend in the Netherlands that her neighbor needed a cook, and was offering wages of 20 to 25 dollars a month: "you would only have to cook and clean the house."[51] The pattern of women not working outside the house (much) was much more widespread in the United States at a much earlier date and hence was almost invariably labeled "American."

In rural areas of the Midwest where most Dutch immigrants settled, work in domestic service in this period was typical of many European immigrants and their children. Unlike conditions in many European countries, however, there were opportunities for those who began as servants to move up both socially and economically. The rigid class divisions disappeared, replaced in some places by racial ones in which northwestern European groups like the Dutch gained a particularly useful asset with migration—"white" skin. In the Netherlands, where seeing someone with dark brown skin was a major public attraction, people were used to other visible indicators of *stand* (caste/class).[52] In the rural Midwest, these were largely gone. Even in urban areas, immigrants indicated they were not nearly as prevalent as in the Netherlands. Between the labor shortage for domestics and the rise in racial status, Dutch immigrant women could expect much better working conditions.

There was one major exception to these patterns: working for a Dutch American employer in a Dutch American settlement. One woman from Schouwerszijl, Groningen, began working for Dutch Americans at age twenty-five in 1912. Her description of America replicated the conditions in Groningen. At first she earned the equivalent of ƒ50 per year and worked from 3:30 A.M. to 7:30 P.M., milked the cows, hauled wood, and cleaned the milk pails with lime: "Oh, that was work!"[53] But newcomers rapidly learned their options and even Dutch American employers either had to offer better conditions or lose their help. Working for a Dutch American employer frequently was a first job. Later, particularly after women had a better grasp of English, they could pick and choose, knowing the advantages and disadvantages of various employers. As one domestic reminisced about working in Pella, Iowa, Dutch employers were "more particular," requiring scrubbing the floors with a brush and regular oven cleaning. Another reported that when she switched to an American employer in Grand Rapids, Michigan, her main responsibility was cooking.[54]

Whether or not a young woman went into domestic service depended on the family more than on her own wishes. If the family budget required money and there were enough hands at home to keep things running, then a daughter could be sent off to domestic work. As one interviewee recalled, she had no choice in the matter. Her father placed her as a domestic with an American family, hoping she would learn English. "It was terrible that first summer. . . . I had nobody, and I was just a young girl."[55] For others the opposite was true: they wanted to go into service, but their parents required that they stay at home. A few, generally those such as Anna Kuijt who did not have parents in the United States, could make their own decisions about employment. But even in Kuijt's case, her married sister organized her first job in a Dutch family.[56] The Dutch American press underscored the need for such supervision: "[F]ather and mother can see to it that their daughter does not enter into service, except with their consent, and does not go to work in a factory, without their assurance that the moral atmosphere is good."[57]

Few of the Dutch American women whom I studied considered domestic service a profession unless they were widows who became housekeepers. Neither did they generally have positions in households with several servants, which could have fostered solidarity among the household staff.[58] Rather, the employers they mentioned, if not farmers, tended to come from the class of professions which did not have the discretionary income to have a full household staff, instead hiring one or two domestics for part of the family life cycle—ministers, doctors, school principals, and college professors. Young women in the Netherlands, at least if they did not anticipate staying in domestic service long (and most did not), often looked favorably on these families as potential employers as well.[59]

When Joan Younger Dickinson wrote about domestics in *The Role of Immigrant Women in the U.S. Labor Force 1890–1910*, she described the pattern that reigned for Dutch immigrant domestics well: "a typical girl entered the labor force after her education was complete and remained there until marriage or shortly thereafter."[60] Domestic service for most Dutch Protestant immigrant women was a life course event, something temporary, a preparation for marriage. A young woman could earn some money as well as learn household skills, American style. If she lived in the countryside, she could learn the tasks needed to keep a farm running. Domestic service also had the distinct advantage of offering continuous employment. In a labor market plagued by sporadic unemployment, employers, at least in this period, continually registered a shortage of domestics. Domestics' letters and reminiscences confirmed this. They could get a job almost immediately after arrival, could change practically at any time, and never mentioned having difficulty finding a new position. If an employer imposed unreasonable demands or left a young woman with less pay during vacation, she could quit. Frequent changes constituted an "American" pattern according to Trijntje Kooiman, a domestic in Hawarden, Iowa, who wrote back to her friend Anna de Vries, a domestic in Andijk: "Maids earn a lot of money here but generally don't hire out for an entire year. Mostly you go for four of five weeks at one place and then on to another. That way you learn more."[61] This was yet another advantage of the American system, for in the Netherlands the verbal contract for service generally entailed a year of work, and while the employer could fire the domestic at any time, the domestic could not leave until the end of the contract without jeopardizing her chances of getting another position.[62] Getting a "good" job as a domestic might require several shifts, but the seller's market in domestic service meant steady employment for those women who could work and wanted to work.

There was one other, much smaller category of paid domestic service, that of "housekeeper." This was a job often reserved for older women, including widows. It was in fact one of the few positions where a widow could hold and make a living on her own, because she received room and board as well as wages. Such women might place classified ads specifying a number of conditions of employment.[63] If letters and classified ads are any indication, there was a strong demand for such women. *De Hollandsche Amerikaan* included eight ads seeking housekeepers in 1919, but only two from persons offering the service. A small sample of classified ads from *De Volksvriend* in 1920 included seven ads for housekeepers. Yet the ads also indicated that a change in nomenclature was underway. In some cases the writers asked for a "housekeeper" (*huishoudster*) yet described tasks (such as washing) for what in the Netherlands would have been termed a "domestic" (*dienst-meisje, -meid, -bode*). Since housekeeper was a title with more respect (and better wages) in the Netherlands, this could have been a way to attract workers or to give the impression that one's family was bourgeois. Further, housekeeper was a term the papers sometimes used to refer to wives, particularly in advertisements aimed at the person in charge of buying things for the house. The two roles also mixed in ads where the person requesting a housekeeper was a widower, since these were sometimes combination housekeeper/wife ads.

In the United States the changing economic profile around the turn of the century meant that many women who formerly went into domestic service began entering clerical and service jobs.[64] Immigrant and ethnic women formed the bulk of those who remained in household service. Dutch American women, because they did not face much of any racial discrimination, had the option to move into other occupations once they acquired the linguistic and cultural parlance of the world around them.[65] But for most of the first generation this step was rather steep. Furthermore, their own cultural prohibitions against "immoral workplaces" and their predominantly rural settlement patterns made domestic service a much more likely option.

Women's historians who have written about domestic service frequently decry the ethnic exploitation, long hours, and poor working conditions.[66] Those writing about northern and western European immigrant women, however, generally shared their subjects' overall positive interpretation of domestic service.[67] In comparing working conditions in the United States to those in the old world, these women frequently found the former much more inviting. They also appreciated the chance to learn new skills and perhaps "American" ways, including a more limited number of tasks for women and a different ideal of womanhood. Immigrants for the most part had humble beginnings and had not adopted the bourgeois standard, which associated service with "lower" types. While the Anglo population may have considered them "other," for the most part these groups settled in areas where they did not compete with African American or Asian immigrant domestics, groups which faced much stronger prejudice, which in turn resulted in a stronger association of domestic service with poverty or ethnic status. It was something European immigrants would (perhaps) learn within a generation or two. Meanwhile, as their English language skills improved, they might turn to another occupation, an option not available to those less "white." Discrimination also worked in their favor in other areas of employment, particularly in factory and office jobs.

Factories and Shops

In the Netherlands official employment statistics indicate that women engaged in wage work rarely held jobs in industry, and that this number grew only slightly between 1880 and 1920. Just over 15 percent worked in the industrial sector in 1889, almost 17 percent in 1899, and about 18 percent in 1909.[68] Moreover, most of the women workers were unmarried and were concentrated in the textile and clothing industries. While this meant that women rarely competed with men for jobs, it also meant that they had to organize their industries separately if they wanted to improve conditions. The National Exhibition of Women's Work in the Netherlands (1898) spurred an organizational drive, but it had limited success prior to the end of the study period.[69] Wages in the cities were low, but in the countryside they could be even less. One guilder a week for more than sixty hours' work was common in the 1890s.[70]

Opportunities for women's work in industry varied significantly from place to place. One can get an impression, though admittedly a flawed one, of factory work opportunities for women from the introductory map to Marie Jungius's index to women's industrial occupations from 1899.[71] Her data did not differentiate between establishments employing three women or three hundred; nonetheless, it provides an idea of the kinds of work possible within a region. According to this, more than half the workplaces employing women in Friesland were involved in dairying or butter- and cheesemaking. In the province of Groningen, flax processing and dairies predominated in the west, but the more important pattern was the concentration of women's workplaces in regional centers, especially in the city of Groningen, where women worked in industries producing everything from chocolate to bicycles. But there, as in Winschoten and Sappemeer, clothing and textile manufacturing shops were most common. By contrast, in Zeeland, the island province of the southwest, few workplaces employed women.[72] Other jobs, particularly in food processing, also employed Dutch women at least sporadically.[73]

Few Dutch American Protestant women worked in a "factory" prior to migration, though many had engaged in dairying or cheesemaking. But in the United States, factory work, whether in the silk mills of Paterson or in the food-processing industry around Holland, Michigan, offered an increasing range of jobs at relatively good wages for women. Yet, as with domestic service, women generally viewed this work as temporary, something for young women prior to marriage. Employers especially sought workers who adhered to strict Reformed theology, which classified joining a union or striking as sinful—a cause for church discipline.[74] The Dutch generally had a reputation as good workers (in the eyes of employers).

The Banner promoted "the Christian solution" to the "industrial problem," that is, its idea of how to fight radical socialism and improve industrial conditions. As the articles stated, the problem was at heart an ethical one. Nothing was wrong with the system, it was just that employers needed to pay their employees a "just and equal" wage, and employees needed to "render conscientious Christian service to those that employ them."[75] Though the press ostensibly had sympathy for the immigrant worker, when pressed to make a decision, as in the Grand Rapids furniture workers' strike of 1911, community leaders stood against such activity.[76]

To what extent Dutch immigrant women tried to find factory or shop employers from the same background, or to what extent they considered "Yankees" better, was unclear to me. Certain orthodox Calvinists tried to live and work only within their own group, and the sense that parents should insure a moral workplace for their children promoted this trend, yet this was not always possible. Need and opportunity faced off with questions of propriety. Albert Koning wrote to his sister Derkien, who had been living in an orphanage in Groningen, trying to convince her to emigrate: "There are several girls here who work in factories. But you probably would not like that."[77] There were various reasons for this hesitancy. One was the impression that such jobs spoiled women, or at the least did not prepare them to become housewives: "Women who have always worked in factories know little about preparing meals and nothing about how to make a house comfortable."[78] Further, some worried about the moral atmosphere on the factory floor.

Lini Moerkerk de Vries, a second-generation Dutch American, made it clear why this was the case. She joined a large number of "Dutch girls" in the mills of northern New Jersey. According to Moerkerk de Vries's autobiography, her mother forced her to go to work in a silk mill in Prospect Park at the age of twelve, though she wanted to continue her education. To get her first job as a "bobbin girl" they had to lie about her age in order to avoid child labor restrictions. In this position she took full bobbins from the winders to the warpers and empty bobbins in the other direction, ten hours a day, six days a week. Next she moved into a better paid position as a quill winder at a cotton mill in neighboring Haledon. This job consisted of threading cotton from the bobbin to quills on the loom. Like many Dutch women, she continued up the hierarchy of mill jobs. Her next position was as winder in a Paterson silk mill, which she preferred because of the lack of dust. Working conditions were not good, however, and because of the economic downturn at the end of World War I, no one dared complain. Her winding partner, who had long red-gold hair, was scalped and killed by a machine. Moerkerk de Vries moved immediately to another mill, this time a silk ribbon mill, where she stayed until laid off. Her next job was as a picker, one who picked out loose threads on silk crepe de chine. At that job she faced sexual harassment: "Those three sons of the boss seemed to take turns touching my body as they leaned over me and the machine to check my work. Both my hands were busy. . . . I was afraid to slap their hands, afraid to tear the cloth, and afraid to lose my job."[79] There were few Dutch workers in that mill, which may have contributed to the problem. In any case when Moerkerk reported this to several workers of various national backgrounds, a group formed which challenged the practice successfully. When Moerkerk de Vries was laid off from that job, she was old enough, white enough, and savvy enough to land an office position.[80] Later she went on to nurse's training. Moerkerk de Vries, as a second-generation woman, had greater aspirations than some, but she worked at jobs which were typical for Dutch immigrant women in that region, and she was a "Cheesehead" or one of the "damned foreigners" as far as many were concerned.

One 1911 government report on women and children in the silk industry focused on Paterson, New Jersey, as one of its study areas, meaning that Dutch women in that industry garnered close attention.[81] The patterns were relatively clear: large families, children over thirteen (both boys and girls) often working, those sixteen and older almost always working for wages, fathers employed, and mothers not listed as wage-earners.[82] Of 595 Dutch women working in New Jersey silk mills, 548 were single, and of these over 80 percent were under twenty-five. Another 11 women were in the widowed, divorced, separated, or deserted category, meaning only thirty-six married women were listed as working. While the widows were spread out at different ages, the married women workers were young, mainly under thirty.[83] The implication was that these were newlyweds without children.[84] Interviews with immigrants from this area also confirmed this pattern. Many women continued in the mills after marriage until they were pregnant.[85] Most of the Dutch women workers in silk earned between five and eight dollars a week. The best paid Dutch women earned less than half their "Yankee" counterparts, and in general the Dutch ranked low among nationality groups in skilled silk occupations.[86] Despite this, the Dutch had fairly high family incomes in comparison to other ethnic groups in the study. It was a combination of the number of family workers, the consistency of work, the mixed occupations in the family, and the consistency with which the children turned over their earnings which made the difference, not higher wages.[87] Dutch women constituted 15 percent of the labor force in silk factories for those under sixteen years of age and 11 percent for those sixteen and older.[88]

In other areas of the country, factory work also existed, especially in urban areas after the turn of the century. *De Hollandsche Amerikaan* listed a variety of factory jobs available to women in Kalamazoo, Michigan, in 1919. The local glass factory advertised for "strong girls to put mirrors in frames."[89] Another company sought "girls" for various kinds of sewing, some by hand, some by machine, as well as for enameling and bookbinding. Likewise a company sought "girls" for stuffing and sewing furniture. The Holland Biscuit company sought "girls" to work in baking. Jobs were clearly demarcated by sex, given the nature of Dutch language designations. Further, the consistent use of "girls" in ads made the intended population clear. None of the factory jobs were listed as either for men or women. While there were some jobs advertised for "boys," particularly for certain farming tasks, factory jobs for men tended to take adult designations.[90]

Women writing about their activities generally included what kind of factory it was where they worked, but little beyond that. Whether their relatives could imagine what this work included depended largely on the type of product and whether this kind of factory existed in the region of the Netherlands where their correspondents lived. Yet in comparison to other areas of their lives, where the women immigrants described with some detail the kind of equipment they bought or used, the lack of information on this topic was striking. Women on farms would explain the functions of hay binders, threshers, and the possible uses of motors, but women in factories rarely even mentioned there were machines present. In a factory, the technology did not necessarily constitute a marvel, nor something which made life easier. Language operated as a barrier to such descriptions, at least if the machinery was something the immigrants did not know in the old country, but that did not stop them from discussing other equipment, simply giving the English name, sometimes with a rough Dutch equivalent, and explaining what it did. Perhaps the immigrants assumed their relatives would not understand if they went into detail; perhaps they lacked the knowledge to give a good description of what the factory did; perhaps they felt it was not important or even shameful. Or perhaps it is just that women factory workers were less likely to write letters. In the letters by women that I looked at, they represented a minority.

The absence of detail about factory life, however, appeared in women's interviews as well. The one exception was an immigrant woman from Apeldoorn who described her work schedule at a sock and stocking weaving plant: ten hours a day Monday through Saturday, including holidays, and if she took a day off she lost her machines. She began this work in 1912, at age thirteen.[91] Her description, more detailed than most, still left out much more than it included. Women reminiscing about their activities sometimes merely stated they had worked at a factory, with no further elaboration. For them, perhaps, "factory work" became a category unto itself. Those who did talk at more length about the work were more likely to describe wages, whether employment was continuous, the ages at which they worked, and whether other family members or friends worked there. The fact that most described factory work in economic terms only, often in the context of saying it was necessary financially to work for wages, indicated their general attitude.

Many young immigrant women engaged in factory work as a seasonal opportunity for good wages. Food processing best fit this category. It was also closely related to many women's seasonal employment opportunities in the Netherlands and hence was somewhat familiar.[92] Young women could combine seasonal work with other jobs or education. "[Steentje, in California] wants to work at the canning plant putting up fruit this summer and then in the fall she will go to school."[93] For many like Steentje, such work could bridge the time between arrival and the point at which they could speak enough English to get a different position. It was also a good way to supplement family finances, including money which might be used to procure a dowry.

Women's evaluation of retail sales or small business work differed according to whether it was wage work for an employer or work in the family business. Generally shop help came from within the family. Everyone assumed this would function so, though many married women complained about the double burden of housework and long hours in the shop. Daughters also gave the negative impression that the "unpaid" work in a family business allowed them neither the spending money nor the freedom of work for someone else. There were few Dutch immigrant women who worked in businesses. When the labor department did a survey of women and children wage-earners in Chicago in 1910, only two Dutch women appeared among the thousands of employees in retail stores whom they surveyed.[94] For the most part, jobs in shops required a good command of English, and in Dutch American communities of Dutch as well. In some cases Dutch immigrant women were clerks in the women's departments of stores which were carrying women's clothing by the 1910s. In a few cases they had their own businesses. Dutch American newspapers regularly included the name of a milliner who would create a hat along the lines of the latest fashions or, after the turn of the century, of a woman storekeeper who stocked the latest in women's fashions.[95] One of the better-known women in the history of Pella, Iowa, was Sebrietje H. Viersen, a woman who never married and managed to do very well in business, eventually using some of her profits to help fund a library for Pella.[96]

A Career Calls

For a tiny minority of immigrant women, the United States offered job oppor-tunities which either did not exist or would have been difficult to achieve in the Netherlands. The relatively early start of women in professional careers in the United States compared to the Netherlands, and the general acceptance of wom-en in higher education, meant that women could get advanced training and could practice in various professions more readily in the United States than in the Netherlands.[97] In both countries, this option was primarily open to the eco-nomically well-off. But opportunities shifted rapidly during this era. The call of the career came most often in the second generation or later, as the immi-grants' financial circumstances improved and the children became proficient in English.

The debate over women in professions in the Netherlands reflected a differ-ent demographic reality than that in Dutch American communities. In the old country, political leaders, particularly from the confessional parties, faced the difficult task of justifying women's entry into careers. Demographically they recognized that many daughters of the bourgeoisie could not marry. From this some adopted the position that every woman could still use her "mother's heart" to serve others. Likewise, the generation and a half and second generation in the United States, particularly those from educated backgrounds, adopted this line of reasoning, which predominated in American Progressive ideology as well, but tempered it with their particular religious beliefs.

Nel, a woman who migrated at age twenty-two with her family from Rotter-dam in 1908, reminisced that her mother enjoyed all her activities—teaching Sun-day school and participating in various organizations—vicariously.[98] For Nel's mother, whom everyone in the family described as someone who would have been a great lawyer if she had been a man, migration came too late in life to take advantage of professional opportunities. Young women taking on the professional careers offered in the United States were still exceptional in terms of numbers, but less so in terms of acceptance by 1920. Within a church-related world, nurs-ing, teaching, and missionary work (often interrelated) opened educational, marital, financial, and other doors for immigrant women. In the United States, Dutch-born women could earn a living, and not just with domestic service. Immigrant mothers sometimes took pride in their daughters' doing what they could not or would not have dared do, though among the Dutch it was fathers who were more often central to decisions about daughters' careers.[99]

Cornelia De Bey

Cornelia De Bey (anglicized from De Beij) illustrated the degree to which a Dutch-born woman could take advantage of American opportunities and be-come "American." De Bey migrated as a child with her family from Groningen to Chicago, where her father had accepted a call as a dominie to a congregation of people from that province. Rev. Bernardus de Beij gained nationwide stature in the Dutch Reformed denomination, partly for his theological views which stressed allowing the church to adapt to new times and surroundings, as was evident in Chicago in his support for the use of English in his church and for women praying aloud in public.[100] He also showed an interest in education. In all of these, his daughter adopted the pattern and took it much further.

A fictionalized account of De Bey's childhood based on her reminiscences showed her interest in helping the poor of other ethnic backgrounds, as well as in gaining political power, becoming evident early in life.[101] De Bey's father described her in 1884 as a good student in science and art, to whom the family would "not deny the opportunity" to continue her studies.[102] In this she differed from most Dutch immigrant women, though the daughters of dominies often had greater access to education, as did members of the generation and a half—born in the Netherlands but having migrated with their parents—to which she belonged. She attended Cook County Normal School, graduating as a teacher in 1889. Had De Bey been typical, she would have taught for a few years and then quit to marry and raise a small family. Perhaps her ambition went beyond those goals, perhaps she was too strong-willed to attract a suitor she liked, or perhaps she was not attracted to men. In any case, her life from this point onward began increasingly to diverge from the lives of other Dutch immigrant women. Her interest in social reform came into play quickly, and she worked closely with John Meyers, a member of the Illinois State legislature and a friend of the De Bey family, to secure passage of a bill legalizing kindergartens as part of the Illinois public schools in 1890. This reflected a position with support in the Dutch American population, one similar to state policy in the Netherlands.[103]

After teaching briefly in the Chicago schools, De Bey went on to study at the Art Institute and at Northwestern University and then at Hahnemann Medical College and Hospital. Her interest in medicine came partially through two of her brothers, one a doctor, the other a pharmacist. She received a medical degree in 1895 as a doctor of homeopathic medicine and opened an office in Chicago.[104] Somewhere in this process of higher education it seems she left much of her Dutch American life behind. She fostered connections with the Hull-House settlement, the best known and most influential settlement house in the United States, and with its residents, including leader Jane Addams. Much of her medical practice was with the poor and with other immigrants in Chicago's neediest neighborhoods.[105] She also remained active in school politics, campaigning for the right of married women to teach in the public schools.[106]

In 1903 De Bey worked for passage of an Illinois child labor law. During the next year she came to the attention of Chicagoans for her role in settling a strike in the meat-packing industry.[107] De Bey was again involved in a labor dispute in 1905, when she, together with Jane Addams and three other local leaders, was appointed by Mayor Edward Dunne to a citizens' committee to try to resolve a citywide teamsters' strike.[108] In the wake of this unsuccessful attempt, Mayor Dunne asked De Bey (along with Addams) to become a member of the Chicago Board of Education. Margaret Haley, leader of the Chicago Teachers' Federation, recommended her.[109] De Bey and Addams worked together, but not always on the most congenial of terms. Haley described De Bey as "a thorn in Gentle Jane's side. . . . She had an uncanny ability in finding Jane's fallacies and of prodding her with the consciousness of them, even though she shielded them wherever she could from public discovery. The doctor, tall, thin almost to the point of emaciation, wearing clothes as mannish as Dr. Mary Walker's, knew . . . that Jane Addams was a social rather than a moral leader."[110] Not only was De Bey a close friend of Haley, for many years she shared her home with Kate Starr Kellogg, an activist teacher and later a principal in the Chicago school system. De Bey, like many educated women of her time, never married. She dressed in masculine fashion, wearing tailored suits and men's hats.[111] At about the same time she was gaining public attention, one Dutch-language paper which circulated in Chicago wrote a decidedly negative article about "masculine women."[112] It does not take much imagination to guess the target.

Chicago's newspapers regularly identified De Bey as the spokesperson on the Board of Education for the Chicago Teachers' Federation. This in itself spoke volumes about her move away from her ethnic background. Most Dutch Calvinists looked askance at labor organizations, particularly at those without some specific Christian connection. De Bey was an active and outspoken (too much so from the standpoint of several newspapers) member of the school board during her term and successfully fought her dismissal from that post by a political rival of Dunne.[113] What was striking was that the newspapers, even in their most vicious attacks or nastiest cartoons, never mentioned she was an immigrant, or ethnic, or anything of that nature. They could attack her for her cloth-

This drawing of Cornelia De Bey appeared in the Chicago Teachers' Federation *Bulletin,* 16 Sept. 1904. De Bey's style of dress often attracted attention.

ing, her attitude, her viewpoints, and various other things, but her being Dutch-born was not a part of that attack.

Issues surrounding education were De Bey's passion, as was clear from her speech to the Social Economics Club shortly after her appointment to the school board: "Until the last two or three years there has been hardly a day in twenty years that I have not visited one or more public schools, and I knew changes were necessary. These were my purposes: To clean up the book situation, to secure modification of the present promotional plan and to inaugurate a demo-cratic method of administration in the school system."[114] During her four-year term she worked to get the American Book Company out of the schools, to in-crease teachers' wages, and to reorganize the schools along district lines. In this last effort she spearheaded the attempts of Ella Flagg Young, the school super-intendent, to make the school system more democratic.

At the same time, De Bey was active in other political fields. During hearings for a new Chicago charter in 1906, De Bey spoke on behalf of including wom-en's suffrage. Her address, published in the *Record Herald* and reprinted in the Chicago Teachers' Federation *Bulletin,* explained that suffrage was "not the outgrowth of a fad among feminine idlers but is a right demanded by modern conditions." De Bey conceded that many women did not yet want the vote but then argued that votes for women would benefit society on two grounds: first, because women were more moral than men, and second, because women's brains would evolve. "Brains are developed only by experience, and there is no such thing as the vicarious adsorption of mentality."[115] Her interest in suffrage put her in touch with national and international leaders in the women's move-ment. De Bey corresponded with Anna Howard Shaw, head of the National American Woman Suffrage Association, and through her gained news of the suffrage campaign in the Netherlands.[116] In addition De Bey was an early mem-ber of the Chicago Peace Society and had a reputation as a radical pacifist. On both suffrage and peace, her arguments were far out of step with most of the Dutch Protestant community.

Once political currents ousted her from the school board, De Bey took to writing moral tales for the *Chicago Magazine.*[117] After retiring from her medi-cal practice in 1928, De Bey moved to California for a few years and then to Grand Rapids, Michigan, where she could live with relatives. She died in 1948 and was buried in the Pilgrim Home Cemetery in Holland, Michigan, the cem-etery holding many of the leaders of the Holland settlement.[118] For all that she returned to her roots in old age, De Bey was a quintessential American Progres-sive Era reformer in Chicago, a city boasting many such women. She used her Dutch connections initially in getting into politics, and some of the issues she pursued had connections to family concerns and topics also prominent in the Netherlands. In most of her work, however, there was no trace of being Dutch, and her friends and colleagues as an adult were often not part of this group.

Helping Professions

Women like De Bey were extremely rare among the Dutch in the United States. Professional jobs for women, however, were becoming more available, both on a national and an ethnic community level. The turn of the century was a period of phenomenal growth in women's professions in the United States, with nursing and teaching leading the way. The number of trained nurses increased sevenfold from 1900 to 1910. Programs for nurse's training expanded in the Netherlands as well, even more rapidly after the turn of the century. By 1920 there were over 140,000 nurses in the United States, compared to 16,000 in the Netherlands, but relative to the population that meant more in the Netherlands. While Dutch women of the lower middle class or wealthy farmers' daughters could enter into the professions by the 1910s, it remained difficult for those from the agricultural laboring class or small farmers.[119] Those who did get into the professions had somewhat less incentive to emigrate, though the call for Dutch-speaking professionals, especially for the aging Dutch American population, grew.[120] The language barrier operated as more of an obstacle than in factory or domestic work, for unless professional women learned English well, their work opportunities were strictly limited to the Dutch American community. Still, the chances existed. "Eisse wrote me that you had a notion to come here . . . you can earn enough to cover your expenses because professional nurses are paid very well . . . so I say, pack your bag quick if you have your diploma and come on over."[121]

Nellie Mazereeuw, an immigrant from Opperdoes, Friesland, described becoming a nurse in several of her letters dating from 1913 to 1915 to friends in the Netherlands.[122] She attended nurse's training in two hospitals, where she was the oldest among her peers. During this time she reported earning thirty dollars a month plus room, board, and washing. Like most nurses she lived in, first at the hospital dormitory and later in private homes. She changed positions several times, though always in the Grand Rapids area. Her work hours and living quarters differed little from those of a housekeeper or privileged domestic servant. Her sense of how to cope with homesickness, however, showed a considerably divergent evaluation of her work from that of domestic servants. "[N]ursing is wonderful work but it is also difficult work. . . . I have the feeling that I have my work and my calling here and thus I would not be satisfied in the Netherlands in the long run."[123] Mazereeuw was not alone in labeling nursing a calling. For some in the Dutch American community, it was easier to support women in nursing on this basis than it was on the more bourgeois argument that it was an extension of the mother role.[124] Young women in various professions used both kinds of arguments to justify their higher education and career plans. For the immigrant generation, however, the numbers remained small.

Some Dutch American daughters, the second generation, due to the prosperity of their parents and the relative lack of discrimination against them on the part of the American population compared to those of other ethnic backgrounds, took advantage of professional opportunities. The proliferation of separate institutions, sometimes joint ventures of the two major Dutch denominations but especially within Christian Reformed circles—nursing homes, psychiatric institutions, a hospital for tuberculosis sufferers, and more—each requiring professional staff, meant many job openings for nurses, attendants, and social welfare workers.[125] By 1914 the Pine Rest Christian Home, an institution for the mentally impaired, was training its own nursing staff. Women earned five to nine dollars a week during the three-year program, provided they did not marry.[126] Most importantly, the demand for separate Christian schools, combined with the high birthrate, meant a tremendous need for Dutch American teachers. Given that both nurses and teachers often had to quit their jobs after marriage, the number of young women needed rose even more.

When Suzanne de Graaf Betting arrived in Grand Rapids from Vlissingen, Zeeland, in 1907 at age twenty-seven, she found a job teaching in one of the (Dutch-language) Christian schools.[127] Men filled teaching positions to some extent, particularly in Dutch-language schools, but school districts generally were shifting over to women teachers, seeing this as acceptable work for the unmarried. Not only that, wages were lower for women.[128] The stumbling block for women's employment was interpreting biblical passages on women. Churches moved in their debates from whether women could teach at all, to at what grade level they had to stop, and likewise to whether women could teach one another as adults. All positions along the spectrum found representatives among Dutch American congregations at the turn of the century.[129] Few school boards in Dutch American communities, however, would accept a female principal.[130] Both the Reformed and Christian Reformed churches supported education in their academies and colleges for women on these grounds. If there were to be female teachers, then at least they should have a proper education. One article in a CRC publication in 1906 complained "our graduates are not all placed as yet. And, what is especially painful, . . . we hear of school boards employing young ladies who have had *no professional training at all,* least of all in our own school."[131] State laws differed on requirements for teaching, though in the Midwest they generally required completion of high school and perhaps a brief "Normal" course. In reality many schools simply ignored these rules early in the period and only adjusted when standards rose after the turn of the century.

Dutch American women also went into the public schools. Specifically those in the Reformed Church, which was less tied to separate institutions and more interested in running the local public schools, formed a major contingent of teachers in their communities. Few were immigrants. The Dillingham Commission reported seventeen foreign-born teachers as opposed to 103 second-generation Dutch teachers in their study of selected public schools.[132] The need for public school teachers of the "right" background pushed Dutch Americans to train their daughters. Rev. Ale Buursma went to the General Synod of the Reformed Church in Albany, New York, in 1883 and requested funds for their academy in Orange City. Along with needing a preparatory school for boys, he noted that there were twenty public schools in the county, nearly all the one-room variety and most serving Dutch American children exclusively.[133] Yet the teachers tended to be Roman Catholics because they were the only ones available. He could hardly have come up with a stronger justification for support. The academy (later Northwestern College) expanded its enrollment rapidly in the early years and soon it attracted Dutch American women teachers as well as students. In 1888 it added a specific education curriculum, but not until 1908 did it officially train teachers for specific subject areas. Most of the teachers it trained in its first decade were men, and most of the women who attended married not long after graduating (a status which precluded teaching at that time). Women, however, became a larger part of the student body interested in teaching in subsequent decades.[134]

In addition to nurses and teachers, Dutch immigrant families raised their daughters (and sons) to be missionaries, positions which generally included nursing or teaching along with evangelism to greater and lesser degrees. The years from 1900 to World War I were the "halcyon years" of missionary activity in the United States, and some Dutch Americans participated actively.[135] The multiple mission societies of many Reformed and (to a lesser degree) Christian Reformed congregations supported numerous persons to go forth in the United States and to other countries. By following an "American" pattern they carved out roles for themselves not only as mission wives but also as teachers and nurses in expanding mission endeavors. These in turn made higher education more available to women. Interest in missions also led to the creation of groups in local congregations where women could meet, discuss, organize, and otherwise learn about the world.[136]

In 1918 at the annual meeting of the Women's Board of Domestic Missions of the Reformed Church in America, Hendrina Hospers appeared "wearing a beautiful Indian beaded buckskin costume" and "vividly portrayed the daily living of the Jicarilla Apaches at Dulce—their appalling lack of everything—the ravages illness is making among them, the great helpfulness of the Mission and its workers as it ministers daily to them."[137] Hospers's presence was not out of the ordinary for the Reformed mission world; she was from a prominent Dutch American family in Orange City, Iowa.[138] Her hometown was the locus of the Dutch-language mission publication *De Heidenwereld* (Heathen World), and her financing as a missionary came from the almost exclusively Dutch American Synod of Chicago. Hospers had the title "community worker" or sometimes "field worker" and in this capacity spent part of the year visiting scattered Apache families who moved with their sheep. Not officially an evangelist, she like many of these women could fulfill that function as part of other duties: "She smooths out family misunderstandings, distributes layettes and soap for new babies and simple medical supplies and takes the story of Jesus to many a camp home."[139] In an official mission publication of the Women's Executive Board of Missions, the author hinted at the connection of Dutch American workers to their charges: "The present generation of all tribes is facing a period of transition that only second generation foreigners in our country can understand—confused between old tribal loyalties and awakening ambitions."[140]

The generational comment was apt, for it was largely second-generation Dutch American women who undertook this task, specifically the daughters of leading community members.[141] Nellie Zwemer, whose family was strongly associated with missions, attended Northwestern Academy in Orange City, Iowa, in preparation for her work as a missionary in China from 1890 to 1930. When her brother Samuel M. Zwemer, also second generation and himself a missionary (and later professor of missions), addressed the Old Settlers' Picnic in Zeeland, Michigan, in 1907, he noted that twenty-seven men and twenty-four women who were the children of the first settlers in Holland had served in foreign missions.[142]

More information appeared on missionary women in the Dutch American press than on any other group of women. For example, in 1903 Henry Beets wrote of "Miss Nellie Noordhoff." After naming her date and place of birth in the province of Friesland, he described her family's trip to America, settlement in Zeeland, Michigan, and her interest in getting an education, which was impossible beyond the public schools at first. Six years after making her confession of faith she went to Grand Rapids to study nursing, graduating in 1901 at age twenty-nine. Meanwhile the Christian Reformed Church had established a mission including a boarding school among the Navajos, and they needed a matron. She took the position.[143]

Many of the women who went as missionaries were mission wives. As with other groups in earlier periods, women interested in mission work could marry men headed for missions.[144] When the CRC Navajo mission opened in 1896, one of the wives was particularly well suited for the work: "[Effie Hofman van der Wagen] passed the exams to be a teacher, got a diploma in nursing at the same time, and studied for half a year at Moody's mission-institute in Chicago. She will primarily be in charge of work among the women, for which her knowledge of and interest in medicine can contribute much."[145] Churches preferred married missionary couples because of the need for a formal evangelist, by definition a man in this period, and if the wife had skills as well, so much the better. Women interested in mission work might prepare, which would be useful whether or not they would be married. The emphasis on missionary couples was even stronger for foreign missions. When Jane Walvoord wrote that her daughter Edith got married and left shortly thereafter for Japan, she illustrated a common pattern. Edith's husband would teach in the Christian school, while Edith gave music lessons in the "girls' school."[146] A male (and married) missionary could run a compound where single women served, but women as heads of missions were rare. Mothers like Jane Walvoord justified their daughters' work (in Dutch) fairly consistently in terms of religious activity or calling, not in terms of motherhood or a separate woman's duty.

The push for education on Indian reservations in the United States tied in well with mission interest there. The Reformed Church opened several missions to American Indian groups around the turn of the century, each of which required women teachers, often women nurses, and sometimes women social workers. In 1909 the Christian Reformed Church took over a day school in Zuni, New Mexico. Teacher Nellie De Jong's public letter after one year described how the staff gave the children weekly baths and provided them with Western clothing (which the missionaries arranged to have washed as well). "They look respectable now and we don't have to stay at a distance on account of the bad odor."[147] Similar comments about stealing, tardiness, and other "Indian ways" peppered the text. De Jong boarded with a CRC missionary couple living nearby.

Overall, mission work opened doors for Dutch American women. The focus on American Indians combined with the contemporary practice of boarding schools as a major part of this mission field, meant openings for teachers. Likewise the difficulty of male missionaries reaching women in foreign lands, added to restrictions on outright evangelism in some areas, meant a call for women to go as teachers and nurses, and later even doctors, to overseas institutions.[148] Dutch American women were active in setting up schools, medical facilities, and women's education and health programs overseas.[149] The openings helped justify women's education, and women's mission organizations offered opportunities to women to join one another and discuss (among other things) the status of women in various part of the world. I found no evidence that Dutch American women learned to admire their mission subjects' gender roles, but they certainly adopted many of those of other American Protestant women. Missionaries generally earned poor financial recompense, but they did gain higher status and better informal "insurance" than from most jobs open to women at that time.[150]

Mission work was a religious calling for either men or women, and in this it embodied the closest most women could get to the ministry, the most highly esteemed occupation among Dutch Americans. Only a tiny minority of women could participate in the missions, however. For the majority, they were something about which they could read and for which they might save and scrimp, adding their own monetary efforts to the cause. Saving and scrimping, however, were not just something to do in order to add to missionary coffers. They were part of everyday life.

Pinching and Saving a Penny

Earning money did not exhaust women's ability to contribute to the family economy. Saving, making do, budgeting, carefully choosing the products to buy, looking for bargains, all these operated to keep the family budget in the black.

And whether a woman's family worked in agriculture or not, if they had access to at least a plot of land women generally kept a garden and small livestock. Further, women in both urban and rural settings continued to do some of the food processing themselves in order to cut down on expenditures and still fill family needs. Even after packaged products filled the shelves of "Yankee" neighbors, Dutch Protestant immigrant women often stuck to homegrown and home canned, at least according to their accounts. Consumption generally took place in the household, involving the tasks over which women had control, and by careful management, women could assure the greatest returns for the least money. When Dutch Americans talked about financial matters they used one term consistently: *zuinigheid,* which translates as either frugality or miserliness. In the Netherlands and in the United States, the Dutch lauded those who had the ability to get by on little and those who could contribute much. One report from the Netherlands stated: "In a certain sense every worker is also a farmer, . . . one buys a few acres of land, cultivates them, and puts up a cottage . . . the following year when one returns after haying season in Holland or Friesland, the facade of stone is put up, and later improved, all according to one's energy and ability to save—*especially that of the wife*—. . . if the woman is frugal and careful, then even in their simple lifestyle they will know no poverty."[151] Reading between the lines: if the wife did all the farming as well as the housekeeping and child care for several months of the summer while the husband was out earning seasonal wages, the family could be relatively self-sufficient in foodstuffs and could use the husband's meager wages for home improvement.

The refrain that women could manage to make even the lowest of wages enough was on the one hand a compliment to those women who put food on the table and clothes on the children. On the other hand, it was an indictment of women who did not manage this. The ideology that women were responsible for making sure that the cash in the family budget was "enough" developed as wage labor increasingly superseded agricultural work on a family lot for men as the primary source of income. The Dutch had a long history of a market economy, even in rural areas. Yet the extent to which families relied on cash to procure what they needed changed in the late nineteenth century. Well before this change occurred women had primary responsibility for food and clothing; after it, they simply had to do so under different circumstances.

Women frequently handled at least part of the finances among the group of people most likely to emigrate. When Dutch government researchers surveyed the budgets of working families in 1891, they handed the forms out to wives and included a category "pocket money for husband."[152] This was more the ideal of the elite who designed the survey, since practically no one filled it in. Even when women did not have primary control of money in the family, they generally were responsible for some purchases. Sociologist Ali de Regt described the situation for proletarian families even more strongly: women often had the dominant position in finances, either as breadwinner with home work or as the leader in the emotional and fiscal battle against poverty and apathy. If the family had to make do with less, women tended to make the largest sacrifices themselves. "Whether the family managed to grasp a standard of living which could be considered 'proper' hung primarily on [the woman's] capabilities as housewife."[153] Under these circumstances, it was in a woman's own best interest to assure a solid financial base—she stood most at risk to suffer otherwise.

How to manage differed. For those with chronic cash-flow problems, shopping at stores where the proprietors would offer credit solved some problems. Others turned to pawning on a regular basis to put food on the table. In many cases a woman could barter some of her own handwork or produce for other items she needed. But many married women assumed seasonal or occasional wage-labor employment was necessary for the family.[154] Few women kept formal budgets.[155] But specific knowledge of family finances allowed an informed decision on when and whether a wife or daughter should work for wages. Married women generally assumed the wages they could earn could not finance household help and child care.[156] Finding cheaper goods to purchase (like garbage from the butcher's or leftovers from the market), doing more home-weaving and sewing (including for others), growing more in the family garden, all of these offered plausible alternatives to working for minuscule wages, particularly since women continued to be responsible for housework, whether they were employed for wages elsewhere or not.[157] For the working poor, however, there simply was no choice. "[My mother] always had to work—my father earned very little."[158]

In the United States this changed little. Once married, a Dutch immigrant woman might consider taking in laundry or sewing as money-earning activities if the family required extra income. Anna van Zanten de Valk began earning some money soon after arriving in the Chicago area by washing shirts for her husband's boss. With the money she bought a cow and then began selling milk in town. The profit from that allowed her to buy another cow and the business expanded.[159] Dutch American women did not take in unrelated boarders often; more frequently they took in relatives and friends who then contributed to the household finances or helped with household tasks. The Dillingham Commission commented on the relative absence of boarders in Dutch families, at 6.3 percent the lowest of all groups reported.[160] Yet many immigrant letters and family histories noted children staying with their parents after marriage for a period, or elderly parents moving in with a married child. In growing metropolitan areas, immigrants often reported a housing shortage that led families to share apartments or houses, at least at first. Thus the situation of Derkje van Deel, who acted as the housekeeper for her brother, his children, and several boarders, all part of a six-family house-sharing arrangement.[161] Still, some women turned to taking in boarders as a way to make ends meet, as was evident from a number of classified advertisements in *De Hollandsche Amerikaan*.[162] These tended to be older women, sometimes widows.

For other women, renting land and working as a family for wages on a farm was also possible. Dutch Americans as late as 1919 still advertised for "a family" [*gezin*] to work in the celery and onions, or "a family" to take over a farm.[163] Whether they rented or bought, women's production on a farm took on added importance in the success of the migration venture. Anna van Beek Peters, from Baarn, reminisced that her mother brought cheesemaking forms, a butter churn, and a wirewicker for toasting bread from the Netherlands when the family emigrated. Besides being able to make familiar dishes, this meant money-making opportunities. Once in Iowa, Van Beek's mother, with help from her daughters, made and sold both cheese and butter in the nearest village.[164] Nearly every immigrant woman who described life on a farm mentioned selling milk and/or butter, eggs, and sometimes cheese and garden vegetables in addition to the "main" money-making crops.[165] Typical was Maaike Huigen, living in Galesburg, Iowa, in 1880, who reported that "[Farmers] usually have so many chickens that in the summer they can trade the eggs for such things as coffee, tea, sugar, soap, and everything they need besides."[166] Through much of this period, Dutch American newspapers such as *Pella's Weekblad* and *De Volksvriend* carried ads from stores which took various farm items in trade for other products.[167] Eggs, cream, or butter were the most common items to sell, while groceries were the most common item for which one might trade, as attested in the ad "Hens Paid Grocery

The Van den Brink company of Hull, Iowa, offered the services of their milliner in exchange for produce in this advertisement from *De Volksvriend* in 1919.

LADIES!

Thans wenschen wij uw aandacht te vestigen op de nieuwe **VOORJAARS MILLINERY**. Als ooit een hoedemaakster reden had om tevreden te gevoelen, dan is het voorzeker Mrs. Work over haar Millinery dat zij dit Voorjaar vertoont. Maak gebruik van haar voortreffelijke Millinery kennis en kunstigen smaak. Het zal Mrs. Work zeer aangenaam zijn, en het zal een Bron van Tevredenheid zijn voor u, beide in waar en prijs, indien gij u door haar wilt laten bedienen, wanneer ge uw Millinery uitzoekt.

WIJ NEMEN PRODUCE IN RUIL

A. VAN DEN BRINK

HULL, IOWA

Bills."[168] But there were other combinations: at the Van den Brink store in Hull, Iowa, for example, women could bring in "produce" and get a new spring hat.[169]

Women included price lists in their letters, partly because it was something they knew and something about which they considered it appropriate to write, and partly because this was information that potential emigrants in the Netherlands wanted to know. In 1881 Martje Smit wrote: "Coffee costs 25 cents per pound, white sugar 10, candy 45, dried sour apples 25 for 3 pounds, 1 pound of butter 10, 12 eggs 7 cents . . . [Marten] earns 1½ dollars a day."[170] These women used American currency and measures, and on occasion an American name, to describe prices and products. Reciprocally, they too asked for the current information on prices from the Netherlands. In both directions the correspondents needed the information in context—wage levels or crop and livestock prices, the earnings of the farm. Whether they got this information from shopping themselves, or from their spouses, or from Dutch American newspapers, however, was not always clear.

At least according to the sources I consulted, few women handled land or home sales in the city, nor acreage, grain, or livestock sales in the country, though many could report the exact prices. Dutch immigrant men tended to pass on their farms at retirement rather than death, meaning fewer widows left with this task. Still, none of the women I studied reported that their husbands left them uninformed about financial matters. Just the opposite, the detail women used to report finances indicated they discussed such matters openly and sometimes made joint decisions. "This spring we paid off part of our land. We also had to spend 50 dollars to fix our house."[171] Nor was the information limited to the parents. Older children knew the family circumstances as well: "We aren't milking much at the moment . . . so no big money from the creamery, yesterday we got 143 dollars and 34 cents, [checks] come every two weeks, half is for us and the other half for our cousin, the landlord."[172]

Putting together the money to buy farm equipment often required borrowing money. Farms almost inevitably had a mortgage in the early years. The danger of losing one's land because of poor crop prices spurred many women to their frugality. As one widow wrote: "Most farmers here in Dakota are poor and started out very poor, but they took the land because they could get it for practically nothing. The first thing they required was horses and farm machinery, . . . [now because of high interest] many have already had to mortgage out their few possessions again."[173] Yet women also recognized the advantages of such investments. Horses and machinery also meant less manual labor, either for men or women, and the opportunity for more extensive farming. "Everything is done with horses or with steam. Hay-loading and mowing are all done by machine . . . here they have bigger farms for man (and woman)."[174] Her mention of haying was particularly of note for women since in the Netherlands women generally gathered and stacked the hay which men cut.

I do not want to exaggerate women's control of the purse strings. In urban areas men generally brought home the largest paycheck, and the decision to hand over all or part of it to their wives remained in their hands. Men could make the ultimate choice in most major financial matters, particularly where to move, when to sell, and how much land to buy. But even on such issues women often had a voice, illustrated by a family that tried farming in the area around Nordeloos, Michigan. The entire family, from the province of Zeeland, arrived in western Michigan in 1880 and began working. "Then my father got it into his head that he had to go to the country. . . . Dad was green here, you know, he didn't know anything . . . [after two unsuccessful years]. Then my mother said: now Toon, this is enough, now we are going back to the city because there is work in the city."[175] The family moved and father, mother, and daughter all got jobs in Grand Rapids.

In urban areas women were more likely to do regular shopping than on farms, where they required transportation. Yet even if women did not do the purchasing, they could decide ahead of time what went on the list. Ads from grocers, including prices, were not uncommon in several of the Dutch American newspapers I consulted. At times they also carried comparative articles. In 1916 *Pella's Weekblad* carried an article on the tremendous rise in prices in the Netherlands for foodstuffs, particularly since the beginning of the war.[176] In the 1910s and especially with the advent of war, prices rose in the United States, but still most women felt they were better off in America. A few years later Harmanna Schoonbeek Rosenboom noted that the papers in Grand Rapids had been filled with news of hard times in the Netherlands during the war: "Here in America there was still a surplus, but everything was expensive. Prices rose, and that is still the case, but fortunately the war is over."[177] Anna Kuijt Bates, whose husband was earning little in 1918, still bragged about life in the United States: "we pay 1.39 for 50 pounds of flour and we can bake a whole lot of bread with that, the eggs are 35 cents per 12 (dozen) and I just bought *10 pounds* of sugar for *42* cents that is a big difference from Holland eh? there it is 25 cents for *1 pound*."[178] Women's letters made clear that certain products were more expensive in certain areas, yet the refrain continued that "groceries are cheap."[179] In Chicago, Grand Rapids, and Paterson, immigrants reported getting produce from the store or from Dutch truck farmers in the area. Still, women could be actively involved in these family operations.

In the United States the lack of day laborers for cheap rates, and of domestic servants who could double as field workers, meant that farm wives and daughters took on many of the tasks which otherwise might have gone to wage workers. The presence of hired men, but no domestics, or of a threshing crew, but no extra help to cook for them, illustrated how Dutch American families frequently solved the dilemma of too little money and relatively expensive day labor. Men got some extra help, and women worked harder. This changed to some extent with mechanization. One interviewee from Orange City, Iowa, described how girls and boys would work side by side picking corn around the turn of the century. Then, farmers bought corn-pickers and the work was gone. With this some elements of women's field work slowly disappeared, but women's work in barns and gardens generally continued.[180]

Women's agricultural work on the family farm, their assistance in family business, their work for wages when young, and household management when older, all contributed to the family economy. Writers and interviewees stressed that the success of a family migration financially depended on a woman's management of finances—on her ability to be frugal. When Jo Dann carried out interviews in Dutch American communities in the 1960s the stereotype was still present:

—You still make your own soap?! . . . Why do you still do that?
—Because we have the fat, you see, and we are of Dutch ancestry, we are frugal, and we couldn't throw the fat away.
—Isn't that terrible work?
—Yes, that it is.[181]

These women carried their frugality further than some, but the stress on women being frugal was echoed many times. As in this example, frugality frequently meant women doing or making something which other people would buy. "It's Always the Woman Who Pays—Always," read the subtitle on a 1918 article in *The Banner*, which fictionalized (in exaggerated form) the trials of a self-sacrificing minister's wife. In the story the woman gave extensively of her own time and energy, skipped meals and clothing, in order to fill all the challenges she faced. Women reminiscing about their early years in the United States frequently adopted this kind of tone as well. From the perspective of the 1960s their efforts seemed somewhat heroic: the mother who got up before daybreak to start the fire, do the milking, fix something to eat . . . "and sometimes she would still be spinning at midnight."[182]

For those living through the times, the letter writers, the tasks were less heroic and more a matter of hard work and doing what had to be done. "Hunting for eggs and milking I do myself. Good thing that I learned how to climb and scramble so well as a kid, otherwise I would have broken an arm or leg."[183] Those with small children and low finances complained that without domestics or daughters old enough to help the work was overwhelming. Darning, sewing, knitting, crocheting, spinning, and other clothing-related tasks usually fell behind first. Housecleaning and washing came next. Rarely could women neglect food preparation. Neither could they abandon their duties in animal and poultry care, certain aspects of field work, or gardening.

The stereotype of American women as whiling away their time in rocking chairs and spending money on unnecessary items appeared often in the pages of Dutch men's letters: "The women sit here in big rocking chairs and smoke, even pipes—they are the color of . . . milk."[184] In the Netherlands this went so

Dutch American women generally assisted with field work, though plowing was unusual. Photo from the Feringa family of Highland, Michigan, courtesy of Archives, Calvin College.

far that some people would say that a woman they considered a lazy wife "belongs in America."[185] In comparison to the American women around them, Dutch American women did certain tasks more often, especially milking and field work, darning, and certain types of food production. The absence of cheap household help and of sufficient funds to live like the American middle class kept Dutch Protestant immigrant women working when their American counterparts might have stopped. Yet there is a incongruence between the wonderful things women reported buying and their reports of frugality. For many, frugality could be an excuse for not buying something as well as a cultural tradition. Conversely, the riches and technological wonders of the United States could justify a purchase. Easing a woman's labor spurred purchases and mechanization in the household. The distinction of wage and non-wage labor made its mark here. Within the Dutch American community there were a few who resisted buying products to help in the household because this was women's work. More frequently families invested first in products which would help generate cash, on equipment for the farm or business, and only later in labor-saving devices for the home.[186]

Dutch American husbands generally proved adamant about not helping with housework, regardless of the scope of their wives' work. The husband who quipped "everyone in his place" had a wife who clarified that though he never dried a dish or set the table she worked side by side with him in the family store.[187] For some orthodox Calvinist men engaged in waged work, church policies on strict Sunday observance meant that on the one day they had free from the factory, they also would not do any work around the home. Women also had Sunday off from regular tasks, but the consequence was more work other days. Activities which generally fell to men in "Yankee" households were more often left to the wife and children because men had "no time" to do them.[188]

Only in certain circumstances did Dutch immigrant women comment about the gender roles within "Yankee" households. Domestics gave the most detailed descriptions, and generally favored the assistance "Yankee" men gave their wives. They also discerned a tendency among Dutch immigrants who came before marriage to adopt some American patterns, whether cleaning American style for women or learning to cook for men. Working-class Dutch immigrant men often perceived American gender roles with horror: "There are many places you can find here where the husband works all day in the factory and has to take care of the housekeeping."[189] In light of this, allowing a woman to buy certain things became a lesser evil. This helped spread the ideal of the middle-class family where the husband earned a sufficient salary that the wife could buy the products, aids, and services she needed so that the household ran without a husband's "help."

The kind of work women reported depended largely on where they lived and whether a family business or farm required assistance. Over time, the prosperity of part of the Dutch American group meant a negative evaluation of women, at least of married women, who worked for wages. Under these circumstances, frugality became even more the watchword for successful housewives, with the stress on staying at home and making do. This changing evaluation also made its way into people's thoughts about women working on the farm. By the mid-twentieth century many Dutch Americans embraced—in theory—the bourgeois idea of separate spheres of work and home. When a woman from Nijverdal and her husband from Brabant reminisced about their early days on a farm in the Midwest, the husband proudly stated his wife never had to help with farmwork. The wife contradicted him, "well, but" and went on to explain that she milked the cows (about a dozen), took care of the chickens, and did the gardening.[190] His equation of "farmwork" with work in the fields rarely appeared in letters from the turn of the century.

* * *

In a speech before the "Willing Helpers" society in Paterson, New Jersey, the orator noted that women could do important work in the world, citing the example of Florence Nightingale, yet he warned against competing with men for jobs and stressed the importance of housekeeping and raising children rather than acquiring money. "The poorest dwelling presided over by a virtuous, thrifty, cheerful and cleanly woman is the abode of comfort and happiness."[191] The speaker's views reflected at least partly a reaction against increasing numbers of Dutch American daughters who sought their calling outside the home.

The social reproduction of families and homes as Dutch immigrants knew them depended on the money-earning and money-saving activities of women. As was the case for other immigrant groups, the distinction between paid and unpaid work was often blurred, and it became clear primarily in retrospect when the family sought to project mid-twentieth-century views backward. Rarely did a Dutch immigrant woman support herself, yet rarely did she not take part in a large variety of activities to make the family economy work. Exactly what these women did depended on age, for young women more often worked for wages to strengthen the family economy, and on location, since job opportunities were quite different in rural and urban locations, and on time period and general economic conditions. In general women had greater opportunities to earn money in the United States than in the Netherlands. They also began to adopt technological shifts and attitudes about "work" which were part of middle-class life in America. Yet some of the older patterns continued, particularly of women doing various outdoor activities and taking on certain tasks in the home which people of other ethnic backgrounds delegated to men. These gender role distinctions, which also applied to several other northwestern European immigrant groups of the time, as noted by Jon Gjerde, caused people of long-standing Anglo descent to look slightly askance at these immigrants and their children.[192] As my grandmother said: the Dutch expect a lot of their women.

CHAPTER 4

In Sickness and in Death

"**W**e are in good health and hope the same is true for you." Health was the topic that introduced nearly every Dutch immigrant letter and was a prominent theme in most. Sickness was more than an inconvenience, for it could endanger the lives of members of the family and the functioning of the family as a financial unit. Women reworked their schedules, rearranged their homes, and otherwise shifted their lives to accommodate care of those family members who needed it. Sickness drained an individual physically and put greater strain on the caregivers, and it taxed the family emotionally and financially. Dutch immigrant women oversaw their own and their families' health, providing care in the home and mediating between the one who was ill and medical professionals. Informal nursing constituted a major social reproductive task. Exactly who did what and under what circumstances differed over time, yet in the western European world, for the most part it was women who handled issues relating to the health of their families. The gendered nature of the nursing profession developed in this context.[1] By the turn of the century many Dutch Americans entrusted "serious" health matters to professionals, though there were some who still feared and avoided hospitals and doctors. In either case it did not stop women from caring for the ill, the incapacitated, and the aged, and from providing emotional encouragement. Informal care could put heavy demands on women caregivers. Both in cases of persons who were old and infirm and when a person faced a terminal illness, the caregiver had to handle extensive nursing tasks as part of the daily routine. At the death of an individual both women and men shared in grieving, in arranging a funeral, and in sharing the news with others. In the realm of health care, the Dutch resembled Anglo American society quite closely, more so than many ethnic groups.

The language surrounding age and aging was intimately intertwined with health. In this, the old world and the new held quite literal connotations. For a potential Dutch woman migrant, one of the most convincing grounds not to emigrate was her duty to care for her parents. But younger women were also vulnerable if illness struck the family. They relied upon family and friends both in sickness and death, to provide the support and assistance they needed. They also relied upon them for information concerning health, how to deal with childbirth and illness, and particularly as people with whom they could share their burdens of care, suffering, and grief. From this standpoint, the lure of the new and uncharted became the fear of being alone when need struck. Because family and chain migration played such an important role in the Dutch case, migrants could mitigate this danger.

Still, migration meant finding alternatives for extended family and the knowledgeable older women who would otherwise figure prominently in health care. It also meant creating institutions which would serve Dutch Americans in a way they felt was appropriate. This entailed recasting the gender role divisions of American philanthropy to suit Dutch American tastes and creating a separatist Christian world of institutions which have continued to this day. The institutions which Dutch immigrants formed in this period were based on the philosophy of soul/body connections in treatment of illness, a major distinction which set most Dutch American Protestants (and many other ethnic groups) apart from more established American patterns.[2] Further, though the Dutch for the most part went along with professional training, they generally avoided arguments about the "scientific" basis for social assistance in the form of aid to the poor, mentally ill, elderly, and children which was characteristic of many Progressive activities.[3] Belief in professional medical care and the recognition that it was as good in the Netherlands as in the United States set them apart from some immigrant groups and helps explain part of the generally good reputation the Dutch enjoyed as an immigrant group.[4]

Belief in separate (religious) institutions and the religious ideology which supported them helps explain why women were relatively absent from Dutch American philanthropy. Unlike other ethnic women, who used their positions in churches as a base to form parochial schools and hospitals, as well as homes for the aged and mentally impaired, Dutch immigrant women could take part only to a limited extent in a world of formal institutional care which remained the province of men.[5] The social reproduction of formal care on a communal level, in other words, remained primarily in men's hands. Moreover, the church frequently provided "insurance," both monetary and emotional. At times the more orthodox Dutch Protestants forbade for-profit insurance, insisting that such expenditures went against the communal responsibility of church members. Rather, church members organized their own benevolent and burial societies to take the place of commercial policies.[6] Women's close ties to both family and church related in part to their financial, emotional, and sometimes legal reliance on these institutions in cases of sickness and death. The development of these patterns had their roots in the Netherlands, as is clear in the case of Jacoba Beuker Robbert.

Jacoba Beuker Robbert

Jacoba Beuker Robbert spent most of her adult life in one of the most revered positions available to a Dutch American Protestant woman, as the wife of a dominie. That meant that in addition to supporting her husband in his ministerial work, housekeeping, raising children, and entertaining guests, she would have as large a role in church activities as was generally possible for women at that time. Her family background prepared her well for this role. Her father was Henricus Beuker, born in Volzel, Graafschap Bentheim (a Dutch-speaking district just across the border in German territory).[7] He had joined the pietistic revival, the *Afscheiding* (Secession), early, working directly with several of its leaders to gain his training as a dominie. His connections to leaders of the Secession continued after he began his own ministry, and later as the next major religious revival, the *Doleantie,* began he came into close contact with Abraham Kuyper. Henricus Beuker became editor of *De Vrije Kerk,* a leading Seceder monthly, and in this capacity earned credentials as a theologian as well as a reformer.[8] In 1881, in a series of articles on Freemasonry in the Netherlands and the United States, he argued that the Reformed Church in the United States had not taken a strong enough stance against this secret society, and hence that the Dutch should separate and have an entirely "Dutch" church.[9] The debate, which then coalesced with growing interest in the Doleantie in the Netherlands, took Beuker into the wings of those who supported the Christian Reformed Church as a separatist alternative in the United States. It also was one of the issues which Abraham Kuyper, a friend of Beuker, used to steer migrants away from the Reformed Church in the United States.

Henricus Beuker's interest in separate institutions also applied to his work in the Netherlands. As part of the Vereeniging ter Christelijke Verzorging van Krankzinnigen en Zenuwlijders (Society to Promote the Christian Care of the Insane and Neurotics), he became a leading figure in founding Veldwijk, a mental institution which opened its doors in 1886.[10] In subsequent articles in *De Vrije Kerk* he continued to stress the need to combine proper Christian commitment with good medical training, and he supported training the institution's own personnel on site to ensure this combination.

Jacoba Beuker, born in Zwolle in 1863, grew up in the midst of this atmosphere. As one commentator explained, it was her "privilege to serve tea to her father in his study and to a frequent visitor, Dr. Abraham Kuyper. She recalled vividly their conversations,"[11] and she became a party to at least some of their theological differences. In addition to her regular formal education, about which we know little, she attended lectures by Seceder luminaries. Her own interest in theology was keen, yet according to her minister, late in life she felt inadequate in this regard. "If I cannot understand such a great mind as Dr. Bavinck's, how can I expect to understand God's ways with men?"[12] At twenty-two, in 1885, she married Jan Robbert, a dominie born in Graafschap Bentheim (like her father) and trained at the theological school at Kampen (a leading Seceder institution), and they began a round of service to church congregations in the Netherlands.

In 1893 the Beukers and Robberts all headed for the United States, where the demand for Dutch-speaking dominies was growing with every shipload of immigrants. Henricus Beuker took his column "Een en Ander" from *De Vrije Kerk* to a leading Dutch American theological journal, *De Gereformeerde Amerikaan.* Both dominies began serving Christian Reformed congregations: Beuker beginning in Muskegon, Michigan, and Robbert in Roseland (a suburb of Chicago).[13] Beuker continued his journalistic efforts to promote separate institutions, writing extensively in *De Wachter* (another Dutch-American journal tied to the Christian Reformed Church) in support of Bethesda, a tuberculosis sanitarium in New Mexico.[14] Beuker soon took a chair as professor of systematic and practical theology at Calvin College, the Christian Reformed seminary in western Michigan. He remained there until his death in 1900.

Because of this pedigree, it is easier to explain why Jacoba Beuker Robbert, dominie's wife and mother of several children, became one of only a handful of women who managed to get published in *De Wachter.* In the years immediately after her father died, Beuker Robbert lived in Kalamazoo. Her interest in a Christian mental institution, according to her story, came when a woman appeared at her door one Sunday asking for the "Dutch church." When Beuker Robbert found that this woman regularly escaped from the state mental institution on Sundays looking for a religious service, her social activism progressed. Beuker Robbert began leading religious services for women in the institution twice a week, and combined her efforts with those of John Keizer and Peter Jonker, both dominies, to alert the Christian Reformed community more broadly to the need for a Christian mental institution along the lines of the one her father helped organize in the Netherlands.[15]

The call for a Christian mental institution had sounded several times in the Dutch American press, notably when Rev. Idzerd Van Dellen wrote a series for the *Reformed American* in 1897, and when Rev. Keizer had called for it in *De Wachter* in 1903. But others, especially Rev. Henry Beets, indicated there was no need since the state hospitals were not against religion (as they were in the Netherlands).[16] Jacoba Beuker Robbert joined the debate largely to counter this image. In 1906 an article by "Mrs. J. Robbert" appeared in *De Wachter.* Her title was significant, for normally authors were only identified by first initial, even if they were dominies or possessed other advanced degrees. Beuker Robbert chronicled the advances in separate Christian institutions which the denomination had achieved: a seminary and junior college, a mission to Jews and one to "blind Indians," primary schools in many locations, Christian literature (especially for the young). "There is *one* area which remains totally barren, a major field to be cultivated, specifically the part of that work of philanthropy: the Christian care of 'mentally ill and neurotics.' Is there not *one* among all those who are ill, who does not ask for our help and devotion, and most of all for our Christian love?"[17] Beuker Robbert went on to stress that the mentally ill were sick in the soul, a literal reading of the term *zielsziek,* which was sometimes used to describe this group. She noted the lack of prayer or Bible reading in state institutions and the presence of dancing parties (at a time when dance was denounced as immoral in some church publications).

Her comments highlight how ideas common among mental health professionals at that time conflicted with Dutch American Protestant worldview: "How can someone who laughs at a sense of guilt; who considers a complaint about intrusions from Satan as 'ravings'; who does not know or understand how Jesus alone can heal the 'broken hearted'; how can such a person deal professionally with the souls of these unfortunate ones who have to fight against Satan's tricks?"[18] Along with her references to the Bible and admonitions about Satan working against recovery for the group without proper spiritual care, she also hinted at one of the major obstacles to a separate institution: "is it not our great [*dure*] calling to bring 'our' sick ones of the soul to God's word?"[19] The term *dure,* however, also meant expensive, and money was the main obstacle to support for such an institution. She ended the article with a call to form a Christian institution for such care.

Three years later Beuker Robbert became part of the first planning committee for the institution, the Christian Psychopathic Hospital Association. As with other institutions, this group had backing from both Reformed and Christian Reformed denominations. The group bought a farm in Cutlerville, south of Grand Rapids, for the home. Beuker Robbert concentrated her efforts on contacting and winning the support of church women's groups. Her efforts resulted in some financial support but also in auxiliaries which provided canned goods, bedding, furniture, and other items for the institution. The facility opened in 1910 with four nurses and a cook. One year later it added a doctor/administrator.[20]

Meanwhile Beuker Robbert had to curtail her organizational activities for the hospital because her husband took another position in Niekirk, Michigan, a small farming town too distant from Grand Rapids for her to commute often. In subsequent years the family, which eventually included ten children, moved to three other Dutch American churches.[21] Beuker Robbert spent thirty-three years of her life as the dominie's wife, which meant as a leader for certain women's activities and provider of coffee and conversation for congregation members and other visitors who stopped in during the week.[22] A eulogist reported that she was known for saying, "If the coffee pot is on the stove [in the parsonage] there will most likely be peace in the congregation."[23] Though it meant at least eight moves in her lifetime, being a dominie's wife was a role she adored.

The family faced a difficult situation during World War I. Four sons fought, and a fifth was awaiting a call to go overseas in 1918. The Netherlands was not directly involved in the war, but because Jan Robbert was from a Dutch-speaking region of Germany originally, his relatives were on the other side of the conflict from the United States. One son had a cousin with a name identical to his, against whom he fought, not knowing the situation until after the war. The emotional toll, in addition to physical problems, led Jan Robbert to retire in 1918.[24] He died four years later.

When her husband died in 1922, Beuker Robbert lost not only her spouse but also her role as dominie's wife. She missed the activities of the parsonage sorely in the subsequent thirty-five years of her life. Living in Holland, Michigan, where she moved after her husband died, she discussed missions, divorce, and other issues of interest to the denomination with her dominie there, and she continued to read (and later have read to her) denominational publications. The surviving materials indicated she took an active part in the Prospect Park Christian Reformed Church but did not engage in any further major public campaigns. She died in 1957 and was buried in the cemetery in Graafschap, Michigan, between her husband and her father.

Beuker Robbert exemplified what the conservative pundits of the Christian Reformed Church, the rising force in Dutch America, lauded. When she wrote a speech on women's role to present to one of her women's study groups, she provided a clear example of how conservative Dutch Protestantism, whether in the Netherlands or in the Dutch communities of the United States, differed from the ideology which American social reformers espoused. Beuker Robbert wrote about "woman": "She is a help in the family, a help for the ill. She can be a help in the church of God. She can be a special help in the Christian School, where her influence on the little ones will never be forgotten."[25] Nowhere in her writings was the woman the leading figure in the home; nowhere was she the primary moral force of the family or society. She could enrich her children's souls, and she should (even it meant neglecting the mending). Beuker Robbert, in other words, followed the vision of patriarchal families in which men reigned morally in the home as well as in other arenas of life. She also followed the Dutch ideal of patriarchy in the church. She taught Bible studies for women, including studies of women in the Bible, but she felt strongly that women should never teach men and that there should be male teachers for older boys.

Beuker Robbert was the daughter of a well-known social reformer and church leader, but her status as a dominie's wife also assisted her in pushing the barriers of women's roles to advocate social reform. Moreover, she had the examples of other women active in missions and in founding Christian institutions. Beuker Robbert, by virtue of her marriage to a dominie, earned respect and the expectation that she would advance the cause of the church among women members. Few of her activities took her beyond that charge, and when the dominie was gone, so was her role. She represented the ultimate degree to which women from the more conservative Protestant group could be involved in formal philanthropy, a pattern which had its base in gender dynamics in public health care in the Netherlands in the late 1800s.

In the Netherlands

Up until the 1880s Dutch society consisted of two groups in terms of health care: the poor and those who could afford medical treatment at home. Hospitals, in this system, were places for the poor. Deaconesses and nuns, along with medically untrained but somewhat educated women of the bourgeoisie, handled most nursing. This changed around the turn of the century, partly as a result of advances in surgical techniques and partly in response to the needs of those who were neither poor nor rich enough to afford private nursing, a (largely urban) middle class. Trained nurses handled much more of the care in these new hospitals, which gained their foothold in urban areas first, then spread to the countryside, especially under the umbrella of religious organizations.[26]

Research advances, the discovery of the bacilli causing tuberculosis and cholera (in 1882 and 1883 respectively) and an understanding of how to fight them, spurred further development. At the same time the professionalization of medicine in terms of formal training, both for doctors and for nurses, meant the denigration of nonprofessional help, particularly of those with knowledge of herbs and folk medicine.[27] Women in the family, however, continued in their roles as informal nurses for those recuperating from an illness or operation. The medical profession divided along hierarchical lines, embodied in gender distinctions between male doctors and their female assistants (nurses), and concurrently into the class hierarchy of educated women (trained nurses) from bourgeois backgrounds to the lowest level of health care, untrained female aides who emptied bedpans and changed linen. In the home women took the latter kinds of activities as givens. A further hierarchy reflected ideas about the development of medicine on a national scale. In this, educated Dutch individuals assumed their standard of medicine rivaled any in the world. Only Germany provided close competition, and the United States fell into a lower category entirely.

The relatively high cost of medical care in the Netherlands and the general lack of insurance (only about 10 percent of the population had health insurance in 1900) meant that the less affluent did not always call a doctor when someone was ill. There were also some who relied on folk remedies or on the patent medicines which also were widespread in the United States. Yet most Netherlanders, including the group which emigrated, believed in modern medicine and relied upon doctors to the extent that they could afford to.[28] Both allopathic and homeopathic doctors found a clientele. One of the major divisions regarding Dutch health care (one that also existed elsewhere) was the juxtaposition of scientific, professionally trained medical staff, which basically ignored religious (including emotional or psychological) implications of disease, and a part of the population which refused to disconnect these elements of experience. In the context of religio-political developments at the turn of the century, this led to an upsurge of church-related hospitals. In these, professional health care could retain a denominational flavor which included "spiritual" and emotional support, and Christian women would find opportunities for nursing.

The role of church-based organizations in public care generally was quite different in the Netherlands than in the United States. According to the constitutional changes of 1848, care for the poor was officially a state responsibility, but at the local level the deacons of the Calvinist churches staffed the committees which made decisions on who received care. In practice, they tended to approve support only if the church first refused. A revision of the poor law in 1870 did not change this noticeably. The local poor relief board still worked with religious authorities, and even more liberal members of government did not challenge the role of churches in handling much aid for the poor. Orthodox Protestants generally assumed people should rely on the church rather than the state for such aid, and thus a state poor allowance was "double begging."[29] The poor law of 1912 allowed for more oversight of church practice, but in principle churches retained their position. This situation had two major consequences for women. First, women, who were more likely than men to become poor because of lower wages or widowhood, generally turned to churches (and the male authorities in them) for assistance first. A woman who regularly attended church and did not challenge the church's moral strictures was not only more likely to receive aid but likely to get more aid than someone who did not have those characteristics. Second, Christian women would be largely excluded from social work. As historian Berteke Waaldijk put it: "Religious philanthropy had little room for ambitious women."[30]

The aged also faced a similar situation. In some towns the same institution housed the poor and the elderly. Homes for the elderly had a long history in the Netherlands, but not as a place most people wanted to spend their last years.[31] At of the beginning of the twentieth century one entered such an institution after having sold all one's possessions. In a typical institution men and women slept separately, even married couples. Often people had to wear institutional clothing, and generally there were strict rules to follow regarding behavior, visitors, and possibilities to leave the premises. Despite the conditions, many such homes were constantly full. Poverty and old age went hand in hand for much of the working-class and farm-laboring population. Unless family could provide, there was no choice. Older individuals who could handle some of their own housekeeping and who already had a place to stay might continue on their own with only some assistance in the form of food or fuel. As of 1912 all persons had a right to ask for help (if the family could not provide) and in 1919 every person below a certain income level gained the right to a pension after age seventy.[32]

From the beginning of my period of study (1880), people in the Netherlands had access to a greater range of welfare institutions than was typical of the United States, but under church auspices. The Dutch welfare state would continue to outpace that of the United States thereafter, but again, with a religious twist. What that meant was that the Dutch, like other ethnic groups, would take the initiative in the United States to set up their own institutions. The lack of state intervention, which on the one hand opened possibilities for some women to get involved in philanthropy, also allowed other visions of communal responsibility to take root.[33]

The Trip

While the institutions of philanthropy and care were important to Dutch immigrant women, their encounters with sickness and death often came on a more mundane level. Even before a woman set foot on the boat to cross the Atlantic, issues of health came into play. Health formed one of the criteria for those going to America. Immigration control designated that those whom the authorities branded as likely to become a public charge could not enter the United States. In 1891 the new superintendent of immigration formulated minimum health standards for immigrants, barring "persons suffering from a loathsome or dangerous contagious disease." When the entry station at Ellis Island opened in 1892, it helped make inspections possible for those crossing the Atlantic. Steamship companies had to return those who did not pass this inspection, meaning they began running their own physicals prior to departure. In 1903 another measure barred epileptics. That same year the list of "common causes" for people who could become public charges included things from hernia to varicose veins, poor physique, or chronic rheumatism.[34] Thus the elderly, as well as the mentally or physically impaired, could only come in the context of family migration, where the younger or more financially established family members supported them, and even then if their condition was obvious they might not make it through Ellis Island. In practice this meant they sometimes stayed in the Netherlands. Liefiena Bos, age nineteen, of Sappemeer, Groningen, wrote to her aunt and uncle in Grand Rapids, Michigan, in 1888: "Uncle, we are stuck here. As far as I am concerned, I would gladly come to you, and father would also be game for it. But what would we do with mother? She can barely walk any more and, uncle, father is old and stooped too. Work: that would hardly be worth much any more."[35] The theme of leaving behind those who could not work or who were plagued with frequent illness appeared in several letter collections. Such was the case of Derkien Koning, of Groningen (city). A letter from her brother in 1910 indicated that Koning was living in an orphanage when her brother emigrated. While he thought of sending for her, there was the problem of a stomach ailment, for which she received free treatment in the Dutch institution. From the tone of the letter it was clear the siblings were not close, and in Groningen Koning stayed in contact with a sister who lived in the area. Poor health, plus government health care for the poor, plus family ties combined to keep Koning in the Netherlands.[36] Likewise Gerrit Kuijt and his spouse Letha Retel Kuijt had already made most of the preparations for emigration, intending to join his three siblings in Chicago in 1907, when Gerrit's chronic illness disqualified them.[37]

The ocean served as a barrier for others, for even in the age of steam transportation the crossing was arduous. Some ships had a staff of "lady helpers," as one immigrant called them, to assist those who were ill, while on other vessels the cabin stewards took on this role.[38] In most cases, however, women generally reported taking care of the queasy themselves. At least one or two members of nearly every large family experienced sea sickness. Though the Netherlands was a seafaring nation, most of the emigrants lacked sea legs, having little or no regular contact with ocean-going vessels. They wrote back to family and potential emigrants to let them know that seasickness, while uncomfortable, was not dangerous. Dutch women immigrants with children generally spent much of the voyage in the cabin taking care of the young ones, while older children and men explored more of the ship and went on deck more often. Since women got on deck less often and were confronted with the sight and smell of regurgitation more, they were more susceptible to seasickness.[39] One of those sufferers was Etje Houwerzijl, who wrote her mother that "[For two days] I was so seasick, when I was upright I had to vomit continually, and was giddy. Oh I felt so sad and lonely then."[40] An otherwise healthy person could withstand illness, but the Atlantic could claim victims among the less hearty. The sad stories of those who died during passage acted as a warning to others: "The 17th of April the boat with Frisian emigrants arrived. . . . It was not a pleasant reception . . . [father] had died two days before on the boat. . . . They wanted to take along father's body but that was not allowed and thus he had to be left to the sea. Horrible."[41]

The loss of an adult during the journey struck so hard partially because the immigrants were accustomed to funerals which included extended family members in a somber ritual and to visiting grave sites as a way of remembering and honoring the dead. A burial at sea also contradicted the optimism and anticipation that usually accompanied a trip to America. This was even more the case since children were the most likely to succumb.[42]

In immigrant letters, the most frequent notices of death during the crossing concerned children. On the one hand their youth made the loss easier, since people recognized that infant mortality and childhood diseases knew no borders. On the other hand, children were part of the new, part of the future, and when they died it embodied the lack of control migrants had over that future and foreshadowed disillusionment. Whether of a child or of an adult, any death at sea made the survivors reflect on death, specifically on death in a foreign land.

Illness and Home Care

Once in the United States, when women immigrants (and many men as well) wrote to their relatives, they included information about health. For women doing so combined two of their roles in social reproduction: maintaining family connections through correspondence and also describing women's work. How much information they included depended on the recipient and on certain tabus about what topics people could discuss. For example, despite the extensive information about health issues, women did not typically write about menstruation, sexuality, or menopause in direct terms.[43] Instead their letters remained ambiguous: "In earlier years I suffered a great deal, especially from my 46th to my 49th year, but now I am much healthier."[44] If they needed assistance for health problems related to these issues perhaps they relied on relatives in the United States—if they were available, perhaps they asked professionals, or perhaps they simply suffered.

Women reported major health events. Generally they knew when many people in the area had a disease, particularly a dangerous one, or if there was an epidemic taking place in their vicinity. For example, the 1918 flu epidemic was a standard part of women's letters that year.[45] Just as men might report the general political events, women frequently provided a health report. I do not mean this in absolute terms. Some women reported on political events, and men generally mentioned health. The difference lay in degree and detail. Because women took care of the ill, both adults and children, they could and did provide more information. In cases such as the Schuilings of Manhattan, Montana, where both husband and wife wrote sections of most letters, the wife provided the details of health, whether about sickness or measures to avoid it such as vaccinations.[46] Married women with children in particular would note which diseases plagued the area. And if women had access to international news, whether they lived in the United States or the Netherlands, this was one piece of information they frequently discussed. One woman, thanking her relatives in the United States for an overdue letter, chided: "Mother sometimes thought that none of you was alive any more since the fever has been so widespread in America."[47]

General news about health in the United States punctuated women's letters in other ways. Just as immigrants assured relatives and friends in the Netherlands about the soil and weather conditions in the context of farming, so too they reported about the climate in terms of health. "I have never wanted to be here [Texas] that much. In the summer it is hot here and in the fall we have much too much sickness for it to be pleasant."[48] Basically for some immigrants any climate that did not resemble that of the Netherlands was "unhealthy." One young woman wrote a friend that the continued warmth of southern California had left her tired and drained, whereas the seasons of western Michigan suited her well. She wrote this letter on a cold, damp, December day when the sun never appeared.[49] Others disagreed about California, though they too discussed the climate in terms of health. One's own health, including the effect of climate, was a major factor in deciding if one would migrate, and later in evaluating migration. This was a common experience for other immigrant women as well.[50]

Letter writers chronicled various attempts by relatives and friends in the area who assisted in cases of incapacity. When one Dutch farmworker arrived in California he spent his first few days with a family he knew from Overijssel. Thereafter he went to work as a milker. When he got kicked by a cow, causing a leg injury, he left his quarters and employer and went back to recuperate with the family he knew. "He stayed with us for three weeks and then he left again although his foot wasn't better."[51] Most single men and women reported going either to their own relatives or to families they knew. In some cases the caregivers went to the patients, as with Gezina van der Haar Visscher, who mentioned going to stay with her daughter Marie for several days when Marie was ill.[52]

Home nursing, a standard women's task, was a requirement for these immigrants, one which they met primarily through networks similar to those of the Netherlands. The distances involved became longer, and the number of individuals upon whom someone could call narrowed. Still, chain migration set up at least the parameters for some informal care. Married immigrant women expected to act as unpaid nurses at times for recuperating friends and relatives. The trouble was that the narrower the networks, the smaller the number of women upon whom these tasks fell, until it sometimes became too much of a burden. Migration, by decreasing the number of potential informal caregivers and by increasing other burdens on those exact individuals, pushed the immigrant community toward a greater reliance on professional medicine and organized care. Availability and the wherewithal to pay played important roles in this process, but I could not discredit the significance of migration itself in this change.[53] One of the clearest cases of how the process operated was that of Anna Kuijt.[54]

Kuijt had two married siblings who, like her, lived in the Chicago area. Kuijt's relatives took her in frequently when her leg condition made work impossible. Her employers for domestic work might have been paternal, but not so paternal that they would nurse her through eight weeks of recovery. Instead her sister Jeannette and family took her in for five weeks, and then her brother Coen[raad] and family for three. After a few months at work her leg acted up again. This time she went to the hospital for a time, but when they refused to keep her any longer her relatives faced another period of weeks in which they would need to provide care. Kuijt's sister reported: "She has to take cod-liver oil and lie still. We will have to see, because if it takes *too* long then she can't stay here because that is too much for me since I am not well either and I have to think about my own children."[55] Child care was also on the mind of her brother Coen, whose wife Nellie had just had a baby. The siblings considered sending Kuijt back to the Netherlands. There she had other relatives, further into their life course, older married women to whom families liked to turn in such circumstances. Furthermore Kuijt's relatives labeled her a "cripple"; her health frequently did not allow her to work, and the United States was a land for those who were physically able to work. She generally did not earn enough between bouts of illness to pay off her doctor bills, and hence she was a frequent burden financially. Despite the complaints, Kuijt's extended family continued to care for her, though after repeated illnesses they were less particular about what kind of work she took when she was well.[56] Loss of wages, inability to carry out farming or wage-earning tasks, money spent on doctors and medicine, all added up to one thing: sickness was expensive.

Pieternella Cevaal, a domestic servant from Middelburg, Zeeland, was less fortunate. When she fell ill in Indianapolis in 1914 her only close relative in America was her unmarried brother in Wisconsin. From the letters it appeared that neither she nor her brother considered her coming to live with him so he could oversee her recovery. The best she could hope for was special delivery return on her plea for assistance: "I am sick. I don't have anyone here that I know and I don't know what I should do. Would you be so good and send me money so that I can buy my food and medicine and pay the doctor."[57] Nearly a year later she sent the thank-you note for the money along with a report that she was well, had thought about his admonitions, and would try to pay him off soon.[58]

The examples above outlined the pattern of Dutch American home nursing for wage-earning adults. When there were relatives' or friends' families which included adult women, then the patients went there. In some cases an adult woman relative would come to the patient's home: "[Albertha's] sister stood by her faithfully during her last suffering. This was great favor for us."[59] Men did not consider taking care of sick women or children for very long, nor did women expect that. Under the gendered task divisions of Dutch immigrants, men's work consisted of wage-earning or running the farm, while married women's work included nursing sick relatives and friends. Unmarried women fell somewhere between these categories, either serving in the home in the same capacity as an unpaid domestic or replacement for a wife or in the labor market as wage-earners, with each requiring a different scenario in case of illness. If wage earners, they, like Anna Kuijt, needed to return to the workforce as soon as possible, as did unmarried men. If wives or unpaid housekeepers, the women could only anticipate rest and recuperation in the presence of others who took on the household tasks, and that meant women. Women relatives, under these circumstances, were indispensable, for others would rarely take on the housekeeping and child care along with nursing.

Much of the health care that Dutch immigrant women reported dealt with calling doctors and administering medicine, but there was also an emotional element to this home nursing. When Geertje Schuiling wrote that she could hardly write anything because her sick son kept yelling "mama," she illustrated a common phenomenon.[60] Children demanded attention when ill, more so than otherwise, and mothers generally provided it. They talked to the little ones, told them stories, sang to them, and reassured them, as well as taking care of physical needs. The later the time period, the more likely the women were to consider the emotional needs of the children, but in principle they assumed both young and old needed moral (what also might be termed psychological) support in times of illness. Thus Etje Houwerzijl faced a terrible decision as her husband lay on his deathbed at the same time her son Koos went to the hospital for an operation. She stayed with her husband, sending her other children to visit the son, "Jakob goes there every evening, but that is not right, [Koos] keeps asking for mama."[61]

Houwerzijl's description of her husband's last days illustrated several recurring patterns. Like many dying Dutch immigrants, he wanted to sing and to hear singing, specifically psalms. Since Dutch Calvinists sang psalms frequently in church, churchgoers generally knew many if not all of them by heart. Singing constituted one of the common pastimes in Dutch immigrant families. The religious content of the psalms (and for some also hymns) as well as the music contributed to a more pleasant atmosphere for the terminally ill. Etje Houwerzijl talked, sang, prayed, and otherwise did what was in her power to make her husband more comfortable in his illness. Her role was not that of a medical professional, nor a religious one, but of the one caregiver who stayed for weeks at her husband's bedside, providing the ongoing care that he needed.[62]

Another means of cheering the ill was through the visits of concerned friends and relatives. Visitors might bring things to eat, to ease the burden of cooking for the person involved in nursing. The visitor could also provide emotional support for both patient and informal caregiver. Here the advantages of church membership weighed heavily, since churches had officers whose duty it was to visit the ill. Members of the local church congregation passed on news of those suffering from serious illness, along with encouragement to visit and assist those persons and their families. What that meant was that church members expected the dominie, deacons, and other members to visit the seriously ill, at least the adults.[63] The Houwerzijls had repeated visits from the dominie and others from the congregation. Since the Houwerzijls had only one extended family member in the state, these visits took the place of much familial support.

Emotional care was also a way of taking much of the responsibility for health decisions away from the patient, yet not turning them completely over to a professional. The caregiver became a concerned intermediary, using her emotional link to the patient as the basis for demands on the more emotionally detached professional. The caregiver thus took on some of the burden of making the patient well, and specifically of supervising what kind of professional care he or she received. As health care moved into hospitals, women caregivers had a smaller role in supervision because they could not always attend their relatives. In the Houwerzijl case the mother felt guilty for not overseeing her son's operation, particularly when she realized the surgeon operated on the wrong leg.[64] The need for emotional support and for advocacy in the face of unrelated professionals continued, but for female caregivers it became more difficult to provide.

As Dutch American communities matured, their networks of care also expanded geographically, and the Dutch American press reflected this. *De Volksvriend*, for example, regularly carried reports in the 1910s from a variety of locations in

Iowa, Minnesota, Michigan, and Washington which often included who had been ill, with what, and if he or she was getting better or worse. Such reports could range from a nasty splinter under a fingernail to an operation for cancer. When the measles broke out in Lynden, Washington, people in Orange City, Iowa, would know about it. Along with these reports were news of visits to the invalids by family members and friends. Most Dutch American papers also played upon women's roles as caregivers through their ads for medicines, including patent medicines. In 1916, for example, *Pella's Weekblad* carried ads not only for Dr. Pieter's Zokoro (the most widely advertised medicine in Dutch American papers) but also for things like Dr. King's cure for consumption and Chamberlain's cure-all for colic, cholera, and diarrhea.[65] *De Huisvriend* in 1905 carried not only such American fare but also Dutch staples.[66] *De Wachter* carried a series of articles denouncing patent medicines in 1907, but for the most part Dutch American papers carried the ads without comment.[67] By the 1910s, in some papers the ads began picturing nurses in uniform as a symbol of trust, just as news reports included cases of trained nurses taking over the care of sick individuals. Classified ads included notices not only of doctors but also of specialists, from a surgeon to an eye, ear, nose, and throat doctor. While many of the readers of a paper like *Pella's Weekblad* must have been third- or fourth-generation residents of the United States, it and others also sought to attract readers in the newer Dutch American settlements. Thus newcomers had their views about American medical practice filtered somewhat through the more acculturated.

Depending on whether one looked to newspapers or letters, women were more or less sick than others. In scanning newspaper notices, women were more likely than men to appear as suffering from an injury or illness. Yet according to women's letters there was a double standard in how Dutch immigrants treated illness. Basically, women could not be ill enough to quit work. Only with "permission" in the form of a direct order from a doctor could they stay in bed for a short time. In most cases they simply worked through the illness or discomfort. R. Smit wrote about his wife, who had just died: "She felt very sick—She still wanted to fix meals for me from the beginning of the month but her illness that last day kept her away from the table. She wanted to keep on doing until she almost fell."[68] Likewise, Zwaantje Becksvoort wrote that she suffered and was worried about her continually swollen legs, "but we have to be satisfied with our lot."[69] Others echoed this sentiment that even if work made them ill, they had to continue. Geertje Schuiling, writing to her in-laws in Friesland, complained that after doing a big wash she "had a good deal of pain in my back by evening and now it has gone into my head" but still reported she was preparing the next meal.[70] These were part of a peasant tradition, by which people could complain of health problems, but to take to one's bed meant a truly debilitating illness.

Because women might not want to report being "lazy" to others who placed a cultural value on hard work, I tried to find confirmation for the pattern of not taking off time for illness. Looking back through the interviews yielded similar results. Further, the frequency with which women reported not going in for medical help when they needed it, whether suffering from possible appendicitis or cancer, made the likelihood greater that many Dutch American women, for a variety of reasons, continued to carry on life as normal when they were ill, at considerable physical cost to themselves.[71] "We were ailing a bit for a few weeks. We had a throat and chest ailment which hindered us from speaking. I did my work despite it but Arend had to stay in bed but is a little better now."[72] I encountered several such cases where both husband and wife were ill, and the husband stayed in bed to speed recovery while the wife continued to prepare food and take care of the children as well as her husband.

There was one other exception to this pattern. Women could stay in bed for a few days after childbirth. Exactly how long depended on their physical condition, but a week was common. The availability of help, usually from female relatives or neighbors, to keep the household going during this time also played a role. But culturally, people accepted that a woman needed that time to recover.

Medical Advice

Women's ideas about being ill and about home nursing came out of a gendered medical world where women treated minor illnesses at home without the assistance of professionals. The relationship of informal to formal care, however, was in flux during this period. Physicians, overwhelmingly male, assumed an increasing role in family health care, encroaching where midwives and home remedies were once standard. By the 1910s women occasionally reported taking relatives long distances to obtain better medical care. Further, they switched from operations at home to allowing their relatives to go to the hospital. They faced a changing medical landscape, where doctors took a larger role, nurses assumed some of the functions of the home caregiver, and hospitals became a place where everyone (not just the poor) went for medical treatment. These changes were underway on both sides of the Atlantic. Migration contributed to the shift in several ways.

Migration meant that women had to relearn medical terminology, make do without certain remedies and learn others, and, most importantly, get by without the medical advice of older women they knew in the Netherlands. Immigrant women could write and request information concerning health problems, but they had to find replacements for the persons in the Netherlands who might have helped make a diagnosis, suggest a treatment, or send for a professional.[73] If someone was ill, they could not wait for a letter to cross the Atlantic and for someone to answer. In this way, migration accelerated the shift toward having doctors handle more aspects of health care.

When an immigrant woman wrote she had called a doctor, it generally meant the illness was serious, probably threatening to life or limb. Either that or it prohibited someone from performing his or her given tasks. Three other factors played a role: time, location, and class. By the 1910s immigrants relied more heavily on professional medicine than in the 1880s. Further, those in or near urban areas could take advantage of doctors more easily, particularly specialists. And those without funds rarely would call on a doctor, while those with money to spare could afford this "luxury." Beyond this, the letters I read indicated a hierarchy of who received what kind of treatment, ranging from adult men to adult women and then over young adults to the elderly to young children, and lastly to infants. I do not want to imply that parents did not call doctors to care for ailing octogenarians or newborns—the issue here is to what lengths a family would go to cure an illness.

In their letters women (and men) prayed and hoped that the elderly would enjoy good health, but they expressed no surprise when their older relatives suffered from the effects of aging and disease, and letter writers frequently pointed out in such cases that everyone must die at some point. Likewise, though infant mortality rates went down in the late nineteenth century, families still could not be assured a new baby would survive the first few years, and they approached childhood illnesses with resignation. Basically, people expected the very young and very old to be ill at times, and hence handled some aspects of care themselves and believed doctors when they said there was not much to be done, rather than going for second and third opinions. Middle-aged adults, especially those with children, however, should not be seriously ill according to this ideal, and hence made the rounds to the best medical professionals the family could afford. This was especially true of persons suffering from unknown ailments for an extended period. In these cases immigrants also reported their astonishment with advances in medical knowledge and technology. "Hendrik is not doing well at all. He has already been to 3 doctors in Modesta, but they can't seem to find the problem. Now he has been in San Francisco for about 3 weeks to see a specialist, who checked him out thoroughly, and with a thing where they can look all the way inside you . . . and he had a black spot there."[74] The belief in medical wonders and a general skepticism about the training of any individual doctor led Dutch immigrants to go to increasing lengths to preserve health for adults, particularly by calling for second and third opinions and consulting specialists.

The possible loss of income or work capacity, in addition to the emotional loss, meant the death of an adult entailed higher stakes materially. As one writer stated, "It is difficult for the flesh because we can't do without him."[75] Other immigrants used the biblical metaphor—the "flesh" part of the phrase—to refer to the loss of children, but I encountered no writers who referred to deceased children with this sense of indispensability. The death of a child was different than the death of an adult. Zwaantje Becksvoort wrote quite matter-of-factly in 1902 that her three children had been ill with a hard case of the measles, and while two were now better, the third might not recover. "Willempje is not strong.

She has a continual fever and has suffered so much that she can't get over it."[76] Likewise, when Jantje Enserink van der Vliet lost a baby and nearly her life in childbirth in 1910, her sister-in-law reported: "Though it was a disappointment that the hope was gone to have a new little darling, still it would have been a hard blow if we had lost Jantje, so my lamentation was O Lord spare her life."[77]

Along with financial status and ideas about who should be ill, the family's skills in English helped determine whether they would consult a doctor. For newcomers and for those who never mastered English well, the prospect of going to a "Yankee" physician was unpleasant. If possible, they preferred to handle medical matters in their native tongue. The frustration of one woman who went to a pharmacy seeking quinine to treat a family member and coming home empty-handed because she could not communicate was not uncommon.[78] Likewise, with English skills came the ability to understand, and thus better to critique medical professionals. Anna Kuijt, whose ill health frequently put her in a doctor's care, wrote that she ignored a doctor's warning that she had to go to the hospital at once because of appendicitis. "I said I wanted to sleep on it first. . . . Doctors don't frighten me quite as much any more. They like to operate a great deal here."[79] Her ability to criticize stemmed from experience, particularly experience with American doctors.

Kuijt also had adjusted to the sense of hospitals as places where specialized medicine took place. When Wilhelmina Woudenberg became ill in 1912 a little over two years after arriving in the United States, her husband and children sought out various opinions, including a homeopathic doctor and several specialists. Finally their regular doctor convinced them that surgery was the only option for what was probably an advanced case of breast cancer. The doctor, however, then had to convince the family that the surgery could not take place at home, which another doctor had recommended and which the family wanted. The family's faith in modern medicine hardly rose when Woudenberg died on the operating table.[80] Though Willem Woudenberg was part of several of the discussions with doctors about his wife's declining health, it was two daughters who went with their mother to the hospital. "[T]hey were sufficiently conversant with the English language to take knowledge of the nursing procedures, etc."[81] The two factors of women traditionally nursing the ill and of the younger generation acting as the go-betweens for their elders intertwined. The Woudenbergs had relatives in the area who served as interpreters for the family in various other settings, but care for the ill remained the job of women in the nuclear family whenever possible.

Dutch doctors did not migrate often, but when they did they found a community willing and able to pay for their services in the United States. More common was the second- or later generation man who gained his medical training in the United States but continued to serve a Dutch American community. Some doctors made the trek to America to serve the Dutch immigrants short-term. The kind of reception they might expect appeared in a letter describing Albertha Muis Gortworst's demise.

When [Bertha] approached 50 she gradually began to languish and sometimes complained of pain. . . . on the farm this once became so severe that we thought that she wouldn't last long. . . . Since that time, Bertha always was ailing. We had the most capable doctors call on her and they said that they couldn't do anything. . . . [Bertha] read in *De Grondwet* that a certain doctor, who was a urologist, had come from the Netherlands and was in Grand Rapids. By urinalysis he could determine what was wrong with a patient. Thousands and thousands had been to him, Dr. Bysterveld, and he had performed wonders, though not for everybody. . . . So it went with Bertha [she died].[82]

The prevalence of charlatans offering wonder cures concurrently with medical "wonders" in the form of patent medicines and new technology made the decisions difficult. Language difficulties exacerbated the process immensely. For some individuals with difficult health problems, such as Lini Moerkerk de Vries's mother, the only option was to return to the Netherlands. "I don't trust these foreign American doctors. I am sure that if I go to Amsterdam, the doctors there can cure me of my deafness so that I can hear again."[83] The family made two extended trips to the Netherlands in order to have better professional medical care.

An article in *De Gereformeerde Amerikaan* in 1899 by H. van Hoogen presented yet another aspect of the question of whether to seek Dutch or American doctors. Van Hoogen claimed that medical help was readily available in the United States, especially in the cities, where there was one doctor per thousand inhabitants. He went on to argue that the United States had come to a level equal to Europe in terms of medical training: "in earlier times persons who had their medical training in the Netherlands or Germany were preferred over those who had studied at an American university. From this standpoint there has been a rapid advance. . . . In every field the medical knowledge on this side of the ocean is up to date."[84] Van Hoogen was perhaps a bit optimistic. While state licensing boards were in place by 1894 in all areas where the Dutch settled in any numbers, there was still a great deal of variety in medical education.[85] In the case of serious illness, what was at stake made trust in the unfamiliar hard.

Women's knowledge of formal medicine was generally limited, more so due to migration. When they wrote about disease they used the terms they knew: dysentery, measles, lung or kidney disease. Frequently they had to explain treatments for which they did not know the terms in Dutch, whether X rays or specific operations. In terms of medicines, most women knew of cod-liver oil, which was to some nineteenth-century households what aspirin is to an early twenty-first-century one. Folk medicine made the transatlantic passage at only a very limited level, for it was already in sharp decline in the Netherlands. Some did maintain a household pharmacopeia of herbal remedies and used these effectively. One woman described the herbs used by her great-grandmother, among them several imported from Europe, including purple loosestrife, for blond hair dye or to treat diarrhea and dysentery, and "Bouncing Bet" or soapwort as soap or bleach, and also for rashes.[86] Somewhat unconventional treatments, particularly administering wine or whiskey for anything from a head-ache to seasickness, did appear in letters and interviews. Only a few women, particularly the educated, wrote their relatives about specifically which medicines doctors put in the little bottles and hypodermics their patients received, though nearly all informal caregivers could report what each dosage cost and whether it helped.

Comments and complaints about the cost of doctors' visits and medicines often appeared in letters which discussed a recent bout with illness. In cases such as that of Arendje Bergman Akkerman, the comments remained on a general level: "dear sis, with the doctor things are a little different than planned. Otherwise I had hoped to send a little present with this. May it be better next time."[87] Frequently, however, immigrants provided the exact costs. Nellie and Coen Kuijt's daughter underwent surgery at home for a throat infection. The Kuijts wrote: "We expect the doctor's bill any day. It will probably be around 50 dollars. Doctors get 50 cents a visit."[88] Such an expense could easily break the family budget.

Dutch immigrants, given the opportunity, often turned to doctors rather than midwives for assistance in childbirth. For some, especially among the farm laborers in the Netherlands, midwifery remained the standard, whether by a professional midwife or at the hands of friends and relatives. For others, the reliance on doctors may have already taken place to some extent in the Netherlands.[89] When Lena Boer Bardolf, an immigrant to Holland, Michigan, discussed medical care on one of the islands in the Dutch province of Zeeland, for example, she mentioned that her mother assisted when the next-door neighbor gave birth to twins: "Yes, they all did that. They helped each other. . . . If one delivered a baby, then the neighbor woman would help and if the neighbor woman had a baby then the first [would help] the other, see . . . they were so poor, they could not afford a doctor."[90] Even if the family was not poor, family members would arrive to assist after a birth. A woman in Kolijnsplaat, Zeeland, reported to her relatives who lived in Kalamazoo, Michigan: "Mother went on vacation with Aunt Mietje and Aunt Vina and Aunt Pietje to see Aunt Neeltje, who delivered a girl."[91] If they did not serve as midwives, such relatives could provide necessary home nursing care. They might also serve other functions. The celebrations surrounding childbirth represented a communal support network of individuals who dropped by with food and advice. Aside from the emotional support of having people around, the woman could nap and know someone would always be there to help. This was one of the practices that was difficult to replicate in the same form in the United States. In the Netherlands midwifery continued throughout this period, and became a licensed specialty, though doctors also increasingly attended births.[92] In addition a specialized group of nurses arose to handle postnatal care (*kraamvrouwen*). These women spent days if not weeks in the home. As in the United States, women's rights advocates there called for this kind of assistance for mothers as a state entitlement.[93]

Informal midwifery made the transatlantic passage to some extent. Recall the earlier examples of Jantje Modderman Negen, who assisted her daughter-in-law, and Elizabeth Menkens Schreurs, who traded birth assistance with her neighbor. They appear to have practiced only among family or friends. At a somewhat more professional level was Maartje Lautenbach Zondervan, who turned to midwifery along with taking in washing and boarders after her husband deserted her in 1907.[94] She was probably not the only midwife in the Paterson, New Jersey, area. Most of the Dutch American men interviewed in the area by the WPA in the 1930s recalled that at the turn of the century midwives attended the birth of their children.[95] Other sources indicated Dutch midwives continued to practice in various parts of the country, and that the pattern of neighbors assisting, with or without a midwife or doctor present, was common.[96] In the United States more generally physicians attended only about one-half of home births at the turn of the century.[97] Yet over time, immigrants began to question the qualifications of midwives compared to doctors.[98] Dutch Protestant immigrant women began to have sufficient funds to pay for medical assistance in childbirth, either a professional midwife or doctor, at the same time that doctors began to offer several professional services: forceps, morphine, antiseptic techniques.[99] Dr. Bertha van Hoosen, a third-generation Dutch American, contributed to this trend.[100]

As one of the leading advocates of twilight sleep (anesthetized delivery using scopolamine) in the United States, Van Hoosen regularly performed deliveries using this technique at Mary Thompson Hospital in Chicago, beginning in 1914. Like so many medical developments, twilight sleep had originated in Germany, and women such as those at the Chicago Women's Club found it disconcerting that American doctors did not adopt it more quickly. The controversy surrounding the method in 1915 did not deter Van Hoosen from pursuing what she considered the best in obstetrical care, not to mention a major advance in women's rights. The method required that birth take place in the hospital, where the medication could be administered and monitored.[101] The cost of a hospital birth as compared to a home birth meant that it remained primarily a method for the affluent, and doctors assumed those used to manual labor could handle the pain. Midwives had no part in twilight sleep, though Van Hoosen herself teamed up with a (Swedish American) midwife for a ten-year practice in suburban Chicago.[102] Their situation, where the midwife checked in with the family for weeks before and after the birth, while the doctor was present only at the delivery itself, was closer to the European counterpart of the time.

Various aspects of these debates had a direct impact on immigrant women. Migration combined with the shift from midwives to doctors in the United States meant that there were fewer women present during parturition who knew something about childbirth and could negotiate between the doctor and the patient, acting as advocates for the woman giving birth. When Fie Woldring wrote to her sister-in-law Anje that once Anje had her obstetrics certificate she should emigrate, Woldring did so partly out of personal interest. She wanted the best of both worlds: a family member and friend who would be an emotional support and a professionally trained midwife.[103] Not many women could find this combination, so they turned to others. In *Brought to Bed,* Judith Waltzer Leavitt argued that it was loss of community which largely eliminated midwifery in the United States. For Dutch immigrant women, that loss was seen in the demographics of migration.

Dirk Nieland chronicled the shift in a story written in Yankee Dutch in the 1920s. While fictional, his story accurately portrayed the themes of change in childbirth. The story centers on the main character's daughter, Loesie (Lucy). She went to the hospital to have her child, staying for a couple of weeks. The narrator explained: "When I was young it was a lot easier. Mrs. Hipstra [the midwife] was there for all of us kids, and she fixed up the business really nice, without doctor or nurse or fashion. And she did the washing and cooking as well."[104] When Loesie was afraid the child had been switched at the hospital, the family called in Mrs. Hipstra, who assured her that the child was her spitting image, at which point the daughter was satisfied and the narrator again showed his appreciation for a person who knew her trade. What was perhaps more appalling to the narrator was the lack of household help which a hospital birth entailed. He and his wife arrived at the newborn's home to find the family fully unprepared for a visit, with the husband washing diapers. "But she [the narrator's wife] could not say much besides it was a shame that a man still had to do housework after his job."[105]

In lieu of the Dutch midwife, and later the postnatal nurse, who generally remained in the home for several days and attended to household tasks as well as nursing, Dutch immigrants relied on family or friends, or if they were unavailable, on hired help for this recovery period. I ran across several incidences of immigrants paying for household help where there were no adult women in the extended family in the area. In 1900 G. H. Holmer, a Dutch immigrant in Michigan, reported his daughter earned two and a half dollars in two weeks by doing housework for a friend of the family, a new mother, or as he put it, someone "who has something in the cradle."[106] Hannah Bruins vander Velde reported that after her mother gave birth in July of 1883 they brought in a young woman to help for several months.[107]

The turn of the century was the period when both Dutch and American society moved toward increased professional health care. Migration to the United States speeded the process for the Dutch for several reasons. First, they lost a significant segment of the extended family who might have been part of this network. Second, the distances between relatives made casual visiting to provide home care impossible or at least impractical in some cases. Third, the decision to migrate already entailed an acceptance that the migrant would not participate in certain caring tasks for the family, setting a precedent for placing nuclear family or individual needs above those of the family more generally.

What might be advantageous for the family economically rarely was as positive in terms of care networks, and much of the reluctance of women to migrate, narrated in various immigrant stories, highlighted exactly these issues. If home nursing and medical networking with family constituted an important task for women, migration often meant abandoning or slighting that task. Correspondence could still bridge a part of that gap, but only a tiny part.

Growing Old in a Different World

If health provided a consistent topic of interest for most Dutch immigrant women, aging generally stood as an important component in setting parameters of what they would report. Or to put it another way, life course helped set the topics in immigrant letters. Younger women, particularly unmarried ones, generally suffered less from disease than older women and were less likely to be charged with the care of children. Theirs was a world of the new, whereas the Netherlands was the "old world."

Herbert Brinks, historian and curator of a major Dutch American archival collection, has proposed a simple yet profound idea, namely, that the sense of the "new world" had a basis in demography. Because the emigrants tended to be younger than the general population, and since their letters often went to their parents' generation or to their siblings and rarely continued after that generation died out, the sense Dutch Americans got of the Netherlands was of a land where people were old, frequently ill, and dying. In comparing one hundred collections where correspondence from both sides of the Atlantic was present, Brinks noted that 56 percent of the mail coming from the Netherlands included news of at least one death, compared to only 19 percent of the American letters. Letters that reported multiple deaths were even more skewed—25 percent of the Dutch letters reported two or more deaths, compared to 2 percent of the stateside mail.[108] Moreover, Brinks stated, "the [Dutch] letters reporting death and disease were not freighted heavily with gloom. Instead, death, like the weather, seemed to constitute the inevitable stuff of daily life."[109] Another factor playing into the youthful image of American life was the fact that nineteenth-century settlement in the United States coincided with a decline in infant mortality rates. While a similar process took place on both sides of the Atlantic, because the percentage of young adults and children on the United States side was relatively higher, the impression should have come through more clearly that children generally survived. Further, the sickly in the Netherlands had less chance of migrating.

In general my sources replicated Brinks's findings, but with a somewhat less skewed picture. Men were more likely the correspondents in his sample, whereas I looked at women, and there were several gendered factors in why they might have slightly different outlooks. One was language, since women were more likely to lack English-language skills as they aged and hence had greater incentive to continue the correspondence over time. Many of the Dutch American women's letters I consulted dealt with aging. Several letter collections involved women who were married and outlived their husbands by many years. Their letters in old age recounted impending death, the death of loved ones, and remorse concerning those who had died. Also, because women dealt with nursing the ill more directly, their letters could and often did describe in painful detail the suffering of their spouses and siblings, as well as of their children. If anything, these women suffered from disillusionment concerning the collective ideology Brinks described. They grew old, lost the loved ones of their generation, and often spent years thinking about how they had to die in a land they sometimes still considered foreign. Men generally could die secure in their achievements as breadwinners, with all the positive connotations of success along the lines of the American dream which that entailed. Women, less tied to the financial rewards and more likely to interpret migration in terms of familial roles, sometimes had time to contemplate their lives in their older years. America was still the new world, but women, especially in old age, did not always find comfort in the "new."

What kind of guilt did it engender for women who had left their elderly parents behind in the Netherlands when they tried to convince their own children to care for them? It was an almost unanimous wish of adult women emigrants that their parents would have family to care for them. Klaaske Noorda Heller, who lived in Oak Harbor, Washington, frequently expressed her thanks to her sister who remained in the Netherlands for housing and caring for their mother. She also stressed these familial roles in her letters to her mother: "to have comfort and companionship from one another in these few days that one has here on earth, you have already found out much about that in the last few years . . . the Lord grant you still more restful days, mummy, in your old age and may you eat your bread with pleasure."[110] One of the tragedies of migration for immigrant women was that they could not provide this service to their elders.

In the oral tradition of one Wisconsin family, the decision to migrate was specifically one between duties to nuclear family and to extended family. The daughter retold the poignant story of her mother, whose husband decided to leave for the United States. The father knew it would be a difficult decision for his wife to make, but posed it in terms of "I am going to America . . . will you come along?"[111] The wife agreed, much to the chagrin of her parents. Among their reasons for opposition to the move was the fact that she was the only daughter and hence a prime candidate to care for them in old age. On the docks the grandfather held his grandson in his arms: "my father walked up to him and took that child and went onto the boat."[112]

In other cases the parents either migrated with adult children or migrated after the children were settled. The latter was often the wish but less often the reality of immigrant letters. Rather, most recognized that the journey itself was strenuous and dangerous, and migrating to a different country, even to an ethnic enclave in a different country, required a mental flexibility which the elderly did not necessarily possess. The last years could be bountiful in number, as in the case of one woman from Zeeland. Lena Boer Bardolf's mother moved in with her daughter when she was eighty-two and remained until her death, fifteen years later.[113] Boer Bardolf spoke with fond remembrance on those years when the two would chat in Dutch dialect. One of the positive aspects of life in the United States was that by the time many immigrants' parents reached "old" age, the younger generation could assist them financially, whether the parents lived in the United States or the Netherlands.

There were many parts of the "new" world ideology about economic promise and freedom which women shared. Older immigrant women, however, sometimes pined for a romanticized Netherlands of their childhood. Dina Maria Oggel represented the extreme. Her letters to her brother in Axel elaborated on everything she missed. After receiving a local paper she wrote: "I cannot tell you how happy I was to see the [picture in *De Axelsche Courant*]. There by the church where our house stands. Yes I sat there and looked at it until I couldn't look any more. The tears came into my eyes [and] I remembered everything. The trees by Piet Meertens's under which we always used to play, and [paragraph of reminiscences] . . . Above all it is and remains a dear place. Our cradle stood there once, and the graves of our cherished parents are there."[114] The last line plays upon a Dutch song which stated, here my cradle stood, here I will find my grave. Other immigrants picked up that line as well. Oggel frequently wrote about how old and gray she had become, how much she missed Axel, and about the one woman with whom she could talk about this—her cleaning woman. "Things are good for her here in America she says, but it is nicer in Holland."[115] For Oggel, who did not have as close contact to her Dutch American relatives as some other immigrants did, even living in a hub of Dutch American life was insufficient. The "new" of America lacked exactly the "old" she treasured. She wrote several letters indicating how she looked forward to death and to a heaven where there would be "no more parting" and where she could meet her "dear relations and friends who have left for there already."[116]

If Oggel was an exception in terms of class (she was from a bourgeois background) and of emotion, others shared her concern with growing old and, particularly as they grew older, with maintaining family ties to the Netherlands. Hendriene Mensink Bos wrote her family and friends: "I am old and the time goes on how long I know not or if we are ready for eternity. . . . Now you must write about your children to me—if any of them are married and who is still at home."[117] This kind of information was exactly what Dutch Americans needed in order to balance their views of the Netherlands.

What exactly did these immigrant women mean when they stated they were "old"? One woman, from Sibley, Iowa, wrote to her uncle in a letter on aging, that her hair was just as gray as the lock of her grandmother's hair which she had as a memento.[118] Gray hair and grandchildren might qualify them, though age generally operated as a factor. "All is well at sister Trijntje's but she is beginning to get old. She turned 69 this summer."[119] Physical impairments related to age, whether loss of hearing or of mental capacity, also fell under the rubric of "getting old." Yet many immigrants also viewed old age as a time when they could quit working and enjoy their grandchildren. In Dutch American circles, it was common practice for the parents to turn over the farm or business to the children before death, with some stipulations as to providing for the parents. The effect was not only to ensure continuity of the family (and ethnic group) but also to create a period of retirement. It was a pattern common for German immigrants as well, and it resulted in greater continuity for groups which practiced it than the "Yankee" standard of inheritance at death.[120]

Financial circumstances as much as physical ability determined whether someone could retire. One woman reported that her husband and son worked together on the farm: "but I think Uncle, [my husband] will not farm much longer, as [he] wants very much to take a rest. He cannot do much more either. Perhaps we will go to California as well and rent our farm."[121] The rest of her letter indicated that their children, three of whom lived in California, while not exactly prosperous, all managed quite well financially. Implicit in this report was the sense that one or more of the children could afford to care for the writer and her husband, that she was in regular contact and on good terms with these children, and that they could look forward to a familial care setting for their last years. Exactly how they would handle inheritances, if any, was unclear.

Inheritance disputes were a common problem in immigrant letters, and one which transatlantic correspondence had trouble bridging. The Smit family of Oosterwijtwerd, Groningen, had contacts with several individuals in the United States related to inheritance matters. Cornelia wrote to her uncle in 1888 pleading that he release her share of her father's inheritance because she was getting married and wanted to build a house. Likewise, L. Timmer wrote asking for his new wife Geeske's share of another inheritance so they could set up a tailor shop. In each of these cases the individuals not only had to ask but had to ground their requests in concrete circumstances, hoping that the executor would find the proposed expenditures worthy. Legally the women only had to prove they were married, but to satisfy the family they felt they had to prove they were justified.[122] Even if everyone was on good terms, problems could arise in dealing with an inheritance. In one case a woman wrote her uncle in 1907 that she had sent a notarized proxy for him to handle her parents' inheritance question four years ago, and according to her reckoning several letters must have gone amiss in the meantime. "Two months ago I sent you a letter, perhaps that did not come into your hands either since we have not had any answer back. I hope that you don't have trouble . . . be so good and write us about that, the distance is so far."[123]

The distance was very far by the standards of the day, and that made difficulties concerning inheritances more problematic. Klaaske Noorda Heller wrote her family that she had unknowingly engendered the ire of a relative by asking for a particular picture from an estate. The relative's negative reply stung Noorda Heller, who countered: "It made me very unhappy that I had asked about [the picture] because I really thought that she did not care about it."[124] With months passing between the exchange of letters, little disputes like this could escalate. In the Netherlands, family members normally met at the funeral and discussed sometime thereafter how to divide remaining items. These face-to-face confrontations could be fraught with tension, but the danger of misunderstandings was less.

For many Dutch immigrants, just as in the Netherlands, old age meant relying on children as one's financial assets vanished. Not all were successful, either because their own finances were inadequate or because they had no children or none who could make such contributions. Providing for them in an appropriate manner became part of the social reproduction of care for the aged. By the 1880s the population in some Dutch American communities was aging, and an increasing number of persons needed a place to live out their last years. Many descriptions of Progressive Era reforms noted the importance of women in organizing and maintaining various institutions, even the creation of a women's political culture.[125] When I went looking for it in Dutch American circles, I found that the patterns they describe applied to a limited degree, if at all. The differences were glaringly clear in the case of the Holland Home (for the aged) in Grand Rapids, Michigan. There, social reproduction of care for the elderly blended gender ideals in a typically Dutch American way.

Holland Home

In 1892 a group of Dutch American men and women from around Grand Rapids, Michigan, drew up the constitution and bylaws for the Holland Union Benevolent Association, a legal step necessary before founding a home for the elderly. The origins of what from the beginning was called the Holland Home were not particularly unusual in light of similar activities in care for the elderly in this period. Yet the social reproduction of gender roles and ideas about culture based on ethnicity imbued various aspects of the Holland Home with a distinctly Dutch American flavor, and helps explain its development in subsequent years. This also highlighted an alternative pattern in the creation of nonprofit homes for the elderly. The Holland Home in Grand Rapids became a model for other Holland Homes among Dutch Americans.[126] The Dutch brought with them ideas about elder care which sometimes blended and at other times conflicted with developing American patterns.

When the Holland Home came into being, its founders based aspects of its organization on several precedents. One came from the Netherlands, where community homes for the poor and aged were commonplace by the mid-1800s.[127] Yet the trustees also wanted a specific religious tie, so they used as their model Veldwijk, the Christian home for the mentally ill which was the brainchild of Henricus Beuker (father of Jacoba Beuker Robbert). The idea was for the two primary Dutch American denominations, the Reformed Church and the Christian Reformed Church, to cooperate in establishing an institution which advanced the basic theology shared by these two groups and yet was not tied to one denomination, and one which would get state support.

On the American side, the precedent was even more specific. The constitution and bylaws of the Dutch group were an almost verbatim copy of those of the Union Benevolent Association (UBA) of Grand Rapids. The UBA began in 1847 when a group of prominent women met to discuss the needs of sick and needy persons in Grand Rapids. The group worked through women's organizations in various churches, dividing the town into districts and assigning two visitors for each. When the state opened a school for needy children shortly after the Civil War, the women of the UBA focused their efforts on a home for the "aged, infirm, and helpless."[128] In 1873 they filed a charter as the Union Benevolent Association. This then was the local predecessor of the Dutch American group.

Several aspects of the UBA highlighted gender ideals for the group. The Anglo American UBA originally consisted only of women. By 1873, when they drew up the bylaws for the new home which would serve both the sick and aged, they stipulated, "The number of Trustees of the corporation shall be ten, one-half of whom shall be men and one-half shall be women."[129] Another section noted that the head of the home would be the matron, "standing in the same relation to each member of the household as the mother or mistress of a private family."[130] In tasks that prefigure social work casework, women continued for some time to handle visitations and recommendations of persons to enter the home.

By all accounts the driving force behind the Holland Home was Reverend Adriaan Kriekard. Few women took part in the formal organization in 1892. Of the twenty-eight original subscribers, only four were women, and as far as I was able to discern, all were married or at least related to men who were also part of that twenty-eight.[131] That the bylaws called for a board of trustees of twelve, one-third of whom were to be women, was very unusual among Dutch Americans. In order to meet that number, one woman had to be summoned from her home to sign the document. Compared to the Union Benevolent Society, where women had organized the association and then granted men one-half the seats, the Dutch American practice was considerably more conservative. Given the role of Dutch American women in reform generally, however, this was a major step. As the editor of *De Standaard,* a local Dutch-language newspaper, wrote of the inclusion of women on the board: "That testifies to real progress among our Dutch people and the framers of the constitution have earned a compliment."[132]

What made the inclusion of women on the board even more astounding was the type of work the board undertook in coming years. It is not surprising that the board operated at least part of the time like a church consistory. The president and vice president were ministers, and several (if not all) of the male board members were on the consistories of their various churches. In the surviving board minutes from the period 1896 onward, the group debated in their monthly and then bimonthly meetings whether individuals should be allowed into the home, partly based on their financial situation but also on their moral character.[133] Frequently the board took up disciplinary measures concerning "inmates" in the home. In disciplinary matters the board mimicked consistory policies most closely.[134] Rarely did the board have to go beyond a reprimand. But what broke gender traditions among the Dutch Americans was the fact that women were present at these discussions of disciplinary measures. Further, Emma Heyboer, the woman who served the longest in the most positions on the board in these early years, served on the committee of inquiry, which did the background research on people seeking admission.

Still, in the early years women's functions on the board generally were limited to areas considered "women's" concerns. All board members served on at least one committee related to the home. Women made up the management committee for the most part, which oversaw conditions in the home and handled complaints about or from staff.[135] This committee could employ cleaning personnel after the full board approved of the financing for this, and they handled which resident went into which room with which roommate, clothing distribution, and funeral arrangements for those without relatives nearby. It reported on deaths, and sometimes on activities in the home, and its members relieved the house "parents" when they went on vacation. For several years this committee was made up exclusively of women. A related area, another where women actively took part, was the committee on necessities, which handled issues of supplies and furnishings. Women were not officers for the board in the first thirty years. Board women also served as liaisons with women's groups in various churches. This they coordinated through the efforts of the Ladies Home Circle, which I will discuss later. In any case the "Lady trustees" as the minutes referred to them by the 1910s, remained limited in the kinds of functions they performed.

Because in nearly all cases the board minutes did not elaborate on who said what or who got involved in issues of debate, I could not discern how active women trustees were in meetings. The chairs gave their committee reports, so at least one woman had to speak at nearly every meeting. All meetings opened and closed with prayer, and women trustees never led these devotions. Neither, however, did most male trustees get the chance. Prayers for the most part in the first twenty years were left to one of the ministers or another religious leader, first Rev. Kriekard, and then his successor Rev. Kolyn or Professor Broene.

The women on the board were not the only ones active with the home. A women's auxiliary started shortly after the home opened "to make life easier for the inmates of the Home."[136] The minutes for the auxiliary have disappeared up to the 1930s, and the first mention of the auxiliary in existing board minutes appears in May 1897, when the board thanked the "Ladies' Home Circle" for their good services. Thereafter the board thanked the group periodically, though rarely more than once in a year. Like the name Holland Home itself, from the outset the "Ladies' Home Circle" sported an English name, despite use of Dutch in its meetings and minutes up through the 1930s. Basically, the auxiliary united representatives from various women's circles at the Dutch American churches, particularly in Grand Rapids.[137] Its main functions were to promote fundraising among these women's groups and to encourage women to donate goods and time to the home. Lists of contributors, published in the *Holland Home News* (also in Dutch, despite the name) as well as recorded in trustees' minutes, indicated that various women's groups contributed to the home periodically.[138] They held "annual" rummage sales, though the existing records do not confirm if they actually were annual. The Ladies' Home Circle took over paying the nurse in 1903, a commitment of fifteen dollars a month. In any case, they were financial contributors to the home on a regular basis by the turn of the century. They even gave "pocket money" to residents who otherwise had none.

When the home opened its major new facility in 1912, the Ladies' Home Circle provided the furniture, household supplies, curtains, bedding, and other supplies either directly or through financial gifts which bought most of the furnishings.[139] The group continued to be a major support for furnishings and for volunteers. The circle also served to bring together the women of various congregations periodically. The December 1917 edition of the *Holland Home News* reported on a recent meeting of the circle at which seventeen churches had representatives. Each brought a donation, as did a few individuals. In addition the *News* reported how various women had donated a large amount of food to make Thanksgiving a feast for home members.[140]

The contributions specifically by women's groups, while welcome, were not solicited as assiduously as one might expect. By 1899 the board had hired a fundraiser working on salary plus commission. How often they had such people on staff was unclear, but frequently there was a man out visiting the various denominational strongholds around the country and sending back funds.[141] One attempt by a woman who had been active with the home to use her contacts with "hundreds of women" around the country to raise funds for a new building, much along the lines of what took place with children's homes and hospitals, met a quick refusal from the board.[142] Rather, a month later, they hired a local (male) solicitor to do the same—but not targeting women's groups. They later hired other men for similar purposes. So while the Ladies' Home Circle could work to organize women in Grand Rapids churches to assist with the home, men, not women, were the main target for philanthropic fund-raising as far as the board and the solicitors were concerned.

By the 1920s the role of the Ladies' Home Circle was somewhat ambiguous. In particular, the board sought to make it an official auxiliary, which would mean loss of some autonomy.[143] Up through 1922, the circle remained officially outside the home's formal organization. Its gifts, while numerous, remained gifts which the group donated from time to time, including the salaries which they paid some years. The trimonthly meetings contrasted with the board's biweekly (and frequently more often) gatherings.

In addition to board trustees, circle members, and a young women's willing workers (the junior version of the circle), a fourth group of women involved with the Holland Home were the staff. Of these, I could uncover the most information on the matron and later the nurse, though records note cleaning women who stayed for varying periods of time. For cleaning women, the primary characteristic which the board specified was "as cheap as possible." Like many "homes," this one sought a familial atmosphere. But while the "Yankee" counterpart called only for a matron to serve as the house "mother," the Holland Home constitution called for a matron and a superintendent, to act as "parents." The board even referred to the matron and the superintendent as "mother" and "father" in many early writings. To fill these roles the board specifically hired couples without young children.

Though the home did not accept persons with major physical problems requiring special care, the board soon recognized the need for medical assistance on a more than sporadic basis. Local doctors (all male) donated their services, but the board knew from a early date that it would be advantageous to hire a nurse. It debated the issue for several years, primarily because of the expense involved. Finally, in 1907 "Miss Kriens" joined the staff. She not only improved medical care and record-keeping but soon took over the role of mother (and superintendent) as well. Kriens particularly impressed the board when she turned down a raise of five dollars a month (one-third of her salary at the time), indicating she was involved in "the service of the Lord."[144] Her Christian atti-

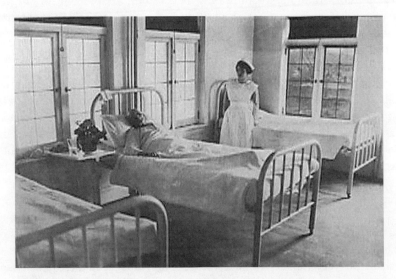

The Holland Home hospital ward, which recruited nurses from the Netherlands, around 1920. From the *Holland Union Benevolent Association: A Home for Aged People,* Grand Rapids, 1922.

tude conflicted with that of the home "parents" and helped create support for her on the board, which dismissed the matron and the superintendent and promoted Kriens to "director" of the home. She remained in this position for several years. Needless to say, this saved a substantial amount of money, but it also indicated a willingness by the board to allow a woman to serve as the head within the home, at least temporarily. By the time the home moved to its new quarters in 1912 she was joined by a male superintendent. The board listened to her request for another nurse—one from the Netherlands—and by 1919 the home had three women nurses. They were paid at the same rate as the janitor.[145] Through these early years, the home was shifting between the ideal of "parental" supervision and one of expert care. The Dutch pattern was to combine the two, finding persons who would act paternally or maternally and yet also had the training to fulfill the more demanding tasks.

The other group of women prominent in the history of the home were "inmates." In the early years men were the majority of the home residents. Financial policy was one factor in this imbalance. While the Dutch Americans tried to accommodate some less fortunate individuals, most of those accepted into their home from an early date paid a significant admission fee and/or agreed to pay a regular upkeep fee (or—frequently—had someone pay for them).[146] Once someone was accepted it was generally for the remainder of that person's life. The contracts stipulated this as well. In practice some people moved out (and on rare occasions back in) as family circumstances changed.

In 1901 the trustees of the home published a notice aimed at the Dutch congregations of Grand Rapids, indicating they would take someone for one dollar a week. The congregations, in addition, had to agree to hold special collections twice a year for that individual. In practice, however, the minutes from around this time indicated that many people had contracts stipulating $2.50 per week.[147] This combined with competition for space, which was present from the outset, and led to the building of a major new facility in 1912 and its expansion again in 1917.[148] Within the first decade, it was clear that many of the residents of the home were not exactly poor. Perhaps they would have eventually faced that prospect, but when they entered the home, many paid a substantial sum. Whether they had to sell all their belongings, as was the case in the Netherlands, was unclear. In any case, the home preferred taking individuals with some means at the outset. Because women generally had fewer financial resources, this meant women were less likely to be able to afford the home on their own.

Those who entered the Holland Home faced strict policies, including ones against strong drink, later one against smoking, and various restrictions on where one could go and when. These replicated those in the homes for the elderly in the Netherlands. The board heard complaints on all these policies and others more often than they appreciated. Legally, they could always dismiss a resident, and yet they rarely did even in extreme cases. One exception was a man who complained often and publicly about the food at the home. He was transferred to the county poorhouse.[149] Women and men residents faced a similar move into dependency when they entered the home. They had to follow the rules as set by the home and the requests of the "parents" or face discipline.

In all, the case study showed how a group of Dutch Americans managed to combine aspects of two cultural traditions, the Dutch idea of religiously based care with public support and the American one of female philanthropy. At the Holland Home, women helped launch the home, but it was primarily the work of male religious leaders. Women were members of the board of trustees from the outset, and they continued to provide many of the volunteers, all the nursing staff, and a significant proportion of both group and individual financial supporters through the home's early years. Men, nonetheless, determined many of the key policies, including the degree to which women could be involved in the home activities. Men kept control of the administration, avoiding the feminizing of philanthropy which was notable in Anglo American organizations of the time period. Patterns of men's and women's participation related to larger ethnic and religious ideals. By limiting women's options, men in the group not only retained their own power, they also reinforced a particular form of patriarchal relations. By creating a broad spectrum of institutions in which people could live "in, but not of the world," or more specifically with few important contacts outside the ethno-religious circle, the Dutch Protestants managed to limit gender role shifts. In the process they created what by the late 1900s was the largest nonprofit provider of care for the elderly in Michigan. This was not a pattern the Dutch had to follow—they could have gone to the American institutions and found a reasonable reception. They chose separate and religiously related facilities. In this they mirrored other ethnic groups, some who chose to support their own and others who had no options.[150] Unlike German American women, who had a stronger premigration history of women's organizations, and who used this in organizing philanthropy, Dutch American women for the most part had to develop their organizational skills in the United States.[151] When Jacoba Beuker Robbert helped found Pine Rest Christian Home (for the mentally impaired), she was following in an already established Dutch American tradition of social reproduction in terms of philanthropy.

Dealing with Death

The provision of death benefits followed a similar path. The lack of standard state allowances to cover death benefits for the poor led many to join burial funds through their churches. The financial realm of death fell largely to men. Formal intervention by spiritual advisors was also the realm of men, as ministers and other church-related individuals offered a variety of assistance. By the end of the period at least some Dutch immigrants were turning to funeral directors to manage arrangements for the deceased.[152] But even before that they were often used to a male undertaker handling care for the body, a replication of the pattern of a village undertaker in the Netherlands. In Dutch American communities it was one of the businesses which developed. The *Holland Home News* regularly carried ads for two Dutch American undertakers in the Grand Rapids, Michigan, area in the 1910s, as did other Dutch American papers. One oral history described a Dutch undertaker who set up shop and had a thriving business in Paterson, New Jersey, even before 1880.[153] Thus in older Dutch American community settings there was a good chance that families would have access to a Dutch-speaking undertaker who was also familiar with funeral patterns in the Netherlands. Women, thus, had limited roles in the formal realm of death arrangements and care, primarily as consumers. On the informal level, however, they were part of the grieving circle. In the face of death, people wanted extended family members around them. After migration, correspondence had to suffice for many.

Obituary letters, sometimes clearly identified by their black borders, may have been more common from the Netherlands to the United States because of the demographics of the population, but they were similar in both directions. Nelly van der Maas provided a typical example in her 1898 letter from Wissekerke to Kalamazoo: "With this [letter] we have to fulfill our sad duty [to inform you] that our dearly beloved son and brother Aart has died at the young age of 19."[154] The letter went on to describe Aart's final months, making particular note of his going to the doctor, his symptoms, and his mood. Like most writers, Van der Maas mentioned both family support and religious belief as the ways she was coping with the loss. The same was true on the American side of the Atlantic. The difference was that while most Dutch immigrants could still rely upon their religious background for assistance, not all had extended family connections in America. Further, obituary letters of those involved in migration tended to stress the theme of meeting the departed once again in the afterlife.

Distance and time widened the gulf between family members who were at odds with one another or who had never been particularly close. In such cases Dutch Americans had to hope their relatives would be conscientious enough to send important information about loved ones. Maaike Huigen, after years of writing how she hoped to have her father join her in Iowa, learned rather abruptly of his death. Like many Dutch immigrants, she would occasionally receive a local newspaper from the Netherlands as it made its rounds from hand to hand among migrants from that community: "You wrote that Uncle Cornelus wrote us that father was dead. No he never did that. I never got any report from anyone, I read it in *De Biltse Courant,* which Klaas van der Mei sends me. What do you think of that?"[155] Huigen noted that she sent the obituary along with a note to further family members in the United States. Klaaske Noorda Heller reported a similar case concerning her Aunt Kattarina's death: "E. K. Nienhuis read it in the paper and told me that news from afar . . . here in America the families are not connected to one another I think."[156] Since close family members generally went into official mourning for a year, the lack of information was particularly troubling.

Noorda Heller's observation about distances in the United States echoed in the letters of others. Not only distances between the Netherlands and the United States but also those between families within the United States could make family tasks such as gathering for a funeral impossible. In the Woudenberg family, two older sons set off to make their fortunes in the West against their parents' wishes. The two did not remain in close touch, hence the family could not reach them to inform them of their mother's death or to summon them for the funeral.[157]

While the ordeal of saying good-bye to a dying loved one was hardly a pleasant experience, the comfort of family and friends for the person dying, and a chance to say good-bye for the others, was an important part of Dutch traditions around death. When Gezina van der Haar Visscher's husband had a stroke, she called the doctor. The next day he was worse, and after consulting with her daughter, they called all the children who lived in the area to come. When it appeared that the husband would die soon, Van der Haar Visscher sent telegrams to the other two children. One, a daughter who lived in the same state, immediately decided to make the trip. "The boys came and also our son's wife and despondently we all stood around the bed. We couldn't do anything but wipe away the phlegm from his mouth. . . . My husband lay that way for three or four hours and during that time either Sena or I held his hand. . . . Many friends and relatives came to see him. . . . The children all came to see their old father die."[158] The deathbed scene formed a standard component of obituary letters. It was a common practice to give close relatives a lock of hair from someone who had died. These also made their way into obituary letters.[159]

At funerals, the mourners sought the comfort of extended family members. Beyond that, the details of funerals differed considerably. As with other issues of health, a funeral for the very young did not attract as much attention as that for an adult. Etje Houwerzijl described her young daughter's burial in 1917, to which she asked four family members and two neighbors:

> We had not sought to have anyone else at the funeral, . . . and when the dominie held the eulogy here in the house there were 48 people all together. Here things are very different than in the Neth., most bring a body to the church first, but we did not like that, and had everything as regular and simple as possible. The song leader took care of everything to a letter, even down to bringing chairs and everything. . . . [Janetje] had a white coffin with white silk lining. You can't get anything else here, and it looked so nice, Janetje with her prettiest white dress on and a broad white hair ribbon.[160]

Six years later, when Houwerzijl's husband died, she felt differently. Though sixty people came for the funeral she noted "Jacob Kort and his wife were the only family members here."[161]

Houwerzijl's descriptions from the 1910s and 1920s highlighted that the laying out tended to take place in the home, a pattern that also appeared in other sources. Gezina van der Haar Visscher noted in her diary that "All our relatives and several friends were there [for the funeral] and our house was filled."[162] While corpses and caskets in "Yankee" society generally were moving into funeral parlors, and "parlors" were becoming "living rooms," the more familial-based tradition remained among many Dutch immigrants, with church contacts and friends taking the place of family.[163] Obituaries in Dutch-language papers rarely included information on funeral arrangements, perhaps in part because most papers did not appear often enough for such notices to be useful unless there were several days between death and ceremony. Rather, they served as information for others, and sometimes were followed by thank-you notes from collective family members for support during their time of grief. While few families spent the money for a formal obituary, newspapers such as *De Volksvriend* and *Pella's Weekblad* regularly carried news of the deaths of people in various Dutch American settlements simply as a service to their readers. These notices, like birth and marriage announcements, were part of knowing about the far-flung Dutch American community.[164]

Other commentators noted the details of funeral customs. Johan Woudenberg, only nine when his mother died, described how the body lay on display at their home, and a stream of relatives and friends came to offer condolences. The family tacked a ribbon of black crepe to the front door to signify that someone had died. The body of Wilhelmina Woudenberg, dressed in a plain gown with high collar, lay in a wooden casket. When they went to the cemetery, the coffin rode in a black coach, followed by several other coaches carrying family members.[165] Though the child did not notice, the number of coaches signified something of the wealth and importance of the person. This was yet another example of how the loss of certain family contacts due to migration reinforced the need for other contacts in the local community.

Traditionally, the family of the deceased ordered and paid for the coaches, and the larger the number the greater the display of wealth. In the United States friends and family tended to own their own horse-drawn carriages, and later automobiles, making for an elaborate parade. An article in *De Gereformeerde Amerikaan* in 1899 provided details on this and on several other aspects of funerals:

> Here, people put great emphasis on an honorable funeral. In the Netherlands, by contrast, especially in the countryside, they do things rather roughly. Here the coffins of average citizens are no less elaborate and decorated than those of the rich in the Netherlands. The corpse is dressed and placed in the coffin and arranged so that the interested may view it. They try to eliminate the shocking aspects of death as much as possible. The hearse goes forth with the mortal remains, followed by various hired coaches and vehicles belonging and friends and acquaintances. When one arrives at the grave site the pallbearers, who are recognizable by their clothing, carefully take the corpse out of the hearse. . . . And here one does not hear of throwing clods of dirt on the

coffin. . . . They do not arrange a costly meal . . . as we have often experienced in the Netherlands. In everything this appeals to us greatly.[166]

In the United States burial patterns shifted slowly and unevenly toward American standards. G. J. Holmer, writing from Holland, Michigan, in 1902 mentioned that the family held a large funeral for Albertha Muis Gortworst in church there. While the dominie presided, Muis Gortworst herself had chosen the text for the sermon.[167] Jane Walvoord made a point in her letter of 1915 that at her brother's burial the service took place in the church, not in the home, and "they dress the dead here in a black suit just like the ones they wear in life."[168] Walvoord did not explain who "they" were, but presumably she meant the undertaker.

The same logistical problems that kept migrants from going to funerals applied to visiting grave sites. Though the Dutch did not consider tending family graves often an absolute necessity, they nonetheless found it important emotionally to be able to visit and for someone to maintain the site. Words of gratitude crossed the Atlantic to those who checked on the graves of parents and siblings left behind. Dina Maria Oggel, who lived in Pella, Iowa, reported the visit of a friend, whose child had died there years earlier. "[W]e also went to the cemetery and found the grave where a little marker stood. It was really a wonder. That was 34 years ago. The stone had broken into three pieces. She also wanted to see Rozien's grave again."[169] The desire to visit the grave site meant, in the case of Jennie Frijling, one half of a missionary couple working with the Navajo in Arizona, that after her death her "mortal remains" returned to Grand Rapids, Michigan, for burial.[170]

While visiting a grave often was something a correspondent noted doing alone, grief required sharing. Emotional support from family members for those closest to the deceased constituted one of the reasons people wrote obituary letters. If the extended family could not be at the funeral, they could at least send appropriate condolences. Houwerzijl shot back a thank you to her in-laws after she received their letter of condolence on her husband's death: "[M]y heart hungers so for your sympathetic words . . . when I read I[da]'s letter, I thought: we are really bound closely together, and it is almost as if I felt your kindly handshake, I., and saw your tears flowing Because our hurt here is your loss as well, eh? It was our dear husband and father, but it was also your brother, right?"[171] In emotional crisis situations women expected to hear from family. This operated in both transatlantic directions. When Arendje Bergman Akkerman received a letter that mentioned one of her sister's children was sick, she quickly wrote a letter: "Dear, we learned from Betje's letter that your Jan has been sick . . . oh how frightened you must have been. Is he well again now? Write back something about all of you soon."[172] A year later the roles were reversed, her son had just died, and again the tone she used made clear that she was on close emotional terms with her sister: "Oh sis, my heart is still so full with mourning over my darling of 3 years and 5 months. His prattling is in our memory every day."[173]

Attempts to garner support, however, did not always succeed, as in the case of Harmanna Schoonbeek Rosenboom, from the Grand Rapids area. Three months after writing her brother of the death of their sibling, she noted that she had gotten no response and hence would write once again. "You already know about our sister Jekje, who has died. That caused me such grief that I could not get over it. We loved each other so much."[174] While this woman could express her grief to her brother, the lack of reciprocated emotion exemplified a tenuous tie. Other letters in that collection pointed to a similar conclusion. The same kind of emotional distance could have developed had both been in the Netherlands, but the physical distance and the lack of contact it inspired increased the probability of people growing apart.

* * *

The story of Jantje Enserink van der Vliet illustrated the importance of illness and death, and particularly of how they could have an impact on migration patterns. Jantje Enserink spent a good part of her young adulthood in Eefde, Gelderland, caring for her eight younger brothers after her mother died. In 1909, at age thirty, she married Cornelis van der Vliet and they headed off to Canada, where many Dutch migrants who wanted to farm were looking for land. Enserink van der Vliet arrived in Fort William with her new groom Cornelis to find an unfinished house, no Dutch church, and a group of male boarders for whom she was supposed to cook. Since she knew little about the circumstances in advance, she was understandably disconcerted. When she fell ill shortly thereafter, her husband hinted that the hot weather was bothering her. "Jantje has not been well for the last week. She can't eat, and when she tries she throws up, [she is] terribly tired. . . . we decided that if it doesn't get better soon to send her away, since it is difficult to take care of sickness as it should be cared for so far from everything. And it is difficult because I can't get away because of my work . . . [a relative] will bring my wife to sister M[aria van der Vliet Verbrugge]."[175] Heat stroke, however, was not the most likely cause of her discomfort. Enserink van der Vliet went to her brother- and sister-in-law's home in Chandler, Minnesota, a Dutch American settlement, where Maria took over informal care. Six months later Enserink van der Vliet gave birth "too early, to a dead girl." Maria wrote that they were thankful because Jantje, who had been in grave danger physically, was now better.[176] The grieving parents planted a tree on the grave, on a hillock close to the house.

Cornelis van der Vliet left again for Canada a little over a month later, only to die suddenly of acute appendicitis in April 1910. The in-laws broke the news, and Enserink van der Vliet, despite her strong religious faith and the support of the local congregation, took it hard. She focused her attention on the Verbrugge children, especially the seven-month-old baby. She continued to stay with the Verbrugge family, helping in their home during her period of mourning, but she also began doing housework for other local families, probably in order to earn some money. The other family letters indicate she had a hard time thinking of Minnesota as anything but a "veil of tears." Two years after Cornelis's death she reemigrated to the Netherlands where she became the housekeeper for Rev. Harm Brouwer and his two children. Three years later they married.[177]

Between the losses of the baby and her husband, Enserink van der Vliet suffered more sickness and death in her short stay in America than most. While she probably could have remained and remarried, the lack of consanguine kin and the negative associations of the place made it difficult. She clearly missed the Netherlands and had no one who kept her from doing what she wanted, namely going back. Having been the housekeeper in her father's home, and then briefly in her own, she probably had a hard time adjusting to adjunct status. With eight brothers along with her father in the Netherlands, she had a reasonable safety net waiting.

Dutch immigrant women's basic roles in reproducing informal care did not change in theory, but they did in practice with migration. The lack of extended family, a village midwife, or a doctor who spoke the same language could be problems of major proportions. Dutch immigrant women sometimes helped promote institutional solutions to societal problems of care for the aged, mentally ill, and those suffering from long-term disease. This related both to their sense of responsibility for this kind of care and to the general development of social welfare in this period. The church based institutions of the Dutch model became ethno-religious entities on American soil. In the process women gained a slightly larger role in philanthropy, but nothing close to the "Yankee" models. In this, the ethno-religious community kept many of them "in but not of the world" of shifting gender roles tied to Progressive Era reform which surrounded them.

CHAPTER 5

Learning Language
and Worldview

One of the biggest adjustments most immigrants made was learning to live in another culture where people spoke a different language and had
a different view of the world. That different view could be small things such as
the songs people sang, or the cut of their clothing, or the common experiences
they had growing up. It could also be much larger issues which were taken for
granted, such as gender roles or class status. Replicating language and worldview was one of the tasks of social reproduction which fell to women in many
contexts. This also was the area of life where young women were most likely to
seek change. Long before discourse analysis, immigrant women and their daughters recognized the power of language in creating or dispersing ideas and personal networks. The Dutch ethnic community faced this dilemma head on and
sought to retain the worldview while switching the language.

The disciplines of anthropology and sociology developed in part to chart
differences in worldviews, and not surprisingly, immigrants were some of their
first subjects. In the late nineteenth century, national culture was evident in the
Netherlands and in the United States, but less so than it would be by the 1920s.
Public education in both the Netherlands and the United States had as one of
its goals a basic knowledge and appreciation of the homeland. Around the turn
of the century mass marketing and mass media in the United States extended
the reach of language and image tremendously. Further, the connections between Dutch Americans and their Dutch origins meant regular reports going
back and forth, with both familial and national news. What this meant is that
migrants lived in largely local worlds with an increasing degree of knowledge
about other places. Dutch American Protestants sought to control those worlds
by producing their own institutions and replicating their views. Women had

ambiguous roles in this process. In responses, they ranged in attitude from outright rebels who adopted American culture and language wholeheartedly as a challenge to Dutch gender roles and proscriptions, to those who sought valiantly to maintain language and life as it had been before migration. In this process, education was the primary battleground. The life of Cornelia De Groot illustrated several aspects of this.

Cornelia De Groot

Korneliske de Groot (later anglicized to Cornelia De Groot) was born in Dearsum in the province of Friesland in 1878. Her parents owned a cattle-breeding farm and employed a number of hired hands and servants. She described her youth in an autobiographical text published in the United States in 1917, *When I Was a Girl in Holland*.[1] As the daughter of a relatively well-to-do family, something she downplayed in her text, she had opportunities beyond those of many girls. Her formal education began at age five, when she started attending the local two-room schoolhouse. Like most Frisian children this was her first extended contact with the Dutch language. People wrote and heard religious services in Dutch but on the streets and at home the families spoke Frisian.

For the early grades De Groot had a woman teacher, who concentrated on basic reading, writing, and arithmetic, then adding knitting and grammar. According to De Groot there could be up to forty students in a class. The school provided the books, which could not be taken home, and the teaching materials consisted primarily of pictures posted around the walls of the room. The classes met from about 8 to 10 A.M. and 1 to 3 P.M. during the summer (and began half an hour later in winter), with Wednesday and Saturday afternoons off. Misbehavior netted the culprit, including De Groot, lengthy writing assignments of "I may not talk," though corporal punishment was also a possibility.[2]

When De Groot entered fourth grade she moved to the other classroom and to a male teacher. The curriculum expanded to include more compositions, but also measures and lessons in anatomy, botany, civics, Dutch history, geography, and music. Girls also had (in addition to knitting) sewing, crocheting, darning, and cross-stitching. De Groot, along with several of her friends, took additional sewing lessons from a seamstress after school. Like most country schools, hers had six grades, and when a pupil finished the material for one she advanced to the next, meaning that a reasonably good student might run out of material long before she reached the age to leave school. De Groot's family supplemented her education with private lessons in arithmetic, grammar, reading, geography, and composition. After her brother left for the United States, De Groot and her sister also took English lessons.[3]

De Groot tried to convince her parents to allow her to attend an advanced school in the town of Sneek in order to become a teacher, but the distance and her parents' desire that she should train at home to become a farmer's wife left that wish unfulfilled at first. At least in retrospect De Groot claimed she want-ed independence. "Why should I live my life as my mother was living hers? Up at four or half-past each morning. All day making butter, cooking, cleaning, polishing, knitting, with few people to see and fewer books to read."[4] De Groot continued her studies on her own, borrowing books from her local Reformed Church and reading late at night. She concentrated on languages and litera-ture—French, English, and German—and sometimes neglected her housework in the process. As she described her ambitions: "I did not seem to think of myself as a girl, but as a boy. . . . I read biographies of great men and wanted to emu-late them. My hero and example was always a man, never a woman. . . . Yet I was not a tomboy, due perhaps to my not being very robust. Neither did I regret my being a girl; on the contrary, I was proud and glad of it, but I believed myself to be on a perfect equality with boys and having the same rights."[5] Her one "her-oine" was the aunt of a friend, a teacher in the Dutch colony on Java. This be-came her goal. Meanwhile she increasingly faced problems with her health which she described as rheumatism, neuralgia, and a heart condition. These she cred-ited to her lack of exercise and hunger for pleasures. "The company of my former playmates now bored me. The books I had read, my ambitions, my dreams had estranged me from them. Nearly all their thoughts and their talk centered around finery and boys. . . . Also, my strong sense of justice and love for free-dom rebelled against the domination of woman by man."[6] According to De Groot's account, her parents finally allowed her to enter the Hooger Burger School in Sneek at age seventeen. There she continued her studies of French, English, German, and Dutch, along with mathematics, history, geography, chem-istry, physics, bookkeeping, and drawing. This was not the *gymnasium*, which prepared students for college, but it was a program which prepared young wom-en to be teachers. After one year De Groot had to quit due to poor health, but she continued her studies at home.

Meanwhile her brother Lolke was still in America, working as a market gar-dener, and her sister had also migrated there in 1893, first working as a steward-ess for the Holland-America Line, and then as a nurse until her marriage to a (non-Dutch) engineer. Her sister sent her copies of American magazines like *Ladies' Home Journal* and *Youth's Companion,* along with poetry, history, and novels. De Groot read these and other materials in the local papers and decid-ed she would like to become a journalist. She went to Amsterdam to work at an unspecified job. According to family tradition she, like her sister, served as a stewardess for the Holland-America Line. Although De Groot gave no hint of this in her book, one of her reasons for leaving was that her fiancee ran out on her in the Netherlands, absconding with her savings, which soured her on mar-riage. De Groot's emigration, which she claimed occurred at the age of twenty-one but which other sources indicated took place when she was older, spared her the life of a "spinster" in a rural farming community.[7]

After migration she settled in San Francisco with her sister and sought to

Cornelia De Groot migrated in
part to gain more independence,
especially from rural gender roles
for a *boer*'s daughter. Photo from
When I Was a Girl in Holland.

pursue a dream of becoming a journalist.[8] According to her account she immediately enrolled in a business college. One of the articles she wrote in later years,
published in an unknown paper, described her participation as a "farmerette"
at the model farm of the University of California at Davis. Her views on wom-
en's roles were clear: "Of course not all farm work is pleasant, some of it reminds
one too much of house work." The same was true in her description of their
clothing: "we donned our new farm clothes, a blue one-piece suit consisting of
blouse and bloomers, . . . for the first time I enjoyed the delight of taking long
manly strides without being hampered and tired by the friction of skirts!"[9]
According to an interview she gave in the 1950s she was a suffragist in the successful 1911 fight for women to get the right to vote in California.

De Groot wrote periodically for the *San Francisco Chronicle,* primarily in the
"World Topics Section." Many of these stories dealt with the Netherlands: windmills, dikes, alcohol consumption, the position of women. She made a point of
showing positive aspects of American women:

many American women work harder than the Dutch, as theirs is a double job
of both wage earner and housekeeper. It was hard to make [a young Dutch
woman] understand that every grown daughter, not a society girl, has a voca-

tion and makes her own living. . . . When the Dutch gossips were referring to a lazy wife, they would say: "She belongs in America," or, "She would make a good American." I found however, after a good deal of observing, that laziness is not a characteristic of the women of any one nationality, nor is the spoiling of wives characteristic of some American husbands only.[10]

It appears De Groot's writing remained an avocation while she made her living as a secretary/stenographer. She traveled widely, living in the mining boom town of Tonopah, Nevada, and in Miami and Havanna. She eventually returned to San Francisco and in later years worked in several Dutch offices in the city, including the Netherlands-American Chamber of Commerce and (briefly) the Dutch consulate. De Groot went back to the Netherlands a number of times to visit, including for her parents' sixtieth wedding anniversary in 1927. She had a falling out with her brother-in-law but remained on good terms with her brother, who also remained single all his life. The two lived together in Berkeley after they retired. When he died in 1950 she moved to an apartment and then, when her health declined, to a rest home. De Groot died in 1978 in San Pablo, at age one hundred.

To say that Cornelia De Groot was an exceptional Dutch immigrant woman would be an understatement. She did, however, indicate the ability of a Dutch American woman to blend into the rest of the American world much in the same way as Cornelia De Bey did. Education was one of the key factors in both her lack of interest in following the role set out for her in the Netherlands and her ability to make a living in the United States. She used this knowledge much of her life to bridge the gap between the land of her birth and her adopted homeland.

Education in the Netherlands

Education attracted attention and debate both within individual migrant families and in society more generally. Historian M. J. Maynes referred to schooling as "one of the central and most politically and socially charged routines of growing up."[11] For the Dutch and Dutch Americans at the end of the nineteenth century this certainly was the case. Dutch immigrants sought to control their schools from the outset. In isolated communities they could achieve this by running the school board. Mandating Dutch-language education and hiring teachers from their own ranks made these public schools amenable to the local population. Later, as state bureaucracies tried to gain further control and put limits on foreign-language instruction, the Dutch split. The group which adhered to the Christian Reformed Church generally sought separate Christian day schools, run by families in the church and staffed with church members. They sometimes had the cooperation of Reformed Church members as well, but often those in the Reformed Church were willing to have their children attend public schools, trying to supervise and integrate their members into the staff and curriculum. As one commentator put it "civic neglect is sin."[12] This was only one of the points of divergence between the denominations, but it was one of the most important.

The debate replicated a major controversy, the *schoolstrijd,* in the Netherlands. The interest in private Christian schools acted as a motivating force for some in the migration.[13] That changed somewhat with the school law of 1889 in the Netherlands, which provided government subsidies for private schools, not exactly on the same basis as public ones but setting the stage for this.[14] At that time 29 percent of Dutch elementary education took place in private schools, and the rate had been rising for several years. The growth in private education continued thereafter, as further legislation strengthened the place of private schools in the overall educational system, forming the foundation for pillarization. With the revision of the Dutch constitution in 1920, private and public schools stood on an equal financial basis in terms of government subsidization. In a time period when religious affiliation and party politics went hand in hand, the issue of religious education involved much more than simply teaching one religious doctrine as opposed to another. Both political and social power flowed through religious organs. Getting control of schooling was one way the political parties as well as local groups of parents sought to maintain and strengthen their sway.[15]

The Dutch parliament also intervened in education by passing a mandatory school attendance law in 1900. The law contained several exceptions, most notably a six-week reprieve for children assisting in agricultural pursuits, and an allowance for those who lived more than four kilometers from a school. Since school attendance in 1900 already ran in the 90 percent range, the new law registered a minor impact, but that impact primarily affected girls. It made it more difficult for families to withdraw daughters from school at an earlier age than sons, which had been a common practice.[16]

The three provinces which had the highest rates of emigration, Groningen, Friesland, and Zeeland, led the country in terms of literacy by 1910. In all three, rates of basic literacy for children aged nine to twelve were close to 98 percent in 1900. With the exception of (predominantly Catholic) Limburg, boys consistently ranked higher than girls in terms of literacy at the provincial level during this period. Dutch elementary schools tended to be co-educational, but their curricula were gender specific, with more attention to household tasks for girls. Both boys and girls learned basic literacy, beginning with reading, then progressing to writing, and only if time allowed moving on to arithmetic. Schools for the elite, which were separate in large cities and provincial centers, offered a different curriculum for their children. The school books produced at the turn of the century for the public schools stressed the existing *standen,* or social castes, indicating the virtues and vices that belonged to each.[17] Orthodox Calvinist schools tended to stick more exclusively to the Bible and to catechetical texts as sources for instruction.

At the advanced end of the educational spectrum, women slowly made their way into a variety of settings in higher education in the Netherlands. High schools which stressed college preparation were nearly all closed to girls prior to 1880, and generally women had to petition to gain admittance to college programs until there was a precedent for "lady students."[18] Two- or three-year programs for daughters of the well-to-do stressed language and handwork, but they reached a small audience.[19] Opportunities for girls to attend high school and even college expanded during the period of this study, partly as a result of battles over who would run the schools. Cornelia De Groot was one who benefited from the changing educational climate.

Education in Dutch America

For the majority of the migrant group, who did not have the financial resources the De Groot family did, education was more rudimentary. They, much like her less wealthy counterparts in Dearsum, would attend a one-room or two-room schoolhouse, a phenomenon also common in the rural areas of the United States where Dutch Americans settled. The Dillingham Commission report on the children of immigrants in schools in 1911 showed large numbers of Dutch children in primary and grammar grades but few in either kindergarten or high school.[20] Most would not have the advantage of extra lessons, except religious ones which the churches provided. Neither would most attend a high school, though establishing academies which would train budding ministers and teachers became a priority for Dutch American communities early in their existence. Some of these academies were based on European models to the extent they could be, such as the choice of subjects in the curriculum and letter-based levels. Some Dutch Americans felt that the American education system was not as good as the Dutch one, at least in terms of training an elite.[21] But others appreciated the open attitudes, even if they could not learn Latin.

In the United States Dutch American families continued the pattern of making sure their children gained a basic education. Nearly all children between the ages of six and fifteen enumerated in the 1910 sample appeared as "in school." Owing to mandatory attendance laws, few parents were likely to admit not sending their children to school, but the fact that so many fourteen- and fifteen-year-olds, girls as well as boys, could still be found in school indicates the willingness of parents to allow them to pursue education despite the costs (lost wages or assistance).[22] As the letter writers indicated, children needed extra time to make up for the shift in language. Though they might already have learned the material in the curriculum, they still needed to relearn it in English.

By far the biggest difference in education practices among Dutch American Protestants was the split between those who supported Christian primary schools and those who did not. As historian Jacob van Hinte stated, "our countrymen took their school controversy with them to America."[23] Christian schools supported by independent associations were a replica of those advocated by

Abraham Kuyper and the Anti-Revolutionary Party in the Netherlands. This period constituted the waxing of the Christian school system on both sides of the Atlantic. For all that the schools were "independent," they enjoyed substantial moral support and organizing impetus from the Christian Reformed Church. Depending on the location, however, Reformed Church children might attend in small numbers as well.[24] Many women were part of the campaign and support network behind Christian schools. In a paean to Albertha Muis Gortworst, the family historian wrote: "Bertha chose the side of God's people and she proved this by being a promoter of Christian Schools."[25] As in other areas of community organizing, however, women tended to hold supporting rather than primary roles. Decisions about where to send the children, both in terms of the moral implications and in terms of the financial cost, which could be substantial, also fell in principle and often in reality to fathers.

The Christian schools which some members of the Christian Reformed Church supported nearly all included some training in Dutch. A few carried out all instruction in Dutch in the early years, but more generally by the turn of the century the schools would have a combination of Dutch and English, often with English predominating. The fact that Abraham Kuyper encouraged Dutch Americans to train their children to become "solid, truly American Calvinists" rather than stress the Dutch language and topics in schools helped move the language issue in this direction.[26]

Learning formal English or Dutch for children took place to a large extent within the context of the school. Schools reflected the ideology of the local population and the age of the settlement. Thus those who organized Christian schools were more likely to have formal instruction in Dutch. When two dialectologists asked their interviewees in the 1960s how they managed to keep their Dutch intact, or to learn it (a relevant question for those who spoke dialect or Frisian at home), they received a variety of answers, nearly all variations on a basic pattern, with church and Christian school being the primary purveyors of official learning.

An early photo of the Baldwin Christian School of Baldwin, Wisconsin. Only the male teacher and the names of the pupils hint at the ethnic background. Photo courtesy of Archives, Calvin College.

The division of public as opposed to "independent" schools continued (and still continues) long after schools switched to English-language instruction. By the 1920s those who advocated separate Christian schools (run officially by parents) had established a national network, publishing *Christian School Magazine* to keep in touch with one another. The group included more than eighty elementary schools with three hundred teachers and over ten thousand children. This was still a minority among Dutch Americans, though a significant one.

The Dutch education system assured that most potential emigrants learned to read, and the Dutch American system reinforced this trend. According to the 1910 Public Use Sample, about 96 percent of Dutch immigrants as a whole, and 94 percent of Dutch women above age fifteen could read. Likewise 94 percent of Dutch immigrants and 91 percent of Dutch women could write according to the census takers.[27] So literacy rates were high, with only a minor difference between those for men and women. In general the standards for boys and girls in the United States were the same, with one major exception. Higher education was much more likely to go to boys. Boys could go on to become dominies, doctors, or other professionals, whereas Dutch Protestant families generally expected girls at some point to marry and leave the workforce. Under these conditions education for girls was a luxury. Thus Hannah Bruins vander Velde wrote in her reminiscences how she had to quit school at age twelve to help in the home. Her brother Will continued during the winter until age fifteen, though he too had to work on the farm during the other seasons. At fifteen he got to go on for further education at Hope College, along with several other boys from Alto, Wisconsin.[28]

Most Dutch immigrant children attended school for approximately the length of time or until the age required; if they went beyond this they generally attended courses to learn English. The Dillingham Commission noted this pattern for some Dutch children. If they came to the United States when they were six or more, they might be placed in a grade below that which one would expect for their age, at least until their language skills increased.[29] When Cornelis Kooiman wrote his aunt he noted: "Aafje and Wim go together regularly to school, though it really was not necessary for Aafje in terms of reading, writing, and arithmetic. But it is mainly to learn the language, because it is necessary here to know the language. . . . We only live ten minutes away from the school, but in March we will move, then we will be 35 minutes from the school. That is too far because the road here is often in bad shape."[30] The refrain of distance the children had to travel to go to school and of conditions that prevented them was a common one on the plains of America, but a somewhat less common one to Dutch ears. To overcome the distance children acquired mobility early. The distance to school determined whether children could attend school, or more specifically how often. Lubbigje Schaapman reported that children of all sizes made it to the local schoolhouse: "They take a buggy to school or go on a donkey, or bicycle. Young children go along because the horses usually are very tame."[31] Not everyone, however, could do that. As one woman reminisced, when she was five, "my mother did not want to send me to school. It was too far for me to walk, you see."[32] Weather conditions, the

need for help on the farm, and other things could get in the way of school attendance, but the basic desire for the children to get at least a rudimentary education spurred parents to find some way for their children to make it to the schoolhouse. Mandatory school attendance laws also contributed.

Over the period young women also began filling the ranks of the high school
and college bound, though the numbers remained skewed. As the need for and
acceptance of female teachers increased, more women joined the ranks of students at the "academies," which were college preparatory schools. In 1881 Gezina
van der Haar Visscher wrote an unusual entry into her diary: "Sena graduated
the 28th of June [from Hope preparatory school] and had to make a speech
before a large crowd in the college chapel. She did very well."[33] This was not the
only one of her daughters to speak at commencement. Van der Haar Visscher's
interest in education, which carried on in the family, spurred her to support her
daughters and later her granddaughters in their endeavors to become teachers
and missionaries. The fact that they lived in Holland, Michigan, near the denominational college, helped as well. Hope was not the only institution opening its doors to women in the 1880s. Northwestern Classical Academy opened
in Orange City, Iowa, in 1882, and from the outset sought to serve not only as a
feeder to Hope but also as a teacher-training institution for the area.[34] Few
women (or men for that matter) attended college in these years however. The
Dillingham Commission's figures for selected students in institutions of higher learning included thirty male and two female Dutch-born students, and
thirty-three male and seven female Dutch Americans of the second generation.[35]
For the tiny minority of women who went outside Dutch American circles, there
were many opportunities to pursue higher education. Even before the first
woman gained admittance to a university in the Netherlands, women could
attend most of the midwestern state universities, including Iowa, Indiana, Michigan, Minnesota, and Wisconsin.[36]

The shift to college attendance for women was not an easy one to make. In
an editorial for *The Anchor,* college paper at Hope College, the women editors
of the January 1900 edition explained their situation:

> Please do not expect too much of the Women's edition. We have done our
> best . . . but it should be remembered that we are very weak in numbers, and
> more than two-thirds of us are in the preparatory department. And, while the
> women of the college department have the same class-room work as the men,
> they are obliged to do all their literary society work with the preparatory girls,
> and thus miss much of the helpful stimulus as well as criticism which our . . .
> brothers enjoy. When the college women can meet with the college men in true
> co-educational fashion, then may equal work be expected of them.[37]

That the paper divided editions, allowing male students to edit it most of the
time but periodically having a women's edition, illustrates the degree of social
separation, one exacerbated by the absence of a women's dormitory on cam-
pus, meaning female students had to board with local families.

Migration required new language skills. Even for someone moving into the midst of a Dutch community, learning some basic English was useful. For a single individual it was almost a requirement in order to take advantage of the new economic opportunities. For a family it was more problematic, and it often became a source of generational imbalance because children generally learned English in school. They learned it quicker than their parents and could use it more fluently. Thus they became the go-betweens, the translators of language and culture.[38] Dutch remained the language of the majority, of church activities, but English became the language of wagework opportunities, different gender roles, and of the future.

Language Shift

Change language, change perception. Sociolinguists and linguistic anthropologists have chronicled such shifts extensively, and at times have sought to describe the meaning of such shifts in terms of changing social relations within the minority-language or bilingual communities, including gender dynamics.[39] Others have explored gender roles and their relations to language in a wide variety of settings.[40] Their most common methods, participant observation and questionnaire, however, are not available for past populations. Among historians studying gender, the interest in language and the creation of meaning through language has less often addressed language shift among immigrant populations.[41] Because of the existence of a large body of data collected by linguists, I have been able to partially trace this shift among Dutch immigrant women.[42]

Learning a foreign language effectively requires utilizing the patterns of thought which the language embodies.[43] Whether one agrees with the patterns is another matter, but to become fluent one must recognize them. Language shift in an immigrant population takes place at different levels—individual, family, and ethnic community, to name the most prominent.[44] Within those categories people have different access to language acquisition, different levels of incentive and compulsion to shift, and different evaluations of language shift. At each level the difference is gendered, but other factors, most notably age, also affect who shifts and why.[45] Crossing a linguistic boundary, in other words, can have very different meanings.

The educational background of most Dutch immigrants, which included basic literacy but not much beyond that, meant that most had only limited competency in Standard Dutch. In the Netherlands, a dialect of Dutch was the most common mother tongue for residents of rural areas, including the main regions of emigration. There were a wide variety of local dialects. Linguists have grouped them into five or six families of dialects plus Frisian, which gained the status of a separate language (with its own dialects) in the mid-twentieth century.[46] One of the early linguistic developments in Dutch American communities was a convergence toward Standard Dutch, a process that Caroline Smits chronicled as taking place in the period up to World War I, concurrent with learning English for many. The dialects spoken by most immigrants resembled one another and Standard Dutch relatively closely, which assisted in this process.[47]

In general Dutch and Dutch dialects also resembled English in many ways. Like English, they developed out of the West Germanic family of languages, and Dutch in most instances had an intermediate position between Standard German and English. For speakers of Dutch and its dialects, English was a relatively easy language to learn. Yet Standard Dutch differed from English in a number of ways, some of which were important to perceptions. In Dutch, all nouns had a gender: masculine, feminine, or neuter. The definite articles combined masculine and feminine in one form (*de*) and had neuter as a separate category (*het*), but to choose a pronoun or decline an adjective, one had to know the word's gender. References to people in various occupations or activities grammatically required specifying the sex of the individual (*schrijver* = male writer; *schrijvster* = female writer). As in German, plurals referring to people would be in feminine plural form only if all members of the group were women. If one or more men were included, regardless of the number of women, the plural form was "generic," that is, masculine. Dutch people used titles or lack thereof to indicate *stand* or caste/class much more extensively than was typical in American English. This applied not only to members of the nobility but also to the distinction between employers and employees, bourgeoisie and working class. These distinctions also governed who used which form of address. Two levels of formality existed grammatically, a formal "you" (*u, gij* [old fashioned or dialect]) and an informal "you" (*jij*). Dutch immigrants to the United States generally came from the class of people who were the informal "you" in many social settings in the Netherlands.

For the Dutch, English embodied a new world. English was the language of freedom—free from conventions, free from many aspects of gender, free from levels of formality which could reinforce class distinctions.[48] I am not arguing that this was so automatically. There are many other ways besides grammar for a language to impose class and gender differences.[49] New speakers of a language, however, were less likely to notice those distinctions, particularly if they were used to others which were much more overt. Further, the social circumstances in which the Dutch lived reinforced the freedoms they experienced in grammar.[50] What in their eyes was a society with relatively few class divisions, which offered women and men many more opportunities than in the Netherlands, was reflected in the grammatical changes they encountered. As immigrants lost their proficiency in Dutch, one of the first elements to fall by the wayside, even before the shift into English, was grammatical gender.[51]

The perception of freedom and of new opportunity was partially a function of migration. While the immigrants' knowledge of what they left behind was not static, increasingly they missed the new developments of the "old" world. English was also literally part of the association with newness, as can be seen in the pattern of loan words for new inventions creeping into the letters of immigrants (threshing machine, picture show, telephone, automobile).[52] This reinforced the association between innovations and "America." Trends which took place concurrently or with limited time lapse in urban areas of the Netherlands and the United States, immigrants read about and experienced in their new setting. Since the turn of the century was a period in the Netherlands in which earlier class patterns were breaking down as industrialization reached more rural areas, and one in which the women's movement began to make rapid progress, especially in opening up occupations for women and improving working conditions for some female employees (not to mention in gaining suffrage), the impression immigrants had of their homeland became outdated rapidly. That did not make the perception any less real to them. Young immigrant women often embraced American opportunities, and the language which provided them, while women who arrived as married adults were some of the least likely to learn English and the strongest opponents of linguistic shift. On the spectrum of language conservators and language innovators, women occupied the extremes.

According to my research, the women who most challenged Dutch gender roles, women like Cornelia De Groot, all switched to English relatively quickly after migration and lived most of their adult years primarily among English speakers, in some cases almost abandoning their Dutch ethnic contacts. Cornelia De Bey, the subject of the vignette in chapter 3, had a commitment to the English language which reflected that of others in this group. A children's book based on her childhood described language use in her family when she was young: "Though Dutch was spoken in the family, and familiarly among the people of the parish, Cornelia was thoroughly, nay, almost aggressively, American. She spoke English, and a great deal of it, among her companions."[53] The pattern of women consciously choosing to leave behind the language *and* some of the gender role conventions was consistent for women who pushed linguistic innovation. This is strikingly similar to more recent research on ethnic minority women.[54]

These women formed one extreme. That they lived in urban areas was not surprising. The kind of challenges they posed were more difficult to replicate in the small and insular Dutch American settlements in rural areas. In those regions, young women were more likely to make moderate demands for change, and less likely to achieve them due to communal pressure. For the more rebellious in rural areas, the better option was to leave town. Speaking English was also related to that possibility. Further, the "rebels" illustrated a pattern noted on both sides of the Atlantic for young single women to switch more quickly than male peers into the dominant language, whether Standard Dutch as opposed to dialect in the Netherlands or English as opposed to Dutch in the United States.[55]

Another distinction was age. An essential part of the age difference was the access young women had to the private life of people outside their ethnic group. Serving as a domestic was one of the few ways of learning nursery rhymes and patterns of child socialization, names for household items, cooking and other aspects of food preparation specific to American usage, and customs of American household organization. Adult women, unlike adult men, did not have access to the American version of their workplace. Only very close friendship with

Americans might have provided this. The idea of a division between private and public spheres in American life meant that men were more likely than women to have access to (public) male roles in English at later stages in life. Young women, on the other hand, had the greatest access to American life possible.

At the other end of the spectrum were the women who opposed shifting language. Sociolinguists generally view European women of the kind of background which produced most Dutch emigration as conservators of language. Women trained young children in basic language skills. They passed on their household knowledge with terminology as well as training and equipment. They used the terms and experiences they had to imbue the next generation with a religious worldview, one where the father ruled the home. Certainly this was also the case for many Dutch immigrant women, who used Dutch in their homes. For those who came as adults with children, particularly if they entered rural communities, their chances for learning the new language were minimal. They might learn some English from their children in a generational role reversal, or through a laborious comparison of Dutch and English Bibles. Parents often switched to an English Bible at home at some point after the first or last child began school, trying to maintain religion for the following generation, even if the language was lost.[56] A few immigrant women took opportunities related to Americanization programs. But official statistics reaffirm the inability of older Dutch immigrant women to speak English. In the Dillingham Commission reports of 1911 focusing on employees, Dutch women who arrived before age fourteen were listed as speaking English over 99 percent of the time. This was opposed to just over 34 percent of those who were above age fourteen at migration. In contrast, over 80 percent of Dutch men in the category of those older at migration were listed as knowing English.[57] For those not in the paid workforce, most household tasks did not require English language skills. Only in purchasing was it a major issue, and that might be handled by the father or a child. The standard comment in women's letters that men's needs always came first in terms of farm equipment, household items, and other purchases had a basis not only in familial power but also in some cases in differential access to consumption due to language skills.

Information about women who sought to maintain Dutch is harder to come by than that about the rebels, for the latter group attracted and sometimes demanded attention, whereas the more conservative group was both more busy with raising children and keeping households and running farms and also less likely to voice their sentiments in public settings. For some women, as for some men, Dutch was strongly related to religion. One woman reminisced about a discussion in her Holland, Michigan, church women's group at the time when some younger women wanted to form an English-language group. "And one of the ladies in the Dutch group said, but in heaven they will have to speak Dutch."[58] While the sentiment was religious, it also highlighted the trend of older women losing their status as advisors to younger ones in one of their main social outlets. Women were also likely to enforce language retention in the home, at least if their husbands agreed. One author quoted her mother as scolding: "This is a Dutch household, and you will speak Dutch here."[59] The mother, "Betje" Moerkerk, was also the driving force in sending her children to Dutch catechism classes and trying to keep them out of contact with American life, which she frequently labeled as immoral.

Dingena T. van Beek Berkhout's reminiscences typified the slow shift out of Dutch and into English which commitment to mother tongue promoted. Van Beek Berkhout was born in the province of Zeeland in 1893 and migrated to the United States with her parents in 1908. The family settled in Grand Rapids, Michigan, a heavily Dutch American community. She worked in the family bakery, where they did business in both Dutch and English, and she attended church services in both languages. In reminiscing about her linguistic background, Van Beek Berkhout stressed that it was her mother who ingrained in her an appreciation for her native tongue, so that nearly sixty years later she was still fluent in Dutch and proudly recited the Dutch poem:

> I was raised in the Netherlands
> I learned to speak in the Netherlands
> I will continue to promote the same
> kind of love for the language
> Not that I revile the foreign
> Everything has its worth
> But I say, for me, Dutch
> is the most beautiful language on earth.[60]

The interest of women such as this in maintaining their Dutch and passing it on to the next generation did not preclude learning English, but it did slow language death. That many older women, especially those who came as married adults, tried to maintain Dutch in their homes and communities was not simply a matter of access to learning English. Their (limited) roles of authority, status, and power were often linked to Dutch.

Dutch was also the language needed to maintain ties to the Netherlands. There was an irony in the English word "family" for Dutch speakers. As I noted in chapter 1, in Dutch *gezin* referred to nuclear family, while *familie* indicated extended family. It was extended family contacts which were harder to maintain after migration. Retaining Dutch could be a way for a woman to maintain contact with her extended family left behind. Men also faced these problems, but not to the same degree because of the difference in gender roles. Men had a variety of roles apart from the family; married women had few. Women may have conserved the mother tongue more often than men, but I would argue that this was as much a matter of pragmatism as one of conservatism. Whereas young women saw opportunities opening to them through English, older women saw more lost than gained.

Older Dutch immigrant men faced similar circumstances of generational shift which occurred for their female counterparts. A major difference, however, was the degree to which they *could* learn English and thus maintain their position in the new as well as the old language. Immigrant men also adopted English to make sure religious orthodoxy would continue. One of the reasons men gave for switching was to be able to teach Sunday school.[61] Immigrant ministers were often leading proponents of the shift to English for this reason as well, seeking to ensure that the next generation would remain in the church. Given that churches held three different services each Sunday, switching one service to English provided a way to ease the congregation into the language.

But even those who advocated the shift found aspects of American religious practice creeping in with the language: "Many women as well as the men pray publicly."[62] The common practice in the Netherlands was for women to be silent in mixed settings. Likewise, one dominie who opposed switching a service to English explained that he felt those interested in the switch actually were less interested in the language than in the "more informal" style of service.[63] The minister of a Christian Reformed Church in Holland, Michigan, reported in a denominational publication about leading the "Young Ladies' Mission Circle" in studies of biblical women and in writing essays critical of the Campfire Girls, YWCA, and WCTU. The article made the purpose clear: "There is a tendency especially among our English-speaking churches, to conform to the church life as it evinces itself in the broad American church world. Our young people in general, even of our Dutch congregations, show that tendency. All are afraid to be called narrow and bigoted. . . . the Reformed truth is as broad as the universe. . . . Our young people must be indoctrinated, thoroughly indoctrinated."[64] Still, however, many ministers sought to use English in order to preserve religion.

Preserving religion and preserving patriarchy went hand in hand. To maintain the father-dominated homes that many orthodox Dutch Protestants sought to create and replicate, fathers had to keep control of language; thus the need for fathers to learn English rapidly enough to stem dissension among the younger generation was also more acute than for mothers. It was primarily the father's decision whether the children would attend religious education programs featuring the Dutch language or whether they would attend public schools. When religious understanding started to slip, it was often the time for a shift. In the case of one Lynden, Washington, family, the father demanded Dutch in the home until his daughter described her (totally incorrect) understanding/translation of one Dutch psalm.[65] In familial roles thus, as in economic roles, men—to a greater degree than women—required skills in English.

Within Dutch Protestant America, language itself was changing in this period. Migration had begun on a large scale in the late 1840s, and hence a second and even a third generation existed in some of the older settlements. Newer migrants sometimes joined these communities, and in most cases at least had ties to them. On the one hand, they were learning Standard Dutch, particularly in Iowa, in order to speak to those of different provincial backgrounds. This operated as an important aspect of ethnic group cohesion. On the other hand, communities began to use English on more formal levels: a church service here, advertisements and then articles in the paper there, a form of language on the street which some called "Yankee Dutch." In linguistic terms, English became the dominant language in more domains of activity.[66] For the ethnic group as a whole, Dutch remained dominant until around World War I, when attacks on foreign language and confusion of Dutch and German were rampant. Thereafter Dutch and English mixed. As of 1930, over 133,000 people in the United States still spoke Dutch as their mother tongue. Only after World War II did linguists begin to see signs of imminent language death, and even then the results were mixed.[67]

In the process of switching from Dutch to English, the ethnic group was moving away from a language with formal gender to one without. For obvious reasons, it was easier to do more things in the United States if one knew English. Thus people associated speaking English with activity, particularly new activity. This had important psychological implications. "And mother said, Nel is a born American, she wants a bit of everything, she does a bit of everything, and mother got pleasure out of that, that I did all those things. Well, then I was a Sunday school teacher and that was in English and I belonged to various organizations."[68] The association of English and activity sometimes found in interviews such as this replicates the sense that language allowed the young to challenge the normal generational hierarchy and, particularly for women, prescribed gender roles, at least in terms of economic endeavors and certain opportunities outside the home. It also illustrates that in some cases mothers supported their daughters in these efforts.[69] Male community leaders, from ministers to fathers, sought to control the meanings of English-language life in this context. In the face of challenges, they made compromises, allowing women a more public voice, the possibility to teach Sunday school, opportunities to go to denominational colleges and to become missionaries. Increasingly they endorsed a new vision of womanhood, not the "New Woman" by any means but a vision which allowed for greater individual ambitions. As the leaders of the next generation went on for education, learning Dutch at high school or college was a common phenomenon for the young men. Because the language was primarily associated with the study of theology, the absence of women, who were barred from such training, was not surprising. Women who crossed the boundary into English were not likely to go back.

More importantly, crossing the boundary into English brought a shift from a more class-based world into one in which, despite economic distance between migrants, there was greater adherence to one common (bourgeois) standard of language. In nineteenth-century Dutch, titles were used to create class distinctions. A domestic servant, even one from roughly the same economic background as her employer, referred to her employer as *mevrouw*, whereas the servant was called by her first name.[70] The same was true for both male and female farmhands. In English, the class element largely disappeared. In the Midwest and on the Great Plains, where most Dutch immigrants settled, jobs of this sort were on a much more egalitarian basis. Dutch American domestics and farmhands described their employers by their first names, or sometimes by title and last name, but not by a title only, which was seen in the letters of Dutch domestics to the United States. Their employers called them by their first names and "you," which sounded like the Dutch formal "you" [*u*]. This combination was the kind two adult family members might use in the Netherlands in talking to one another.

In addition to servants and hired hands, the other group of people consistently referred to by the informal "you" in Dutch were children. Within the family, addressing one's parents and siblings with the formal "you" could be a sign of respect or it could be a sign of putting distance between one another. Around 1900, at least in the bourgeoisie, Dutch parents in the Netherlands began allowing children to call them *jij* (informal "you"). After World War I this went a step further, so that parents would allow their children to call them by their first names.[71] Among the immigrant letter writers a formal "you" (*u*) continued to predominate, though the more old-fashioned *gij* ("thou") began to fade by 1920. Young people, those writing late in the period of study, and those who frequently spoke English were more likely to use the informal "you." The switch reinforced a lack of hierarchy in the United States and the association of English language usage with innovation in Dutch language use as well.

Much of the Dutch American community tried to adopt middle-class norms in referring to men and women in English. This meant a standard "Mr." for most men, with other common titles for ministers (dominie), doctors, and professors. Titles of professional status were basically identical. Again, the major shifts came in referring to women. In church consistory minutes, obituaries, and newspaper stories, women went from birth names followed by marriage information (Minke de Vries, married Brouwer) or first name and married name followed by birth name (Minke Brouwer, née De Vries), to simply title and husband's name (Mrs. Gerrit Brouwer).[72] The best example of this shift I encountered was in an entry to the minutes of the Holland Home board meeting. This group kept minutes in Dutch until the 1930s, but English words and phrases kept creeping in. At one meeting board member Emma Stoel Heyboer was listed as "Mrs. Joh.," then the "Mrs. Joh" was crossed out and "Emma" written over it followed by "Heyboer."[73] Single women became "Miss." Shifts in names showed once again a growing acceptance of American middle-class standards.

In a systematic survey of local news in *De Hollandsche Amerikaan* in 1919 and 1920, the paper consistently referred to the parents of newborns in the form of "Mr. and Mrs. Charles Dykstra" and referred to married women as "Mrs." followed by husband's names much of the time.[74] In cases like "Mrs. Johanna Boskamp," the notices appeared to refer to widows about one-half the time. There were still many individuals listed by initial only, a pattern common in the Netherlands but one which made it difficult to know whose initials were there. In all, just over 60 percent of the sample listed married women's names clearly in an Anglo pattern. Young women, on the other hand, rarely had the title "Miss." Rather, somewhat older women in professional jobs—nurses, missionaries, teachers—gained that title. When a family paid for a larger obituary notice, however, women's names were much more likely to be hyphenated or otherwise include a woman's birth name.[75] Considering that this paper continued to print almost exclusively Dutch text, the lack of Dutch titles was striking. If there was a title or abbreviated title for a woman, it was consistently in English.[76]

An overview of several other Dutch American papers confirmed the general trend, but with slight variations. In *De Heidenwereld,* the mouthpiece of the missionary movement, readers found many reports about women's mission societies, often translated from English and using titles in American fashion.[77] *De Hope* out of Holland, Michigan, followed a similar pattern.[78] In the latter case reports of women's mission societies were abundant. *Pella's Weekblad* from Pella, Iowa, seems to have made the shift to American-style titles for women even earlier. By 1916 it almost exclusively used the form "Mrs. Charles Houck" even for obituaries and generally did not include birth names for women. Unlike *De Hollandsche Amerikaan,* it almost always included the title "Miss" for young women as well as for older unmarried women. Because *Pella's Weekblad* contained many more names in the form of short news items about people from various Dutch American settlements, including reports of illness and visiting, readers would have seen these patterns often.

Still, the older bilineal tradition remained evident. All the papers at least periodically in the 1910s had reports sent in by family members which included birth names for all women. When Onne van Stedum and Geziena van Byssum celebrated their fortieth anniversary in 1920, they listed both their birth names in the paper, along with the names of their children, including all the married daughters with hyphenated names.[79] Which name to put at the front of the hyphen was a problem. Dutch tradition was to hyphenate with the husband's family name first, then the wife's name. All the Dutch American newspapers I consulted utilized this tradition throughout this period if they included any hyphenated names. The few American women who hyphenated at that time used the opposite order.

Translating gendered job titles into English also required a new way of thinking. Given that many Dutch immigrants settled in rural areas, titles referring to farming were some of the most common. Without the class system and without so many servile servants, the *boer* and *boerin* could not exist in the United States. While "farmer" described what a man did reasonably accurately, "farmer's wife" in the American connotation did not describe Dutch immigrant women and their more extensive activities on farms. Thus when Cornelia De Groot, herself the daughter of a *boer* and *boerin,* went to write about women working on farms, she labeled them "farmerettes."[80] The term did not catch on, but the distinction of women's activities in rural areas continued. As titles changed, two continued to hold on in Dutch: *dominie* (minister), and *juffrouw* (minister's wife or teacher). The first was already adopted into English formally, and the second no longer had the marital or class status components it originally held in Dutch. Both, notably, were titles of respect.

Clearly anglicization meant adopting different class ideals. Long before Dutch American publications switched to English, they began to use "ladies" as a loan word to refer to women. This borrowing signified a shift toward a bourgeois American ideal, a move into the middle class ideologically if not economically.[81] Advertisements, in particular, would use "ladies" in an otherwise Dutch-language ad to attract women readers. Dutch Americans used the Dutch equivalent for ladies, *dames,* more sparingly, in part because in some migrant circles it continued to have a somewhat negative (aristocratic, snobby) connotation, one associated with the caste-like *standen* of the Netherlands.[82] Women's church groups followed this pattern as well. Those adopting Dutch titles generally used some form of *vrouwen,* the generic term for women/wives, not *dames.* Yet even those groups which used Dutch exclusively in their meetings frequently took the title "Ladies' Aid." Like most linguistic borrowings, it referred to a group for which there was no precedent in Dutch. In an editorial for *The Banner,* the author explained their origin: "The present-day societies are noble successors to the organizations started about a century ago by Elizabeth Fry, Florence Nightingale, the German Frauen Verein of 1813, and the women's associations which arose in our country during the Civil War and the decade following it."[83] The ethnic group as a whole viewed such women's organizations as American.

Many of the women's activities which Dutch-language religious newspapers reported originally appeared elsewhere in English. *De Heidenwereld* (Heathen World), for example, regularly carried reports from the Women's Executive Committee of the Reformed Church, a group dominated by colonial-descended Dutch. They also carried reports from English-speaking missionaries, including some by Dutch-descended men and women who went into the mission field. These, as well as articles from English-language publications such as *Mission Field,* helped reinforce the association of activity, especially for women, and English. The ministers who edited church-related (and often general) magazines found their clientele expanding as women's missionary societies took root in Dutch American communities.

Reaching out to this new clientele, however, entailed a different tradition of reporting on women, one which was unfamiliar and which made some editors uneasy. The editor of *The Banner,* for example, wrote that he was pleased with much of the work of the Ladies' Aids or Dorcas Societies, but that these groups sent in far too much information about their activities for the paper, particularly about how many pieces of clothing or bedding they produced. He also warned that such groups could become "Talking Clubs," a common fate of "American" women's church groups.[84] The editorial as a whole hinted at a problem these women faced, and at why they have since received so little attention. Much of what the papers published concerning religion dealt with theology, sometimes in excruciating detail. Women were not supposed to delve into this subject, certainly not for a mixed audience. Yet what women did in their groups aside from discussion of religious topics was questionable as "news."

For many who did not have formal training in English, the result of the linguistic shift into English was often "Yankee Dutch," a mixture of English words spoken with a Dutch accent, anglicized Dutch words, English words altered to fit Dutch grammar, and other variations on a combination of the two languages.[85] When Jacob van Hinte wrote his classic *Nederlanders in Amerika* in the 1920s he discussed the Yankee Dutch writings of Dirk Nieland: "One of the points he makes—and it is a very significant phenomenon—is that especially women, particularly the young girls who think that the use of English sounds very distinguished, are the first ones who prefer to forget the language of their fathers."[86] Van Hinte confirmed this, noting that in the early 1920s the young women of Grand Rapids and even the daughter of the founder of Pella, Iowa, would not or could not speak Dutch. As an illustration of Yankee Dutch he used the poem "Zwaantje spreekt geen Hollandsch meer" (Zwaantje No Longer Speaks Dutch). The poem poked fun at Zwaantje, who after only two years in the United States refused to speak Dutch. She ran into problems ordering shirt baize fabric—*baai* in Dutch, getting instead a red-headed boy. What was perhaps even more telling, however, was Zwaantje's interaction with her mother:

> And if she has to talk with her mother
> Who does not even understand "yes" or "no,"
> —Whether it be in a streetcar or in a store—
> Then she avails herself of whispering.[87]

The language Nieland used exemplifies gender role stereotypes all on its own. In *'n fonnie bisnis* (no funny business), the main character works in his own name on various occasions but rarely mentions that of his wife. She is *"mijn wijf"* (my wife) in tale after tale. Likewise, other characters like Sikke Pit and Bik Nik appear with their wives in some short stories, but the wives never have names— they are someone's wife or *"de woemens."*[88] Only in the case of *dominie* and *juffrouw* did both spouses have titles which obviated a need for further names. Likewise, in the preface to Nieland's *'n fonnie bisnis,* Frederick ten Hoor points out that the lead female character in the book assumes she is always speaking pure English, just as the main male character thinks he is speaking Dutch. Yet both actually are using a Yankee Dutch mixture.[89]

It was in this context in 1920 that a young Dutch American man sought to impress possible girlfriends/spouses with the following English ad in the otherwise Dutch-language *De Hollandsche Amerikaan* of Kalamazoo, Michigan: "A Naturalized Hollander, 26 years old, mechanic, would like to become acquainted with a girl or lady of from 22 to 27 years, who will form a congenial, intelligent companion. Simplicity instead of arrogance desired. Religion no exigency. Photo desired, which will be returned immediately. Address [this paper]."[90] The same man had placed a very similar ad two weeks earlier in Dutch, but with a few noticeable differences: "would like to meet a simple, understanding, and goodhearted girl. No specific denomination required."[91] The English ad sought to use a vocabulary which strained the author's competency, while the Dutch ad remained in more everyday terms. To reach some young women, this author probably felt the need to try to use their preferred language.

Many Dutch American parents reinforced the desirability of English for their second- or third-generation offspring by using Dutch as the "secret" language, primarily to decide on punishment for children. As one man explained: "the children would say: eh, we mustn't talk that way because they couldn't understand that. And we said: no, maybe we didn't want them to, right."[92] Children in this kind of setting began to associate the Dutch language with spankings, long church sermons, and distant older relatives. In many cases the language of the home could be the language of intimacy, of family, of caring, and it was in some families in Dutch America. But I was surprised by how many cases where it was not.

For those Dutch Americans who shifted to writing in English, gendered standards also applied, and those standards differed according to the audience. The autobiographies of Edward Bok and Cornelia De Groot were aimed at a non-Dutch-descended audience rather than at those of the same background. While Bok's fit the ideal for a contemporary American autobiography, winning a Pulitzer Prize, De Groot's was a children's book, a typical genre for women writers.[93] In both cases they blended into an American "white" identity, yet could still refer to their ethnic background. Those writing for the Dutch American group in English had different limitations. Arnold Mulder, for example, wrote novels which at times ridiculed the strict orthodoxy of many Dutch immigrants.[94] While he encountered some resistance, he continued to live in Holland, Michigan, and find an audience among the ethnic group throughout his life. The same was not true of Cobie de Lespinasse. Though from a prominent family in Orange City, Iowa, De Lespinasse did not remain there but moved to a non-Dutch setting on the West Coast. Her novel, *The Bells of Helmus,* clearly based on her own youth in Orange City, also challenged religious orthodoxy, particularly as it had an impact on gender roles. The novel was published by a non–Dutch American press and gained scathing comments from commentators within the community who read it.[95] Yet the novel had difficulty attracting a broader audience, for it was too heavily interlaced with disputes and jargon which only those in the group could appreciate. In the literary culture of Dutch Americans, religion and gender were both important themes, but how far you could challenge them before losing the audience on grounds of apostasy was a difficult calculation. Just as Dutch America generally had more difficulties with women than men taking an active role in determining religious policy, so too the community had less tolerance for a woman writer attacking either religion or gender. The offshoot was a very limited range of acceptable genres for Dutch American women wanting to write for the group. Further there was the somewhat accurate perception that there were few Dutch American women writers— rather there were American women writers of Dutch descent.

Language shifts also affected literature in other ways. The switch to English generally accelerated the loss of archaic language. While some replaced their Dutch Bibles with the King James Version in English, the rough equivalent to the old *Statenbijbel* authorized by the Synod of Dordt and published in 1637, many adopted a more modern version. The desire for sermons, devotional literature, and other materials geared for the Dutch American audience but no longer available in Dutch helped support the foundations of three major religious publishers which exist to this day: Zondervan, Baker Book House, and Eerdmans. These became the publishers of Christian school materials, for example.

What people could read, particularly after migration, was another question. Protestant households generally had a family Bible and perhaps some devotional literature. Dutch American women might read *De Heidenwereld* (Heathen World) or the feuilleton sections which many Dutch American papers carried around the turn of the century. All of these targeted women as readers to a degree. Yet in comparison with the resources for other European ethnic women, the lack of materials specifically targeting women was striking.[96] Sermons, printed regularly as booklets in the United States and in the Netherlands, also circulated widely in Dutch American Protestant circles, and women mentioned reading them. Dutch American women also could read newspapers from the Netherlands, and judging from their letters, they did.[97] Immigrants passed these around from person to person. Nearly all the Dutch-language papers published in the United States I consulted regularly carried national news from the Netherlands, and most carried news of Dutch settlements around the United States. This meant that immigrants in Grand Rapids, Michigan, were as likely to know about the activities of Dutch Americans in Orange City, Iowa, or Manhattan, Montana, as they were to know what the local Anglo Americans were doing. It is a trend that has continued to some extent to this day through church-related publications.

For the most part Dutch American children learned to function in English with their parents' and churches' active support. For all that Dutch American communities wanted to maintain a degree of isolation from the rest of the world, they also wanted to function economically in a broader American context, and that required skills in English. Religion rather than language was generally considered the crucial part of group identity, and hence one could shift language supposedly without giving up the core. And yet language shift did help create a different world, one in which women could do more (even in the church) and in which class distinctions faded in importance for both men and women. The lack of gender and (easily discernible) class distinctions in English did not create those patterns in the United States, but the language reinforced what people saw and helped them create a mental world in which neither gender nor hierarchy had the same meaning as before. In the time of transition, before the patterns of words as symbols of class and gender systems had ingrained themselves into people's lives, when they still remembered a different way of thinking, language assisted in changing life. And language on the individual level,

perhaps more than any other area, illustrated the direction women wanted social reproduction to take.

Worldview

Perhaps the most important role of language in women's lives was the one hard-
est to document: in providing a prism with which to interpret life and a way of
viewing the world through a Calvinistically tinted lens.[98] This was less a matter
of indoctrination, though there was some of that, but more a matter of pretheo-
retical suppositions. What words and concepts did people have at their disposal?
For late nineteenth-century immigrants, who learned their written Dutch primarily from the Bible and religious texts, this meant a rather specific kind of language.

Most of the information conveyed in Dutch immigrant women's letters appeared in conversational form. In keeping with limited schooling most women
had received, and with the practices of the time, there was little punctuation in
the frequently stream-of-consciousness dialogue. Women shifted into a formal
biblically based language for certain topics. I had a hard time translating these
passages adequately, since the difference in levels of language involved was profound.[99] For some individuals it seemed as though two different people were
writing. "Marten has a letter ready to send to you, now I must write a little bit
of the everyday news. Otherwise I am always so busy, our Sieuwke has been very
ill for a week, it is much better this morning, from the time he was born he
wanted to sit and play on the floor . . . [three lines later] And when our heav-
enly Father comes to call you from this earth then I hope that the parting will
be a gain for you, and that our Holy Maker may be a refuge and comfort for
you."[100] This pattern of short declarative sentences (without punctuation) con-
veying news of the family interspersed with sentences displaying structural com-
plexity and a larger (biblical) vocabulary appears in many letters, particularly
those of the less well educated. Writers switched to more religious language and
metaphors most often when dealing with matters of life-threatening illness or
death. "A few years ago I suffered a great deal with rheumatism and that took
much out of me. This winter I have been spared from that. Well uncle, we received news that Uncle Arend has traded the temporal for the eternal. . . . many
have been called from their course of life to appear before the God of the living
and the dead. . . . Ana lives close to us, her property and ours lie next to one
another. She has a nice farm."[101] The distinction between the conversational tone
of most of this woman's letter and the formalized phraseology of the sections
dealing with death make this mental distinction of levels of language clear.
People could describe what happened in someone's last days in concrete descrip-
tive terms, but the passages dealing with serious illness or death for Dutch Protestant women were generally couched in biblical phrases and religious vocabulary.[102] Through the lens of religious belief, what seemed unfair, unbearable,
and catastrophic became less of a burden.

The connection of religious reference to the topic of health also appears in other settings. Writers frequently included this kind of association with New Year's greetings and birthday wishes: "We wish you from the heart the Lord's Best Blessings for 1909."[103] Even the ritualized greeting which opened most letters, noting the good health of the writer and hoping the recipient enjoyed the same, was often combined with a word of thanksgiving or a prayer for the recipient's health: "Our health is blessed by the Lord, so is yours I hope."[104]

Letters of condolence and reports of death tended to contain the most extensive amounts of religious language, combined with several standard biblical explanations or coping strategies. Thus Johanna Heinen of Gibbsville, Wisconsin, wrote after her husband's death: "the Lord rules and he does not explain his deeds. . . . I hope that the Lord will give us the strength to carry with patience the cross he has laid upon us."[105] In these cases, letters from the Netherlands show identical patterns, making them indistinguishable from those of the immigrants: "Oh, dear ones, what shall we do under such sad circumstances? What other than to accept God's doings with quiet resignation and pray."[106]

Elderly women tended to write more frequently in religious terms, partially a matter of more frequent illnesses but also as a conscious preparation for death. Such letters often contained references to meeting again in a world beyond: "I am old and time goes on, how much longer I do not know . . . we will not see each other again here on earth, I hope that we may view the many mansions in our Father's house, that is my wish for you and all your kin."[107] This theme became standard among Dutch Protestant immigrant women by the turn of the century, a philosophy which compensated for leaving family behind: "we may believe that we will meet him again, never more to be parted."[108] The letters coming from the Netherlands that I consulted did not pick up this theme as often.

It is notable in immigrant reports that many writers automatically assumed the salvation of their family, rather than expressing the doubt a stricter interpretation of predestination might have warranted. "What could we consider better for our children than to wish they are safely with Jesus. Naturally our flesh does not want that, but through God's grace we can understand."[109] Though church theologians during this period struggled with issues surrounding when, not if, predestination took place (and the debate received considerable attention in church-related publications), women's letters indicated that many of them perceived salvation as a given for themselves, their spouses, and their children.[110] One's "elect" status in these terms was evident in belief, church membership, and descent from Christian parents.

The ideologies they espoused assumed that heaven was a place where good Christians, and sometimes good non-Christians, could meet after death. One of the climaxes in obituary letters was the deathbed affirmation of life after death: "He himself could testify that he was going to Jesus where things were better."[111] Or in another version: "I told her that she was going to die, and if she knew where she was going. Without hesitation and I should say with a joyful voice she called: 'I go to Jesus, Mom.'"[112] Dutch Protestant immigrant women relied heavily on religious belief to see them through times of sorrow, yet that belief in most cases reflected a kind of filtering that ameliorated the most severe aspects of predestination.

While according to Calvinist theology a person needed to keep track of her life, just as God did, keeping a diary was not part of that introspection for many female immigrants. Moreover, there was no Dutch Protestant autobiographical tradition coming from the Netherlands.[113] Letter writers and interviewees did not refer to writing journals or memoirs of any kind. Most diaries and memoirs I consulted were produced by the second (or third) generation. The first generation was much more likely to write letters. Those who did pen other personal writings either were detached from the Dutch American community or used these writings at least partially for religious reflection. The latter was the case for Gezina van der Haar Visscher, who not only listed her participation in various church activities in her diary but interspersed family news with snippets of psalms or biblical texts which held her interest on that particular day. She commented sporadically on sermons and speakers, but primarily in terms of whether they were inspiring or whether they brought new converts to the church. Her notes rarely dealt with theology, and when she wrote of a sermon topic it was most often to explain how this affected her: "The preacher took as his subject, from the Songs of Solomon, these words . . . Oh, how wonderful it felt to know that this was true from my own personal experience!"[114]

* * *

The worldview which radiated from church teachings influenced the lives of Dutch American Protestant women in unfathomable ways. One important component was the form of patriarchy which the church supported. Dutch Protestant immigrant women, many living in a world in which the language and worldview they knew came largely from a religious base, could examine American life on these terms. Education in Dutch American communities sought in large measure to replicate many aspects of these worldviews, if not always the language at first associated with them. The ideological filter of women's upbringing was not always enough to keep them following this way of thinking and acting, however. For some, circumstances or personality prompted a move away from the ideals they had learned. In these cases the church might try to bring them back to the "right" way by coercion. The same applied to Dutch immigrant men. Because people's picture of the land they left was more static than that of the one in which they lived, change tended to be associated with America. English for some became the vehicle for a new way of thought. It was a major change in terms of social reproduction.

CHAPTER 6

Our Father,
Who Art Everywhere

Churches were the most important institutions outside the family for Dutch Protestant immigrant women. For many in rural areas, church activities represented the primary if not the only social contacts they had on a regular basis. In addition to worship, churches generally provided a form of social control and a safety net in times of need. Depending on the denomination, they sometimes offered separate women's organizations for intellectual and/or philanthropic purposes. In this chapter I explore religion, and more specifically the two largest Dutch American Protestant denominations, the world they sustained, and how women functioned in that world. Churches were the bedrock of community, which made an ethnic culture possible for many. It took a critical mass as well as the desire to maintain ethnic identity, and for a group as small as the Dutch, a church congregation often fulfilled these roles.[1] Women based various efforts at social reproduction around these institutions, yet in many cases they worked within parameters over which they had little control. From 1880 to 1920 women gained many roles in these churches, some of them replicating developments in the Netherlands and others coming out of the American context. Trying to maintain the belief system, and yet expand their opportunities for service within it and perhaps even have a voice in theological debates, became a characteristic of women's lives in the American context.

In the introduction I described how the nineteenth-century Dutch migration to the United States began among congregations of Seceders (*Afgeschiedenen*), who migrated en masse under the leadership of their dominies (ministers) to the new world. As the founders of the Michigan and Iowa colonies, the Seceders attained a prominence far beyond their actual numbers in the immigration.[2] Further, their legacy of religious orthodoxy even in the face of opposition, sometimes called obstinacy, continued among Dutch American men (and women to a lesser extent). As the saying went: "One Dutchman a theologian, two Dutchmen a church, three Dutchmen a schism." Women had little voice in the impassioned conflicts which split congregation after congregation and led to a wide variety of splinter groups. They did, however, have to reorder their social worlds when the denomination changed.

The first major religious schism in the Dutch American colonies occurred in 1857, seven years after Van Raalte and the Classis of Holland had joined the Dutch Reformed Church (later Reformed Church in America), whose members, and particularly ministers, had offered them aid from the outset. Those who opposed aspects of the union formed the core for a new denomination, the Christian Reformed Church. A second schism, over the issue of Freemasonry, led to an upsurge in membership in the Christian Reformed Church beginning in the 1880s. Just as a new wave of migrants was getting underway, dominies in the Netherlands warned emigrants not to join the Reformed Church.[3]

The Doleantie, the neo-Calvinist religious movement in the Netherlands begun in the 1880s under the leadership of Abraham Kuyper, which helped bring about the pillarization of Dutch society along religious lines, also added to Christian Reformed ranks, since Kuyper advocated emigration to relieve population pressure. Dominies in the United States frequently came from the Netherlands, especially early in this period. The members of the Christian Reformed Church in the United States and Canada sought to follow the separatist path forged in the Netherlands, albeit less successfully in the political arena, whereas the Reformed tended to opt for working within the existing political and religious institutions. As I noted in previous chapters, both the Reformed and Christian Reformed supported certain separate institutions such as homes for the elderly, though the Christian Reformed were much more committed to this path, particularly in regards to schools.

Religion and Daily Life

Among Dutch Protestants religious belief entailed certain actions. For those who lived in Dutch communities, many were simply taken for granted. Thus it was more likely those who lived outside who noticed the difference. A young woman, newly arrived in California, wrote: "Americans don't think much of Sunday. Even though they are such fine people, they don't pray before they eat. They just come sit by the table and then step away again. Pitiful."[4] Prayers at mealtime, one before and a second afterwards, often coupled with Bible reading, were common fare for Dutch Protestants.[5] An elderly Frisian woman, asked about whether she continued to read Dutch, proudly stated she and her husband had read the Dutch Bible together every day of their married lives—fifty-three years.[6] Daily family devotions were common, though as I demonstrated in the last chapter, the switch to an English Bible took place much earlier for many.

To find information on personal devotions was more difficult. The diary of
Gezina van der Haar Visscher was an exception. After her daughter left for Africa, for example, she wrote: "We can do no more than entrust them to God in
prayer which I do in private and my husband prays for them at the meals."[7]
Many letter writers made a point of asking relatives and friends to pray for them
in times of trouble, or noting they were praying for someone. Etje Houwerzijl
wrote during her husband's final illness: "Pray for us a lot mother dear, that we
may not turn from the Lord in this difficult time."[8] Notices of illness or death
in the Dutch American press either directly or indirectly asked for prayers.[9]
Prayer served not only as a spiritual exercise but also as a way to cement familial and community bonds.

Another aspect of religion in daily life was the weekly and yearly calendar of
ritual observance. Sunday was strictly a day of rest for many, punctuated by
church attendance. "People tend to go to church a lot here, you are more respected
here if you go to church, although I don't go so much. I find it too warm. But
Jeanette, W.C., and Nellie go faithfully every Sunday—J. and W. two times."[10]
Dutch American churches typically offered at least two and often three separate
services each Sunday. If a woman did not attend she could anticipate probing
questions from (male) church authorities. In several of the church records I con
sulted, "profaning the Sabbath" stood out as a sin which the ruling elders fought
with vigor. Depending on the congregation, inappropriate activities could include
anything from having a picnic or playing games to visiting someone in the hospital. As one woman put it: "We couldn't set foot outside the house on Sundays,
only to go to church."[11] For her and her mother "keeping the Sabbath" also meant
doing all the cooking and other preparations for Sunday on Saturday, and then
getting up early on Mondays to do the Sunday dishes. Not everyone considered
women's activities as work however; many pressed instead for lighter duties on
Sunday, less cooking and no major housecleaning or washing. One thing people
could do on Sundays was to catch up on correspondence, and they did. Immigrant women frequently mentioned that they started or finished or simply wrote
the letter on Sunday. "I thought I would answer your letter since it is Sunday and
it has rained the whole day so that I cannot go to church."[12]

Church attendance and church activities frequently appeared in the letters
of immigrants. For those in rural areas the distance to the nearest church held
particular importance.[13] For some, weather and/or limited transportation could
cause difficulties. "Father and mother and Wim went to church and Wout and
Aafie and I had to stay home because there wasn't enough room in the buggy."[14]
Churches often held additional meetings during the week for catechism, Bible
study, or missions, and women sometimes frequented these as well.

Dutch American women rarely went into theological detail about what went
on in church, but they might discuss their dominie. Since many of the dominies,
especially in the Christian Reformed Church, continued to go back and forth
from the Netherlands to the United States, letter recipients frequently knew of

them even if they did not know them personally. Grietje Rubingh in Wilder-vank, Groningen, for example, asked her relatives in the United States to greet her former dominie, who now served their area. "Our dominie is a good man but he can't come close to preaching like Dominie van Hoogen."[15] Women tend-ed to note if the congregation was Dutch, sometimes going into provincial back-ground, and which language they used in services. For the most part women did not engage in theological debates by mail, a common feature of men's let-ters. This was not for lack of knowledge.

Girls as well as boys went through a rigorous catechism at church. Both were tested on their knowledge of the Bible, the catechetical texts, and their own conversion before they could become communicant members of the congre-gation. But as adults women encountered mixed messages in theological terms. On the one hand their churches talked of equality before God, yet they saw the family rather than the individual as the basis of society. In the church interpre-tation of family, wives should submit to their husbands, and women in general should listen to men concerning theology. For some that meant women should not vote in the church, despite individual membership, and for Dutch Protes-tants generally it meant no women in church offices. In some churches it meant women could not teach Sunday school, and at the extreme should not speak in any mixed settings.

For some women the church's stance on women led to avoidance of theo-logical questions: "My parents went to the Reformed Church at first. And then later they changed to the Christian Reformed Church . . . but what the differ-ence was, I don't know."[16] For others it meant resignation about having to change denominations when a husband switched, or tolerance of women who switched Calvinistic denominations, especially because of marriage. One wom-an, whose letters had a greater than average share of biblical quotes and refer-ences to dominies in the family, wrote that her daughter had joined the Presby-terian church: "Well I think it's pretty much the same, at least I don't worry about it."[17] Yet there were some for whom such a switch was difficult. Hendri-ka Rientjes Berendschot, from Nijverdal, met a young man from her village while studying in Holland, Michigan. They started courting but he was Reformed and she Christian Reformed so there was opposition in her family, which they over-came with good character references from a doctor the family trusted. Still, changing to the Reformed Church was difficult for Rientjes Berendschot: "it was still a hard blow for me . . . Because I was very Christian Reformed."[18] One of the few situations in which a woman was expected to challenge her husband was if she was religious and he was not. In Maartje Lautenbach Zondervan's letter providing the reason why her husband of twenty-eight years deserted her, she noted: "Whenever I wanted to go to church he would act up like the devil him-self, but I went anyway."[19]

Besides church attendance there were various activities for women and girls in the Dutch American Protestant churches. At the turn of the century women's groups burgeoned. Ladies' Aid societies and mission groups, both foreign and domestic, were the focus of many of these groups, but other groups devoted to Bible study, local philanthropic causes, or sewing had a place within some churches. By the turn of the century the Dutch American press frequently had notices of activities of women's organizations. A Chicago church reported: "Our Ladies' Aid Society is, as ever, still doing its work. . . . Only a short time ago the Society gave $10 to our Bethesda Sanatorium, for the benefit of those that need it to be restored to health."[20] Even more common were the yearly reports or results of annual festivals. In 1919 the Vrouwen Zendings Vereeniging (Women's Mission Society) of the Westfield Gereformeerde Kerk held its annual mission festival. They raised $330, a large sum at that time.[21]

Women's groups were both more numerous and freer from male control within the Reformed Church than those of the Christian Reformed. In both denominations, however, women's groups often met under the supervision of an elder (sometimes the dominie).[22] In some cases these groups had to repeatedly ask permission to use the physical space in the church. While they were quite successful on some fronts, especially in promoting Christian institutions, the Christian Reformed women had less say in handling the monies they collected and the projects they initiated. They also had a more difficult time convincing churchmen to promote women teachers (for Christian schools), or women in positions as Sunday school teachers, or single missionaries. Unlike the Reformed, who had the direct example within their denomination of (colonial Dutch-descended) women active in these fields, Christian Reformed women had to create their own examples. This story was most clearly seen in the life of Christine van Raalte Gilmore, daughter of the leader of the *kolonie* in Holland, Michigan, Rev. Albertus Christian van Raalte. Van Raalte Gilmore, Netherlands-born and United States educated, inherited from her father an interest in church organizing and missions.[23] She became the driving force behind women's mission groups in the nineteenth-century Dutch branch of the Reformed Church.

Christine van Raalte Gilmore

Christine van Raalte embodied the shift between two worlds. From the outset her life was not typical of Dutch immigrants, yet she set a standard which other women would emulate to greater or lesser degrees. After the Van Raalte family had been in the United States a few years they sent Christine east to a girl's school in order that she would learn correct English—that is, without a Dutch accent—as well as American social graces. Thereafter she attended Olivet College for a short time. Her education befit her class standing, for the Van Raaltes were well-to-do from the outset, even bringing along their maid when they migrated. The presence of household help also meant Christine could concentrate on her studies, and not on housekeeping. At age twenty-four she married William B. Gilmore, not Dutch, but a recently ordained Reformed minister. The couple went to her father's mission in Amelia, Virginia, for a couple of years. There she had to adjust to a different lifestyle: "We are having very warm weather here and it is especially hot in the kitchen over a hot stove. There we spend most of our time since we do not have a maid. So there is always plenty of work for us and it is fortunate that we learned to work, at least if we hadn't learned more about work than these southern girls, things would be in a mess. What poor creatures they are—don't know anything—not even how to make a bed or how to sweep."[24] Van Raalte Gilmore had two children in Amelia, one of whom died in infancy. Her husband then took up a position as teacher for "primary and female instruction" at the experimental school in Holland, Michigan, which would become Hope College. This lasted only a year, until he received a call from a congregation in Spring Lake, Illinois, which he served from 1873 to 1882. There the couple had two more children, both of whom died in 1879. In 1882 William accepted a call to a church in Havana, Illinois, and as was expected of any minister's wife, Christine made the move yet again.[25] When William Gilmore died suddenly in 1884, Christine van Raalte Gilmore had only one surviving child, already a teenager. Her personal tragedy left her a widow with incredible talents but few avenues to use them. She returned to Holland, Michigan, and three years later became "Lady Assistant and Matron of the Preparatory School" of Hope College, a newly created position at the denominational college. She was the first woman on the faculty. Her style of working with the administration was clear in her letter of acceptance: "Please accept thanks for the honor conferred (through your instrumentality) upon one who feels so undeserving. . . . I am perplexed to know how I can teach any class three or four times a week without exceeding the hours required by Council, and if those hours are devoted regularly to teaching, how can I devote any time to the young ladies? If you can assure me that I am not to exceed the required time stated by Council, I will accept the appointment."[26] Women's attendance at Hope was a recent innovation when Van Raalte Gilmore took the position there. The college was established largely to train ministers for the new Dutch American branch of the Reformed Church. Rev. Philip Phelps, the first president of the college and of the older branch of the Reformed Church, however, also sought to open the school to women.[27] As Frances Phelps Otte, one of the first two women graduates, later wrote: "Although the academy and College were denied to females, my father persuaded the Dutch worthies to experiment with his two daughters and two American girls who lived in the House now known as Gilmore Cottage."[28] Though the young women were not allowed to sit on the graduation platform, the university administration and advisors deemed their performance satisfactory.[29] Five years later Van Raalte Gilmore was ensconced as lady assistant and matron, and Dutch American daughters were allowed to attend both the prep school and the college.

While the college council referred to Van Raalte Gilmore at first as the "Matron," within a few years she became known as "Lady Principal." She lectured

Christine van Raalte Gilmore became a leading
force for women and mission activities in the
Reformed Church. Photo from the Western
Seminary Collection of the Joint Archives of
Holland.

regularly in addition to giving instruction on "Good Morals and Gentle Manners."[30] Her female students had no on-campus housing, so Van Raalte Gilmore
entertained them at her home on a regular basis. A story in 1901 about "Our Lady
Principal" in the college paper illustrated that the young women had learned
her style of accomplishing things: "For thirteen years Mrs. Gilmore has been
wielding an influence over the character of the women students of Hope with
her own beautiful culture and rare tact. We are earnestly looking forward to the
time when her gracious presence will preside over [a] women's hall. A daily and
more intimate contact with such a woman as our Lady Principal would be a great
privilege to the young women."[31] The article went on to say that she was the one
who managed to get people to conform to the "unwritten rules" of Hope. It also
hinted that Van Raalte Gilmore had received offers to go elsewhere (for more
money) but had remained loyal to Hope. In 1907, Van Raalte Gilmore was able
to write to the paper of the opening of a new women's residence, the Elizabeth
R. Voorhees dormitory. She also used the article to expand on her vision of
womanhood in the time: "The need of today is a well-rounded Christian womanhood. How many of you, dear girls, will avail yourselves of the opportunities
afforded to prepare for greater usefulness, and for a life of sweeter service for
the Master? . . . The power of choice rests with the young girl who reads."[32] At
that point in time Van Raalte Gilmore's title had ascended to dean of women
for both the college and prep school. Two years later she resigned the post, citing poor health. Her other career, however, continued.

The same year Van Raalte Gilmore took the Hope College position, 1887, she
also became a vice-president for the Women's Executive Committee of Domestic
Missions of the Reformed Church, a position she held for decades. She had already been active in the mission societies of both First Reformed and Hope

Reformed churches in Holland, taking notes for both.[33] She became the first president and served for thirty years in that capacity for the Women's Union Missionary Conference of the Classis of Grand Rapids, Holland, and Muskegon, organized in 1898.[34]

As vice-president for the Synod of Chicago, she used her credentials as daughter of the *kolonie* founder to good advantage. Thus while "Mrs. C. V. R. Gilmore" signed reports to the Women's Executive Committee, she frequently spelled out "Van Raalte Gilmore" in materials to Dutch Americans. Yet she faced a general unease with women's separate organizations and with women's activism, even for such causes. The annual report of the Women's Executive Board in 1890 hinted strongly at the kind of conditions Van Raalte Gilmore faced:

> It is almost impossible for those near the centre of interests to understand the difficulties of carrying on the work successfully so far from headquarters: but the Vice-President of this Synod brings to her work wisdom and tact. She is at home on the field; she knows the people, their needs and their hopes; she has their confidence in the highest degree. Among ministers of Western churches, her presentation of our work has found courteous reception; where they could, they have brought the matter before the women of their respective churches; where for the present that has seemed impossible, they have still shown kindly interest in the cause, and have promised to interest their people in it as opportunity offers.[35]

Despite opposition, Van Raalte Gilmore "personally organized seven of the Women's Classical Conferences in the Particular Synods of the West and was instrumental in the organization of several others."[36] As one history of the Women's Board explained: "She was a wonderful platform speaker, gifted in the use of both the English and Holland languages."[37] The position she held at Hope College gave her great visibility for leaders of the denomination and allowed her to recruit potential women missionaries. Not only could she recruit women but the Women's Board of Domestic Missions generally provided scholarships for "girl students."[38]

In 1919 Van Raalte Gilmore organized the Federation of Women's Societies of Holland and Vicinity. Not surprisingly, she was elected president. The group decided at their first meeting to collect money for a medical facility to serve lepers in Inhambane, Portuguese East Africa. They did this, buying an estate and establishing what would be called the Christine van Raalte Gilmore Home for Lepers.[39] The home itself would disappear, but the interest would not.

Many persons who described Van Raalte Gilmore likened her to her father, which among many Dutch American Protestants was a very strong compliment. Physically, however they were quite different. One friend described her as a "sturdily built woman, always neatly and conservatively dressed."[40] Pictures showed her in clothing which by most Dutch American standards would have been rather elaborate, outfits trimmed with feathers and lace. They might not have lived up to an elite American fashion statement but neither were they something common. It was also quite noticeable, especially in later years, that she dyed her hair.[41]

Van Raalte Gilmore died at age eighty-seven in 1933 and was buried in the Van Raalte family plot in Pilgrim Home cemetery in Holland, Michigan.[42] Because of her status as a pioneer for women, in organizations, education, and careers, she would tower among Reformed women (and men). Hope College erected a women's dorm called Gilmore Hall in 1963. In all, she represented a somewhat different path in Dutch America. Because of who she was, daughter of the colony founder and widow of a minister, she could push Dutch American women toward American patterns without seeming to step out of her place. She served directly as the model for many young women in college, in mission societies, and in churches. She shaped social reproduction in one realm of community life far beyond the means available to most immigrant women.

Women and Church Mission Societies

The interplay of Dutch and American gender roles continued over the years, following the pattern of American innovations which some Dutch Americans eventually accepted. For example, *De Hope,* a Dutch-language paper based out of Holland, Michigan, and closely related to Reformed thought, began a series of articles on women's mission work in 1899. The author of the articles was Kate B. Horton, corresponding secretary for the Women's Executive Committee of the Board of Domestic Missions, and her series was translated into Dutch. I looked through several years' worth of issues from this newspaper, and I found no regular articles written by Van Raalte Gilmore or any other Dutch American woman. There were however many reports by women of activities from various churches, including reports of mission societies, which appeared in small print at the end of the paper. Though the advertisements made clear that *De Hope* was aimed at least as much at women as men, the text was written almost exclusively by men, and among them, by ministers.[43]

This was less true of *De Heidenwereld,* a mission magazine which carried news of both Reformed and Christian Reformed missions, though somewhat more on the latter.[44] Though the original editors were two ministers from Orange City, Iowa, and ministers and male missionaries wrote many of the articles, reports from women missionaries and women's missionary societies also had their place. Kate Horton contributed regularly (again translated). News of women in "heathen" societies regularly filled the pages, as did profiles of the missionaries. But it was the presence of articles about the concerns of women in local congregations which distinguished this publication. Women often found it difficult to say or write things publicly.[45]

To understand the role of women in the missionary activity of the denominations, one first has to know a little about the mission activities of the group generally. Both the Reformed and Christian Reformed increased their presence in domestic missions to persons other than those of their own background beginning in the 1890s. The Reformed also took an increasing role in foreign missions, one which the Christian Reformed were somewhat slower to support. Comparing the activities of women in the two denominations illustrates different modes of accommodation to American patterns.

Among the Reformed, the Women's Board of Domestic Missions was organized in 1882. In the first years they largely served Dutch American congregations, sending Christmas and mission boxes, reading material as part of the "paper mission" and other items for the newcomers, and reporting on the progress of their missionary, Frederick Zwemer, who traveled from church to church in the Dakotas, preaching to the Dutch Americans.[46] In 1893 representatives of the Women's Executive Board of the Reformed Church in America (RCA) went to the World's Fair in Chicago and to the World Conference of Missions. Van Raalte Gilmore was among the delegates to the latter. The denomination received money from the exhibition to found a "Columbian Memorial" for domestic work among American Indians. The group then set out to find missionaries and get support for them.

The result was Colony Mission to the Cheyenne and Arapaho.[47] In 1900 the group began to serve the (Chiricahua) Apaches from "Geronimo's Band" at Fort Sill, a mission which continued when the Apache got their freedom and moved to the Mescalero reservation. Another of the RCA women's American Indian endeavors was the Mission to the Winnebago in northeastern Nebraska, which the group took over in 1908. A Dutch American minister and his wife initially staffed this mission. One more RCA mission field, at Dulce, New Mexico, opened in 1914, seeking to convert the Jicarilla Apaches. Among the missionaries who had served at least five years at these missions by 1932 were not only two Dutch American couples but also ten Dutch American women (of sixteen "workers").[48] Sharing skin color, ancestry, and religion with many "old stock" Americans, Dutch immigrants could downplay the mission efforts to their own members and join the Anglo interest in converting "others."[49] At some of the early meetings of the Woman's Board of Domestic Missions, the group displayed both United States and Dutch flags, and an orange banner as well, letting the new members of similar background know that they were welcome, while at the same time providing (at times condescending) suggestions for adjustment, including rapid language shift in new RCA congregations.[50]

The Christian Reformed Church (CRC), even more closely tied to Dutch American identity, also began their domestic mission work among their own. At the turn of the century there were many new congregations which needed support. In debating what to do beyond this, the CRC considered joining in the mission work to Java supported by churches in the Netherlands, setting up a mission to African Americans in the United States South, or joining with other churches (notably RCA) in already established mission work, but in 1886 the group chose to serve American Indians: "because we were occupying and holding as our own their former homes and hunting grounds. For the material we would return the spiritual!"[51] Articles on the early mission in *De Heidenwereld* took an even stronger position, comparing the situation of the Dutch in the United States to that of the Dutch Reformed Church in South Africa, where interest in the natives was negligible. "God brought us to this good land and if the original inhabitants of it die out or are lost . . . and we look on with indifference or make only lukewarm efforts to save them, will not their blood be on our hands?"[52] Aside from the religious sentiment, there was also an element of creating a new home by taking on roles of cultural imperialism.

Women's efforts were much less coordinated among the Christian Reformed than among the Reformed. The CRC itself had a less organized mission structure, and within that even fewer administrative roles for women.[53] As late as 1917, in reporting on the annual meeting of the Council of Women for Home Missions, part of an interdenominational group which coordinated which denominations served which American Indian groups, *The Banner* included an explanation of what this group did: "Perhaps some of us may not know that some of the large denominations of our country are leaving the work of providing the Indians with missionaries, to the organization of women interested in this field of Christian effort,—hence the existence of this 'Womans' Council for Home Missions."[54] While individual CRC congregations had women's mission societies, they never gained the organizational strength or stature of the women's groups among the RCA during this time period. The readers for the mission publications, the monetary and moral support for various missions, and the young women who became missionaries generally came out of local congregations with an interest in missions.

Women's mission societies affected Dutch American women in their local congregations in a variety of ways. One was in learning organizational and public presentation skills, though at least some groups remained partially under the oversight of male church leaders. For example, Gezina van der Haar Visscher, whose diary was filled with news of mission society meetings and special church services for missions at her local Reformed Church, frequently noted giving reports of her children (three of whom were missionaries) in her women's mission group and how the group then supported them with prayers, money, and letters. She also made the observation in 1896: "Last week we held our ladies mission society meeting. There were only a few present and it was decided that it would be better to hold our monthly meetings in the evening in the church. Then the minister could lead and men could pray too. How this will work out I don't know—the collections will very likely be less."[55] But women also had the opportunity to speak, and women missionaries, when in town, would report of their work.[56] At the First Reformed Church of Holland, Michigan, the presence of Christine van Raalte Gilmore ensured that visiting missionaries made this a stop on their agenda. Still, the average meeting was spent reading letters from and assigning who would write to various missionaries, learning about mission fields and who was working in them, talking, praying, and singing (sometimes in Dutch, sometimes in English), and taking up a collection.[57] The women often got to choose where to send the money, and a special object, that is a missionary from their own congregation or one with whom they corresponded regularly, was often the recipient, though a group might also send smaller amounts to general missions.[58] This was typical of the heydey of Anglo women's mission groups but was dying out in other denominations as they switched to more "scientific" management beginning in the 1890s.[59]

Mission societies were also one of the main areas where women could gain some notice in the denomination. Women missionaries (mainly single, though some were married) sent news of their work and if they continued in the field might expect to write a memoir which would become reading material for these groups. Mission societies over time increasingly published notices about upcoming events or reviews on their major annual activities. In addition they sent in long obituaries of their members in various Dutch-language papers, and the obituaries generally did not concentrate on women's roles as wife and mother but as Christian and mission supporter. It was a small but important shift in thinking. Moreover, information about women missionaries and organizers for missions became a part of the regular reading material in Dutch American homes.

The degree to which information on women was mediated by men reflected the gender role ideals of the group. When Mr. C. Dosker spoke to the Woman's Missionary Conference in Holland, Michigan, in October 1911, a speech which the Women's Board of Domestic Missions later printed, he opened his remarks on "mothers and missions" with an aside: "I realize that this message should come from a mother, who is deeply conscious of the meaning of this subject. . . . I shall speak for her, yet it will be her message."[60] In other words, it was the son who could speak for the mother. This was also the gist of the text, which told the story of how a woman deeply interested in missions had, by creating the right atmosphere in a Christian home, encouraged two of her sons to become missionaries. In the pamphlet, interspersed with pictures of women missionaries, women active in mission organization, and the mothers of missionaries, the male author told of homes brimming with missionary literature, where a mother wrote letters to missionaries and prayed for them, took part in missionary groups, used money frugally so they could have more to give to mission work. Moreover, he described one woman's vision of meeting Christ in church, and her transformation thereafter: "things became new for myself and family. This is only the beginning of obedience, and there is still much imperfection; but I have learned to appreciate, first of all, the privilege of being a Christian mother; secondly, the privilege of training children for His service; and thirdly, the thought that all we possess belongs to Him, and we may gladly give thereof for His service."[61] This praise of Christian motherhood set only in the home contrasted the section in which the woman (through Dosker) described her life "until it pleased God to open my eyes," a period in which she enjoyed the Women's Missionary Society meetings and was active in the group but was still not cognizant of "how much I owed to Christianity as a wife and mother."[62] While the text mentioned a woman missionary and the possibility of daughters becoming missionaries, the focus was more on women making their contributions to missions in the home. This was also a topic which appeared in other publications. Reports of the problems faced by women in other lands, common among Protestant publications, also reinforced the ideal that in western Protestant Christian lands women had great privileges, and they should be grateful.[63] The implication was that women should focus their attention on helping "other" women rather than changing their already high status at home. Minutes from women's missionary meetings illustrated that women clearly embraced the desire to help "others," but that they also, through Bible study, were seeking precedents for more active church roles.[64] While this was hardly radical, it was something new in Dutch American experience. Thus it was not surprising that some churches preferred a male elder in attendance at these meetings.

When there were several missionary societies in a single church, especially larger urban churches, the groups tended to differ according to the ages and sex of the participants rather than the composition of the leaders, at least in those churches I studied. For these churches, the women who held office in the societies tended to be wives and daughters of men who were respected, thus not only the dominie's wife but also those of the store owner and the successful farmer. Over time the Dutch American women's mission societies increasingly resembled American ones, taking up quilting, putting together age-specific mission groups for girls, and organizing mission festivals where they sold handwork and food.[65] These activities made women's mission societies suspect in some eyes.

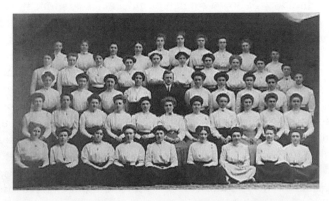

The young women's group at Eastern Avenue Christian Reformed Church in Grand Rapids, Michigan, had a man in charge, as did many Dutch American women's church groups. Photo courtesy of Archives, Calvin College.

An article in *De Gereformeerde Amerikaan* in March 1907 illustrates why. It claimed mission festivals and other such "fun" gatherings, while they could earn a significant amount, led people away from the correct path of giving at regular church services and led them to believe they should get something in return for their money. Hence the gatherings were bad and should not be tolerated in the church.[66] An underlying current was that of financial control, for women's mission societies might encourage women to give to causes and individuals of their own choosing.

While there were many women's mission organizations, the role of men in churches did not diminish much. The feminization of congregations was a major theme in other denominations, and one which attracted attention though less concern for Dutch Protestants. According to the United States church census of 1906, "Reformed" women (included German Reformed, Dutch Reformed, and Christian Reformed) constituted 57 percent of their denomination.[67] This was the second lowest representation of women for Protestant groups. Within the Christian Reformed denomination, the percentage was much closer. For communicant members it was divided almost evenly, with 52 percent female. For the Dutch Reformed the difference was greater: 62 percent female, though this included the colonial Dutch descendants as well as the newcomers.[68] *The Banner*, as well as other publications, took up this theme sporadically, calling other churches to follow various strategies to win back the men, while congratulating itself for maintaining orthodoxy and a family orientation.[69]

While mission societies were not the only organizations in Dutch American churches for women, they illustrated the basic pattern. In small congregations a Ladies' Aid might take up all mission and philanthropic endeavors. In other cases it was the women's mission society which did various tasks in addition to mission work. A striking characteristic was that many of these groups had their origins in this period, somewhat earlier for Reformed congregations, somewhat later for Christian Reformed ones on average. In all cases they served social as well as spiritual and philanthropic ends. For the most part they undergirded the principles of religion with which women grew up. They also, however, opened opportunities for women to do things somewhat separately within the church, something which disturbed at least some men. Dutch American writer Dirk Nieland was not alone in noting that a woman was likely to pick up ideas, like ones about how men should act, at the Ladies' Aid.[70] Male leaders tried to allow women service opportunities (like the chance to clean the church for free) without seriously challenging the vision of patriarchy which was enshrined in their religious worldview.

Women and Church Discipline

Though the Reformed Church and the Christian Reformed Church possessed nearly identical hierarchies, they used those structures differently, and their responses to changing gender roles at the turn of the century differed significant-ly. Both churches provided a safety net in times of trouble and a sheltered haven of social life and spiritual support, but they also demanded obedience to their understanding of proper conduct. The space women could carve out for them-selves within the churches varied, most importantly, according to each church's definition of patriarchy and its will to put this into practice. The stronger the male supervision in a congregation, the weaker the role of women's organizations. Klaaske Noorda Heller summed up part of the difference in her description of the churches in Oak Harbor, Washington: "There are two churches here, one Christian Reformed and the other Dutch Reformed [RCA]. Their teaching are almost alike but discipline is more strictly exercised in our church [CRC]."[71]

The Reformed and the Christian Reformed churches operated within a sys-tem of church government where the ruling body at the local level was the con-sistory, or board of elders (the minister was also an elder). At the turn of the century the consistory usually oversaw the actions of the deacons, who had the task of assisting those in need.[72] Only men in good standing with the church qualified for either of these church offices. The consistory might refer certain issues, especially regarding theology and general church policy, to Classis, the regional body of the denomination; which in turn could refer it to Synod, the next higher level; or finally to General Synod, an international body.

The consistory carried out most church business for a congregation. One of its functions was to admit and dismiss members, and further, to make sure that current members walked a straight and narrow path of good behavior. It fulfilled this partially by regular visitation (*huisbezoek*) of all members. As one church history reported: "There was fear and trembling when the minister and elder came on 'huis bezoek' (family visiting). In the early years this was held in the daytime and children stayed home from school. The elder and minister would begin at 9 o'clock, and end at four. It was a formal affair, and the children were frightened by the minister's direct questions about their spiritual welfare."[73] Such visitation could uncover a variety of problems which required discipline. At other times elders received complaints from congregation members about bad behavior on the part of others. In these cases the consistory could operate as a religious court, where defendants brought their witnesses and elders sought out evidence. Punishment went according to a series of steps, beginning with a reprimand, going to denial of communion, and ending in excommunication.[74] Trying to leave one church and join another to avoid the problem generally failed since one had to provide a letter of dismissal from one church in order to join another of the same denomination, and the elders used this letter to elaborate on any problems with that member.[75] Church discipline operated on the as-sumption that people wanted to remain within the denomination, and since for many immigrants the church was a large part of their world, the threat of ex-communication could engender considerable fear.

Depending on one's "sin," one would have to take various actions to avoid or be relieved of punishment. Most often one had to confess the deed and agree not to commit it again. Where the confession took place depended on the church and on the transgression. In some cases a confession before the consistory sufficed, particularly in Reformed congregations.[76] In other cases the confession before the consistory was only a precursor to a confession before the full congregation at one of the Sunday services, sometimes on one's knees.

To find out the role of church discipline in women's lives, and especially to uncover how women worked through these proceedings, I turned to consistory minutes. I gained access to records from a dozen churches in the period from 1880 to 1920. These records represent a spectrum of older and newer congregations, rural and urban locations, five of the top six states in terms of Dutch American populations, and various regional backgrounds from the Netherlands. The average consistory met twice a month, with additional meetings as necessary. In a large congregation the consistory often met weekly, in a small one monthly. As one might expect, some consistory secretaries wrote almost verbatim descriptions of the meetings, while others summarized cases briefly. The discipline cases they handled tended to be exceptions, but instructive ones.[77]

Premarital sex was one of the most common disciplinary issues, particularly for Christian Reformed consistories. Any couple requesting baptism of their first child born "early" had to come before consistory and admit their transgression against the Seventh Commandment. Christian Reformed consistories generally required confession at the baptism, that is in a service before the congregation, as well. Christian Reformed consistories were also less likely than Reformed ones to allow a child born somewhat "early" to go unnoticed.[78] The couple suffered the humiliation of public confession and the knowledge that few in the congregation would forget it, while their punishment served as a reminder to others that premarital sex could have unwanted consequences. The frequency of "early" children compared to the near absence of illegitimate births indicated that if the woman got pregnant, the couple got married. The exceptions illustrated this point as well as giving clues to prevailing thought patterns. Single mothers always had to make confessions or face excommunication, but unmarried fathers could expect the same treatment. As part of the interrogation of a woman, elders asked (and sometimes demanded on threat of excommunication) the name of the father of the child. Then the consistories generally meted out at least as much blame on the man as on the woman. In one Michigan church the consistory threatened excommunication of a young man for "seducing" a young woman. But the consistories did not assume women were victims or unwilling partners.[79] If men received strong reprimands, it was because of their responsibility for being in control of the courtship. The double standard was a bourgeois phenomenon, and the immigrants neither had their roots in this background nor had they generally adopted the ideology in the United States regardless of their economic standing at this time.

Illegitimacy cases also reinforced the Calvinist patriarchal ideal of family:

young adults were "children of," even if they lived apart from their parents, until marriage. An Illinois church member presented public confession for "treading upon the honor of the daughter of Mrs. [F]."[80] This was more than a linguistic convention. When "children" of any age acted improperly the consistory went first to the parents, to find out if they were fulfilling their parental duties. In an article on young people, immorality, and venereal disease in *De Gereformeerde Amerikaan*, J. W. Brink wrote: "Where does the responsibility lie? In ninety-nine out of a hundred cases with the parents."[81]

The patriarchal ideal of the church appeared glaringly in cases of marital strife. On this issue Dutch immigrant women also faced some of the strongest contrasts between their ethno-religious cultural background and that of the surrounding "Yankee" world. This also represented a major distinction between the two denominations. The Christian Reformed Church, the more conservative denomination and the choice for the majority of immigrants arriving in this period, maintained a stricter policy. The Reformed Church, while not agreeing totally with the liberalization trend in state divorce statutes, nonetheless allowed greater freedom. I should note that marital strife rarely came to the attention of consistories, and when it did it was usually at a critical stage. A woman who suffered with abuse, alcoholism, or desertion did not automatically "deserve" sympathy. Rather, she received part of the blame. The injunction to stay with her husband regardless, given in both denominations but enforced more strictly in Christian Reformed ones, led some to look outside the church for aid.

Frouwke Pul Schoonbeek faced particularly sad circumstances. Her husband died suddenly, leaving her with debts for the house they had built and with several children, including one mentally impaired son. After struggling to survive on public poor relief along with some money from her grown daughters and neighborhood assistance, she remarried. She identified her new husband only as "Berend" to her relatives in the Netherlands, and they received little news of the family until conditions became intolerable. As her son-in-law reported: "They lived in a good relationship for eight years, and then he began to leave her. Between times he would be at home, and then he would be with someone else . . . they struggled along for a couple of years until [your brother and sister] said to her that if she was going to put up with that man any longer they were going to leave. After that he left again and she would not take him back."[82] While he was at home the husband would beat both his wife and the mentally impaired son. At one point the neighbors reported him for child abuse, and he had to spend the night in jail. This, according to the son-in-law, was the cause of the problems in the first place. Pul finally locked her husband out of the house permanently in 1884.

Pul begged her children and her relatives in the Netherlands for financial help. Her older daughters were both married with children, and both indicated they could send little. The two youngest children stayed at home to support her.[83] Pul had attended a Christian Reformed Church with her first husband and during her years as a widow. Whether the church provided assistance in this latter case, however, was questionable. Though officially she could charge him with adultery, he could counter the charge by saying he had repented and returned but she had barred him from the house, and this a consistory would not allow. In every case of wife abuse I encountered, the consistory sought to discipline the husband and gain a promise of better conduct. Yet this could become a cycle, and the consistory expected the wife had to continually take him back if he repented and asked forgiveness. Only if he persisted over a long period of time, or was recalcitrant in not wanting to change, was he likely to face excommunication.[84] The difference between how many times a woman (or her children) were willing to put up with abuse, compared to how many times a consistory would give such a man another chance, became a major point of contention.[85]

An abused wife who had to deal with the consistory could also find that she became the accused. In one case in Illinois the husband admitted beating his wife and children. After he promised to do better the consistory committee questioned the wife. She claimed to be innocent of having incited her husband, and because she would not admit guilt the consistory put her under discipline. They did not take this step with the husband.[86] Throughout this time period, wife beating often garnered less reprimand than going to the lake on Sunday.[87] Further, abuse did not constitute grounds for divorce according to either denomination. This certainly contributed to the number of desertions by wives, which in my sample outnumbered those by husbands in the period 1880 to 1900. The tide changed as women began to seek civil divorces, where abuse often was an accepted grounds. This became an increasing problem for consistories after 1900, especially in Christian Reformed congregations.

Separation was grounds for church discipline, though usually the consistories of either denomination were slow to enforce this. Further discipline might follow, to the point of excommunication, but again at a deliberate pace. Whereas a consistory often handled other discipline cases on a biweekly or monthly basis, separation cases could easily stretch over several months or even years. In such cases consistories generally assumed that the couple needed time to work out their problems themselves and hence would warn the couple of the consequences of not reuniting and then wait. Financially women rarely had the means to remain separated for long, since the church normally refused assistance.[88] If a woman wanted to support herself her options were limited, more so since consistories frowned upon separated women housing male boarders. A Michigan Christian Reformed consistory case exemplified this. Though the consistory had not begun discipline for a couple that had been separated for a couple of months, it took the first step against the woman immediately when it found there was a male boarder (who had been in the house before the separation) still living in her home.[89]

No consistory disputed that adultery was a biblically sanctioned ground for divorce. In practice, however, there was only one circumstance which generally prompted divorce on grounds of adultery: venereal disease.[90] Like the rest of the American population around the turn of the century, Dutch immigrants were not immune to this "plague." A consistory would discipline a man who committed adultery, but rarely would they consider a divorce necessary on these grounds alone. They would, however, sometimes grant a divorce if the woman proved she had venereal disease and they believed that her husband was responsible.

Two cases illustrated this process. In 1885 a Michigan Christian Reformed consistory member went to visit Mrs. R., who was living with her sister. She informed the elder that her husband "suffers from a disease" and had infected her as well. The consistory agreed immediately to support her financially, but required proof of the disease to grant a divorce. Her doctor, a "Yankee," refused to reveal anything to the elder, but testified on her behalf in a civil divorce case. Thus assured, the consistory went ahead in requesting a divorce from Classis.[91]

In 1902 a young married woman petitioned the local church for membership after she moved back in with her parents. Her doctor, a Hollander, explained to the elders that she suffered from venereal disease and that her husband was her "spiritual murderer." On these grounds they should give her a divorce. The woman's husband, however, had his own witnesses. His doctor testified that he was an upstanding young man, and that she must have picked up the disease before their marriage.[92] The consistory let the matter drop for the moment, and like many other cases it simply disappeared from the records. What is instructive from this second case is that the Dutch American doctor considered the consistory the proper authority to notify concerning venereal disease, and that the consistory would take seriously the charge that the woman had the disease before her marriage, rather than assuming that it had to be the husband who infected the wife.

The second biblical grounds for divorce, at least according to some, was desertion (*moedwillige verlating*). In practice the Reformed Church accepted this by 1880, though individual congregations could make their own decisions. In a 1909 case a Reformed Church consistory in Wisconsin agonized over whether to allow a man who was divorced and then remarried to join their congregation. His first wife had gotten the divorce on grounds of abuse, which the consistory agreed was not a biblical reason, but then she left him, and that the consistory considered proper grounds. So they wrote to Classis for advice.[93] Classis reported they would "not countenance any compromise with the evil of unscriptural divorce," however if he had biblical grounds then they could approve his membership.[94] In general the Reformed Church simply left divorce cases on grounds of desertion up to the local congregation.

Since the Reformed Church generally worked more in conjunction with civil authorities than did the Christian Reformed, it sought actively to change divorce laws to make them more amenable to its own views. On the national level this involved cooperation with seventeen other denominations in the "Committee on Inter-Church Conference on Marriage and Divorce." They lobbied Congress to pass a uniform (national) system of divorce laws which would make divorces more difficult than they were in many states. Their program included desertion as grounds for divorce, but only if it continued for at least two years.[95] Congress left this prerogative to the states.

Meanwhile the Christian Reformed hierarchy spent a good deal of time around the turn of the century agonizing over how to interpret 1 Corinthians 7:15, the biblical passage concerning desertion and divorce. The main discussion centered on the divorce of a minister and his wife. In 1892 the woman left her husband, claiming psychological abuse, lack of financial support, and a dictatorial atmosphere in the home. In sum, she stated: "he doesn't know what love is, at least not love for me."[96] The western Michigan consistory dismissed this perfunctorily and put her under discipline. But when she refused to return to her husband, the minister sought a divorce on grounds of desertion. He became a leading proponent of divorce on these grounds, usually without mentioning his personal circumstances.[97] Meanwhile the minister found another pastorate in the West and went to the appropriate Classis there for support. Regional animosities added to the furor of the debate.

A lengthy editorial in *The Banner* in 1920, "Our Divorce Problem and the General Synod of the Reformed Churches of the Netherlands," illustrates how this issue kept surfacing.[98] The General Synod of the Christian Reformed Church ruled in 1894 that desertion was biblical grounds for divorce; in 1896 it reversed the ruling. In 1904 they returned to the 1894 ruling; in 1906 they reversed the ruling again. In 1914 a Synod committee expressed the opinion that the church could accept as members those who confessed their sins of getting civil divorces and then allow them to stay with their new partners. But there was significant opposition, and the 1916 meeting "outlawed" all divorces on these grounds, making the remarriages adultery again. The 1920 editorial chastised the minister who had contributed to this confusion and then stated its position: "we think that a lowering of the bars, be it ever so little at first, will in the long run bring our Church to the sad condition of many Protestant denominations in our land."[99] In sum, the Christian Reformed Church by 1920 still found desertion a problematic grounds for divorce.

The strict stance of the Christian Reformed Church combined with changes in state laws to make divorce outside the church an increasingly viable option for women in bad marital situations. There was a gradual trend in Christian Reformed consistory records from women deserting their husbands to women being excommunicated because they went outside the church for a divorce.[100] Obviously the state and the surrounding "Yankee" community had an impact; women became more aware of their civil options and were willing to risk life outside the church community. From this standpoint the church functioned as a place where women could learn about these issues, but it offered little space for women who took advantage of their civil rights.[101]

Bigamy cases illustrate the uneven church practices concerning desertion as well. Since neither the consistory nor the state considered such a second marriage legal, officially these cases did not involve divorce. In the instances I found in consistory records, bigamy involved one partner living in the Netherlands and one in America. Transatlantic church connections and chain migration meant that the culprits could be discovered at any time. A consistory would never allow the situation to stand, though in the cases I found the partners left the church and pursued civil divorce and remarriage rather than separating. In two cases of men whose wives refused to accompany them to the United States, a Reformed Church consistory, but not a Christian Reformed one, would consider divorce on grounds of the wife's "desertion." A woman who left her husband in the Netherlands had no such recourse; she was expeditiously excommunicated.[102]

Divorce was uncommon among Dutch American Protestants in this period, but policies concerning it were also a means for the churches to uphold their patriarchal ideal of family. Because the church policy disagreed with the surrounding community on this issue, it became an arena for cultural clash. In this battle women could choose the culture of their birth or that of a somewhat unknown America. Excommunication meant life outside the church and the church community. The more inclusive that community was, the more difficult the decision to leave. Men often faced a similar choice, but in general also had more leeway to err and still return.

Women and Church Aid

The way consistories dealt with widows also reflected the patriarchal ideals, not to mention their attitudes toward poverty. Not everything churches did appeared in consistory records, as was clear from the letters of Etje Houwerzijl, a middle-aged farm widow. After her husband's death, one of the elders informed her of a mother's pension in Michigan, to which she was entitled.[103] The minister and an elder drove her and her children to the office where she applied for this money. Moreover, Houwerzijl's religious belief supported her emotionally through a troubling time:

> We people always think that things must go in certain ways, but oh, if we pray for our daily bread, then the Lord remains free to decide *how* he wants to support us eh? the biggest care is only that we must stay close to Him in everything. The seeds were all gone, but this week a man came with his horses and plowed the land again, . . . he offered me all the plants that we needed out of his hothouses for nothing. The same man, one of the leading persons in our congregation, now took over management of all our farm affairs voluntarily and tells us exactly how and what we must do.[104]

The patriarchal hand of the elder in such cases rarely made it into the consistory notes. When the assistance involved money, though, consistories were scrupulous bookkeepers.

Consistories, through the deacons, provided assistance for widows fairly frequently. If a deacon noticed the need rather than the woman asking for help, the consistory was more amenable to the request. That did not mean that they did not respond to direct pleas, and hence widows were willing to face disapproval if it achieved their goals. Still, they could best send their requests via a third party (a man, and preferably a deacon) to the consistory.[105] If the persons were not well known in the congregation or the circumstances of their problems not already obvious, the process could take quite a bit of time as the deacons did their study.[106]

The kinds of assistance were multifarious. One widow was left in a financial bind because a debtor refused to pay her, so the consistory began censure proceedings against him. In another case the consistory agreed to buy the goods it distributed to the poor at a woman's store to help her business pick up. Consistories frequently arranged mortgages or loans for widows. The case of a widow who deeded her house to the church in return for a promise that she could stay in it until her death and that the church would provide for her during that time was no exception.[107]

For widows with few or no means, help came in the form of direct financial aid or payment in kind. A consistory would often authorize delivery of goods to a widow and her children: coal or wood for heating, potatoes or other foodstuffs in bulk. They would pay one-time expenses such as doctor's bills or funeral expenses more willingly than ongoing bills, though they sometimes contributed to rent.[108] Within the Christian Reformed Church, with its emphasis on Christian (separate) institutions, the aid could go further. Christian Reformed consistories would usually waive Christian school tuition for the children of impoverished widows, or if the school was not under their jurisdiction, might pay the tuition.[109] They would also support a widow in a Christian home for the aged if there was no relative available to care for her.

Other widows received a weekly dole from the church. Providing direct financial aid for widows proved difficult because special collections frequently fell short of the prescribed amount. The Christian Reformed committee to support retired ministers and their widows and orphans illustrated this dilemma. In 1904–5, when the number of persons to support rose and the sum of contributions fell, the committee sent letters to several widows, asking if they could not get by on less. They replied (through their deacons) that this was not possible, but the committee reduced the amounts nonetheless.[110] For most years the ministers' widows could anticipate the full amount promised, though it was not particularly generous. The amounts were still slightly above what local congregations gave to impoverished widows. In the period 1905–10, for example, Christian Reformed ministers' widows generally received around $200 per year, depending on the number of children. At the same time congregations reported giving out pensions of two dollars per week to widows in need. In both cases the women could rely on assistance in kind for additional support. Widows who were not church members did not generally receive regular aid, though under certain circumstances (such as long-term regular church attendance) they might receive something.

The amount any widow received depended on her circumstances, and the consistories knew these well before extending any aid. They could always report how many children were working and for what wages; how much each child contributed financially to the household; whether the widow could earn anything herself; if there was a possibility to get aid from other relatives or friends. When it came to convincing family members to do their duty, a consistory could be rather persuasive. Widow V. complained that her son-in-law went back on his promise that she would have a room upstairs in his house until her death. He claimed he neither said this nor intended it. The consistory, without corroborating witnesses on either side, ruled in favor of the widow, informing the son-in-law she would stay. It then instructed the two that they "must make peace with one another."[111]

Phrases such as "if she really needs it," and no additional assistance until she is "more needy," in the consistory minutes made it clear that churches sought to be frugal with their outlays to widows. Theologically they might attribute poverty to a person's sin, but in the case of widows they rarely assumed the woman should take on a job outside the home if she was elderly or had children.[112] The stress generally fell on children to support their mother. Consistories would not expect children of primary school age to work, but they assumed teenagers could earn something. They also assumed that children, even those who lived far away, could contribute a substantial amount, and they would acquire the cooperation of other church consistories in getting it.

The church took over not only the patriarchal role of breadwinner for widows, it also took over the oversight of moral conduct in the family. This corresponded to the prevailing ideal within the group of the father as the leading moral force in the family. Widows and their children deserved special attention in the eyes of consistories. A widow had to be doubly careful not to consort with "improper" types, and members of the consistory had to supervise the children's discipline and spiritual training more thoroughly.[113] Though I found no cases where the consistory cut someone's support because of bad conduct, the threat was always there.

Widows, like other women, experienced the church in its dual functions of caregiver and disciplinarian. The minister might come to give communion to a homebound elderly woman, or he might arrive with an elder to inform a widow she could no longer take communion because she had done something wrong. Women knew that if they stayed within the parameters of good conduct the church would provide a safety net.

* * *

Though both churches had similar hierarchies, their social practices exhibited significant differences. The Reformed Church allowed women more space in a physical as well as metaphorical sense.[114] Thus the Reformed Church congregations boasted more women's organizations, with greater independence. In their bazaars and suppers, many Reformed churches by 1920 resembled the surrounding "Yankee" ones. Still, even within the Reformed Church, the role of men and of a more strict patriarchal ideology was evident.

The theological shift underway, spurred by the women's movement generally, gave women greater individual rights within churches (such as voting) and greater opportunities for religious service as something more than a helper. In the more conservative Dutch American community there was concern about the *vervrouwlijking* (feminization) of society generally.[115] Here the example of the Netherlands retarded shifts in that direction. There, it was the male church hierarchy and their political allies who took over the tasks of caring for the ill, the old, the poor, and even (to a lesser degree) the "heathen." Men, in other words, set the terms of social reproduction for many communal-level care functions, and women had little input.

Beyond that, the absence of a network of women's groups within Protestant churches in the Netherlands until this time period meant that women immigrants had to overcome older ideas to increase their religious roles. Research on other ethnic groups highlights the difference. Norwegian and Jewish women, for example, who had more old world precedents of women's organizations, organized relatively quickly in the United States into separate women's spaces.[116] Dutch American women had to justify that their organizations were something more than just social ones.

Missions were one of the main areas of congregation-level organization for Protestant Dutch American women. There women could learn organizational and fund-raising techniques. Though by American standards supporting missions was hardly pathbreaking in this period, it meant a shift in women's roles in Dutch American churches toward much greater direct participation. Again the difference between Reformed and Christian Reformed was clear, with the women of the Reformed Church taking a more active role, in part due to the efforts of Christine van Raalte Gilmore. On the other hand, the network of church-supported institutions, particularly Christian schools, which the separatist ideology of the Christian Reformed advocated, also offered positions to women. The Christian Reformed network of church-sanctioned businesses, groups, press, institutions, and activities meant that in many of the clustered Dutch settlements and urban ghettoes, one could live with relatively little contact to non–Christian Reformed people. This meant that the Christian Reformed congregations were more likely to offer support to women in poverty or widows, if only because its consistories were more in touch with most aspects of the lives of the parishioners. For the same reason, and because of somewhat more liberal attitudes, the Reformed Church was less likely to discipline members—it offered more freedom of choice.

The United States offered the denominations the freedom to practice religion as they saw fit; it also offered women freedom from these churches when they saw fit. The legislation of this period protecting wives from abuse and widows from poverty had a significant impact on the Dutch American community, partially by supplementing church social welfare but more importantly by offering some women an option for life outside the church community. For a tiny minority it was one of the clearest choices they would ever have to make, to remain in a group which would tolerate abuse or to leave the community. The church could and would accept a woman's taking assistance from the state if she was widowed or needy but would not tolerate a state policy that allowed nonbiblical divorce or infringed on a husband's rights in its eyes. Most women never faced this dilemma, but for those who did, it became a very difficult choice. In total, concerning church life, women's role in social reproduction was more often one of small innovations, and the degree to which women could pursue such innovations depended on parameters set by others.

Conclusion

When I first drafted this work I referred to it as "Home is where you build it." There were two meanings I wanted to convey with that phrase: one related to the immigrant women I studied and their coping strategies regarding international migration, and a second dealing with how the study of immigrant women fits into a broader academic discourse. What that meant was placing this study of Dutch Protestant immigrant women in the period 1880 to 1920 in context, into its own "home" if you will. The history of immigrant women was a stepchild of both immigration history and women's history for years.[1] More recently, the exclusion of European immigrant women, with the exception of some urban workers, from the "ethnic" category has had a similar effect in women's history. As this and other studies show, while such women were not as "visible" a minority, and hence they benefited from whiteness, still their experiences often did not match those of "American" white women more generally.[2]

In the Midwest, the heartland of Dutch Protestant settlement, different ideas of gender roles coming from Europe clashed in important ways. Jon Gjerde captured one of them in describing the difference of evaluating women's field work, a part of the development of what he called "minds" of the West.[3] The continuing subordination of women's interests to a familial and communal ideal well into the twentieth century had significant consequences in patterns of land development and community continuity.[4] Moreover, the same freedom from state control which allowed elite women of the Progressive Era to create the beginnings of a welfare state also allowed ethnic groups, sometimes with the leadership and participation of women and sometimes without it, to create their own institutions.[5] The continuation of both these institutions and the communal ideal which supported ethno-religious over state intervention impeded stronger state development over time. The Dutch were a part of all of these developments. In the context of the world that they came from, the world that they tried to create made a great deal of sense.

People involved in international migration make choices about what home is and how they want to structure it. Those choices take place in the context of parameters, many over which the choosers have little control. Age at migration, family status, race and ethnic background, size and location of the local ethnic community: these contributed heavily to how a woman might react to the United States. I discuss such choices under the rubric of social reproduction, showing that some migrants would choose new patterns and some would replicate old ones. And when people could not replicate the old, they made choices about how to adjust. I have chosen to look at certain aspects of social reproduction, thus less at the labor market and more at roles in the familial and religious realm. And I have chosen to focus my attention on women, not because they were the only ones involved in social reproduction but because their experiences tell us a great deal more about aspects of it and about the meaning of migration than we may think at first glance. Migration meant challenges to gender roles, shifts in them at least temporarily, and sometimes changes on a more permanent basis. Immigrants were among the trendsetters, the urban working-class innovators, and they were among the staunchest conservatives in the period around the turn of the century. It was the conservators who predominated in the rural Midwest, and this fact contributed to a particular kind of ideal of womanhood there, one which did not match that of the elite. Many evangelical women of the present have their roots in a transnational ideology of family and community which came from this past.

Adaptation to a new racial/ethnic system was also part of adjusting to life in the United States, though this was not always visible to Dutch immigrant women at the time. Their ability to come to the United States at all, and the economic opportunities which both men and women encountered, were related to existing racial categories. The presence of the colonial-descended Dutch in the United States opened doors and supported early activities of the newcomers, just as the example of the Netherlands' colonial holdings in this period made it easier for immigrants to think about U.S. imperialism in familiar terms. Social reproduction of racial categories in this case meant identifying a hierarchy, with some groups being more familiar than others. The mission activities to American Indians served an important cultural as well as religious purpose from this standpoint.

Migration made a difference in several important ways for Dutch Protestant immigrant women at the turn of the century. For one thing, it expanded their opportunities to marry. They entered an international marriage market in which the demand for wives in the United States was higher than in the Netherlands and in which the men who migrated generally had better opportunities to amass enough money to support a family. Women, too, because of better economic opportunities for wage work, could contribute more to the beginnings of a marriage. Taken together these factors led to significantly higher marriage rates than in the Netherlands. This was not a unique experience for women given the skewed sex ratios of many migrant groups of this era. The relative absence of women who would remain unmarried, who might have followed careers or been outspoken advocates for the rights of women based on their own circumstances, had a strong relationship to demography. Further, the high birthrates of the first generation, averaging over seven children, meant little opportunity for such activism until quite late in life. Large families meant not only a labor force and economic security in old age but also the possibility to re-create extended family networks, some of which were lost with migration. The loss of such extended family initially was one of the most difficult aspects of life for Dutch immigrant women, for such individuals took part in one another's lives in many ways.

The relative shortage of domestics and hired hands in the United States, combined with the predominantly rural nature of the Dutch settlement, led the group to rely on nuclear family, including women and children, and on machinery to fill their labor needs. Dutch immigrant women had to trade off the servants and social position allotted a farm wife in the Netherlands for the chance to attain or retain the farm at all. Children took on an added importance in carrying out household work, but that role did not generally come at the expense of a basic education. Distance and the difficulty of reviving extended family ties after migration meant a greater reliance on nuclear families, at least initially. Yet the goal was to re-create a world which was disappearing in Europe, and in this the group was relatively successful until beyond the scope of this period. Among the rural settlers, this was part of a general move of agricultural settlement across the plains and onto the West Coast, and even into Canada.[6] Along the way, they sometimes adapted as much to other ethnic groups as to Anglo patterns, as was clear in the (somewhat over-represented) connections of the women in the biographies to German Americans, though that adaptation could go in both directions.[7]

A major shift for many Dutch immigrant women was the opportunity for a better financial base over time, which translated into better food, clothing, and shelter. These operated as some of the most outstanding motivating forces for migration from the outset, as seen in letters describing the chance to eat meat three times a day. In the United States the immigrants found patterns of life they associated with wealth. Overall they tended to eat according to Dutch patterns, not adopting many American foods, yet they increased the amount, the variety, and particularly the proportion of meat in their diets, thus replicating the food habits of wealthy individuals in the Netherlands. On clothing, immigrants varied, particularly according to age at migration and according to when they arrived in the United States. Those who were younger were more likely to want to adopt the new patterns, as were those who came late in the period. The better economic circumstances that many of their families managed in the United States meant more clothing. But the biggest shift in terms of apparel for the immigrants was the absence (in the areas where most of them settled) of major class distinctions based on dress. Not only could a family eat like the wealthy, their children could dress as nicely. Adapting to some aspects of bourgeois consumption as the family could afford it was typical, though it did not necessarily entail embracing other aspects of "Yankee" bourgeois ideology. While some adopted the term "lady" as a sign of their financial well-being, others would challenge it over time as representing an ideal "more decorative than useful."[8]

In terms of housekeeping, women found it difficult to maintain the same standards of cleanliness that reigned in the Netherlands. This they justified by stating that it was customary to live that way in America, and by invoking the circumstances of settlement, which often did not include a street to sweep. They still upheld a higher standard than the "Yankees," but they could not begin to maintain the patterns of Dutch farmhouses where one or two domestics assisted with the cleaning work. For Dutch domestics that meant that the United States was paradise. Their work hours were fewer, the requirements for cleanliness were significantly less, the wages were better, and the difference in status from employer to domestic was much less than in the Netherlands. Hence the picture of domestic service as degrading drudgery which still seems to haunt women's history needs serious qualification, especially in light of similar findings from several studies of European immigrant women, particularly those in the Midwest.

Work opportunities for women generally were better in the United States than in the Netherlands. Here the difference was one of time. Industrialization was much further along in the United States and, further, there was a difference in gender roles. In the United States jobs in nursing, teaching, and social work opened up to women earlier under the banner of the extension of "mothering." In the Netherlands the churches' role and through it male responsibility for philanthropy remained paramount, even when Netherlanders created new service opportunities for women rapidly around the turn of the century. Careers for women came late enough in the Netherlands that many of the immigrants experienced these patterns as new in the United States and labeled them "American." The example of U.S. women and careers made few inroads among the Dutch in early years, with a couple of exceptions. Colonial-Dutch-descended Reformed churchwomen became role models for newer Dutch Americans in that denomination, who found mission activities one avenue into the American middle class. Likewise, women of the second generation began entering helping professions and gaining a share of (rather than dominating) leadership roles in philanthropic organizations. In both cases, the continued participation of church men and the continuation of ideological precedents from the Netherlands meant women never gained the status which typified Progressive Era female reformers. An individual Dutch immigrant woman like Cornelia De Bey could make that leap, but for most, separatist activism signified only limited cooperation with Anglo American women.

The loss of extended family was perhaps most poignant in the realm of health, for with migration many families lost a particular cohort of women, relatives with grown children and hence more flexible schedules, who could help fulfill informal nursing roles. Contributing to the change was the shift in geographic space, so that distances between family members in the United States could thwart their interest in caring for one another. The area of settlement, whether in a Dutch American community or not, close to a church, neighbors, family, friends, or not—these were crucial factors in determining how satisfied most women were with their new homeland and whether it really became a *home*land.

Health was as important as economics in determining a family's success. Here women continued to carry on their informal nursing roles, yet had to adjust to a new language for medicine and to the absence of those who might have assisted them in informal care. This sped the move toward professionalization, as did the economic circumstances that allowed the Dutch immigrants to go from doctor to specialist. The lack of extended family and of state institutions also led Dutch immigrant women to support the formation of care homes for the elderly and other ethnically based institutions, and to serve in them.

The demographics of migration meant that older and weaker family members were less likely to cross the Atlantic, leaving an impression of the old world as literally old, sick, and dying.[9] Women, especially older women, might have corrected this impression somewhat, yet their attempts to maintain family ties into the next generation foundered on the shoals of language loss and with the continuing absence of face-to-face contact. This habit of thought, associating the new with America, was something which recurred in many areas. The developments in the Netherlands which paralleled those in the United States in many areas did not gain enough attention to counter this view. Whether in technology, women's occupations, or clothing, America was the "new" land.

Migration for some entailed a shift to English over time. Young migrants expected to learn English; and older ones expected it of their children. The changeover, which on the ethnic group level began around World War I, had several important consequences. First, it upended the generational patterns within the family, making the children the interpreters and the experts in some settings. Many other immigration studies have found similar results. Second, the shift to English reinforced an ideal of freedom in the United States: freedom from hierarchies, freedom from the limitations on gender known in the Netherlands. The young Dutch immigrant women who most challenged the expectations their families and ethno-religious community held for them chose to live in an English-language world. Their older female counterparts lost some of their influence on the young, and in the broader U.S. community, due to lack of communication skills. Their lack of opportunities to learn English, even if they wanted to, isolated them from a world beyond their ethnic boundaries. Older women seeking to conserve their mother tongue were also trying to conserve their status, their roles, and their worldview. Language shift thus was gendered in important ways, a characteristic which appears in most of the research on ethnic groups, if they consider gender at all. Religious language, and the world it created mentally, was central to many women's understanding of the world. Conservation, thus, was often embedded in the words women had at their disposal.

The church remained a central part of Dutch communities after migration. Because migration meant in effect the loss of certain extended family and community members, social networks in the church took on greater importance in women's lives. For some, at least, church members took on the roles of extended family left behind. The ideology of the church supported this view, operating as the communal control on moral activities, and as the patriarchal authority in cases where there was no man present. The Dutch Protestant churches differed among themselves according to the degree of separateness they sought to maintain in the new setting. The more conservative group attempted, to a large extent successfully, to live apart from the surrounding society. The implications of this separatist stance meant greater social control over women. In cases of prenuptial births, marital discord, and divorce, these women could expect the strong patriarchal hand of the church to discipline them, and to uphold the patriarchal arrangement of families, even at the expense of the women involved. On the other hand, the activism also meant a greater attention to assisting widows and others in need. For those of separatist persuasion this led to a different model of state assistance and of women's participation in those endeavors.

These changes fell into the category of social reproduction. Yet for all the changes which migration entailed, the extent to which life remained the same for these Dutch Protestant immigrant women was significant. A few used migration to escape the roles and rules of their world in the Netherlands, and that of the developing Dutch American communities, but many more used migration to conserve a way of life which otherwise would have disappeared sooner. All faced situations in which the parameters of the new setting required changes, often changes the women had not anticipated, and those women made choices about how to organize life based on their circumstances, choices which changed according to age and time. Still, for the most part they managed to keep many of the patterns they considered most important—to create homes.

Notes

Abbreviations

HH	Heritage Hall Collection, Calvin College (Grand Rapids, Mich.)
HUBA	Holland Union Benevolent Association
IFWC	International Federation of Women's Clubs
IIAV	International Institute and Archive for the Women's Movement (Amsterdam)
JAH	Joint Archives of Holland (Holland, Mich.)
PJM	P. J. Meertens Institute (Amsterdam)
RL	Rijksarchief Leeuwarden (Leeuwarden, Friesland)
SHSI	State Historical Society of Iowa

Introduction

1. Pierrette Hondagneu-Sotelo suggests a similar conclusion related to another group in *Gendered Transitions: Mexican Experiences of Immigration* (Berkeley: University of California Press, 1994).

2. Catholics were far fewer in number than Protestants among the immigrants. On their experiences see Yda Schreuder, *Dutch Catholic Immigrant Settlement in Wisconsin, 1850–1905* (New York: Garland, 1989); and H. A. V. M. van Stekelenburg, *Landverhuizing als regionaal verschijnsel: Van Noord-Brabant naar Noord-Amerika 1820–1880* (Tilburg: Stichting Zuidelijk Historisch Contact, 1991). On Dutch Jews see Robert P. Swierenga, *The Forerunners: Dutch Jewry in the North American Diaspora* (Detroit: Wayne State University Press, 1994). On socialists see Pieter R. D. Stokvis, "Dutch Socialist Immigrants and the American Dream," in *The Dutch-American Experience: Essays in Honor of Robert P. Sweierenga,* ed. Hans Krabbendam and Larry J. Wagenaar (Amsterdam: Vrije Universiteit Uitgeverij, 2000).

3. For an overview on Dutch immigration which explains the three waves see Suzanne M. Sinke, "Dutch," in *A Nation of Peoples: A Sourcebook on America's Multicultural Heritage,* ed. Elliott R. Barkan (Westport, Conn.: Greenwood Press, 1999), pp. 156–73. See also Robert P. Swierenga, "Dutch," in *Harvard Encyclopedia of American Ethnic Groups,* ed. Stephan Thernstrom (Cambridge: Harvard University Press, 1980), pp. 284–95. By far the most complete study of the nineteenth-century migrants in the United States is Jacob van Hinte's *Netherlanders in America: A Study of Emigration and Settlement in the Nineteenth and Twentieth Centuries in the United States of America,* 2 vols., ed. Robert P. Swierenga, trans. Adriaan de

Wit (Grand Rapids: Baker Book House, 1985), a translation and reprint of the original published in the Netherlands in 1928. Henry S. Lucas also utilized this work extensively for his *Netherlanders in America: Dutch Immigration to the United States and Canada, 1789–1950* (1955; reprint, Grand Rapids: William B. Eerdmans, 1989).

4. Recent works have sought to incorporate more on women, though the general focus remains on public activities typically associated with men. See Rob Kroes, *The Persistence of Ethnicity: Dutch Calvinist Pioneers in Amsterdam, Montana* (Urbana: University of Illinois Press, 1992); and Annemieke Galema, *Frisians to America 1880–1914: With the Baggage of the Fatherland* (Groningen: REGIO-PRojekt, 1996).

5. On using generations as a key to understanding immigrant women see also Judy Yung, *Unbound Feet* (Berkeley: University of California Press, 1995). On women as innovators see especially Kathy Peiss, *Cheap Amusements: Working Women and Leisure in Turn-of-the-Century New York* (Philadelphia: Temple University Press, 1986) and Joanne J. Meyerowitz, *Women Adrift: Independent Wage Earners in Chicago, 1880–1930* (Chicago: University of Chicago Press, 1988).

6. See Robert P. Swierenga, "Local Patterns of Dutch Migration to the United States in the Mid-nineteenth Century," in *A Century of European Migrations*, ed. Rudolph Vecoli and Suzanne Sinke (Urbana: University of Illinois Press, 1991), pp. 134–57.

7. I became more convinced of this approach after I encountered the Hunter College Women's Studies Collective text, *Women's Realities, Women's Choices: An Introduction to Women's Studies*, 2d ed. (New York: Oxford University Press, 1995).

8. An alternative term which included some of the same ideas was cultural reproduction; see Don Kulick, *Language Shift and Cultural Reproduction: Socialization, Self, and Syncretism in a Papua New Guinean Village* (Cambridge: Cambridge University Press, 1992).

9. The literature on immigrant women which stresses conservative trends and acceptance of new conditions includes three on German American women: Linda Schelbitzki Pickle, *Contented among Strangers* (Urbana: University of Illinois Press, 1996); Agnes Bretting, "Frauen als Einwanderer in der Neuen Welt: Überlegungen anhand einiger Selbstzeugnisse deutscher Auswanderinnen," *Amerikastudien* 33 (1988): 319–27; and Carol K. Coburn, *Life at Four Corners: Religion, Gender, and Education in a German-Lutheran Community, 1868–1945* (Lawrence: University Press of Kansas, 1992). Others stress the opportunities of the United States for women and women's new roles. Included among these are Hondagneu-Sotelo, *Gendered Transitions;* L. DeAne Lagerquist, *In America the Men Milk the Cows: Factors of Gender, Ethnicity, and Religion in the Americanization of Norwegian-American Women* (Brooklyn: Carlson Publishing, 1991); and Yung, *Unbound Feet.*

10. Because it focuses on one group, this study could not test the relevance of culture. For an excellent case study of factors related to women's rural-to-urban migration, including culture, see Christiane Harzig, ed., *Peasant Maids, City Women: From the European Countryside to Urban America* (Ithaca: Cornell University Press, 1997).

11. On this see Jon Gjerde, *The Minds of the West: Ethnocultural Evolution in the Rural Middle West, 1830–1917* (Chapel Hill: University of North Carolina Press, 1997), part 3.

12. By far the largest collection on Dutch Protestant immigrants is the Heritage Hall Collection at Calvin College in Grand Rapids, Michigan. The Joint Archives of Holland, at Hope College in Holland, Michigan, also contain various materials on Dutch Americans. I also collected letters from Dutch archives, notably the Rijksarchief Leeuwarden.

13. A selection of these letters appear in Herbert J. Brinks, ed., *Dutch American Voices* (Ithaca: Cornell University Press, 1995).

14. I read several thousand letters in total, but used only about fifty collections (several hundred letters) for the bulk of my information based on correspondence. The collection edited by Ulbe B. Bakker, *Sister, Please Come Over. Experiences of an Immigrant Family from Friesland/the Netherlands. Letters from America in the Period 1894–1933* (Winsum, Fr.: Trion, G.A.C., 1999), appeared too late to incorporate into this book. On using letters see Walter D. Kamphoefner, Wolfgang Helbich, and Ulrike Sommer, *News from the Land of Freedom,* trans. Susan Carter Vogel (Ithaca: Cornell University Press, 1991), pp. 27–35; and David A. Gerber, "'You See I Speak Wery Well Englisch': Literacy and the Transformed Self as Reflected in Immigrant Personal Correspondence," *Journal of American Ethnic History* 12 (Winter 1993): 56–62. See also Ulrike Sommer, "Letters of German Immigrant Women: Attempting a Case Study," in *The Press of Labor Migrants in Europe and North America, 1880s to 1930s* (Bremen: Labor Migration Project, 1985), pp. 48–58.

15. On this phenomenon see Leo Schelbert, "On Interpreting Immigrant Letters: The Case of Johann Caspar and Wilhelmina Honegger-Hanhart," *Yearbook of German-American Studies* 16 (1981): 141–51.

16. For some of the results see Jo Daan, *"Ik was te bissie ..." Nederlanders en hun taal in de Verenigde Staten* (Zutphen: Walburg Pers, 1987).

17. In this comparison I am not alone. Other ethnic groups from the same time period also held to communal values and utilized their churches to maintain order. See, for example, Jane Marie Pederson, *Between Memory and Reality: Family and Community in Rural Wisconsin, 1870–1970* (Madison: University of Wisconsin Press, 1992), p. 7.

18. The literature bridging the fields of immigration and women's history has grown steadily in the past few years. The most comprehensive work is Donna Gabaccia's *From the Other Side: Women, Gender, and Immigrant Life in the U.S., 1820–1990* (Bloomington: Indiana University Press, 1994). For a bibliography consult Donna Gabaccia, comp., *Immigrant Women in the United States: A Selectively Annotated Multidisiplinary Bibliography* (New York: Greenwood Press, 1989); for overviews on research in the fields of history, sociology, and anthropology, see the essays in Donna Gabaccia, ed., *Seeking Common Ground* (Westport, Conn.: Greenwood Press, 1992).

19. Anja Meulenbelt, "De Ekonomie van de Koesterende Funktie," *te elfder ure* 22 (1975): 638–75. See also Selma Sevenhuijsen, "Vadertje staat, moedertje thuis? Vrouwen, reproduktie en de staat," in *Socialisties-Feministiese Teksten 1,* ed. Selma Sevenhuijsen, Joyce Outshoorn, and Anja Meulenbelt (Amsterdam: Feministische Uitgeverij Sara, 1978), pp. 18–64; Johanna Brenner and Barbara Laslett, "Gender, Social Reproduction, and Women's Self-Organization: Considering the U.S. Welfare State," *Gender and Society* 5 (Sept. 1991): 311–33; Evelyn Nakano Glenn, "From Servitude to Service Work: Historical Continuities in the Racial Division of Paid Reproductive Labor," *Signs* 18 (Autumn 1992): 1–43.

20. Micaela di Leonardo, *The Varieties of Ethnic Experience: Kinship, Class and Gender among California Italian-Americans* (Ithaca: Cornell University Press, 1984). See also chap. 5 in Gabaccia, *From the Other Side.*

21. Louise Lampere adopted this approach in *From Working Daughters to Working Mothers: Immigrant Women in a New England Industrial Community* (Ithaca: Cornell University Press, 1987). The basic economic model sought to complement works such as Brinley Thomas, *Migration and Economic Growth: A Study of Great Britain and the Atlantic Economy* (Cambridge: Cambridge University Press, 1973); or Dirk Hoerder, ed., *Labor Migration in the Atlantic Economies: The European and North American Working Classes during the Period of Industrialization* (Westport, Conn.: Greenwood Press, 1985); or Lucie Cheng and Edna Bona-

cich, *Labor Immigration under Capitalism: Asian Workers in the United States before World War II* (Berkeley: University of California Press, 1984).

22. Various scholars of migration have sought to cover both sides of the migratory stream. See the materials answering Frank Thistlethwaite's call in Rudolph J. Vecoli and Suzanne M. Sinke, eds., *A Century of European Migrations* (Urbana: University of Illinois Press, 1991).

23. Siep Stuurman, "Christendom en patriarchaat: De zedelijkheidskwestie, het vrouwen-vraagstuk en het ontstaan van de verzuiling in Nederland," in *Jaarboek voor vrouwengeschiedenis 1982*, ed. Josine Blok et al. (Nijmegen: SUN, 1982), pp. 211–14, 224–26.

24. On this see Hille de Vries, "The Labor Market in Dutch Agriculture and Emigration to the United States," in *The Dutch in America*, ed. Robert P. Swierenga (New Brunswick: Rutgers University Press, 1985), pp. 78–101.

25. Van Gogh quoted in Liesbeth Brandt Corstius and Cora Hollema, eds., *De Kunst van het Moederschap: Leven en Werk van Nederlandse Vrouwen in de 19e Eeuw* (The Hague: De Dageraad, 1981), p. 71.

26. See Pieter R. D. Stokvis, "Dutch International Migration 1815–1910," in *The Dutch in America*, ed. Robert P. Swierenga (New Brunswick: Rutgers University Press, 1985), p. 60.

27. See, for example, W. H. Posthumus–van der Goot and Anna de Waal, eds., *Van Moeder op Dochter: De maatschappelijke positie van de vrouw in Nederland vanaf de franse tijd* (1948; reprint, Nijmegen: SUN, 1977), p. 303. On prostitution and on the related concern for vene-real disease, see Johan P. Nater, *Vigelerende vrouwen, gedienstige meiden: Sexualiteit in Neder-land in de negentiende eeuw* (Rotterdam: Ad. Donker, 1986), pp. 27, 46–67 passim.

28. Marjan Rossen, "Huize Lydia: Alleenstaande Vrouwen in het Begin van deze Eeuw," in *Vrouwendomein: Woongeschiedenis van Vrouwen in Nederland*, ed. Maria Grever et al. (Am-sterdam: SUA, 1986), pp. 102–4; Nater, *Sexualiteit in Nederland*, pp. 70–75.

29. Similar motivations operated in the case of Dutch Catholic migrants, who began a smaller but significant move to Wisconsin at about the same time, under the tutelage of Fa-ther Van Den Broek. For general descriptions of each of these individual congregational movements and their successors see Van Hinte, *Netherlanders in America*.

30. Robert P. Swierenga, "The Delayed Transition from Folk to Labor Migration: The Netherlands, 1880–1920," *International Migration Review* 27 (Summer 1993): 420–23.

31. On placing migration in an international context, or more broadly into world history, see especially the articles by Frank Thistlethwaite on transatlantic connections, Julianna Puskas on personal motivations, and Rudolph Vecoli's introduction, in Vecoli and Sinke, *Century of European Migrations*. See also Virginia Yans-McLaughlin, ed., *Immigration Recon-sidered: History, Sociology, and Politics* (New York: Oxford University Press, 1990); and Walter Nugent, *Crossings: The Great Transatlantic Migrations, 1870–1914* (Bloomington: Indiana University Press, 1992). On the differences in village migration rates see Swierenga, "Local Patterns of Dutch Migration to the United States," and Galema, *Frisians to America*. On the role of the church and chain migration compare June Granatir Alexander, *The Immigrant Church and Community: Pittsburgh's Slovak Catholics and Lutherans, 1880–1915* (Pittsburgh: University of Pittsburgh Press, 1987).

32. On underreporting see Robert P. Swierenga, *Faith and Family: Dutch Immigration and Settlement in the United States, 1820–1920* (New York: Holmes & Meier, 2000), chap. 11, "Dutch International Migration Statistics."

33. See Stokvis, "Dutch International Migration 1815–1910," p. 57, where he estimated 15 percent.

34. Sucheng Chan exposes the importance of earlier arrivals from the same national back-

ground as one of the important factors in immigrants' acceptance. See "European and Asian Immigration into the United States in Comparative Perspective, 1820s to 1920s," in *Immigration Reconsidered: History, Sociology, and Politics,* ed. Virginia Yans-Mclaughlin (New York: Oxford University Press, 1990), pp. 37–75. On the importance of whiteness see especially David R. Roediger, *The Wages of Whiteness: Race and the Making of the American Working Class* (London: Verso, 1991).

35. See Hasia R. Diner, *Erin's Daughters in America: Irish Immigrant Women in the Nineteenth Century* (Baltimore: Johns Hopkins University Press, 1983); Joy Lintelman, "More Freedom, Better Pay: Single Swedish Immigrant Women in the United States, 1880–1920" (Ph.D. dissertation, University of Minnesota, 1991); Carl Ross, "Servant Girls: Community Leaders, Finnish American Women in Transition (1910–1920)," in *Women Who Dared: The History of Finnish American Women,* ed. Carl Ross and K. Marianne Wargelin Brown (St. Paul: Immigration History Research Center, 1986), pp. 41–54.

36. Swierenga, "Delayed Transition," table 12, p. 422. Generally women made up 23 percent of the single migrants to the U.S. in the period 1900–1920.

37. See Jon Gjerde, *From Peasants to Farmers: The Migration from Balestrand, Norway, to the Upper Middle West* (Cambridge: Cambridge University Press, 1985); and Lagerquist, *In America the Men Milk the Cows.* Compare Christiane Harzig, "Women's Work and Family Strategies: Immigrant Women in the U.S. around the Turn of the Century," in *"Why Did You Come?" The Proletarian Mass Migration: Research Report 1980–1985,* ed. Dirk Hoerder and Christiane Harzig (Bremen: Labor Migration Project, 1986), pp. 111–22.

38. On this phenomenon see Caroline B. Brettell, *Men Who Migrate, Women Who Wait: Population and History in a Portuguese Parish* (Princeton: Princeton University Press, 1986); Robert F. Harney, "Men without Women: Italian Migrants in Canada, 1885–1930," *Canadian Ethnic Studies* 11 (1979): 29–47.

Chapter 1: Family Matters

1. Given that the sources I relied upon for most of this study, letters and Dutch language interviews, had an automatic bias toward those with family ties, I need to qualify this. There were individuals who simply "disappeared" in America, perhaps taking advantage of the new setting to abandon family connections, perhaps falling prey to disease or destitution before they had the chance to find a safety net. But considering the familial nature of Dutch migration in this period, combined with heavy concentration in ethnic settlements, the number of individuals in this category must have been small.

2. This debate appeared in various venues. Abraham D. Lavender notes that theorists (such as Juliet Mitchell) who argue that the family is a central institution of women's oppression tend to downplay those positive aspects of familial support which ethnic women valued (*Ethnic Women and Feminist Values: Towards a "New" Value System* [Lanham: University Press of America, 1986]).

3. Scholars who deal specifically with immigrant women and families form the exceptional, but growing, group that fills this gap. See, for example, Virginia Yans-McLaughlin, *Family and Community: Italian Immigrants in Buffalo, 1880–1930* (Urbana: University of Illinois Press, 1982) or Sydney Stahl Weinberg, *The World of Our Mothers: The Lives of Jewish Immigrant Women* (New York: Schocken Books, 1988).

4. See Diner, *Erin's Daughters in America,* and Hondagneu-Sotelo, *Gendered Transitions,* for the Irish and Mexican cases respectively.

5. Terry Meinke, "The Genealogy of Eight Renville County Minnesota Families," 12 Dec. 1997. Manuscript in author's possession. Further information developed through e-mail correspondence with Meinke, who was extremely helpful.

6. This was a region characterized in the late nineteenth century by intensive farming on large *boerderijen* (farms). Crops were primarily for market rather than local consumption. The area was also known for farm worker unrest brought on by the sharp class distinctions. See the description of neighboring Midwolda in Frans van Poppel, *Trouwen in Nederland: Een historische-demografische studie van de 19e en vroeg-20e eeuw*, A.A.G. Bijdragen 33 (Wageningen: Afdeling Agrarische Geschiedenis, 1992), p. 136.

7. Average age at first marriage for 1860–64 was 27.5 for women and 29.4 for men (Hettie A. Pott-Buter, *Facts and Fairy Tales about Female Labor, Family and Fertility* [Amsterdam: Amsterdam University Press, 1993], p. 174). The average age for marriage in the 1860s in neighboring Midwolda, Groningen, with a similar economic base, was about 26 for women and 27.5 for men (van Poppel, *Trouwen in Nederland,* pp. 141–42).

8. Under the Van Houten child labor law, which had passed parliament the year before, only the oldest child was officially able to work in most industry, but farm labor was exempt See Lily E. Clerkx, "Kinderen in het gezin," in *Gezins Geschiedenis,* ed. G. A. Kooy (Assen: Van Gorcum, 1985), p. 126; and Marianne Braun, *De prijs van de liefde: De eerste feministische golf, het huwelijksrecht, en de vaderlandse geschiedenis* (Amsterdam: Het Spinhuis, 1992), p. 73.

9. Pott-Buter, *Facts and Fairy Tales,* p. 174; Van Poppel, *Trouwen in Nederland,* p. 584.

10. Swierenga, "Delayed Transition," p. 407; quote from p. 410.

11. According to a national survey of work, there were no industries employing women in either Oostwold or Oudedijk, neighboring towns which were the homes of the Negens and Schippers (Marie Jungius, *Beroepsklapper, Excerpt uit de "Uitkomsten der Beroepstelling in het Koninkrijk der Nederlanden op den een-en-dertigsten December 1889," aangevende het aantal gehuwde en ongehuwde vrouwen (benevens het algemeen totaal) werkzaam als hoofd of ondergeschikte in eenig beroep of bedrijf, met inleidend woord en eenige supplementen* [Amsterdam: H. J. Poutsma, 1899], summary map). "Domestic service" in rural areas of Groningen, according to another report, consisted of particularly distant relations between employers and servants, with young women learning nothing of household work (W. N. Schilstra, *Vrouwenarbeid in Landbouw en Industrie in Nederland in de tweede helft der negentiende Eeuw* [1940; reprint, Nijmegen: SUN, 1976], p. 60).

12. Martin Schipper sailed on the SS *Kensington* leaving Antwerp 2 Mar. 1901. He listed his destination on the passenger list as German Valley, Illinois, where he was joining a friend.

13. "Heritage of Faithfulness—History of the Emden Christian Reformed Church—Renville, Minnesota 1890–1990" (privately published, n.d.), p. 11.

14. The Moddermans crossed the Atlantic on the SS *Rotterdam,* departing 20 Feb. 1904. Their son/brother Helmer paid their passage and they had only $12 for the family. The Moddermans made the journey with one other family from Oostwold, Groningen, also traveling on prepaid tickets from a son. Both couples were headed for Aplington (near Parkersburg), Iowa.

15. Martin Schipper bought 96 acres in Crooks Township in 1915; Hendrik Negen purchased 128 acres there in 1916; Jurjen Negen purchased 320 acres in the same township in 1920 (Meinke, "Genealogy," and land records, Renville County Courthouse).

16. Henry S. Lucas, *Netherlanders in America* (1955; reprint, Grand Rapids: William B. Eerdmans, 1989), pp. 370ff.

17. Louis M. deGryse, "The Low Countries," in *They Chose Minnesota,* ed. June Drenning Holmquist (St. Paul: Minnesota Historical Society Press, 1981), p. 195.

18. Rev. J. H. Beld noted that the church at that point included 27 families, with 60 communicants and 140 souls ("The Emden, Minnesota, Church," *The Banner,* 2 Nov. 1911).

19. Brian W. Beltman provided a similar if slightly more geographically mobile example in "Nineteenth Century Dutch Migrants Extraordinaire on the Prairie-Plains," in *The Sesquicentennial of Dutch Immigration: 150 Years of Ethnic Heritage,* ed. Larry J. Wagenaar and Robert P. Swierenga (Holland: Joint Archives of Holland, 1998), p. 131.

20. Had they remained in Iowa the problems might actually have been worse. In 1918 Governor Harding forbade the use of foreign languages in Iowa entirely. See Nancy Ruth Derr, "The Babel Proclamation," *Palimpsest* 60 (1979): 98–115.

21. "Heritage of Faithfulness," pp. 15–17.

22. In 1920, Martin Schipper, age forty-four, died, leaving his mother and spouse along with the children to handle the farm (Meinke, "Genealogy").

23. The church did not introduce English for worship services at all until 1925, the year Modderman Negen died. Up to that time the debate was always on how much German and how much Dutch. See "Emden Celebrates its Fiftieth Anniversary," Emden CRC folder, HH.

24. "Mrs. Jantje Negen—Modderman," *The Banner,* 6 May 1925, in HH obituary file; Meinke, "Genealogy." On the Dutch settlement in Renville County, see Van Hinte, *Netherlanders in America,* p. 570.

25. "Heritage of Faithfulness," p. 11.

26. Stuurman, "Christendom en patriarchaat," p. 214. Frans van Poppel reported slightly higher rates, 85–86 percent ever-married for those who were born up through 1885 (*Trouwen in Nederland,* p. 21).

27. In 1889, there were 103 women to every 100 men aged twenty to sixty (Josine Blok et al., *Vrouwen, Kiesrecht en Arbeid. Nederland 1889–1919* [Groningen: SSGN, 1977], p. 141). In 1909, out of a population approaching six million, there were 102 women for every 100 men. Dutch rates of marriage in this period were slightly below those for Germany (Renetta Brandt-Wijt, "Moederschap en Volkskracht," in *De vrouw, de vrouwenbeweging en het vrouwenvraagstuk,* ed. C. M. Werker-Beaujon, Clara Wichmann, and W. H. M. Werker [Amsterdam: Elsevier, 1914], pp. 598, 600, 604).

28. U.S. Department of Commerce, Bureau of the Census, *Thirteenth Census of the United States, 1910,* vol. 1: *Population* (Washington, D.C.: Government Printing Office, 1922), p. 252; U.S. Department of Commerce, Bureau of the Census, *Fourteenth Census of the United States, 1920,* vol. 2: *Population* (Washington, D.C.: Government Printing Office, 1922), p. 694.

29. I calculated the data from the 1910 Public Use Sample using SPSS. The sample included 170 Dutch-born women, compared to 271 Dutch-born men. The 1910 U.S. census listed a little over 120,000 persons born in the Netherlands. See appendix 2 in Stephan Thernstrom, ed., *Harvard Encyclopedia of American Ethnic Groups* (Cambridge: Harvard University Press, 1980), p. 1059. The public use samples underwent further revisions and as of 1998 were available in an integrated version: Steven Ruggles and Matthew Sobek, Integrated Public Use Microdata Series: Version 2.0, Minneapolis: Historical Census Projects, University of Minnesota, 1997 <http://www.ipums.umn.edu>.

30. Salida, Calif., first day of Easter, 1912, HH. The sex ratio for Dutch immigrants in the Pacific region at that time was about 194 men to every 100 women (U.S. Department of Commerce, Bureau of the Census, *Thirteenth Census of the United States, 1910,* vol. 1: *Population,* p. 866).

31. Lubbigje Schaapman, Salida, Calif., to Willamientje Beltman, Jan. 1913, HH.

32. I am researching a larger project on international marriage markets. For a foray see

Suzanne Sinke, "Migration for Labor, Migration for Love: Marriage and Family Formation across Borders," *Organization of American Historians Magazine of History* 40 (1999): 17–21.

33. R. H. Brinks, Orange City, Iowa, to H. Brinks, [Emmen, Drenthe], 17 Feb. 1882, HH.

34. Jan Brouwer, Orange City, Iowa, to Willem Kooiman and Family, [Andijk], 25 June 1888, "Oude brieven uit Amerika," HH.

35. For example, Jan Hofman spent at least six years trying to convince his intended to come to the United States and marry him, but she was hesitant because her parents were solidly against the idea and he could not win them over (Jan Hofman, Grand Rapids, Mich., to Brother, Leens, Groningen, 1 Apr. 1910, HH).

36. Aafje de Vries, Appelscha, Groningen, to Friend [Aaltje van der Wal], [America], 15 Feb. 1914, HH.

37. For a general description of the consistory records, see chap. 6. This case is from a Christian Reformed Congregation in western Michigan in the mid-1880s, HH.

38. Lini de Vries, *Up from the Cellar* (Minneapolis: Vanilla Press, 1979), p. 82.

39. See John D'Emilio and Estelle B. Freedman, *Intimate Matters: A History of Sexuality in America* (New York: Harper and Row, 1988), p. 209.

40. H. Dekker, "Immigration Laws," *The Banner*, 9 July 1914, p. 422. Dekker noted that those men who lived in the Hoboken or New York area should meet their prospective brides, but others could send a notarized statement of intent to marry along with a certificate of good moral character from the dominie or another elder.

41. The cases of the Van der Vliets showed this. Maria van der Vliet's boyfriend could not get permission to marry her until he decided to migrate, at which point her parents agreed and the two married and left together for Minnesota. Her brother Cornelis van der Vliet worked on a railroad crew in Canada, and then came back to marry and recruit more workers for the railroad (Frank Verbrugge, ed., "Brieven uit het Verleden," HH, p. 98).

42. For remigration estimates see Stokvis, who calculated the figure for the period after 1870 as 15 percent ("Dutch International Migration 1815–1910, p. 57); the U.S. secretary of labor's report from 1923 lumped Dutch and Flemish migrants together and listed the remigration rate for 1908–23 at 18 percent (reproduced in Mark Wyman, *Round Trip to America* [Ithaca: Cornell University Press, 1993], p. 11).

43. The two married, went into dairy farming, and had seven children (Galema, *Frisians to America*, p. 82 and related note 67).

44. *De Hollandsche Amerikaan*, 15 Sept. 1919, p. 4.

45. For the years 1919 and 1920, the paper averaged fourteen classified notices per issue and appeared three and then (1920) two times a week. Only two ads were from women, both of whom were widows in their sixties. Because the paper was clearly Christian Reformed in orientation, some writers might have assumed characteristics of the readership, but others specified religious background in their ads. That at least some found such a means suspect was clear in the wording of the ads, such as that of the man who started out his ad stating that he "honestly meant" to find a wife.

46. *Pella's Weekblad*, 23 May 1902, p. 8. Another "Marriage Proposal" appeared in the 28 Mar. 1902 edition, this time from a young man in Lynden, Washington.

47. *Pella's Weekblad*, 31 Oct. 1902.

48. I scanned classified ads for part of 1899, all of 1902, and most of 1916 through 1918 in *Pella's Weekblad*.

49. *De Volksvriend*, 30 Jan. 1919, p. 7.

50. See Marion A. Kaplan, "For Love or Money: The Marriage Strategies of Jews in Impe-

rial Germany," in *The Marriage Bargain: Women and Dowries in European History*, ed. Kaplan (New York: Harrington Park Press, 1985). In the British Isles "wife for sale" in the personal ads (even into the nineteenth century) meant a rare form of divorce. See Samuel Pyeatt Menefee, *Wives for Sale* (New York: St. Martins, 1981).

51. Clerkx, "Kinderen in het gezin," p. 126.

52. Amry Vandenbosch, *Dutch Communities of Chicago* (Chicago: Knickerbocker Society of Chicago, 1927), p. 83.

53. "Minnebrief met antwoord," *Pella's Weekblad*, 22 Aug. 1902, pg. 8.

54. Hilde Berg, "De positie van de boerin op het Hogeland, ca. 1880–1914" (thesis, Rijksuniversiteit Groningen, 1984), pp. 48–50.

55. Compare Jon Gjerde's discussion of night-courting and the pietistic stance against it among Norwegians and Norwegian Americans (*From Peasants to Farmers*, pp. 90, 107).

56. Swierenga, "Local Patterns of Dutch Migration to the United States."

57. Tape 1067, woman from Nieuwe Schans, Groningen, who settled in Hollandale, Minn., PJM.

58. Lubbigje Schaapman, [Salida, Calif.], to Willamientje Beltman, [1911], letter 3 (fragment), HH. Schaapman uses the term "English" to designate nonethnic Americans.

59. Aart Plaisier, Grant, Mich., to Cousin, 6 Jan. 1915, HH.

60. Gerrit Plaisier, Grand Rapids, Mich., to Cousin, 27 Mar. 1911, HH.

61. Gerrit Plaisier, Grand Rapids, Mich., to Cousin, 18 May 1911, HH.

62. Robert Merton was one of the leading exponents. See "Intermarriage and the Social Structure: Fact and Theory," in *The Blending American: Patterns of Intermarriage*, ed. Milton L. Barron (Chicago: Quadrangle Books, 1972). See also Ruby Jo Kennedy, "Single or Triple Melting Pot: Intermarriage in New Haven, 1870–1950," *American Journal of Sociology* 58 (July 1952): 56–59. Kennedy's work had serious methodological flaws, yet her "triple melting pot" terminology continues to have currency. See also Richard D. Alba and Reid M. Golden, "Patterns of Ethnic Marriage in the United States," *Social Forces* 65 (Sept. 1986): 202–23.

63. In this I agree with Paul Spickard's concept of ethnic difference as a continuum which varies according to context; see *Mixed Blood: Intermarriage and Ethnic Identity in Twentieth-Century America* (Madison: University of Wisconsin Press, 1989).

64. For a description of the *oorijzer* see chap. 2. In the nineteenth century women who could afford it would make or hire someone to make a traditional costume in the style of the local community or province. Compare Jane Schneider, "Trousseau as Treasure: Some Contradictions of Late Nineteenth-Century Change in Sicily," in *The Marriage Bargain: Women and Dowries in European History*, ed. Marion A. Kaplan (New York: Harrington Park Press, 1985), pp. 81–119.

65. *De Hollandsche Amerikaan*, 3 Dec. 1920, p. 4.

66. D. Riemersma, Kollum, Friesland, to J. D. Douma, [Galesburg, Iowa], Dec. 1883, HH.

67. The "Record of Marriages" from Ebenezer Church, a Dutch American congregation in western Michigan, illustrated the pattern. Beginning in the 1860s the church recorded information about the bride and groom for every wedding from the congregation. The first entries included marriages where the age difference between spouses was substantial, often fifteen or twenty years but including a few cases of thirty of more years separating the pair. Almost invariably the men were older. By the 1880s such matches occurred rarely. Rather, first marriages took on a more homogeneous pattern, with nearly all men marrying in their twenties, their spouses were women in their late teens or, more frequently, early twenties (Ebenezer Gereformeerde Kerk Records, Joint Archives of Holland [Mich.]).

68. In the 1910 Public Use sample data there were no Dutch immigrants, either men or women, under the age of twenty who were listed as married. For those born in the Netherlands the singulate mean of marriage for women was 23.7 years and for men 28.6 years. To calculate the singulate mean I used the formula in Henry S. Shyrock and Jacob S. Siegel, *The Methods and Materials of Demography* (New York: Academic Press, 1976), p. 167.

69. For example, G. van Nijhuis, Boyden, Iowa, to Friend, Dec. 1890; G. van Nijhuis, Boyden, Iowa, to Friend, 8 Mar. 1891, HH.

70. Jeanette Kuijt Goedhart to Letha Retel and Gerrit Kuijt, Chicago, 22 Sept. 1909, HH. The Kuijt collection is also included in Brinks, *Dutch American Voices,* pp. 443ff.

71. Anna Kuijt Bates, Morgan Park, Ill., to Gerrit Kuijt and Letha Retel, 15 Jan. 1918, HH.

72. Anna Kuijt Bates, Morgan Park, Ill., to Gerrit Kuijt and Letha Retel, 15 Jan. 1918, HH.

73. This is a liberal translation of the Dutch "dat gaat hier zoo maar." J. Boekholt and Aaltje Giesing, n.p., to J. Hoogland, 23 Sept. 1883, RL.

74. Letter [sender unknown], New Sharon, Iowa, to G. N. van 't Sant, Feb. 1898, HH.

75. Jan Brouwer, Orange City, Iowa, to Parents and other family [Willem Kooiman and family], 24 Mar. 1889, HH.

76. "Amerikaansch," *Pella's Weekblad,* 12 Dec. 1902, p. 3.

77. Pieterdina Smit Lever, Chicago, to Uncle and Cousins, 17 Jan. 1892, HH.

78. On the growth of one elaborate wedding ritual see Simon R. Charsley, *Wedding Cakes and Cultural History* (New York: Routledge, 1992). See also John Modell, *Into One's Own: From Youth to Adulthood in the United States, 1920–1975* (Berkeley: University of California Press, 1989), p. 9.

79. This pattern appeared among other immigrant groups as well. Note the cover illustration to John J. Bukowczyk's *And My Children Did Not Know Me: A History of Polish-Americans* (Bloomington: Indiana University Press, 1987). The practice of the bride wearing at least headgear representing her regional background had largely faded out of use by the turn of the century.

80. "Diary of Mrs. Gezina Visscher (van der Haar) 1820–1901," trans. C. L. Jalving, HH.

81. "Diary of Mrs. Gezina Visscher," p. 92.

82. Cornelia De Groot, *When I Was a Girl in Holland,* with "Supplement" by Cor Bakker (Boston: Lothrop, Lee and Shepard, 1917; privately reprinted, Arnhem: C. Bakker, 1991), pp. 185–88.

83. Men might have a separate but less formal celebration, and the long Gouda pipe remained a part of Dutch American festivities in early years.

84. Fie [married Woldring], Pasadena, Calif., to Anje Woldring, 16 Apr. 1918, HH, their translation.

85. The review is of E. Schrenk's *Ken den Heere in al uwe Wegen* (Kampen: J. H. Kok, [1910?]) in "A Few New Dutch Books," *The Banner,* 27 Oct. 1910, p. 677.

86. L. M. Hermans, *De Spiegel der Waarheid: Moderne Moralisatiën over Liefde, Prostitutie en Huwelijk* (Deventer: G. J. Lankkamp, n.d. [1910s?]), n.p. The description comes from section 4 on white slavery. See also Thérése Hoven, "De organisatie van den Arbeid der Vrouw. 1. De algemeene nederlandsche vrouwenvereeniging 'Arbeid Adelt,'" in *De vrouw, de vrouwenbeweging en het vrouwenvraagstuk,* ed. C. M. Werker-Beaujon, Clara Wichmann, and W. H. M. Werker (Amsterdam: Elsevier, 1914), p. 246; Sondra R. Herman, "Loving Courtship or the Marriage Market? The Ideal and Its Critics, 1871–1911," *American Quarterly* 25 (1973): 235–52.

87. Letter and biography, Jantze Buist Schoemakers, manuscript, trans. Gradus Schoemaker, HH.

88. For example, the Woudenberg family's recounting of another family in the same house where they lived: "The man of the house was a week-end drunkard. He would come home sometime Saturday afternoon and be very abusive to his family. The wife would scream in terror as the drunk would carry on" (Helen Westra, "'Fear and Hope Jostled': Dutch Immigrant Life and Death in Paterson, New Jersey," HH, p. 7).

89. For an example of extensive romantic imagery in letters see Fie Woldring, Grand Rapids, Mich., to Anje Woldring, 5 Dec. 1918, HH, their translation.

90. P. Jonker, "De Eere van het Huisgezin," *De Gereformeerde Amerikaan*, July 1906, p. 321.

91. For an overview of Dutch family demography, see Henk de Haan, "Het huishouden in Nederlands verleden: Een studie van de literatuur," *Tijdschrift voor Sociale Geschiedenis* 6 (1980): 45–78; and O. W. A. Boonstra and A. M. van der Woude, *Demographic Transition in the Netherlands: A Statistical Analysis of Regional Differences in the Level and Development of the Birth Rate and of Fertility, 1850–1890* (Utrecht: HES Publishers, 1984), pp. 55–56.

92. Corstius and Hollema, *De Kunst van het Moederschap*, p. 85; J. de Bruijn, *Geschiedenis van de abortus in Nederland. Een analyse van opvattingen en discussies 1600–1979* (Amsterdam: Van Gennep, 1979), p. 42.

93. Chr. Vandenbroeke, "Seksualiteit en vruchtbaarheidskontrole rond 1900: Een terreinverkenning," *Tijdschrift voor sociale geschiedenis* 11 (June 1978): 197, 211.

94. See, for example, the quotes in Ali de Regt, *Arbeidersgezinnen en beschavingsarbeid: Ontwikkelingen in Nederland 1870–1940* (Amsterdam: Boom Meppel, 1986), p. 124. For the demographics of this see E. W. Hofstee, "De demografische ontwikkeling van Nederland sinds 1800," in *Van nu tot nul*, ed. H. J. Heeren and Ph. van Praag (Utrecht: Het Spectrum, 1974), pp. 36–75; and G. A. Kooy, *Seksualiteit, huwelijk en gezin in Nederland* (Deventer: Van Loghum Slaterus, 1975).

95. De Bruijn, *Geschiedenis van de abortus*, p. 69.

96. The bulk of the immigrants in this period did not come from the most heavily populated areas, that is, from the urban provinces of the west but rather from densely populated "rural" provinces. In 1889 the number of inhabitants per square kilometer in the three leading emigrant provinces was as follows: Groningen 116.5; Friesland 102.6; Zeeland 114.7 (Boonstra and Van der Woude, *Demographic Transition in the Netherlands*, p. 26). Compare this to an overall figure of 21.2 persons per square mile in the United States in 1890 (U.S. Bureau of the Census, *Historical Statistics of the United States 1789–1945*, [Washington, D.C.: Government Printing Office, 1949], p. 25).

97. Stuurman, "Christendom en patriarchaat," pp. 211, 224–28.

98. Nater, *Sexualiteit in Nederland*, p. 15.

99. The Michigan Board of Health released a report in 1878 stating that an estimated one-third of all pregnancies ended in abortion. See D'Emilio and Freedman, *Intimate Matters*, pp. 65, 208–21. On this period in America see also Linda Gordon, *Woman's Body, Woman's Right* (New York: Penguin, 1976), chap. 6.

100. Vandenbosch, *Dutch Communities in Chicago*, p. 82.

101. Ruggles and Sobek, Integrated Public Use Microdata Series for 1910. The average was still about seven children per woman over 40 when the 1910 and 1900 data were combined. For the second generation (at least one parent born in the Netherlands, 61 women), the average number of children was 4.18, and for the 1900 and 1910 group combined (70 people), 4.7.

102. Geertje Schuiling, Manhattan, Mont., to Brother and Sister, 11 Dec. 1901, Hoogland Collectie, RL.

103. Max Americanus [pseud.], "No Children," *The Banner*, 21 July 1910, p. 446.

104. Jan Brouwer, Orange City, Iowa, to Mother [Maartje Kooiman-Groot] and Family, Aug. 1893, HH.

105. Jozina Overduin Bruinsel, in a letter to her brother and sister, dated Paterson, N.J., 18 Nov. 1892, noted that her daughter was now five months old and beginning to eat meat and potatoes: "And I have plenty for her to nurse" (HH). Gezina van der Haar Visscher also wrote in her diary in 1900 that her daughter Sena was able to nurse ("Diary of Mrs. Gezina Visscher," p. 140).

106. See De Regt, *Arbeidersgezinnen en beschavingsarbeid*, p. 135.

107. Ali de Regt, "Vorming van een opvoedingstraditie: Ontwikkelingen in Nederland 1880–1918," *Amsterdams Sociologische Tijdschrift* 4 (May 1977): 40–41; Lily E. Van Rijswijk-Clerkx, *Moeders, kinderen en kinderopvang: Veranderingen in de kinderopvang in Nederland* (Nijmegen: SUN, 1981), p. 133.

108. Selections from G. M. van der Wissel-Herderscheê and Egb. C. de Wijs–van der Mandele, "Taak van Moeders," Nationale Tentoonstelling van Vrouwenarbeid, 1898, IIAV.

109. See Nelleke Bakker, *Kind en karakter: Nederlandse pedagogen over opvoeding in het gezin 1845–1925* (Amsterdam: Het Spinhuis, 1995), chap. 9, p. 222.

110. This was enshrined in Dutch law with the Burgerlijk Wetboek of 1838 and not officially abandoned until 1970. See Braun, *De prijs van de liefde*, pp. 12–13.

111. Hannah Bruins Vander Velde, "Early History of the Derk Bruins Family to 1890," manuscript, HH.

112. Compare Colleen McDannell, *The Christian Home in Victorian America, 1840–1900* (Bloomington: Indiana University Press, 1986), chap. 5.

113. For example, "Gedachtenwisseling tusschen twee kerkleden," *De Wachter* 27 (28 Mar. 1894): 1. In this hypothetical situation the two men ("two church members") waited to begin their discussion until their wives had finished their chores, so that the women could be present. The wives were there throughout the discussion, but rarely said anything, and then primarily in response to a direct question.

114. Quoted in Dorothy Koert, *Portrait of Lynden* (Lynden, Wash.: Lynden Tribune, 1976), p. 101.

115. For example, an article in *De Gereformeerde Amerikaan* described how mothers, above all others, were "burdened with the care of the little ones" (H. van Hoogen, "Het Huislijk-en Familieleven der Hollanders in Amerika, VII," *De Gereformeerde Amerikaan*, Aug. 1898, p. 303).

116. See Schelbitzki Pickle, *Contented among Strangers*, p. 50.

117. Rosa Schreurs Jennings, "A Scrap of Americana," *Annals of Iowa* 29 (Apr. 1948): 295.

118. Maaike Huigen to Father and Siblings, Pella, Iowa, 10 Mar. 1884, Familie Archief Huigen, RL.

119. Klaaske Noorda [Heller], Holland, to Mother, Brother and Sisters, Nephew and Nieces, 6 Nov. [1890s], HH.

120. P. Jonker, "Het Karakter der Opvoeding van het Huisgezin," *De Gereformeerde Amerikaan*, Dec. 1906, p. 538.

121. The editorial went on to say "No husband and wife are fulfilling the measure of their bounden obligations to their children until they have deliberately adopted the children's preparation for life as their superlative business in the world" (*The Banner*, 22 Sept. 1910, pp. 592–93).

122. See, for example, Rev. P. A. Hoekstra, "Our Doctrine: Fatherhood," *The Banner,* 2 Dec. 1915, p. 751.

123. Vandenbosch, *Dutch Communities of Chicago,* p. 83.

124. See the Schoonbeek family story in chap. 6. The father in that case landed in jail for child beating. Taken from Brinks, *Dutch American Voices,* pp. 252ff.

125. Cobie de Lespinasse, *The Bells of Helmus* (Portland, Ore.: Metropolitan Press, 1934), pp. 71–72. It is possible that the story was based on the example which follows, since both took place in Orange City, Iowa, and "Kees" was a nickname for Cornelis.

126. "Kennisgeving" and "Algemeene Kennisgeving," *De Volksvriend,* 18 Mar. 1880, p. 3.

127. Braun, *De prijs van de liefde,* p. 13. On the U.S. see Marlene Stein Worthman, ed., *Women in American Law,* vol. 1 (New York: Holmes & Meier, 1985), pp. 117–18.

128. Richard Chused, "Married Women's Property Law: 1800–1850," *Georgetown Law Journal* 71 (1983): nn. 263, 361. Two Iowa Supreme Court Cases upheld the husband's right to butter and egg money in this period: Mewhirter v. Hatten, Dec. 1875, 1875 Iowa Sup. LEXIS 364; and Hamill & Co. v. Henry et al., Oct. 1886, 1886 Iowa Sup. LEXIS 145.

129. See Judith A. Baer, *Women in American Law,* 2d ed. (New York: Holmes & Meier, 1996), p. 132.

130. Klaaske, [Oudebildtzijl], to brother and sister, Manhattan, Mont., [1910], Hoogland Collection, RL.

131. "Heritage of Faithfulness," p. 13.

132. "As 'Families' in the Church" first takes up the issue of pew rents, stating "We do not presume that there are many, if any, of our Christian Reformed churches which have perpetuated the old, obsolete custom alluded to above." The article then argues that families should sit together (*The Banner,* 21 Nov. 1918, p. 840).

133. *De Volksvriend,* 1 May 1919, p. 7. My survey of one year of *De Volksvriend* classified ads from 1919 found housekeeper to be the most common category of work advertised for women.

134. Max Americanus [pseud.], "Morals of Holland Young Men," *The Banner,* 5 May 1910, p. 278.

135. De Groot, *When I Was a Girl in Holland,* pp. 78–85.

136. Ytje Schuiling, [Manhattan, Mont.], to Aunt, 21 Feb. 1900, Hoogland Collectie, RL.

137. Among the more orthodox Protestants some individuals may not have celebrated either holiday with gifts, since this group was more likely to shun such customs, which they felt had heathen rather than biblical precedents. Yet even ultra-orthodox newspapers carried the advertisements.

138. "Eight Books on Delicate Subjects," *The Banner,* 29 July 1909, p. 492.

139. Max Americanus [pseud.], "Prudishness," *The Banner,* 27 Oct. 1910, pp. 677–78. An article in the 24 Oct. 1912 issue of *The Banner* recommends *Het Huwelijk, geneeskundige wenken voor gehuwden en verloofden, een Boek voor het Christelijk gezin,* a translation of a German text Dr. Boeckh's *Ehefragen.*

140. Tape 1018, woman from Geersdijk who migrated in 1905 at age eleven and settled first in Chicago, and then later in Holland, Mich., PJM.

141. Ida van der Flier, in *Van meisje tot vrouw: Raadgever en wegwijzer voor meisjes die den ongehuwden staat vaarwel zeggen* (Rotterdam: D. Bolle, n.d.), for example, discussed menstruation, venereal disease, and various tips from women's hygiene to how to run a home frugally.

142. De Vries, *Up from the Cellar,* pp. 12–13.

143. De Vries, *Up from the Cellar.*

144. "De boers vrouw ging lope / met 'n broek zonder knope . . ." (tape 1102A, man born in 1880, PJM). "Dutch pants" had a large flap in front secured on two sides with buttons, meaning that without buttons they would have revealed more than American ones.

145. "De Koning van Egypte / Die had een ding dat wipte / Tussen de beene en onder 't gat . . ." Quoted in Willem Wilterdink, *Winterswijkse Pioniers in Amerika* (Winterswijk: Vereniging 'het Museum', 1990), p. 75.

146. "Letters from Lubbigje Schaapman to Willamientje Beltman," introduction, HH.

147. Immigrants frequently expressed this sentiment openly. See, for examples, tapes 1071B–1072A, family migrated in 1912 and settled first in Iowa and later in Hollandale, Minn.; tape 1089, couple from Pella, Iowa, of Dutch ancestry, PJM.

148. Tape 1071B/1072A, woman born in Bennekom in 1885, PJM.

149. Tape 1001, PJM.

150. Tape 1097/1101, woman born in 1912 in Pella, Iowa, PJM.

151. Geertje de Jong Schuiling, Manhattan, Mont., to Brother and Sister, 26 Mar. 1899, Hoogland Collection, RL.

152. See, for example, the case of the Brouwer family, where mother and son wanted badly to join an uncle and aunt in Iowa, but the father had to approve of the idea first. In Galema, *Frisians to America,* p. 241.

153. Jan, Matty, and Joan Ten Hoor, comps., "Genealogie van de Familie Ten Hoor," manuscript, Drachten & Assen, 1995.

154. Aaltje, Sibley, Iowa, to Uncle, 6 June 1907, HH.

155. See, for example, Nanco Smit, Chicago, to Uncle and Family, 16 Sept. 1888; and Arendje Bergman Akkerman and W. Nomes, [Roseland, Ill.], 11 July 1882, fragment, HH.

156. "Diary of Mrs. Gezina Visscher," pp. 75, 79, 85, 89, 92, 100, 107, 126, 127, 129, 136, 145.

157. "Diary of Mrs. Gezina Visscher," pp. 118–19.

158. Jozina Overduin Bruinsel, Paterson, N.J., 18 Nov. 1892, HH.

159. Grietje Rubingh, [Wildervank, Groningen], [probably to Brother, Sister and Children], [1890s], fragment, HH.

160. Letters dated 15, 16, 18, and 23 Aug. 1912, Manhattan, Mont., one letter packet, Hoogland Collectie, RL.

161. Maaike Huigen sometimes even signed the letters to indicate her husband Lucas had contributed to them. On the back of one sheet was a letter from fifteen-year-old Nellie, along with her mother's translation. I include the full original here, including spelling errors:

> Dear uncle and ant and cousins I tought I woud try to rote a few lines to you may be you cant read this letter but Mother chang it on the other side just today we got a letter from cousin Nellie she rote thy were all well up there I would rite a holland letter but I cant but I taught I woud rite a few lines any how I wish we could get your pictures o how glad we would be the best respct from all your cousons your couson
>   Nellie Annyas
>
> round as a ring
> What has no end
> so is my love to you my friend.
> (Galesburg, Iowa, 22 Nov. 1888, Familie Archief Huigen, RL, their transcription).

162. The Hoogland collection in Leeuwarden resulted from one such setting, where the official residents at the farm shared the news but kept the letters.

163. Dina Oggel, Pella, Iowa, to Sister, 16 Dec. 1895, HH. There is a letter from Oggel to the family dated one year earlier in the collection, and from the context it is probable that it was the last letter she had written.

164. Aaltje, Sibley, Iowa, to Uncle, 6 June 1907, HH.

165. Maaike Huigen, Galesburg, Iowa, to Brother and Sister and Children, 19 Feb. 1888, Familie Archief Huigen, RL.

166. Vander Velde, "Early History of the Derk Bruins Family to 1890," p. 111.

167. Dina Oggel, Pella, Iowa, to Sister, 16 Dec. 1895, HH.

168. Anje Nieveen Mulder, Stuttgart, Kans., to Uncle and Nephew, Mar. 1889, HH.

169. 26 May 1916, *Pella's Weekblad*, p. 4.

170. Based on scanning a large number of issues of *Pella's Weekblad* sections "Omnibus" and "Onze Correspondentie" for 1916. I also randomly selected two hundred entries and systematically coded and compared the numbers to confirm my impressions. In that selection twenty-two were about women only, and eight of those were sickness or accident reports. Of the ninety notices about men, in comparison, only twelve were sickness or accident reports. A third category of couples included thirty-six reports of visits to family and friends.

171. There is an index to the names listed in the Sioux Center *Nieuwsblad* for most of this period. See Wilma J. Vandeberg, main ed., "Sioux Center *Nieuwsblad*/Sioux Center *Newspaper* Surname Index: *Stad en omgeving*/Local news section 1893–1929," manuscript, Greater Sioux County Genealogical Society.

172. Van Hinte, *Netherlanders in America*, p. 979.

173. See Gjerde, *Minds of the West*, chap. 9, and for a later period Sonya Salamon, *Prairie Patrimony: Family, Farming and Community in the Midwest* (Chapel Hill: University of North Carolina, 1992).

174. Stuurman, "Christendom en patriarchaat."

I use "morality" and "moralization" as translations for variations on the Dutch term *zedelijkheid*. While Stuurman sometimes translates this (in his English summary) with forms of "civilizing," I prefer to use this latter term to translate *beschavingsarbeid*. On women's rights and the civilization effort, see Selma L. Sevenhuijsen, *De orde van het vaderschap: Politieke debatten over ongehuwd moederschap, afstamming en het huwelijk in Nederland 1870–1900* (Amsterdam: IISG, 1987).

175. See, for example, the comparison of arguments about the development of social work in Berteke Waaldijk, *Het Amerika der vrouw: Sekse en geschiedenis van maatschappelijk werk in Nederland en de Verenigde Staten* (Groningen: Wolters-Noordhoff, 1996), pp. 130ff.

176. On this see Braun, *De prijs van de liefde*, chap. 8, esp. p. 179.

177. Many Dutch American communities and newspapers sent formal congratulations to Wilhelmina at the time of the coronation. Information about her filled Dutch American publications. See *De Huisvriend*, Oct. 1898, where the entire issue was on the coronation. For a sense of how some immigrants viewed their relationship to royalty, in this case to Queen Regent Emma, see Janet Sjaarda Sheeres, "Dear Queen . . . ," *Origins* 14 (1996): 38–41.

178. See Candice Lewis Bredbenner, *A Nationality of Her Own: Women, Marriage, and the Law of Citizenship* (Berkeley: University of California Press, 1998), chap. 1.

179. Bredbenner, *Nationality of Her Own*, chap. 3 and pp. 116–18.

180. George Anthony Pfeffer, "Forbidden Families: Emigration Experiences of Chinese Women under the Page Law, 1875–1882," *Journal of American Ethnic History* 6 (Fall 1986): 28–46.

181. Lucy Salyer, *Laws Harsh as Tigers: Chinese Immigrants and the Shaping of Modern Immigration Law* (Chapel Hill: University of North Carolina Press, 1995), p. 128.

182. National Archives and Records Administration, Immigration and Naturalization Records (NARA, INR), record group 85, entry 9, subject correspondence 1906–1932, United States Circuit Court of Appeals for the Second Circuit, 52531/198, p. 4.

183. NARA, INR, record group 85, entry 9, box 107, 52424/13 A–C "Japanese Picture Brides."

184. One or both of the main Protestant Dutch American church denominations maintained a greeter at Castle Garden and then Ellis Island during this period. These individuals sent periodic reports to Dutch and Dutch American newspapers about their work along with suggestions. This included laws relating to women, for example see H. Dekker, "Ladies Traveling Alone," *The Banner,* 28 May 1914, p. 366.

185. Aart Plaisier, Grand Rapids, Mich., to C. VanderWaal, 1 May 1910, HH.

186. Gerrit Plaisier, Grand Rapids, Mich., to C. VanderWaal, 27 Mar. 1911, HH.

187. Letta van 't Sant, Grinnell, Iowa, to Brother and Sister, [Reasonor, Iowa], 6 Jan. 1910], HH.

188. Oddly enough, some of the early advocates of unionization, one of the issues the Dutch American Protestant press attacked vehemently, were of Dutch Jewish descent, namely, Samuel Gompers and Daniel DeLeon. For an overview on this see Pieter R. D. Stokvis, "Dutch-Speaking Peoples," in *The Immigrant Labor Press in North America, 1840s–1970s,* ed. Dirk Hoerder and Christiane Harzig (New York: Greenwood Press, 1987), p. 269.

189. See Marianne L. Mooijweer, "A Socialist Eden in North Carolina? Frederik van Eeden and His American Dreams," in *The Dutch in North America,* ed. Rob Kroes and Henk Otto Neuschäfer (Amsterdam: VU University Press, 1991), pp. 282–305.

190. J. G. van den Bosch, "The Burning Question: The Equal Suffrage Question," *The Banner* 31 Oct. 1912, p. 684.

191. Quoted in Nicholas Huizenga, "Christian Reformed Church Versus Feminism 1912–1913," manuscript, [1983?], HH.

192. "De Beweging om den Vrouwen vol Stemrecht," *De Gereformeerde Amerikaan,* Sept. 1908, p. 506.

193. "Laat ons onze Kandidaat Ondersteunen," *De Hollandsche Amerikaan,* 17 Aug. 1920, p. 4; "Mrs. Helen Curtenius Statler," *De Hollandsche Amerikaan,* 13 Aug. 1920, p. 4.

194. Nynke Gerritsma, "Vrouwen achter 't theeblad vandaan: Gereformeerd denken over vrouwen, 1920–1940," *Jaarboek voor de geschiedenis van de Gereformeerde Kerken in Nederland* 5 (1987): 80.

195. "Bestemming der Vrouw, II," *De Gereformeerde Amerikaan,* June 1916, p. 242.

196. "Vrouwen Stemrecht," *Pella's Weekblad,* 2 June 1916, p. 1.

197. *Pella's Weekblad,* 9 June 1916, p. 1.

198. "De Vrouw en het Kiesrecht," *De Hollandsche Amerikaan,* 14 Mar. 1919, p. 1; 17 Mar. 1919, p. 1; "Het Kiesrecht en de Vrouw," *De Hollandsche Amerikaan,* 12 May 1919, p. 1; 14 May 1919, p. 1; 16 May 1919, p. 1; 19 May 1919, p. 1.

199. Van Hinte, *Netherlanders in America,* pp. 871, 875.

200. Since the Calvinists were by far the largest proportion of the Dutch immigrant group, and since the others were less likely to identify themselves as "Dutch," the Calvinists in a sense managed to stamp their own variety of "Dutchness" into the public eye. One of the leading popularizers of race suicide thought, Theodore Roosevelt, could look to his own Dutch roots.

Chapter 2: The Bare Necessities and Their Elaborations

1. On this see Ewa Morawska, *For Bread with Butter: The Life Worlds of East Central Europeans in Johnstown, Pennsylvania, 1890–1940* (New York: Cambridge University Press, 1985).

2. Andrew R. Heinze, *Adapting to Abundance: Jewish Immigrants, Mass Consumption, and the Search for American Identity* (New York: Columbia University Press, 1990), introduction.

3. Schelbitzki Pickle, *Contented among Strangers*, esp. chap. 2.

4. For comparison see Elizabeth Ewen, *Immigrant Women in the Land of Dollars: Life and Culture on the Lower East Side, 1890–1925* (New York: Monthly Review Press, 1985).

5. This is similar to the developments described in Patricia Williams, "From Folk to Fashion: Dress Adaptations of Norwegian Immigrant Women in the Midwest," in *Dress in American Culture*, ed. Patricia A. Cunningham and Susan Voso Lab (Bowling Green: Bowling Green State University Press, 1993).

6. Wolfgang Helbich presents strikingly similar results from a content analysis of German emigrant letters ("Die 'Englischen': German Immigrants Describe Nineteenth-Century American Society," *Amerikastudien* 36 [1991]: 515–30).

7. The information on Menkens Schreurs in the following sections, unless otherwise noted, comes from Rosa Schreurs Jennings, "A Scrap of Americana" and "Second-Generation Americans," *Annals of Iowa* 29 (Apr. 1949): 589–98. Her birth month and year were listed in the U.S. Department of Commerce, Bureau of the Census, *Twelfth Census of the United States, 1900*, manuscript schedules for Albion Township, Butler County, Iowa. According to the record in Robert P. Swierenga, comp., *Dutch Immigrants in U.S. Ship Passenger Manifests, 1820–1880* (Wilmington, Del.: Scholarly Resources, 1983), she migrated in 1874. The entry for "Elizabeth Menkes" listed her as an unmarried woman, age twenty-five, traveling on the *Minnesota* from Liverpool to New York.

8. Schreurs Jennings, "Scrap of Americana," p. 291.

9. According to *The History of Black Hawk County, Iowa* (Chicago: Western Historical Company, 1878), Kleinsorge began as a missionary in the area in 1858. He served as pastor of the German Evangelical Church in Cedar Falls in 1860 and then returned for two years, 1873–74. This would indicate that Menkens Schreurs probably went to the Clarence Knapp home in 1875 and remained there about a year.

10. Schreurs Jennings, "Scrap of Americana," p. 293.

11. Schreurs Jennings, "Scrap of Americana," p. 294.

12. Schreurs Jennings, "Scrap of Americana," p. 295.

13. Schreurs Jennings, "Scrap of Americana," p. 295.

14. U.S. Department of Commerce, Bureau of the Census, *Tenth Census of the United States, 1880*, manuscript schedules for Cedar Falls, Black Hawk County.

15. The Miner mill ran on both water and steam, producing up to 275 barrels of flour a day (*Historical Record of Cedar Falls* [Cedar Falls: Peter Melendy, 1893], pp. 83–85).

16. Schreurs Jennings, "Scrap of Americana," p. 296.

17. The account did nothing other than state that the third child was born and then changed the subject. At the end of the account of the second birth, however, the author stated that the lack of calling a doctor in that case would cause Menkens Schreurs to "pay dearly" in years to come (Schreurs Jennings, "Scrap of Americana," p. 295).

18. Schreurs Jennings, "Second-Generation Americans," p. 592, and "Scrap of Americana," pp. 296–97. None of their periodicals was in Dutch, though they did subscribe to the *Evangelische Botschafter*, a religious publication tied to their German church.

19. Schreurs Jennings, "Second-Generation Americans," quotes from pp. 589, 590.

20. Schreurs Jennings, "Second-Generation Americans," pp. 590–91.

21. Schreurs Jennings, "Second-Generation Americans," quotes from pp. 592, 593.

22. *The History of Butler and Bremer Counties, Iowa* (Springfield, Ill.: Union Publishing, 1883), described the township in the early 1880s—a few years before the Schreur family ar-

rived—as an area originally platted in 1856. New Albion, with the post office at Swanton, included several general merchandise stores, hardware stores, and boot and shoe stores. Most of the owners had no obvious ethnic backgrounds (pp. 429, 432–36).

23. Schreurs Jennings, "Second-Generation Americans," quote p. 597, text p. 594.

24. *Census of Iowa for the Year 1895* (Des Moines: F. R. Conway, 1896), Township of Albion, Butler County, Schedule 1, Statistics of Population.

25. Schreurs Jennings, "Scrap of Americana," p. 292.

26. U.S. Department of Commerce, Bureau of the Census, *Twelfth Census of the United States, 1900*, Albion Township, Butler County.

27. U.S. Department of Commerce, Bureau of the Census, *Thirteenth Census of the United States, 1910*, Albion Township, Butler County.

28. *Historical Record of Cedar Falls* listed the first electric light company as going into operation in 1886 in Cedar Falls (p. 76). The family history indicates the farm got electricity sometime after the younger daughter took over residence there (Schreurs Jennings, "Second-Generation Americans," p. 597).

29. "Transcript of Deaths in the County of Butler," 1919 and 1929, SHSI. The family history elaborated on the split between father and son, which pushed the younger man into directions other than farming (Schreurs Jennings, "Second-Generation Americans," p. 597).

30. Schreurs Jennings, "Second-Generation Americans," p. 598. The "Gravestone Records of Butler County, Iowa," part of the WPA Graves Registration Projects, included "Gerrit Schrfurs" [*sic*] for Oak Hill Cemetery in New Hartford, Iowa, though it did not list Elizabeth Menkens Schreurs.

31. "Uit Amerika," *De Baanbreker: Sozialistisch Weekblad voor Zeeland*, 13 Jan. 1906, p. 1.

32. Louise Tilly, "Paths of Proletarianization: Organization of Production, Sexual Division of Labor, and Women's Collective Action," *Signs* 7 (Winter 1981): 417. Collective action appeared in the Netherlands during World War I, when food prices and shortages led the housewives of Amsterdam to unite in the "potato revolt" (De Regt, *Arbeidersgezinnen en beschavingsarbeid*, p. 77).

33. Bert Altena and Dirk van der Veen, "Een onbekende enquête naar broodconsumptie in Nederland in 1890," *Tijdschrift voor sociale geschiedenis* 12 (May 1986): 142–43.

34. Tape 1018, woman born in Geersdijk in 1894; family moved to Nauernapolder and then to Houtrakpolder (near the Noordzeekanaal), then she emigrated with parents at age eleven, settled first in Chicago and then in Holland, Mich., PJM.

35. See, for example, "Arbeiders-budgets," in *Bijdragen van het Statistisch Instituut*, 7th ed. (Amsterdam: Johannes Müller, 1891). These indicated that in the countryside expenditures for bread generally were the largest item in the food budget, followed by potatoes and coffee. The amount spent on fat was frequently double that for meat, and fruit belonged to the luxury category.

36. De Regt, *Arbeidersgezinnen en beschavingsarbeid*, pp. 39, 75–76.

37. On Dutch women and agricultural work in this period, see G. H. Bieleman, "Plaats en taak der Vrouw in het Landbouwbedrijf," in *De Vrouw, de vrouwenbeweging en het vrouwenvraagstuk*, ed. C. M. Werker Beujon, Clara Wichmann, and W. H. M. Werker (Amsterdam: Elsevier, 1914), pp. 271–91; J. Rinkes Borger, "De Vrouw in de Zuivelbereiding," *Vrouwenarbeid* 21 (July 1898): 54–56; and Schilstra, *Vrouwenarbeid in Landbouw en Industrie in Nederland,*

38. Blok et al., *Vrouwen, Kiesrecht en Arbeid*, pp. 134–35.

39. Literally this is "female farmer." *Boerin* has a class identification roughly equivalent to "mistress" of a southern plantation in the United States, hence "farmer's wife" is an inadequate translation.

40. This list stems from Berg, "De positie van de boerin op het Hogeland."

41. Bieleman, "Plaats en taak der Vrouw in het Landbouwbedrijf," p. 273.

42. Emigration was heavy from Winterswijk. See Wilterdink, *Winterswijkse Pioniers in Amerika.*

43. Ine van Huet, "Tussen Traditie en Modernisering: Agrarisch Bedrijf, Boerinnentaak en Landbouwhuishoudonderwijs in Verandering, Winterswijk (Achterhoek)" (Ph.D. dissertation, Rijksuniversiteit Nijmegen, 1988), pp. 34–38.

44. "Arbeiders-budgets," in *Bijdragen van het Statistisch Instituut*, pp. 164–67.

45. Maaike Huigen, Galesburg, Iowa, to Father and Siblings, 12 Mar. 1880, RL.

46. One woman joked with her relatives, "in the Netherlands one never gets to taste sturgeon and salmon, our letters are not bacon letters as someone once said because they appear more like fish letters" (Klaaske Noorda [Heller], Oak Harbor, Wash., to Mother, Siblings, Nephews, and Nieces, Aug. 1897, HH).

47. Tape 1086, PJM.

48. Hulda De Jong, [Julius De Jong] Oral History, Earthwatch-SHSI, 1978, pp. 16–17.

49. Klaaske Noorda [Heller], [Oak Harbor, Wash.], to Mother and Siblings, [1890s], HH.

50. See, for example, "Verandering van spijs doet eten," *De Volksvriend*, 23 Nov. 1899, p. 8; Pure Food Grocers ad, "Echte Maatjes Haring, geen beter," *De Volksvriend*, 20 Feb. 1919, p. 7.

51. Letters from Lubbigje Schaapman to Willamientje Beltman; see, for example, Schaapman, Salida, Calif., to Beltman, 19 Mar. 1911, HH.

52. On technological change see Susan Strasser, *Never Done: A History of American Housework* (New York: Pantheon, 1982), pp. 22–23; Ruth Schwartz Cowan, *More Work for Mother: The Ironies of Household Technology from the Open Hearth to the Microwave* (New York: Basic Books, 1983), p. 73.

53. Quoted in Van Hinte, *Netherlanders in America*, p. 269.

54. For example, Dina Maria Oggel: "Oh how I would like to spend the Christmas holidays with you. . . . You have certainly eaten delicious waffles at Balkenende and also had oliebollen" (Oggel, Pella, Iowa, to Brother and Sister, 17 Dec. 1894, HH).

55. See, for example, the ad from John van der Ploeg's bakery in Pella (*Pella's Weekblad*, 21 Nov. 1919, p. 5), or the ad from Sybenga's bakery in Pella (*Pella's Weekblad*, 12 Dec. 1902, p. 2).

56. See Van Hinte, *Netherlanders in America*, p. 917.

57. Compare to the embourgeoisement of Norwegian immigrants in Gjerde, *From Peasants to Farmers*, esp. p. 229.

58. Based on a survey of *De Boodschapper* advertisements from 1913 to 1916.

59. See, for example, *De Huisvriend*, Mar. 1906, for list of products; *De Hollandsche Amerikaan*, 21 Dec. 1920, p. 4 (ad by import company); *Pella's Weekblad*, 19 July 1918, p. 3 (ad by import company offering Frisian cheese).

60. See, for example, *De Volksvriend*, 20 Feb. 1919, p. 7.

61. Van Zante Bros. ad, *Pella's Weekblad*, 1 Sept. 1916, p. 3.

62. Aukjen Pruiksma, Paterson, N.J., to Children, Joure, Friesland, 16 May 1895, HH, their translation.

63. Vandenbosch, *Dutch Communities of Chicago*, p. 83.

64. Quoted in A. G. Bousema-Valkema, "Valk—De Valk—Valkema: 16 Generaties Nakomelingen van Valck Wolters," manuscript, Herrick Library, Holland, Mich., p. 14.

65. Jeanette van Rooyen, "The Story of My Grandfather," Hospers, Iowa, SHSI, and IFWC Essay Contest, 1923.

66. Quoted in Westra, "Fear and Hope Jostled,"

67. *De Volksvriend*, 25 Nov. 1880; *Pella's Weekblad*, Thanksgiving Day, 1902, p. 4.

68. Luyendijk ad, *De Hollandsche Amerikaan,* 24 Nov. 1919, p. 4.

69. *De Hollandsche Amerikaan,* 17 Dec. 1920, p. 4.

70. Klaaske Noorda [Heller], Oakharbor [*sic*], Wash., to Mother, Siblings, Nephews and Nieces, Aug. 1897, HH.

71. See, for example, Van Hinte, *Netherlanders in America,* pp. 223–24. Van Hinte also noted contacts with Native Americans, who introduced the Dutch in Michigan to maple sugar and corn. I found practically no references to maple products in the letters from women at the turn of the century.

72. See D. Ballard and Wife, Sterling, Colo., to Family, 12 May 1894, HH; "Why We'll Miss Her," *The Banner,* 24 Aug. 1916, p. 534. Fishing could have been possible for many Dutch migrants prior to leaving the Netherlands, but hunting would have been unusual given the population and land-use practices.

73. While the refrigerated railroad car, used widely beginning in the 1870s, brought goods from around the country into city stores, few were willing to pay the prices for unknown items (Strasser, *Never Done,* pp. 16–17).

74. Geertje de Jong Schuiling, Manhattan, Mont., to Brother- and Sister-in-law, 22 June 1902, Hoogland collection, RL.

75. See Van Hinte, *Netherlanders in America,* pp. 551, 772, 792.

76. See the letters of Etje Houwerzijl, a widow who took over the farm, HH. *De Hollandsche Amerikaan* as late as 1919 was regularly carrying ads for people to rent farms which specified a married couple, or ads for a Dutch family to work in the celery and onions.

77. For an extensive example of butchering and meat preserving from Sioux Center, Iowa, consult tape 1078, PJM; on canning and food generally see the letters of Geertje de Jong Schuiling, Hoogland Collection, RL; and the letters from Lubbigje Schaapman to Willamientje Beltman, HH.

78. Again this was class-based, since the more well-to-do could afford to buy various beverages, and farmers with sufficient stock had milk for their own uses. For an example of drinking habits see tape 1077, woman born in 1910 in Rotterdam; man born in Barneveld in 1908; both emigrated with parents and settled in Sioux Center, Iowa, PJM.

79. De Groot, *When I Was a Girl in Holland,* p. 106.

80. De Regt, *Arbeidersgezinnen en beschavingsarbeid,* p. 94.

81. Anna Kuijt Bates, Morgan Park, Ill., to Gerrit Kuijt and Letha Retel, 15 Jan. 1918, HH.

82. On stoves see Strasser, *Never Done,* pp. 36–39.

83. De Regt, *Arbeidersgezinnen en beschavingsarbeid,* p. 76. Cowan argued that white bread became a status symbol in the United States because the flour cost more and because it required more work than other bread to bake (*More Work for Mother,* p. 51).

84. Heintje Oggel van Bruggen, Orange City, Iowa, to Sister-in-law Mietje, [Axel], 12 Aug. 1888, HH.

85. One woman from Oostwolde, Groningen, found life in Hollandale, Minnesota, a little lonesome at first. When some friends came to visit the first thing they asked was "is the coffee ready?" Of course she answered yes (tape 1070/71, woman born in 1892, migrated at age 17, PJM).

86. In the Netherlands even the better-off farmers did not always have a sufficient supply of silver spoons to serve guests. See De Groot, *When I Was a Girl in Holland,* pp. 15–16.

87. Vandenbosch, *Dutch Communities of Chicago,* p. 83.

88. Yankee Dutch written by John Lieuwen, *Sweat en Tears,* 2d ed. (Holland, Mich.: Schreur Printing, 1947), p. 67.

89. See, for example, Pieter Stokvis, "Drie emigranten over het leven in Friesland rond 1900," *It Beaken: Tydskrift fan de fryske akademy* 46 (1984): 153–63.

90. Anna Brown, "Life Story of John Tuininga," in *Dutch Immigrant Memoirs and Related Writings,* vol. 2, arr. Henry S. Lucas (1955; reprint, Grand Rapids: William B. Eerdmans, 1997), p. 193.

91. On food exchange in an ethnic community, see Janet Theophano and Karen Curtis, "Sisters, Mothers, and Daughters: Food Exchange and Reciprocity in an Italian-American Community," in *Diet and Domestic Life in Society,* ed. Anne Sharman et al. (Philadelphia: Temple University Press, 1991).

92. That Dutch women enjoyed a leisurely cup of coffee became enshrined in what two researchers called the three K's of Dutch women's lives: *krant, kachel, koffie* (newspaper, stove, coffee). This contrasted the German standard refrain when referring to women's activities. In German parlance the three K's consisted of *Kinder, Küche, Kirche* (children, kitchen, church). See Carli Schuit and Joan Hemels, *Recepten en rolpatronen: Nederlandse kranten en hun vrouwelijke lezers 1888–1988* (Utrecht: Scala, 1988), p. 17.

93. "Hollandsche Thee Gezelligheid," *Pella's Weekblad,* 26 May 1916, p. 4.

94. See Barbara Henkes and Hanneke Oosterhof, *Kaatje ben je boven? Leven en werken van Nederlandse dienstbodes* (Nijmegen: SUN, 1985), p. 153.

95. Koert, *Portrait of Lynden,* p. 68.

96. Geertje de Jong Schuiling, Manhattan, Mont., to Brother and Sister, 10 Feb. 1901, Hoogland Collection, RL.

97. Anna Kuijt, Chicago, to Uncle and Cato, 12 Aug. 1911, HH.

98. Lubbigje Schaapman, Salida, Calif., to Willamientje Beltman, July 1914, HH.

99. On the growth of home economics and especially nutrition, see Glenna Matthews, *"Just a Housewife": The Rise and Fall of Domesticity in America* (New York: Oxford University Press, 1987), p. 151. See also Katherine Jellison, *Entitled to Power* (Chapel Hill: University of North Carolina Press, 1993), p. 16.

100. *Pella's Weekblad* advertised courses at the Iowa State College for public school teachers who were now required to teach home economics, 26 May 1916, p. 7. It also noted that short home economics courses for housewives took place in Pella in the following years; see "Dit is de dag van Huishoudkunde," 24 Aug. 1917, p. 1.

101. Max Americanus [pseud.], "Cost of High Living or—High Cost of Living—Which?" *The Banner,* 19 May 1910, p. 309.

102. A similar fate met the efforts of home economists in the Netherlands. The reformers' attempts to convince working families that peas, beans, and rice were better sources of nutrition than white bread and potatoes fell on deaf ears (De Regt, *Arbeidersgezinnen en beschavingsarbeid,* p. 76).

103. Genevieve Gough, "Iowa's Hollanders," manuscript, p. 12, SHSI, and IFWC Essay Contest, 1923.

104. Quoted in Kitty de Leeuw, *Kleding in Nederland 1813–1920* (Hilversum: Verloren, 1992), p. 180.

105. See Ruth Oldenziel and Carolien Bouw, *Schoon genoeg: Huisvrouwen en huishoudtechnologie in Nederland 1898–1998* (Nijmegen: SUN, 1998), pp. 208–9.

106. Anna Polak, *Leidraad voor Amsterdamsche Meisjes bij de Keuze van een Beroep* (Gouda: Joh. Mulder, 1913), pp. 72–73.

107. Carin Schnitger, "Ijdelheid hoeft geen ondeugd te zijn: De Vereeniging voor Verbetering van Vrouwenkleeding," in *De eerste feministische Golf,* ed. Jeske Reys et al. (Nijmegen:

SUN, 1985), p. 164; on the clothing industry see Selma Leydesdorff, *Verborgen Arbeid, Vergeten Arbeid* (Amsterdam: Van Gorcum Assen, 1977), pp. 80–88.

108. On clothing for domestics, see Henkes and Oosterhof, *Kaatje ben je boven?* pp. 128–29. On class and clothing, see De Leeuw, *Kleding in Nederland,* pp. 180–86.

109. Berg, "De positie van de boerin op het Hogeland," p. 6.

110. See the selections reprinted in chap. 5, "De strijd tegen de gruwelmode," in *Geloof mij vrij, Mevrouw: Een bloemlezing uit vrouwentijdschriften tussen 1870 en 1920,* ed. Inge Polak (Amsterdam: Feministische Uitgeverij Sara, 1984), pp. 161ff.

111. De Regt, *Arbeidersgezinnen en beschavingsarbeid,* p. 96, 113.

112. De Groot, *When I Was a Girl in Holland,* pp. 37–38. Hilde Berg presented a very similar account of clothing for farmer's wives in sections of Groningen: five to six petticoats, a linen shirt, a knitted *borstrok,* a fabric corset, and a woolen skirt and jacket. In Groningen the standard colors were black, wine red, dark purple, and brown ("De positie van de boerin op het Hogeland," p. 27).

113. See the cover of the exhibition catalog, *De Glorie van het Ongeziene: Nationale Tentoonstelling van Vrouwenarbeid 1898, 100 jaar later* (Amsterdam: IIAV, 1998).

114. Circular from the Bemiddelingsbureau tot Plaatsing van Dienstboden, [Amsterdam], Apr. 1903. Van der Mey collection, IIAV.

115. Acqnoij, Gelderland, to Grand Haven, Mich., 24 Sept. 1874, HH.

116. See De Leeuw, *Kleding in Nederland,* esp. chap. 5.

117. De Groot, *When I Was a Girl in Holland,* pp. 40–42.

118. Sheeres, "Dear Queen . . . ," p. 38.

119. G. A. Stout, pub., *A Souvenir History of Pella, Iowa* (Pella: Booster Press, 1922), p. 221.

120. Lubbigje Schaapman to Willamientje Beltman, Salida, Calif., 19 Mar. 1911, HH. When city promoters of Holland, Michigan, decided to organize a tulip festival in the 1930s, they used an American postcard version of Dutch dress as their model. Only decades later did a home economist from one of the universities assist in locating "authentic" Dutch patterns from several regional origins. On the development of the tulip festival see my "Tulips Are Blooming in Holland, Michigan: Analysis of a Dutch-American Festival," in *Immigration and Ethnicity,* ed. Michael D'Innocenzo and Josef P. Sirefman (Westport, Conn.: Greenwood Press, 1992), pp. 3–14.

121. Tape 1004, woman born in Rotterdam in 1886, emigrated at age twenty-two with parents, settled in Holland, Mich., PJM.

122. Van Hinte, *Netherlanders in America,* p. 816.

123. See, for example, *De Boodschapper,* Aug. 1914.

124. M. Smit to Mother and Brother, May 1881, HH.

125. "Goed Nieuws voor de Dames," *Pella's Weekblad,* 22 June 1917, p. 1.

126. Gough, "Iowa's Hollanders," manuscript, SHSI, p. 12, and IFWC Essay Contest, 1923.

127. Jeannette Goedhart, Chicago, to Anna Kuijt, [Hilversum], 16 Sept. 1907, HH.

128. Trijntje Stormzand, Grand Rapids, Mich., to Brother and Sister, 29 Sept. 1888, HH.

129. Trijntje Kooiman, Hawarden, Iowa, to Anna de Vries, [Andijk], 16 Jan. 1910, HH.

130. This complaint applied to the daughters of many ethnic groups around the turn of the century. See Ewen, *Immigrant Women in the Land of Dollars,* and Peiss, *Cheap Amusements.*

131. Letters were most likely to contain portraits, if any pictures at all. Early in the period these tended to be studio prints, very formal in nature. Later there were more informal shots. On this see Rob Kroes, "Migrating Images: The Role of Photography in Immigrant Writing," in *American Photographs in Europe,* ed. David E. Nye and Mick Gidley (Amsterdam: VU University Press, 1994), pp. 189–204.

132. See "Miss Nona Gordy," *The Banner*, 26 Sept. 1912, cover and p. 612.

133. Max Americanus [pseud.], "The Weaker Vessels," *The Banner*, 11 Aug. 1910.

134. Lubbigje Schaapman, Salida, Calif., to Willamientje Beltman, July 1914, HH.

135. Dirk Nieland, *'n fonnie bisnis*, 2d ed. (Grand Rapids: Wm. B. Eerdmans, n.d. [1929?]), p. 46.

136. Tape 1035, woman born in Ooltgensplaat, Zeeland, in 1893, PJM.

137. J. W. Brink, "Wat dunkt U er van?" *De Gereformeerde Amerikaan*, May 1904, p. 235.

138. P. Ekster, "De Hoeden der Vrouwen," *De Gereformeerde Amerikaan*, May 1912, p. 206.

139. "Idolatry," *The Banner*, 12 Mar. 1908, cover story.

140. Taken from *Youth's Companion*, in *The Banner*, 10 Dec. 1908.

141. *De Volksvriend*, 10 June 1880, p. 3.

142. *Pella's Weekblad*, 3 Oct. 1902, p. 4. The shop offered four hundred patterns from which to choose.

143. *Pella's Weekblad*, 14 Nov. 1902, p. 4. "New Home Sewing Machines" ads were in English, 27 June 1902, p. 3.

144. Mail order came into vogue at the turn of the century, beginning with Montgomery Ward, founded in 1872, and followed by Sears, Roebuck & Company in the 1890s. By 1900 Sears offered "nearly every product line that existed" (Strasser, *Never Done*, p. 257). See also Cowan, *More Work for Mother*, pp. 75, 81.

145. Boukje Arjens Dijkstra Schuiling, Manhattan, Mont., to Brother-in-law and Sister, Feb. 1912. The reference to mail orders appears in the same letter, in the section written by her husband Klaas (Hoogland Collection, RL).

146. In Dutch it rhymed: "In de winkel van Sinkel is alles te koop, hoeden en petten, en damescorsetten," quoted in Schuit and Hemels, *Recepten en rolpatronen*, p. 26.

147. Cornelia De Groot, for example, discussed her fourth-grade class: "we had our lessons in knitting, sewing, crocheting, darning, knitting-darning, and cross-stitching from three to four o'clock on four afternoons and from 10:30 to 11:30 on two mornings." She went on to note that she and several other girls took additional sewing lessons from a seamstress after school (*When I Was a Girl in Holland*, p. 52).

148. Geertje de Jong Schuiling, Manhattan, Mont., to Brother and Sister, 9 Jan. 1910, Hoogland Collection, RL.

149. For example, R. H. Brinks wrote about Orange City, Iowa, in 1882, noting that tailors had their own shops and people went to them (To Brother, Sister and Children [in Emmen, Drenthe], 17 Feb. 1882, HH). Van Huet noted the common practice of "farm seamstresses" who spent a few days on a farm making clothing and then moved on ("Tussen Traditie en Modernisering," p. 40).

150. For example, Anna Kuijt, Chicago, to Uncle and Cato, 12 Aug. 1911, HH: "Cato you wrote me in your last letter that you wanted to crochet a skirt for me, I am afraid that it would cost a great deal of money."

151. Gaatske and Johannes, Crookston, Minn., to Mr. and Mrs. Hoogland, [n.d.], Hoogland Collection, RL.

152. Cornelia De Groot, "American and Dutch Maids Are Compared," *San Francisco Chronicle*, 29 Feb. 1929, reprinted in *When I Was a Girl in Holland*, supplement, p. 15.

153. Klaaske Noorda [Heller], Oakharbor [*sic*], Wash., to Mother, Brothers, Sisters, Nephews and Nieces, 19 Oct. 1896, HH.

154. On the expansion of the sewing machine industry see Ruth Brandon, *A Capitalist Romance: Singer and the Sewing Machine* (Philadelphia: J. P. Lippincott, 1977).

155. Jeannette Goedhart, Chicago, to Letha Retel [Kuijt] and Gerrit Kuijt, 23 Sept. 1907.

Previous letter was from Jeannette Goedhart, Chicago, to Anna Kuijt, [Hilversum], 16 Sept. 1907, HH.

156. "De New Home Naaimachine is Koning," *De Volksvriend,* 10 Sept. 1880, p. 3.

157. Ad for branch in Le Mars, Iowa, *De Volksvriend,* 16 Jan. 1919, p. 8.

158. *The Banner,* clipping from 1917, p. 670.

159. P. J. Hoekenga, "For Ladies' Aids and Girls' Societies," *The Banner,* clipping from 1917, p. 670.

160. See report from Prairie View, Kansas, in *Pella's Weekblad,* 7 Dec. 1917, p. 8.

161. "Aan de Moeders, Vrouwen, en Dochters in Onze Stad . . . ," *Pella's Weekblad,* 19 Oct. 1917, p. 1.

162. "Rapport van de Plaatselijk Roode Kruis Vereeniging," *Pella's Weekblad,* 25 Jan. 1917, p. 1.

163. Posthumus–van der Goot and de Waal, *Van Moeder op Dochter,* described some of the conditions in the Netherlands (pp. 225–26). The lapse generally was only a few years, thus the exhibition "De Vrouw 1813–1913" held in 1913 in the Netherlands included most of the American technological wonders which had their premier at the World's Columbian Exposition in Chicago in 1893. But for the women who lived in this period, those few years with or without running water, gas, or electricity were significant (Clipping on "De Vrouw 1813–1913," *Nieuwe Rotterdammer Courant,* [June 1913], Tentoonstelling "De Vrouw 1813–1913," IIAV; Strasser, *Never Done,* p. 73).

164. Standards for washing changed dramatically when compulsory school attendance laws passed. One study of Winterswijk in the Netherlands indicated that women did the wash about four times a year in the early 1800s, this despite having only one or two outfits. By late century, this changed to doing the wash every two to three weeks (Van Huet, "Tussen Traditie en Modernisering"). On washing standards in the United States see Cowan, *More Work for Mother,* p. 88.

165. Ruth Schwartz Cowan, "The 'Industrial Revolution' in the Home: Household Technology and Social Change in the Twentieth Century," in *Women's America: Refocusing the Past,* ed. Linda K. Kerber and Jane De Hart–Mathews (New York: Oxford University Press, 1987), p. 331.

166. Klaaske Noorda [Heller], [Oak Harbor, Wash.], to Mother, n.d. [1890s], HH.

167. Tape 1085, woman born in Pernis, Zuid Holland, migrated with parents in 1890, settled in Sheldon, Iowa, PJM.

168. Tape 1048, woman born in Apeldoorn in 1899, migrated with parents in 1902, settled in Waupun, Wisconsin, PJM.

169. Anna Kuijt, Chicago, to Uncle and Cato, 12 Aug. 1911, HH.

170. Tape 1027, woman born in Zeeland, Mich., in 1905, parents born in Assen and Norg, had migrated in 1870, PJM.

171. Strasser, *Never Done,* p. 105. See also Cowan, *More Work for Mother,* p. 156.

172. See Oldenziel and Bouw, *Schoon genoeg,* pp. 159ff.

173. Jantje Enserink van der Vliet, Chandler, Minn., to friends, 1 Oct. 1909, in Verbrugge, "Brieven uit het Verleden," p. 120.

174. Westra, "Fear and Hope Jostled," p. 5.

175. A standard definition includes sociability, coziness, cheerfulness, conviviality, snugness, companionableness. The German equivalent is *Gemütlichkeit.*

176. L. van der Pek–Went, "Wonen en Bewonen," in *Vrouwen van Nederland 1898–1948,* comp. M. G. Schenk (Amsterdam: Scheltens & Giltay, 1948), p. 80.

177. Berg, "De positie van de boerin op het Hogeland," p. 30.

178. See, for example, the pictures in De Groot, *When I Was a Girl in Holland*, pp. 36–37; Henkes and Oosterhof, *Kaatje ben je boven?* pp. 127, 140, 153; Leydesdorff, *Verborgen Arbeid, Vergeten Arbeid*, pp. 47, 105; and in *Vrouwen van Nederland 1898–1948*, pp. 36–37.

179. Van Huet, "Tussen Traditie en Modernisering," p. 40.

180. De Groot, *When I Was a Girl in Holland*, pp. 22–32 passim, quote on p. 30.

181. Berg, "De positie van de boerin op het Hogeland," pp. 11, 41–43, 55.

182. Tape 1001, woman born in Amsterdam in 1893, migrated with parents in 1914 because of World War I, settled in Holland, Mich., PJM.

183. "Janet Huyser's Recollections," *Origins* 16 (1998): 6.

184. See Suzanne M. Sinke, "Transnational Visions of Gender and Class Ideologies in Dutch Migration," in *The Dutch American Experience*, ed. Hans Krabbendam and Larry J. Wagenaar (Amsterdam: Vrije Universiteit Uitgeverij, 2000).

185. Lubbigje Schaapman, [Salida, Calif.], to Willamientje Beltman, 9 Mar. 1911, HH.

186. W. Nomes and A. Akkerman, [Roseland, Ill.], to Sibling[s?], 11 July 1882, HH.

187. Anna Kuijt to Gerrit Kuijt and Letha Retel Kuijt, Maurice, Iowa, 27 Nov. 1910, HH.

188. H. Schoonbeek, Grand Rapids, Mich., to Brother, Sisters, and Children, 27 Mar. 1894, HH, their translation.

189. Smit Family Correspondence, esp. Cornelia Smit, Grand Rapids, Mich., to Uncle and Nephew, 9 Aug. 1904, HH.

190. H. van Hoogen, "Het Huislijk- en Familieleven der Hollanders in Amerika," *De Gereformeerde Amerikaan*, May 1898, p. 150.

191. Anje Nieveen Mulder, Stuttgart, Kans., to Uncle and Cousin, Mar. 1889, HH.

192. For one example of the shift from sod to frame around the 1870s, see Mabel Eason, [Carol VanderPol] Oral History, Earthwatch-SHSI, 1978, p. 9.

193. Aukjen Pruiksma, Paterson, N.J., to Children, [Joure, Friesland], 16 May 1895, HH, their translation.

194. Gough, "Iowa's Hollanders," manuscript, SHSI, p. 12, and IFWC Essay Contest, 1923.

195. Van Hinte, *Netherlanders in America*, pp. 819, 821, and plat maps supplement.

196. Van Hinte, *Netherlanders in America*, p. 820.

197. Tape 1010, woman born in Nijverdal in 1887, migrated with family in 1912 to Iowa, then later to Holland, Mich., PJM.

198. See, for example, tape 1047, three persons born in Alto, Wis., in 1880, 1882, and 1890, parents from Nunspeet and Elspeet; and tape 1084, woman born in New Holland, Pa., in 1894; man born in Andijk in 1894, migrated in 1909 with parents, settled in Rock Valley, Iowa, PJM.

199. In the 1920s there were about seventy furniture factories around Grand Rapids, employing about fourteen thousand workers, many of them Dutch (Van Hinte, *Netherlanders in America*, p. 816).

200. Klaaske Noorda [Heller], Holland, Mich., to Noorda Family, to Ulrum, Groningen, 1891, fragment, translated and reproduced in Brinks, *Dutch American Voices*, p. 158.

201. *Pella's Weekblad*, 24 May 1918, p. 4.

202. See ad for Home Furnishing Co. in *De Hollandsche Amerikaan*, 7 Apr. 1919, p. 2.

203. H. van Hoogen, "Het Huislijk- en Familieleven der Hollanders in Amerika," *De Gereformeerde Amerikaan*, Jan. 1898, p. 472.

204. Anna Kuijt, Chicago, to Gerrit Kuijt and Letha Retel, 23 Dec. 1907, HH.

205. Ad for Keables' Apotheek, *Pella's Weekblad*, 23 Nov. 1899, p. 8.

206. See ad for the Sioux County Store, *De Volksvriend*, 10 Sept. 1880, p. 4.

207. Described and quoted in Van Hinte, *Netherlanders in America*, p. 986.

208. Geertje de Jong Schuiling, Manhattan, Mont., to brother and sister, 28 Dec. 1902, Hoogland Collection, RL.

209. "Diary of Mrs. Gezina Visscher."

210. See Oldenziel and Bouw, *Schoon genoeg*, pp. 93ff.

211. Klaaske, [Friesland], to Brother and Sister-in-law, [Manhattan, Mont.], [spring 1910], Hoogland Collection, RL.

212. Strasser, *Never Done*, pp. 61–64.

213. *Pella's Weekblad*, 23 Mar. 1917, p. 5; 4 Apr. 1902, p. 5; *De Volksvriend*, 3 Apr. 1919, p. 8.

214. *De Huisvriend*, Mar. 1906.

215. Koert, *Portrait of Lynden*, p. 104.

216. H. van Hoogen, "Het Huislijk- en Familieleven der Hollanders in Amerika, VII," *De Gereformeerde Amerikaan*, Aug. 1898, pp. 302–3.

Chapter 3: Making Ends Meet

A longer version of the section "Cornelia De Bey" appears in Mary Pieroni Schiltz and Suzanne M. Sinke, "Cornelia De Bey," in *Women Building Chicago, 1790–1990*, ed. Adele Hast and Rima Lunin Schultz (Bloomington: Indiana University Press, 2001), pp. 214–16.

1. On the Dutch occupational census see the discussion in Galema, *Frisians to America*, p. 85; on the U.S. census see Margo A. Conk, "Accuracy, Efficiency and Bias: The Interpretation of Women's Work in the U.S. Census of Occupations, 1890–1940," *Historical Methods* 14 (Spring 1981): 65–69.

2. See Corrie van Eijl, *Het werkzame verschil: Vrouwen in de slag om arbeid, 1898–1940* (Hilversum: Verloren 1994).

3. "Arbeiders-budgets," in *Bijdragen van het Statistisch Instituut*.

4. See Louise A. Tilly and Joan W. Scott, *Women, Work, and Family* (New York: Holt, Rinehart and Winston, 1978). The pattern found in the Netherlands in this period actually falls somewhere between what they title the family economy and the family wage economy.

5. Tamara Hareven illustrated this concept in *Family Time and Industrial Time: The Relationship between the Family and Work in a New England Industrial Community* (New York: Cambridge University Press, 1982).

6. For an overview of legal measures relating to women's rights, see Johanna W. A. Naber, "Eerste Proeve van een Chronologisch Overzicht van de Geschiedenis der Vrouwenbeweging in Nederland," in *De eerste feministische golf*, ed. Jeske Reys et al. (1937; reprint, Nijmegen: SUN, 1985), pp. 189–201.

7. Bieleman, "Plaats en taak der Vrouw in het Landbouwbedrijf," pp. 274–76.

8. Janet Sjaarda Sheeres, raw data for "Your Grandmother from Groningen," in author's possession. Of 392 women in the general category of household worker, 283 were *dienstmeiden* and 60 *boeremeiden*. The second title was exclusively for women working on large farms, and the former was used most frequently, though not always exclusively, for women working in rural households. Only thirty-eight were listed as *dienstbodes* and another eleven as *huishoudsters* or housekeepers. The workers category included *dagloonsters* [people hired by the day], *werkvrouwen*, and *arbeidsters*.

9. Polak, *Leidraad voor de Amsterdamsche Meisjes*, pp. 83–84. Women's wages averaged ƒ0.55/day in 1898. Seasonal work generally paid a bit better. See Schilstra, *Vrouwenarbeid in Landbouw en Industrie in Nederland*, p. 123.

10. See de Regt, *Arbeidersgezinnen en beschavingsarbeid,* p. 111; Jeanne de Bruijn, *Haar Werk* (Amsterdam: SUA, 1989), p. 31; and K. Wenthold, *Arbeid en Zorg* (Amsterdam: Thesis Publishers, 1990), pp. 15–21.

11. WPA interview with Arthur Vermeire, in David Steven Cohen, ed., *America: The Dream of My Life* (New Brunswick: Rutgers University Press, 1990), p. 150.

12. Aukjen Pruiksma, Paterson, N.J., to Children, [Joure, Friesland], 16 May 1895, HH, their translation.

13. Maaike Huigen, Pella, Iowa, to Brother and Friend, 20 Nov. 1882, Familie Archief Huigen, RL.

14. Amry Vandenbosch reported that as late as the 1920s, fathers still expected children under eighteen to turn over all wages (*Dutch Communities of Chicago,* pp. 83–84).

15. One of the most common jobs for sons was that of cowherd. See, for example, Klaaske Noorda [Heller], [Oak Harbor, Wash.?], [1890s], fragment, HH; tape 1018, PJM.

16. Arendje Bregman Akkerman, Roseland, Ill., 11 July 1882, fragment, HH.

17. Tape 1100, woman born in 1897 in vicinity of Pella, Iowa, reminiscing about mother, who immigrated with her parents in 1891, PJM.

18. Quoted in Westra, "Fear and Hope Jostled," p. 8.

19. Vander Velde, "Early History of the Derk Bruins Family to 1890," p. 112.

20. Onno and Klaaske Noorda [Heller], Oak Harbor, Wash., to Mother, Brother, and Sisters, [Ulrum, Groningen], [June 1899], HH, their translation.

21. "Diary of Mrs. Gezina Visscher," p. 141.

22. *De Hollandsche Amerikaan* appeared three times a week out of Kalamazoo, Michigan. This study is based on all classified ads of jobs for women which appeared in 1919. In a comparison sample in 1920 from *De Volksvriend,* based out of Orange City, Iowa, I still found housekeeping and domestic service as the primary opportunities, though there were several chances for women to go into teaching or nursing at new Dutch American institutions, and for women as stenographers or clerks in stores which still served Dutch-speaking clientele.

23. Marie W. Rutgers-Hoitsema, "Het wenschelijke van eene regeling van arbeidstijden met al of niet vrije beschikking over de vrije uren," in *Dienstboden-Congres gehouden op 21 Augustus 1898* (Amsterdam: W. Versluys, 1899), pp. 14–18.

24. Tijdeman-Verschoor, for example, includes in her training program for "household work": cleaning and straightening rooms, scrubbing hallways, sharpening knives, cleaning and polishing metal utensils, setting the table and washing china, caring for children, instructing children, doing wash, cooking simple dishes, keeping the fire going, choosing good ingredients from the market, separating clothing to do the wash, folding, ironing, using an ironing machine, getting stains out, etc. ("De noodzakelijkheid van vakopleiding voor dienstboden," in *Dienstboden-Congres,* pp. 42–43).

25. Organizational attempts were largely limited to urban areas at this time. See Henkes and Oosterhof, *Kaatje ben je boven?* pp. 41–49. See also Jannie Poelstra, *Luiden van een andere beweging: Huishoudelijke arbeid in Nederland 1840–1920* (Amsterdam: Het Spinhuis, 1996) chap. 9 on organizational attempts.

26. Bemiddelingsbureau tot Plaatsing van Dienstboden, Amsterdam, brochure dated Apr. 1903, Van der Mey Collection, IIAV.

27. Berg, "De positie van de boerin op het Hogeland," p. 59.

28. Schilstra provided the results in tabular form in *Vrouwenarbeid in Landbouw en Industrie in Nederland,* pp. 121–22.

29. Poelstra, *Luiden van een andere beweging,* p. 46.

30. Anna Polak, "De arbeid der Vrouw," in *De Vrouw, de vrouwenbeweging en het vrouwen-vraagstuk*, ed. C. M. Werker-Beaujon, Clara Wichmann, and W. H. M. Werker (Amsterdam: Elsevier, 1914), pp. 30–31.

31. Henkes and Oosterhof, *Kaatje ben je boven?* p. 61, citing Bond van Huispersoneel, *Moet het zo blijven?* (The Hague, 1914), pp. 13–17.

32. Cited in a letter in D. Elema-Bakker, "Boerinnen en Landarbeidsters," in *Vrouwen van Nederland 1898–1948*, comp. M. G. Schenk (Amsterdam: Scheltens & Giltay, 1948), p. 47.

33. Quoted in Van Huet, "Tussen Traditie en Modernisering," p. 64. The terms do not translate well because in Dutch there is a class as well as marital difference involved. See the discussion on language in chap. 5.

34. Quoted in Henkes and Oosterhof, *Kaatje ben je boven?* p. 132.

35. One domestic expressed this directly: "They treated the workers like . . . dogs." Quoted in "Klassen en klassebewustzijn in de Zaanstreek," in *Arbeidersleven in Nederland 1850–1914*, ed. Jacques Giele (Nijmegen: SUN, 1979), p. 178.

36. Berg, "De positie van de boerin op het Hogeland," pp. 11, 41–43, 55.

37. R. H. Brinks, Orange City, Iowa, to H. Brinks, [Emmen, Drenthe], 17 Feb. 1882, HH.

38. Geertje de Jong Schuiling, [Manhattan, Mont.], to Brother and Sister, [Jan. 1918], Hoogland Collection, RL.

39. *f*1=$.402; U.S. Department of Commerce, *Statistical Abstract of the United States, 1920*, "Monetary Systems and Approximate Stock of Money," listing for 31 Dec. 1918, p. 831.

40. Based on a study of one issue of *De Volksvriend* for each month of 1920. The same was true in other papers: "No washing or ironing. Small family. Good wages" (*De Hollandsche Amerikaan*, 21 May 1919, p. 4).

41. Clare de Jong, Crookston, Minn., to Friends, [n.d.] Hoogland Collection, RL.

42. Henkes and Oosterhof, *Kaatje ben je boven?* pp. 68–69, 75; see also housekeeping plans in Oldenziel and Bouw, *Schoon genoeg*, pp. 68–69, 94–95.

43. Klaas Schuiling, Manhattan, Mont., to Brother and Sister, 21 Feb. 1900, Hoogland Collection, RL.

44. Tape 1078, family living in Sioux Center, Iowa, interviewee born there in 1887 to Dutch parents from Nunspeet and Deventer, PJM.

45. See the family history in Sheeres, "Your Grandmother from Groningen," manuscript in author's possession.

46. Willem Goedhart, Chicago, to Anna Kuijt, [Hilversum], Oct. 1907, HH.

47. See, for example, "De Verlorene, maar weer gevondene Dochter" (the daughter who was lost but then found again), *De Gereformeerde Amerikaan*, Apr. 1911, pp. 215–24.

48. P.C., Middelburg, Zeeland, to J.C., Wisconsin, 26 Oct. 1909, HH.

49. See, for example, A. H. Brechthold, "Iets omtrent den Arbeid aan Hollandsche Immigranten in New York," *De Hope*, 2 Feb. 1881, pp. 3–4.

50. Jacoba Akkerman [Molenaar], Roseland, Ill., to sister, 2 Jan. 1881, HH.

51. Lubbigje Schaapman, [Calif.], to Willamientje Beltman, [July 1911], HH.

52. The one dark-skinned Surinamese woman who took part in the National Exhibition of Women's Work in 1898 in the Netherlands was mobbed by people wanting to see her. See *De Glorie van het Ongeziene "Nationale Tentoonstelling van Vrouwenarbeid 1898" 100 jaar later* (exhibition catalog) (Amsterdam: IIAV, 1998).

53. Tape 1046, woman born 1887 and migrated in 1910 alone to Waupun, Wis., PJM.

54. Tape 1072B, woman living in Hollandale, Minn.; tape 1030, woman born in Kampernieuwstad, migrated in 1888 at age ten with parents to Holland, Mich., PJM.

55. Tape 1071B/1072A, woman born in Arnhem, migrated with parents at age five, PJM.

56. Jeannette Goedhart to Letha [Retel] and Gerrit [Kuijt], 18 Nov. 1907, HH.

57. "Ouders hebt ge wel eens gehoord van de 'white slave traffic?'" *De Gereformeerde Amerikaan*, Dec. 1908, p. 701.

58. Joy K. Lintelman reported this type of camaraderie for Swedish domestics, who did consider domestic service as more of a profession. See "'America Is the Woman's Promised Land': Swedish Immigrant Women and American Domestic Service," *Journal of American Ethnic History* 8 (Spring 1989): 9–23. Similar findings appear for Irish women in Diner, *Erin's Daughters in America*, and for Finnish women in Carl Ross, "Servant Girls: Community Leaders," pp. 41–54.

59. See, for example, Wilhelmina Merizon, Kolijnsplaat, Zeeland, to cousins, Kalamazoo, Mich., 24 Aug. 1889, HH.

60. Joan Younger Dickinson, *The Role of the Immigrant Women in the U.S. Labor Force, 1890–1910* (1975; reprint, New York: Arno Press, 1980), p. 215.

61. Trijntje Kooiman, Hawarden, Iowa, to Anna de Vries, [Andijk], 16 Jan. 1910, HH.

62. Henkes and Oosterhof, *Kaatje ben je boven?* p. 40.

63. *De Hollandsche Amerikaan*, 28 Jan. 1920, p. 4.

64. Domestic service accounted for employment of 60 percent of wage-earning women in 1870 but had dropped to 25 percent by 1910. See Alice Kessler-Harris, *Out to Work* (Oxford: Oxford University Press, 1982), p. 141.

65. See Kessler-Harris, *Out to Work*, p. 237; Darlene Clark Hine, "Lifting the Veil, Shattering the Silence," in *The State of Afro-American History*, ed. Hine (Baton Rouge: Louisiana State University Press, 1986), p. 242; and Nakano Glenn, "From Servitude to Service Work."

66. See, for example, David M. Katzman, *Seven Days a Week: Women and Domestic Service in Industrializing America* (New York: Oxford, 1978); Daniel E. Sutherland, *Americans and Their Servants: Domestic Service in the United States from 1800 to 1920* (Baton Rouge: Louisiana State University Press, 1981); Faye E. Dudden, *Serving Women: Household Service in Nineteenth-Century America* (Middletown, Conn.: Wesleyan University Press, 1983); and Phyllis Palmer, *Domesticity and Dirt: Housewives and Domestic Servants in the United States, 1920–1945* (Philadelphia: Temple University Press, 1989).

67. See, for example, Lintelman, "'America Is the Woman's Promised Land'": Lagerquist, *In America the Men Milk the Cows*; Ross, "Servant Girls: Community Leaders"; Carol K. Coburn, *Life at Four Corners: Religion, Gender, and Education in a German-Lutheran Community, 1868–1945* (Lawrence: University Press of Kansas, 1992); and Diner, *Erin's Daughters in America*.

68. Leydesdorff, *Verborgen Arbeid, Vergeten Arbeid*, p. 16.

69. On the organization of Dutch women in industry see Joyce Outshoorn, "Loondruksters of Medestrijdsters?" Vrouwen en vakbeweging in Nederland 1890–1920," *te elfder ure* 20 (1975): 725–31.

70. See *Catalogus van de Nationale Tentoonstelling van Vrouwenarbeid* ('s Gravenhage: [n.p.], July–Sept. 1898), pp. 95–98.

71. Jungius, *Beroepsklapper, Excerpt uit de "Uitkomsten der Beroepstelling in het Koninkrijk der Nederlanden op den een-en-dertigsten December 1889."* Note that the map does not include either ready-to-wear or fashion clothing makers' shops.

72. One report on textile manufacturing noted that women in Middelburg (Zeeland) wove muslin, while men wove finer cloth. Weaving generally had made the shift out of home production into factories in this province by 1860 (Schilstra, *Vrouwenarbeid in Landbouw en Industrie in Nederland*, pp. 14, 38).

73. A report by the National Bureau of Women's Work in 1902 noted that cleaning and preparing herring was often women's work and was an exception to laws concerning night work for women. Informants made it clear that only the poorest of the poor would take on such a job (Van der Mey Collection, IIAV).

74. The Synod (the ruling body) of the Christian Reformed Church condemned all unions in general and the Knights of Labor in particular in 1886. In 1904 it allowed that there could be some "neutral" unions, though the stance remained negative. In 1912 it condemned socialists and made adherence to this ideology grounds for excommunication (Van Hinte, *Netherlanders in America*, pp. 906–11). The Dillingham Commission report of 1911 listed 2 percent of Dutch men in trade unions (*Reports of the Immigration Commission: Abstracts of Reports of the Immigration Commission*, vol. 1, Senate doc. 747, 61st Congress, 3d session, 1911, "Affiliation with Trade Unions of Males 21 Years of Age or Over Who Are Working for Wages, by General Nativity and Race of Individual," p. 418.

75. *The Banner,* 11 Dec. 1919, p. 776.

76. Max Americanus [pseud.] illustrated this in "Having a Good Time": "Some are even grinding their fellow men in under-paid labor that they may hang around their wives silks and jewels for display in a so-called good time" (*The Banner,* 7 July 1910, p. 418). On the clashing ideology see James D. Bratt, *Dutch Calvinism in Modern America: a History of a Conservative Subculture* (Grand Rapids: William B. Eerdmans, 1984), pp. 74–77.

77. Albert Herman Koning, Holland, Mich., to Derkien Koning, [Groningen, Groningen], 20 Jan. 1910, HH, their translation.

78. "Enquête betreffende de werking en uitbreiding der wet van 19 Sept. 1874 en naar de toestand van fabrieken en werkplaatsen," 1887, part 11, p. 62, quoted in Leydesdorff, *Verborgen Arbeid, Vergeten Arbeid*, p. 30.

79. See De Vries, *Up from the Cellar*, p. 26.

80. The descriptions of mill work are from De Vries, *Up from the Cellar*, pp. 14–27.

81. Chas. P. Neill, *Report on Condition of Woman and Child Wage-earners in the United States,* vol. 4: *The Silk Industry,* Senate doc. 645, 61st Congress, 2d session, 1911. Of note is the absence of Dutch women from other volumes of this report. For example, in the volume on wage-earning women in stores and factories, even in the section on Chicago, another area of heavy Dutch settlement, there were no Dutch women listed in the examples of hundreds of factory workers (ibid., vol. 5: *Wage-Earning Women in Stores and Factories;* See, for example, pp. 254–57). In many government reports, the category "Dutch" as race or nationality did not exist or was subsumed under "other."

82. Neill, *Report on Condition of Woman and Child Wage-earners in the United States,* vol. 4: *The Silk Industry,* "Number and Per Cent of Families Having Each Classified Number of Members, by Nativity and Race," p. 252; "Number and Per Cent of Fathers and Mothers Contributing to the Family Support and of Children in Specified Age Groups at Work, by Nativity and Race," pp. 246–47; "Total Families, Total and Average Membership of Families, and Total and Average Wage-Earners in Families, by Nativity and Race," p. 228.

83. Neill, *Report on Condition of Woman and Child Wage-earners in the United States,* vol. 4: *The Silk Industry,* "Conjugal Condition of Male and Female Employees, by Age and Race. A. Female Employees in All Silk Mills, New Jersey," p. 340.

84. This was borne out in the one Dutch instance listed under specific cases: the woman was twenty-three years old and had been married six months. The couple had no children (Neill, *Report on Condition of Woman and Child Wage-earners in the United States,* vol. 4: *The Silk Industry,* "Married Women at Work: Age and Occupation of the Woman and Economic Condition of the Woman and the Family, in Detail, for Each State," pp. 576–77).

85. David Steven Cohen, ed., *America: The Dream of My Life* (New Brunswick: Rutgers University Press, 1990), for example: "My wife worked in one of the Paterson silk mills for the next year, until the first baby came along" (p. 146).

86. Neill, *Report on Condition of Woman and Child Wage-earners in the United States,* vol. 4: *The Silk Industry,* "Race of Employees with the Highest and Lowest Earnings in a Full Week of 55 Hours, for Employees 16 Years of Age and Over in Selected Occupations," p. 164.

87. Neill, *Report on Condition of Woman and Child Wage-earners in the United States,* vol. 4: *The Silk Industry,* "Average Individual Earnings of Children of Each Sex 16 Years of Age and Over at Work, Average Contributions of Such Children to Family income, and Per Cent of Their Earnings So Contributed, by Nativity and Race of Heads of Families" (p. 260) listed Dutch daughters as contributing over 98 percent of their earnings to the family. In the specific case studies later in the report, the fathers' occupations were listed for young women workers. In most cases they were not employed in the silk mills, but as tradespeople or laborers (ibid., "Single Women 16 Years of Age and Over at Work: Age, Occupation, and Education of the Woman, and Economic Condition of the Woman and the Family, in Detail for Each State: New Jersey," pp. 528–39).

88. Neill, *Report on Condition of Woman and Child Wage-earners in the United States,* vol. 4: *The Silk Industry,* "Number and Per Cent of Employees of Each Race, by Sex and Age Groups, for Each State," p. 68. Dutch boys constituted 15 percent of the under-sixteen labor force, while those over sixteen were under 10 percent.

89. *De Hollandsche Amerikaan,* 29 Oct 1919, p. 4.

90. *De Hollandsche Amerikaan,* based on study of all classified ads for 1919.

91. Tape 1048, woman from Apeldoorn, emigrated with parents at age three in 1902, settled in Waupun, Wis., PJM.

92. Schilstra, *Vrouwenarbeid in Landbouw en Industrie in Nederland,* pp. 9–11, 42, 47–50, 106, 125.

93. Jeanette Kuijt Goedhart, [Chicago area], to Letha Retel and Gerrit Kuijt, 8 July 1908, HH.

94. Neill, *Report on Condition of Woman and Child Wage-earners in the United States,* vol. 5, *Wage-earning Women in Stores and Factories,* Senate doc. 645, 61st Congress, 2d session, Government Printing Office, 1910.

95. See, for example, Miss Haverkamp's ad, "Dames Attentie," placed in *De Volksvriend,* 8 Apr. 1880, p. 3; and the ad placed by "Mrs. J. van Maren," a "modiste" or creator of fashions and milliner, in *Pella's Weekblad,* 28 Mar. 1902, p. 1..

96. G. A. Stout, pub., *Souvenir History of Pella, Iowa* (Pella: Booster Press, 1922), p. 166.

97. For example, the first woman physician in the Netherlands, Aletta Jacobs, entered medical school in 1871. In the United States by 1870 there were a number of medical schools specifically for women, as well as others which accepted woman as students, and the first woman doctor, Elizabeth Blackwell, had begun professional training in 1847. On this development see J. Brok–ten Broek, "Van bewaarschool tot universiteit," in *Van Moeder op Dochter: De maatschappelijke positie van de vrouw in Nederland vanaf de fanse tijd,* ed. W. H. Posthumus–van de Goot and Anna de Waal (1948; reprint, Nijmegen: SUN, 1977), part 1, chap. 4; Regina Morantz-Sanchez, *Sympathy and Science: Women Physicians in American Medicine* (New York: Oxford University Press, 1985), chap. 2; see also Barbara Miller Solomon, *In the Company of Educated Women: A History of Women and Higher Education in America* (New Haven: Yale University Press, 1985). For a few specific examples from other fields see Selma Leijdesdorff, "Vrouwen dragen geen witte boorden maar schone jurken: hoe drie vrouwenberoepen ontstonden: buffetjuffrouw, winkelmeisje en sekretaresse," in *Socialisties-Femi-*

nistiese Teksten 1, ed. Selma Sevenhuijsen, Joyce Outshoorn, and Anja Meulenbelt (Amsterdam: Feministische Uitgeverij Sara, 1978), pp. 204–21; M. Morée, "Waarom de apothekers voor vrouwen kozen: De transformatie van het apothekersassistentenberoep in de periode 1865–1900," in *Derde Jaarboek Vrouwengeschiedenis,* ed. Josine Blok, Mirjam Elias, and Els Kloek (Nijmegen: SUN, 1982), pp. 36–63; Margery W. Davies, *Woman's Place Is at the Typewriter: Office Work and Office Workers, 1870–1930* (Philadelphia: Temple University Press, 1982); and Susan Porter Benson, *Counter Cultures: Saleswomen, Managers, and Customers in American Department Stores, 1890–1940* (Urbana: University of Illinois Press, 1986).

98. Tape 1004, woman born 1886 in Rotterdam, migrated with family in 1908, PJM.

99. Compare Sydney Stahl Weinberg's work on the role of Jewish mothers in facilitating their daughters' careers, fully developed in *The World of Our Mothers.*

100. Vandenbosch, *Dutch Communities of Chicago;* Van Hinte, *Netherlanders in America,* pp. 366, 373, 380, 589; Bernardus de Beij, Chicago, to Pieter A. Lanting, Winsum, [Groningen], 1 Apr. 1870, HH; and Hans Krabbendam, "Serving the Dutch Community: A Comparison of the Patterns of Americanization in the Lives of Two Immigrant Pastors" (M.A. thesis, Kent State University, 1989).

101. Lucy Fitch Perkins, *Cornelia: The Story of a Benevolent Despot* (Boston: Houghton Mifflin, 1919), includes one story where Cornelia steals coal from her father's church to help a desperate (and deserted) Irish immigrant woman and her family, and another where she intervenes in a political rally in her ward in order to make sure a candidate she feels is unsuitable will be defeated. Perkins based her story on childhood anecdotes told her by an adult Cornelia De Bey.

102. Bernardus de Beij, Chicago, to Pieter A. Lanting, Winsum, 25 Nov. 1884, HH.

103. See Van Eijl, *Het werkzame vershil,* chaps. 5 and 7.

104. Homeopathic medicine declined precipitously in popularity in the United States (though not in the Netherlands) after the turn of the century. See Ronald L. Numbers, "The Fall and Rise of the American Medical Profession," in *Sickness and Health in America,* ed. Judith Walzer Leavitt and Ronald L. Numbers, 2d ed. (Madison: University of Wisconsin Press, 1985), pp. 187, 190, 192.

105. Ernest Poole, *Giants Gone: Men Who Made Chicago* (New York: Whittlesey House, 1943), p. 219.

106. "Dr. Cornelia B. DeBey," Chicago Teachers' Federation *Bulletin,* Sept. 16, 1904, p. 5.

107. William Hard, "Chicago's Five Maiden Aunts," *American Magazine* 62 (Sept. 1906): 482.

108. "The Strike 'Peace Commission' . . . ," *Chicago Daily Tribune,* May 1, 1905, p. 14.

109. Margaret A. Haley, *Battleground: The Autobiography of Margaret A. Haley,* ed. Robert L. Reid (Urbana: University of Illinois Press, 1982) p. 102.

110. Haley, *Battleground,* p. 103.

111. Hard, "Chicago's Five Maiden Aunts," p. 482.

112. Brink, "Wat dunkt U er van?" p. 235.

113. For information on De Bey's term on the school board see Mary Pieroni Schiltz, "The Dunne School Board: Reform in Chicago, 1905–1908" (Ph.D. dissertation, Loyola University, 1993).

114. "Dr. De Bey Tell Aims on Board of Education," *Chicago Record-Herald,* 7 Nov. 1906, p. 13.

115. "Dr. Cornelia De Bey Says Woman Should Rise to Full Sense of Her Duty," Chicago Teachers' Federation *Bulletin,* Apr. 6, 1906, p. 5.

116. Letter of Anna Howard Shaw to Aletta Jacobs, 11 Dec. 1909, in Mineke Bosch and

Annemarie Kloosterman, eds., *Lieve Dr. Jacobs: Brieven uit de Wereldbond voor Vrouwenkies-recht 1902–1942* (Amsterdam: Feministische Uitgeverij Sara, 1985), p. 109.

117. See excerpt in "Can the Fraternity Be Made to Serve Moral Ends," *Chicago Record-Herald,* 17 June 1911, p. 8.

118. Obituary, *Grand Rapids Herald,* Apr. 3, 1948.

119. On nursing see Leontine Bijleveld and Adrianne Dercksen, "De roeping van een ver-pleegster: Arbeidsvoorwaarden van verpleegsters in de jaren twintig en dertig in histories perspektief," in *Socialisties-Feministiese Teksten 1,* ed. Selma Sevenhuijsen, Joyce Outshoorn, and Anja Meulenbelt (Amsterdam: Feministische Uitgeverij Sara, 1978), p. 230; and Kessler-Harris, *Out to Work,* p. 116.

120. Just as Dutch congregations tried to obtain ministers from the Netherlands, so too did other church-related institutions try to hire Dutch nurses. For example, Holland Home in Grand Rapids, Michigan, which served elderly Dutch Americans, sought to recruit nurses from the Netherlands in the 1910s (Board Minutes, Holland Home, 1910–17 vol., Holland Home Archives).

121. Fie [married Woldring], Pasadena, Calif., to Anje Woldring, [Groningen], 16 Apr. 1918, HH.

122. The Mazereeuw name was prominent in Opperdoes due to a religious movement in the 1820s. See Van Hinte, *Netherlanders in America,* p. 86.

123. Nellie Mazereeuw, Grand Rapids, Mich., to Friends, [Opperdoes, Friesland], 20 May 1913, HH.

124. In 1911 *The Banner* referred to nurses as public servants and categorized them togeth-er with policemen and firemen. After citing the hazards of the other two professions it went on to nursing: "The hours are long, the duties are exacting. . . . She must hold herself in readi-ness for any call, expose herself to every danger from infection and poisoning, cheerfully deny herself and persevere day and night" ("Keep Our Policemen, Firemen and Professional Nurses," 28 Sept. 1911, p. 605).

125. In a sample of twelve issues of *De Volksvriend* in 1920 there were seven classified ads for teachers and nurses for Christian institutions.

126. Herbert J. Brinks, *Pine Rest Christian Hospital: 75 Years, 1910–1985* (n.p., n.d. [Grand Rapids, 1985]), pp. 13, 27–29.

127. Her father was a shopkeeper in the Netherlands, and the entire family, including sev-eral adult children, migrated together (tape 1036, woman born in 1878 in De Koten, migrat-ed with family in 1898 and settled in Grand Rapids, Mich., PJM).

128. Teaching, in the Netherlands, remained predominantly male until the 1890s. Even in 1909 the number of women per 100 men teaching was only 128. Taken from the brochure "Mannenbond voor Vrouwenkiesrecht," [May 1913], "De Vrouw 1813–1913," Exhibition Col-lection, IIAV.

129. This stance was similar to that of conservative German immigrants, particularly those of the Missouri Synod who formed their own school system, akin to that of the Christian Reformed. See Schelbitzki Pickle, *Contented among Strangers,* p. 82.

130. See the picture of the female teaching staff and male principle of the Grandville Ave-nue Christian School, "Grand Rapids Notes," *The Banner,* 19 Mar. 1914, p. 199. Trijntje Mar-tens Schoonbeek described this pattern in a letter to her brother, a teacher, in 1875. "Here the school teachers are young women, and at each school there is a supervisor. If you could get such a position . . ." (Martens Schoonbeek, Grand Rapids, Mich., to Jacobus Schoonbeek, 27 June 1875, HH, their translation).

131. "The Teachers Employed in Our Christian Schools," *The Banner*, [1906?], p. 224.

132. *Reports of the Immigration Commission: The Children of Immigrants in Schools*, vol. 1, Senate doc. 749, 61st Congress, 3d session, 1911, pp. 129–30. The report did not specify by sex.

133. Gerald F. De Jong, *From Strength to Strength: The History of Northwestern 1882–1982* (Grand Rapids: Wm. B. Eerdmans, 1982), p. 23.

134. Nellie Zwemer and Emma Kollen, the first women teachers at the academy, both began work on the faculty beginning in 1887 (De Jong, *From Strength to Strength*, pp. 41, 48–49, 62).

135. Patricia R. Hill, *The World Their Household: The American Woman's Foreign Mission Movement and Cultural Transformation, 1870–1920* (Ann Arbor: University of Michigan Press, 1985), p. 122. On women and missions generally, see R. Pierce Beaver, *All Loves Excelling: American Protestant Women in World Mission* (Grand Rapids: Eerdemans, 1968).

136. For more specific treatments of women and missions see, for example, Jane Hunter, *The Gospel of Gentility: American Women Missionaries in Turn-of-the-Century China* (New Haven: Yale University Press, 1984); Patricia Grimshaw, *Paths of Duty: American Missionary Wives in Nineteenth-Century Hawaii* (Honolulu: University of Hawaii Press, 1989); Peggy Pascoe, *Relations of Rescue: The Search for Female Moral Authority in the American West, 1874–1939* (New York: Oxford University Press, 1990); Frederick J. Heuser, Jr., "Culture, Feminism, and the Gospel: American Presbyterian Women and Foreign Missions, 1870–1923" (Ph.D. dissertation, Temple University, 1991); Susan M. Yohn, *A Contest of Faiths: Missionary Women and Pluralism in the American Southwest* (Ithaca: Cornell University Press, 1995); Wade Alston Horton, "Protestant Missionary Women as Agents of Cultural Transition among Cherokee Women, 1801–1839" (Ph.D. dissertation, Southern Baptist Theological Seminary, 1991); and Carol Devens, *Countering Colonization: Native American Women and Great Lakes Missions, 1630–1900* (Berkeley: University of California Press, 1992).

137. *Thirty-Fifth Annual Report of the Women's Board of Domestic Missions of the Reformed Church in America for the Year Ending April Thirtieth 1918* (n.p. [New York]: Reformed Press, 1918), pp. 14–15.

138. Hendrina Hospers served in the "Indian American" mission from 1907 to 1946. Her father was a minister, as were two uncles. Her cousin Hendrine Euphemia Hospers was a missionary to Japan from 1913 to 1926. Hendrika (Hattie) Hospers, another cousin from Orange City, who had gotten a teaching degree and then married a minister, also served in the "Indian American" mission from 1908 to 1952 (Peter N. VandenBerge, *Historical Directory of the Reformed Church in America, 1628–1978* [Grand Rapids: Wm. B. Eerdmans, 1978]).

139. Frank R. Southard, *With Pen, Brush and Camera among the Indians*, pamphlet (n.d., n.p.), p. 11.

140. [Winifred Hulbert], *Old Paths and New Trails* (New York: Women's Board of Domestic Missions Reformed Church in America, n.d.), p. 12.

141. It is striking to find, going through the mission directory of VandenBerge's *Historical Directory of the Reformed Church in America*, that practically no women (if any) were born in the Netherlands.

142. *The Influence of the Dutch Emigration of 1847 on Foreign Missions*, address by Rev. Samuel M. Zwemer, at the Old Settlers' Picnic, Zeeland, Mich., 1907, printed manuscript, JAH.

143. Henry Beets, "Miss Nellie Noordhoff," *De Heidenwereld* 7 (June 1903): 83–84.

144. On the earlier period, See, for example, Grimshaw, *Paths of Duty*. On missionary wives generally see Dana L. Robert, *American Women in Mission: A Social History of Their Thought and Practice* (Macon, Ga.: Mercer University Press, 1996).

145. "De Indianenzending," *De Heidenwereld*, 1 (Nov. 1896): 18.

146. Jane and Willem Walvoord, Holland, Nebr., to Brother, Sister, Nephews and Nieces, 8 Mar. 1906, HH. Edith Walvoord married Anthony Walvoord and served as a missionary in Japan from 1905 to 1919, when her husband died (VandenBerge, *Historical Directory of the Reformed Church in America*, p. 243).

147. Nellie De Jong, "Our Zuni Day School: A Letter from the Teacher," *The Banner*, 17 Mar. 1910, p. 171.

148. Joan Jacobs Brumberg in "Zenanas and Girlless Villages: The Ethnology of American Evangelical Women, 1870–1910," *Journal of American History* 69 (Sept. 1982): 347–71.

149. One example of the role of Dutch American women in forming schools and educational programs for foreign women appeared in the history of the Amoy mission in China. See chap. 9 in Gerald F. De Jong, *The Reformed Church in China 1842–1951* (Grand Rapids: Wm. B. Eerdmans, 1992).

150. My impression of low salaries came from missionary daughters, who wrote their parents and siblings about having little or no money, and from general evaluations such as Beaver, *All Loves Excelling*, p. 107.

151. "Arbeiders-budgets," in *Bijdragen van het Statistisch Instituut*, pp. 149–50.

152. "Arbeiders-budgets," in *Bijdragen van het Statistisch Instituut*, p. 145.

153. De Regt, *Arbeidersgezinnen en beschavingsarbeid*, pp. 52–53; quote p. 97.

154. De Regt, *Arbeidersgezinnen en beschavingsarbeid*, pp. 69–70; Van Huet, "Tussen Traditie en Modernisiering," p. 39.

155. "Arbeiders-budgets," in *Bijdragen van het Statistisch Instituut*, p. 145. Immigrant letters gave the same impression.

156. One report from the 1890s noted that a woman earned 12 stuivers (10-cent pieces) per day and paid 9 stuivers for child care. "Then there isn't much left over after a whole day of work." From "Ze benne toch rijk geworden van ons," in *Arbeidersleven in Nederland 1850–1914*, ed. Jacques Giele (Nijmegen: SUN, 1979), p. 205.

157. "Een harde jeugd in Rotterdam," in Giele, *Arbeidersleven in Nederland*, p. 66.

158. Oral history of a woman born in 1889, excerpt found in "Armoe troef op de heide," in Giele, *Arbeidersleven in Nederland*, p. 251.

159. Bousema-Valkema, "Valk—De Valk—Valkema," p. 14.

160. Van Hinte, *Netherlanders in America*, p. 820.

161. Reported in Eisse Woldring, Grand Rapids, Mich., to Parents, Brother and Sister, 2 June 1912, HH.

162. Study of all classified ads in *De Hollandsche Amerikaan* for 1919 included four ads placed for persons offering boarding opportunities.

163. From a study of classified ads in *De Hollandsche Amerikaan* in 1919. All references to "family" were using the Dutch term "gezin."

164. Tape 1086, woman born in Baarn in 1896, arrived in U.S. at age twelve, PJM.

165. For examples see tapes 1025, 1088, 1090, 1097, PJM. The choices of products to sell differed, but the principle was the same for many other rural women of this period. See Joan Jensen, "Cloth, Butter, and Boarders: Women's Household Production for the Market," *Review of Radical Political Economics* 12 (Summer 1980): 14–24.

166. Maaike Huigen, Galesburg, Iowa, to Father, Brothers and Sister, ['t Bildt, Friesland], 12 Mar. 1880, HH, their translation.

167. *Pella's Weekblad* regularly carried ads for the Farmers Produce Co. which stated "Bring us your eggs, poultry and cream for which we still pay the highest prices." For example, 13 Oct. 1916, p. 8.

168. English-language ad for "Wolf's Egg maker," *Pella's Weekblad*, 12 Apr. 1918, p. 6.

169. *De Volksvriend*, 3 Apr. 1919, p. 8.

170. Martje Smit, [East Orange?, Iowa], to Mother and Brother, May 1881, HH.

171. Arendje Bregman Akkerman Burgerbrug, Roseland, Ill., to W. Nomes and A. Akkerman, July 1882, HH.

172. Lubbigje Schaapman, [Salida, Calif.], to Willamientje Beltman, [around 1911], fragment, HH.

173. Widow [K.] Siderius, Ashton, S.Dak., to Mrs. Hoogland, [Het Bildt], 27 Mar. 1889, Sjouke de Zee Collection, RL.

174. Henriette Bos [Mensink], St. Anne, to friends, sister, brothers, nieces and nephews, Sept. 1909, HH.

175. Tape 1020, woman born in 1877 in Noord Beveland, migrated with parents in 1880 and settled in Holland, Mich., PJM.

176. "Het Steeds Duurder Wordende Leven in Nederland," *Pella's Weekblad*, 26 May 1916, p. 3.

177. Harmanna Schoonbeek Rosenboom, Grand Rapids, Mich., to Brother and Children, [Oude Pekela, Groningen], 27 Nov. 1919, HH.

178. Anna Kuijt Bates, Morgan Park, Ill., to Gerrit Kuijt and Letha Retel, 15 Jan. 1918, HH.

179. Jantje Enserink van der Vliet, Chandler, Minn., to Friends, 1 Oct. 1909, in Verbrugge, "Brieven uit het Verleden."

180. Tape 1086, man, born in Orange City in 1894, father from Gelderland, PJM.

181. The process they described involved using fat from the pigs and cows they would butcher and combining it with a lye and water mixture (tape 1086, woman born in Pernis in 1878, migrated in 1890 with parents, PJM).

182. Tape 1078, woman born in Sioux Center, Iowa, in 1887, parents from Nunspeet and Deventer, PJM.

183. Martje Smit, n.p., to Brother, 6 Apr. 1897, HH.

184. S. de Bildt, Lafayette, Ind., to J. J. Hoogland, [Nieuwebildtdijk], 30 May 1881, Sjouke de Zee Collection, RL.

185. Reported in De Groot, *When I Was a Girl in Holland*, "Supplement," p. 17.

186. Compare Jellison, *Entitled to Power*, on the general move to bring labor saving devices into farm homes.

187. Tape 1084, woman born in New Holland, Pa., in 1894, married to man from Andijk; they settled in Rock Valley, Iowa, PJM.

188. A Dutch American community in northern New Jersey made the national news in the 1990s for still having a no mowing on Sunday ordinance on the books.

189. J. J. Bieleveld, n.p., to siblings, [Kolham, Groningen], [1909], HH.

190. Tape 1010, woman born in 1883 in Nijverdal, migrated with family in 1913 and settled in South Boardman, Mich., later moving to Holland, Mich., PJM.

191. "What young women can do as willing helpers in the kingdom," address given at 13th anniversary of the "Willing Helpers Circle" of the Third Christian Reformed Church of Paterson, N.J., 28 Mar. 1911, *The Banner*, 27 Apr. 1911, p. 271.

192. See Gjerde, *Minds of the West*, especially part 3 on the family.

Chapter 4: In Sickness and in Death

1. Here I wish to stress the gendered nature of care as a historical and economic phenomenon. See also Christien Brinkgreve, "De herwaardering van de vrouwelijke zorg: Enkele scep-

tische notities," *Amsterdams Sociologisch Tijdschrift* 16 (May 1989): 67.

2. If they could not found their own hospitals, they could at least bring in "moral authorities" to assist in healing the soul. In this the Dutch had a much easier time adapting to American medical practice than did many other ethnic groups. See Noel J. Chrisman and Arthur Kleinman, "Health Beliefs and Practices," in *Harvard Encyclopedia of American Ethnic Groups,* ed. Stephan Thernstrom (Cambridge: Harvard University Press, 1980), pp. 452–62.

3. For a case study of how these two positions clashed in the formation of social work, see Waaldijk, *Het Amerika der vrouw.*

4. See Alan M. Kraut, *Silent Travelers: Germs, Genes, and the "Immigrant Menace"* (New York: Basic Books, 1994), for contrasts to southern Italian and Chinese immigrants in particular.

5. Compare the activism of several ethnic groups of women in Harzig, *Peasant Maids, City Women.*

6. This stance was possible in the United States partly because of the lack of interest in health insurance on a state or national level. Whereas European countries had begun instituting national health insurance in the 1880s, the debate did not even get started in the United States until the 1910s and it was not enacted during the period under study. See Ronald L. Numbers, "The Third Party: Health Insurance in America," in *Sickness and Health in America,* ed. Judith Walzer Leavitt and Ronald L. Numbers, 2d ed. (Madison: University of Wisconsin Press, 1985), pp. 233–34.

7. On how this German-Dutch connection was replicated in the United States see Swenna Harger, "'Graafschap' fern von der 'Grafschaft,'" in *Jahrbuch des Heimatvereins der Grafschaft Bentheim, 1980,* ed. Hermann Heddendorp (Nordhorn, 1980), pp. 202–4.

8. Henricus Beuker Manuscript Collection, HH.

9. Beuker argued in print about this with Bernardus De Beij (father of Cornelia); see *De Vrije Kerk* 7 (1881): 577; quoted in Krabbendam, "Serving the Dutch Community," p. 79, his translation.

10. H. Beuker, "Veldwijk," *De Vrije Kerk* 12 (Feb. 1886): 106.

11. Jacob T. Hoogstra, "A Mother in Israel," *The Banner,* 23 Aug. 1957, p. 32.

12. Hoogstra, "Mother in Israel." The obituary concentrated on her connections to leading theologians and was written by her pastor at the Prospect Park Church of Holland, Mich.

13. Henricus Beuker Collection; J. Robbert Family Collection, HH.

14. See H. Beuker, "Bethesda te Maxwell City," *De Wachter,* 1 Mar. 1899; "Bethesda," 7 June 1899; "Aan de Leden en Begunstigers van Bethesda," 13 Dec. 1899.

15. Sue Helder Goliber, "Jacoba Beuker Robbert," in *For Such a Time as This . . . Twenty-Six Women of Vision and Faith Tell Their Stories,* ed., Lillian V. Grissen (Grand Rapids: William B. Eerdmans, 1991), pp. 19–20; Brinks, *Pine Rest Christian Hospital,* pp. 13–14.

16. Brinks, *Pine Rest Christian Hospital,* pp. 11–12.

17. "Verpleging van Krankzinnigen," *De Wachter,* 5 Apr. 1906, supplement.

18. "Verpleging van Krankzinnigen."

19. "Verpleging van Krankzinnigen."

20. Brinks, *Pine Rest Christian Hospital,* pp. 16–17; Helder Goliber, "Jacoba Beuker Robbert," p. 21. Pine Rest Christian Hospital is now a multimillion dollar operation, still serving the mentally impaired.

21. Jan Robbert's tenure as dominie in the United States was: Roseland, Ill., 1893–1900; First Kalamazoo, Mich., 1901–8; Niekerk, Mich., 1908–11; East Paterson, N.J., 1911; East Paris, Mich., 1911–14; and Rusk, 1914–18. All but the last are listed in Robbert Manuscript Collection, Heritage Hall. The last is recorded in Hoogstra, "Mother in Israel," p. 32.

22. The Jacoba Beuker Robbert Collection at Heritage Hall includes several of her Bible study notebooks and in one case a list of the women in her class.

23. Hoogstra, "Mother in Israel," p. 32.

24. Hoogstra, "Mother in Israel," p. 32; and Helder Goliber, "Jacoba Beuker Robbert," pp. 21–22.

25. Jacoba Beuker Robbert Manuscript Collection, notebook 4.

26. Cora Bakker–van der Kooij, "Mara. Pleegzuster zijn. Ontwikkelingen in de ziekenverpleging en de organisatiepogingen van verpleegsters in Nederland, 1870–1920," in *Tweede Jaarboek voor Vrouwengeschiedenis*, ed. Josine Blok et al. (Nijmegen: SUN, 1981), p. 199.

27. Bijleveld and Dercksen, "De roeping van een verpleegster," pp. 223–24.

28. This contrasts with other immigrant groups for whom medicine was less well established and an American doctor or nurse was a new phenomenon. See Kraut, *Silent Travelers*, chap. 8.

29. On the degree to which others could get support, see P. Pennings, "Zuilen en lokale subsidies in 45 gemeenten, 1880–1930," in *Van particuliere naar openbare zorg en terug?* ed. W. P. Blockmans and L. A. van der Valk (Amsterdam: NEHA, 1992), pp. 62–65.

30. Waaldijk, *Het Amerika der vrouw*, p. 101.

31. For some general comments on Dutch family patterns of care for the elderly see Monique Stavenuiter, "Last Years of Life: Changes in the Living and Working Arrangements of Elderly People in Amsterdam in the Second Half of the Nineteenth Century," *Continuity and Change* 11 (Aug. 1996): 218–19, 238–39.

32. Hettie Pott-Buter and Kea Tijdens, eds., *Vrouwen leven en werk in de twintigste eeuw* (Amsterdam: Amsterdam University Press, 1998), pp. 99–102.

33. On the strong state, weak state formula for women's participation see Kathryn Kish Sklar, "The Historical Foundations of Women's Power in the Creation of the American Welfare State, 1830–1930," in *Mothers of a New World: Maternalist Politics and the Origins of Welfare States*, ed. Seth Koven and Sonya Michel (New York: Routledge, 1993), pp. 43–93.

34. See William S. Bernard, "Immigration: History of U.S. Policy," in *Harvard Encyclopedia of American Ethnic Groups*, ed. Stephan Thernstrom (Cambridge: Harvard University Press, 1980), pp. 490–91. See also chap. 3 and appendixes in Kraut, *Silent Travelers*.

35. Liefiena Bos, Sappemeer, Groningen, to Uncle and Aunt, [Grand Rapids, Mich.], 16 Sept. 1888, HH.

36. Albert Herman Koning, Holland, Mich., to Derkien Koning [Groningen, Groningen], 20 Jan. 1910, HH, their translation.

37. Brinks, *Dutch American Voices*, p. 446, n. 1.

38. Quote from Lubbigje Schaapman, SS *Ryndam*, to Willamientje Beltman, 31 Jan.–Feb. 1911, HII.

39. This was one of the few times when immigrant men might have to care for their wives and children. See Anne Bandstra, "My Boat Trip to America," HH, their translation.

40. Etje Houwerzijl, New York, to Mom, [1911], HH.

41. J. Boekholt and Antje Giesing, Paterson, N.J., to J. J. Hoogland, 1 Dec. 1882, Sjouke de Zee Collection, RL.

42. Nearly 70 percent of deaths at sea in the period 1820–80 were of children aged thirteen and under, and close to 18 percent were below age one (Robert P. Swierenga, "Dutch Immigration Patterns in the Nineteenth and Twentieth Centuries," in *The Dutch in America*, ed. Swierenga [New Brunswick: Rutgers University Press, 1985], p. 25).

43. This differs from Elizabeth Hampsten's examples in *Read This Only to Yourself: The*

Private Writings of Midwestern Women 1880–1910 (Bloomington: Indiana University Press, 1982). She did note the important role of women as "primary nurses and worriers." See pp. 102ff.

44. F. Brandt Sterenberg, Fulton, Ill., to Uncles and Mother, Nephews and Nieces and their Children, [Goes, Zeeland], 18 Feb. 1885, HH.

45. The most extensive generalized report I encountered was Fie Woldring, Grand Rapids, Mich., to Anje Woldring, 5 Dec. 1918, HH.

46. Hoogland Collection, RL.

47. Grietje Rubingh, Wildervank, Groningen, to Brother, Sister, and Children [Z. Rubingh], [1890s], HH.

48. Anje Nieveen, Denton, Tex., [to Aunt/Uncle and Grandparent], [9 Oct., early 1880s], fragment, HH.

49. Fie Woldring, Grand Rapids, Mich., to Anje Woldring, 5 Dec. 1918, HH.

50. Linda Schelbitzki Pickle included health as one of the crucial factors in German-speaking women's evaluation of life in the U.S.; see *Contented among Strangers*, p. 127.

51. Lubbigje Schaapman, Salida, Calif., to Willamientje Beltman, July 1914, HH.

52. The diary entry ends with: "She is now well again so I went home" ("Diary of Mrs. Gezina Visscher," p. 96).

53. Donna Gabaccia notes the effects of migration on women's health, which has been studied more thoroughly for recent migrant groups, in *From the Other Side*, pp. 121–23.

54. Anna Kuijt's correspondence and some family information was included in Brinks, *Dutch American Voices*. The translations here are mine.

55. Jeannette Kuijt Goedhart, Chicago, to Letha Retel and Gerrit Kuijt, 6 Oct. 1909, HH.

56. See letter of Jeannette Kuijt Goedhart, Chicago, to Gerrit and Letha, 19 Dec. 1911, HH, where Jeannette reported that Anna was working in a hotel, work against which both she and brother Coen had advised prior to Anna's emigration.

57. Pieternella Cevaal, Indianapolis, Ind., to Brother [Jan Cevaal], 31 July 1914, HH.

58. Pieternella Cevaal, Indianapolis, Ind., to Brother, 25 May 1915, HH.

59. G. J. Holmer, Holland, Mich., to Neeltje and Children, 1903, quoted and translated in "Who Is Who in the Brat(t) Relation," p. 25, HH.

60. Geertje Schuiling, Manhattan, Mont., to Brother and Sister, 10 Feb. 1901, Hoogland Collection, RL.

61. Etje Houwerzijl, Byron Center, Mich., to Mother, 13 Apr. 1923, HH.

62. Etje Houwerzijl, Byron Center, Mich., to Mother, 26 Apr. 1923, HH.

63. R. Smit reported several visits by congregation members in R. Smit, Drenthe, Mich., to Friends, 27 Aug. 1885, HH.

64. Etje Houwerzijl, Byron Center, Mich., to Mother, 13 Apr. 1923, HH.

65. This is based on all (legible) issues of the paper for 1916.

66. Among the standard imported items was *Haarlemmer olie,* while they also had American products such as Dr. Pieter's Zokoro and Myers's papaya tablets (*De Huisvriend,* Nov. 1905, survey of all ads).

67. Harry Boonstra, "'For Sale': Advertising in Dutch Immigrant Communities," *Origins* 17 (1999): 20.

68. R. Smit, Drenthe, Mich., to Friends, 27 Aug. 1885, HH.

69. Zwaantje Becksvoort, East Saugatuck, Mich., to Brother [Gieten, Drenthe], 9 July 1902, HH.

70. Geertje Schuiling, Mont., to Brother and Sister, 1 Jan. 1900, Hoogland Collection, RL.

71. The examples come from Anna Kuijt, who reported suffering from appendicitis (later diagnosed) in a letter from Chicago to her Uncle and Aunt, 12 Aug. 1911, HH; and from an immigrant from Harlingen, Friesland, who reported his wife could not eat normally for several years, and they suspected cancer (tape 1042, PJM).

72. Aaltje, Sibley, Iowa, to Uncle, 6 June 1907, HH.

73. For example, Etje Houwerzijl got a letter from her sister in 1929 indicating that someone in the family had shingles. Houwerzijl wrote back noting that she did not know the disease and asking for information on it (Houwerzijl, Byron Center, Mich., to Sister and Brother, 21 Sept. 1929, HH).

74. Lubbigje Schaapman, Salida, Calif., to Willamientje Beltman, Jan. 1913, HH.

75. Jane (and Willem) Walvoord, Holland, Nebr., to sister and children, 28 Sept. 1909, HH.

76. Zwaantje Becksvoort, East Saugatuck, Mich., to Brother, [Gieten, Drenthe], 9 July 1902, HH.

77. Maria Verbrugge, Chandler, Minn., to Parents, 7 Feb. 1910, in Verbrugge, "Brieven uit het Verleden."

78. Tape 1019, PJM.

79. Anna Kuijt, Chicago, to Uncle, 12 Aug. 1911, HH.

80. Westra, "Fear and Hope Jostled."

81. Westra, "Fear and Hope Jostled," quoted on p. 11, their translation.

82. G. J. Holmer, Holland, Mich., to Neeltje and Family, 1903, "Who Is Who in the Brat(t) Relation," p. 24.

83. De Vries, *Up from the Cellar,* pp. 4–5; the author describes a second trip for similar reasons later in the same chapter (pp. 42–43).

84. H. van Hoogen, "Het Huislijk- en Familieleven der Hollanders in Amerika, XII," *De Gereformeerde Amerikaan,* Mar. 1899, p. 60.

85. Robert P. Hudson, "Abraham Flexner in Perspective: American Medical Education, 1865–1910," in *Sickness and Health in America,* ed. Judith Walzer Leavitt and Ronald L. Numbers, 2d ed. (Madison: University of Wisconsin Press, 1985), pp. 153–54.

86. Recollections of the Speet family of Graafschap, Mich. "In the pantry my great-grandma had several square brown tin boxes with covers. Each contained dried plants and herbs. Whenever somebody was sick great-grandma had a remedy" (Shirley Dykema to Suzanne Sinke, 30 May 1995, letter in author's possession). Dykema also speculated her family learned about some of the plants from the local American Indians.

87. W. Nomes and A. Akkerman, [Roseland, Ill.], to Sister and Children, 11 July 1882, fragment, HH.

88. Nellie and Coen Kuijt, Chicago, to Gerrit Kuijt and Letha Retel, 3 Mar. 1909, HH.

89. Cornelia De Groot, for example, whose family was quite well-to-do, noted that when her mother went into labor a neighbor woman with several children was there to help, but they had a doctor present for the birth (*When I Was a Girl in Holland,* pp. 18–19).

90. Tape 1018, PJM.

91. Wilhelmina, Kolijnsplaat, Zeeland, to Cousins, [Kalamazoo, Mich.], 24 Aug. 1889, Merizon Family Letters, HH.

92. For all provinces of the Netherlands the number of births attended by doctors was higher than that for births attended by midwives in 1912 (Centraal Bureau voor de Statistiek, *Bijdragen tot de Statistiek van Nederland, Nieuwe Volgreeks no. 194: Statistiek van de Sterfte naar den Leeftijd en naar de oorzaken van den Dood over het jaar 1912* [The Hague: Gebrs. Belinfante, 1913], p. 31).

93. C. Pothuis-Smit, for example, argued that since motherhood was a function required by society, society had to assist mothers without means, through consultation bureaus to assist pregnant women and new mothers, in the preparation of milk for women who could not breast-feed, by providing food for pregnant women, and by paying for a nurse to assist after birth with household work (Henriette van der Mey Collectie, Internationaal Instituut voor Sociale Geschiedenis). On these kinds of topics in the press see Schuit and Hemels, *Recepten en rolpatronen,* pp. 81–84. The American equivalent resulted in the Sheppard-Towner Act and support for the Children's Bureau. See Molly Ladd-Taylor, *Mother-Work: Women, Child Welfare, and the State, 1890–1930* (Urbana: University of Illinois Press, 1994), chap. 6.

94. Maartje Lautenbach [Zondervan], Paterson, N.J., to Sijds Lautenbach, Tzummarum, Friesland, 27 May 1911, in Brinks, *Dutch American Voices,* p. 302. Charlotte Borst, in a study of Wisconsin immigrant midwives in this period, found this was an acceptable occupation for women who otherwise might have taken in boarders and who came from the same ethnic background as their clients. See Borst, "Wisconsin's Midwives as Working Women: Immigrant Midwives and the Limits of a Traditional Occupation 1870–1920," *Journal of American Ethnic History* 8 (Spring 1989): 32, 47.

95. See "Dutch," in David Steven Cohen, ed., *America: The Dream of My Life* (New Brunswick: Rutgers University Press, 1990), pp. 140ff.

96. See, for example, De Lespinasse, *Bells of Helmus,* pp. 101–5.

97. On this trend and others affecting midwifery see Judith Walzer Leavitt, *Brought to Bed: Childbearing in America, 1750–1950* (New York: Oxford University Press, 1986).

98. See the diary of Gezina van der Haar Visscher, 1820–1901, report from Sept. 1985, p. 119, HH. The woman notes the expectant parents were unsure of the ability of the midwife and decided to call a doctor as well.

99. A Dutch law of 1865 required midwives to receive basic training in the use of forceps and suturing. Medical professionals continued to consider them less qualified than doctors however (E. van der Werff, J. Veenhof-Misset, and F. Jonk Hartman, "Toelichting bij het Adres aan den Minister van Binnenlandse Zaken betreffende verbetering van de positie en opleiding van de vroedvrouwen," n.d. [1918], n.p., reproduced in Wantje Fritschy, *Fragmenten vrouwengeschiedenis. Deel II: Thematisch* [The Hague: Martinus Nijhoff, 1980], pp. 114, 118).

100. Bertha Van Hoosen, *Petticoat Surgeon* (Chicago: Pellegrini & Cudahy, 1947), chap. 2.

101. Leavitt, *Brought to Bed,* pp. 128–10 passim. Scopolamine blocked the perception of pain rather than pain itself. Van Hoosen wrote a text on use of this amnesiac, which could be combined with doses for morphine for other surgery as well—*Scopolamine-Morphine Anaesthesia* (Chicago: House of Manz, 1915).

102. Van Hoosen, *Petticoat Surgeon,* pp. 308–9.

103. Fie [married Woldring], Pasadena, Calif., to Anje Woldring, [Groningen], 16 Apr. 1918, HH.

104. Nieland, *'n fonnie bisnis,* p. 93.

105. Nieland, *'n fonnie bisnis,* pp. 99–100.

106. G. H. Holmer, Crisp, Mich., to Brother-in-law and Sister, 18 Jan. 1900, quoted and translated in "Who Is Who in the Brat(t) Relation," p. 22, HII.

107. "Early History of the Derk Bruins Family to 1890," p. 112.

108. Herbert J. Brinks, "Impressions of the 'Old' World 1848–1940," in *The Dutch in North-America,* ed. Rob Kroes and Henk-Otto Neuschäfer (Amsterdam: VU University Press, 1991), pp. 34–47, esp. pp. 38, 41.

109. Brinks, "Impressions of the 'Old' World," p. 36.

110. Klaaske Noorda [Heller], Oak Harbor, Wash., to Mother, Brothers, Sisters, Nieces and Nephews, 19 Oct. 1896, HH.

111. The family migrated in 1904 (tape 1053, PJM).

112. Tape 1053, PJM.

113. Tape 1018, Holland, Mich., PJM.

114. Oggel, Pella, Iowa, to Brother and Sister, 13 Oct. 1890, HH.

115. Dina Maria Oggel, Pella, Iowa, to Sister Mietje and Family, 11 May 1899, HH.

116. Dina Maria Oggel, Pella, Iowa, to Brother and Sister, 13 Oct. 1890, HH.

117. Bos, St. Anne, Ill., to Family and Friends, [Nyverdal, Gelderland], Sept. 19?9, HH.

118. Aaltje, Sibley, Iowa, to Uncle, 6 June 1907, HH.

119. Harmanna Schoonbeek Rosenboom, Grand Rapids, Mich., to Brother [Jacobus Schoonbeek], [Oude Pekela, Groningen], 27 Nov. 1919, HH, their translation.

120. For the long-term results of this pattern in the Midwest see Sonya Salamon, *Prairie Patrimony: Family, Farming, and Community in the Midwest* (Chapel Hill: University of North Carolina Press, 1992), where she contrasts the German and Yankee patterns in terms of continuity, land use, and community stability.

121. Aaltje, Sibley, Iowa, to Uncle, 6 June 1907, HH.

122. Smit collection letters: Cornelia, Lake City, Mich., to Uncle, 14 Mar. 1888; L. Timmer, Lake City, Mich., to Sieuwke Smit, 19 Mar. 1888; Cornelia, Lake City, Mich., to Brother [Nanco], 29 Mar. 1888; and Cornelia, Grand Rapids, Mich., to Uncle and Nephew, 9 Aug. 1904, HH.

123. Aaltje, Sibley, Iowa, to Uncle, 27 July 1907, HH.

124. Klaaske Noorda [Heller], Oak Harbor, Wash., to Mother, Brothers, Sisters, Nieces and Nephews, Aug. 1897, HH.

125. See, for example, Robyn L. Muncy, *Creating a Female Dominion in American Reform, 1890–1930* (New York: Oxford University Press, 1991); Kathryn Kish Sklar, *Florence Kelley and the Nation's Work: The Rise of Women's Political Culture, 1830–1900* (New Haven: Yale University Press, 1995); Anne Firor Scott, *Natural Allies: Women's Associations in American History* (Urbana: University of Illinois Press, 1991); and Ladd-Taylor, *Mother-Work.*

126. As of 1929 there were Holland Homes not only in Grand Rapids but also in Kalamazoo and Muskegon, Michigan; in Paterson, New Jersey; in Chicago, Illinois; and in Pella, Iowa (with one in Sheldon being built, and another in Orange City in planning) (Van Hinte, *Netherlanders in America,* p. 1019). Other ethnic groups also established homes for the elderly in this time period. For a foray into this issue see N. Sue Weiler, "Religion, Ethnicity and the Development of Private Homes for the Aged," *Journal of American Ethnic History* 12 (Fall 1992): 64–90.

127. In describing the Holland Home in 1900, a Grand Rapids newspaper article stated: "In Holland nearly every city or town sustaining the average population possesses a home for the aged, supported by all the churches of the place consolidated or maintained entirely by a certain denomination" ("Home for the Aged," *Evening Press,* 24 Nov. 1900, p. 9).

128. [Marion Louise Withey], "Historical Sketch of the Union Benevolent Association of Grand Rapids, Michigan," in *Manual of the Union Benevolent Association of Grand Rapids, Mich. 1887* (Grand Rapids: J. Rookus, 1887), p. 5.

129. "Articles of Incorporation," in *Manual of the Union Benevolent Association,* p. 8.

130. "Articles of Incorporation," in *Manual of the Union Benevolent Association,* p. 15. For a brief overview of this organization's history see Richard Harms, "'Welfare' Health Care: Seeds for a Hospital," *Grand Times,* June 1992, p. 31; or look at the more extensive and specialized work by Sybil E. Hole and Jacqueline Anderson, *Blodgett Memorial Medical Center*

School of Nursing History: 'A Century of Caring' 1886–1987 (Grand Rapids: D & D Printing, 1990).

131. Emma Heyboer (née Stoel) was married to John Heyboer (sometimes spelled Heiboer or Heijboer), confirmed by "Wedded Fifty Years," *Grand Rapids Press,* 6 June 1926 and "John C. Heyboer Taken by Death," *Grand Rapids Press,* 23 May 1927, both in Grand Rapids Public Library manuscript scrapbook, vol. 18, p. 105; I did not confirm but suspected the same for Lena Campman and Henri Campman, Anna H. Molenaar and Tjerk Molenaar, and Berendina Grebel-Schonevel and Jacob Grebel.

132. Adrian Kriekard manuscript collection, JAH. Editorial in *De Standard* without title, but follows article "De Holland Mutual Benevolent Home Association."

133. The minutes of the board are found in a series of bound volumes located at the Holland Home archives. The first set of minutes from 1892 on are not present. Of the extant volumes I consulted those covering 1896 to 1900, 1901 to 1910, and 1910 to 1917.

134. First an individual member of the board might hear of something and discuss it with a home resident. Then trustees from the Committee of Order and Discipline (all men) would go to the home to inquire and reprimand the resident if necessary. Finally, the resident might be brought before the entire board. If the resident repented and asked forgiveness the board would generally let him or her stay in the home. Otherwise the resident had to leave under a clause in the contract for care which stated the resident had to follow the rules set by the board. A typical contract in 1905 included the clause "He promises to submit to the supervisors and rules set out for the inmates of the Home, and to be helpful as much as possible in the maintenance of order, and in the activities which are desirable for such an institution." Contract found in board minutes book of 1901–10.

135. Emma Heyboer, longtime chair of the committee, reported that at first the home committee members had to visit the home two or three times a week in addition to the regular committee meetings, "to give the service staff supervision and instruction, and to listen to the many impracticable deficiencies that old people perceive" ("Comm. van Directie," *Holland Home News* 22 [June 1915]: 2).

136. "Living Portraits of 100 years" in Auxiliary History file at Holland Home.

137. HUBA, thirty-year anniversary booklet (Grand Rapids: n.p., 1922), p. 13.

138. Yearly reports in *Holland Home News* indicated the group had difficulty gaining the participation of all the local churches, a fact they frequently bemoaned. For example, see "Jaarvergadering van de Ladies' Home Circle: Het Jaarlijksch Report," *Holland Home News* 22 (June 1915): 3.

139. Auxiliary history file, Holland Home.

140. "Ladies' Home Circle," *Holland Home News* 24 (8 Dec. 1917).

141. To add to these efforts, the board occasionally printed sermons or other devotional literature by ministers and sold them. For example, the home's founding father, Rev. A. Kriekard, published his sermon "Voorhenlieden geen plaats. Leerrede gehouden op den eersten Kerstdag" (no date); in 1914 the group published Rev. C. Doekes's "De Offeranden Gods." Doekes was a Reformed minster in Nieuwdorp, province of Zeeland, in the Netherlands. Kriekard also translated a historical sketch of the history of the Reformed Church in America into Dutch, a pamphlet which went on sale in 1898, HH.

142. Board minutes 1 July 1909, Holland Home Archives.

143. HUBA, thirty-year anniversary booklet, p. 13.

144. HUBA Board minutes, 7 Nov. 1907, Holland Home Archives.

145. HUBA Board minutes, 6 Oct. 1910, 6 Mar. 1919.

146. For example, commissioners from the local Board of Poor required that the two sons of a woman in the home either pay for her or take her into one of their homes. This indicated that local authorities worked in conjunction with the Home Board (HUBA Board minutes, 3 Sept. 1896).

147. HUBA Board minutes, 26 Sept. 1901, p. 41 insert to Jan. 1901 to Mar. 1910 volume.

148. See HUBA, thirty-year anniversary booklet, pp. 23, 30.

149. HUBA Board minutes, 7 July 1898.

150. Compare Kraut, *Silent Travelers,* who notes the Jewish community tradition of caring for their own and building health care institutions to serve their group (p. 165).

151. Compare Christiane Harzig, *Familie, Arbeit und weibliche Öffentlichkeit in einer Einwanderungstadt: Deutschamerikanerinnen in Chicago um die Jahrhundertwende* (St. Katharinen: Scripta Mercaturae, 1991), chap. 6.

152. See, for example, the ad for Jacob Van 't Hof, "Funeral Director," in Grand Rapids, Mich., in *The Banner,* 18 July 1918, p. 524.

153. "A Hollander's Mainstay," in *America: The Dream of My Life,* ed. David Steven Cohen (New Brunswick: Rutgers University Press, 1990), pp. 147–49.

154. Nelly van der Maas, Wissekerke, Netherlands, to J. de Jonge, [Kalamazoo, Mich.], 10 Oct. 1998, HH.

155. Maaike Huigen, Galesburg, Iowa, to Brother, Sister, and Children, 19 Feb. 1888, Familie Archief Huigen, RL.

156. Klaaske Noorda [Heller], Oak Harbor, Wash., to Mother, Brothers, Sisters, Nieces and Nephews, 19 Oct. 1896, HH.

157. Westra, "Fear and Hope Jostled," p. 19.

158. "Diary of Mrs. Gezina Visscher," p. 115.

159. For example: "I assume that Tietje lost her child, the one whose lock of hair she sent" (Maaike Huigen, Pella, Iowa, to Father, Brothers and Sisters, 4 July 1881, Familie Archief Huigen, RL). This was a common European custom in the nineteenth century; see Philippe Ariès, *The Hour of Our Death* (New York: Oxford University Press, 1991), pp. 461–62.

160. Etje Houwerzijl, Walker, Mich., to Mother, 29 Dec. 1917, HH.

161. Etje Houwerzijl, Byron Center, Mich., to Family, 25 Apr. 1923, HH.

162. "Diary of Mrs. Gezina Visscher," p. 116.

163. On this shift in American funeral practice, see James J. Farrell, *Inventing the American Way of Death, 1830–1920* (Philadelphia: Temple University Press, 1980), p. 212.

164. See Van Hinte, *Netherlanders in America,* p. 924.

165. Westra, "Fear and Hope Jostled," p. 20.

166. H. van Hoogen, "Het Huislijk- en Familieleven der Hollanders in Amerika, XII," *De Gereformeerde Amerikaan,* Mar. 1899, pp. 61–62.

167. G. J. Holmer, Holland, Mich., to Neeltje and Children, 1903, quoted and translated in "Who Is Who in the Brat(t) Relation," HH.

168. Jane and Willem Walvoord, Holland, Nebr., to Sister, Nephews and Nieces, 3 Feb. 1915, HH.

169. Dina Maria Oggel, Pella, Iowa, to Brother and Sister, 17 Dec. 1894, HH.

170. "Een eerste graf van ons zendingsveld binnen geschuurd," *De Gereformeerde Amerikaan,* Mar. 1894, p. 69.

171. Etje Houwerzijl, Byron Center, Mich., to Family, 3 June 1923, HH.

172. Arendje Bergman Akkerman, [Roseland, Ill.], to Sister, [Burgerburg, Noord Holland], 11 July 1882, HH.

173. Akkerman, Roseland, Ill., to Sister, 11 July 1882, HH.

174. Mrs. G. Rosenboom, Grand Rapids, Mich., to Brother, 20 Nov. 1913, HH, their translation.

175. Cornelis van der Vliet, Fort William, to Parents, Wilnis, Utrecht, 1 Aug. 1909, in Verbrugge, "Brieven uit het Verleden."

176. Maria van der Vliet Verbrugge, Chandler, Minn., to Parents and other family, to Wilnis, Utrecht, 7 Feb. 1910, in Verbrugge, "Brieven uit het Verleden."

177. Verbrugge, "Brieven uit het Verleden," pp. 156–72 passim.

Chapter 5: Learning Language and Worldview

Much of the information in the section "Cornelia De Groot" was published in Annemieke Galema and Suzanne Sinke, "Paradijs der Vrouwen? Overzeese migratie naar de Verenigde Staten van Friese vrouwen rond de eeuwwisseling," in *Vrouwen in den Vreemde,* ed. A. Dassen, C. Van Eerd, and K. Oppelland (Zutphen: Walburg Pers, 1993), pp. 23–34. The section "Language Shift" first appeared as Suzanne M. Sinke, "Gender in Language and Life," *Gender Issues* 17 (Winter 1999), and is reprinted by permission of Transaction Publishers, all rights reserved.

1. Most of the information in this section comes directly from De Groot, *When I Was a Girl in Holland,* particularly the biographical details given by her nephew Cor Bakker ("Supplement," part 1, pp. 3–8).

2. De Groot, *When I Was a Girl in Holland,* p. 50.

3. De Groot, *When I Was a Girl in Holland,* pp. 52–55.

4. De Groot, *When I Was a Girl in Holland,* p. 177.

5. De Groot, *When I Was a Girl in Holland,* pp. 179–80.

6. De Groot, *When I Was a Girl in Holland,* p. 196.

7. See Stokvis, "Drie emigranten over het leven in Friesland rond 1900"; and Pieter R. D. Stokvis, "Friezen in Amerika: Drie Autobiografieen," in *Geen schepsel wordt vergeten,* ed. J. F. Heijbroek, A. Lammers, and A. P. G. Jos van der Linde (Amsterdam: Zutphen, 1985), pp. 113–19.

8. On her journalistic endeavors for the *San Francisco Chronicle,* see Galema, *Frisians to America,* p. 246.

9. De Groot, "Nine Farmerettes," reprinted in *When I Was a Girl in Holland,* supplement, p. 11, 12.

10. De Groot, "American and Dutch Maids Are Compared," reprinted in *When I Was a Girl in Holland,* supplement, pp. 16–17.

11. Mary J. Maynes, *Schooling in Western Europe: A Social History* (Albany: State University of New York Press, 1985), quote on p. 4. See also pp. 5–9.

12. J. Bovenkerk, "Rev. Bovenkerk's Reply," *The Banner,* 5 Nov. 1926, reproduced in Van Hinte, *Netherlanders in America,* p. 871.

13. Van Hinte, *Netherlanders in America,* p. 870.

14. See J. H. Meijsen, *Lager onderwijs in de spiegel der geschiedenis* (The Hague: Staatsuitgeverij, 1976), p. 127.

15. Hans Knippenberg, *Deelname aan het lager onderwijs in Nederland gedurende de negentiende eeuw. Een analyse van de landelijke ontwikkeling en van de regionale verschillen* (Amsterdam: Koninklijk Nederlands Aardrijkskundig Genootschap, 1986), p. 21.

16. According to the law, children had to attend school "regularly" for six years and to pass

all classes up to the age of thirteen (Knippenberg, *Deelname aan het lager onderwijs,* pp. 53–54, 102). See also Fr. de Jong, "Vermenigvuldiging en deling: De groei van he Nederlandse Onderwijs," in *Honderdvijfentwintig Jaren Arbeid op het Onderwijsterrein 1836–1961,* ed. IJ. Brugmans (Groningen: J. B. Wollters, 1961), p. 112; Van Rijswijk–Clerkx, *Moeders, kinderen en kinderopvang,* p. 68–69. Mandatory school attendance came later to the Netherlands than to several other European countries, for example, England (1876) and France (1882) (Meijsen, *Lager onderwijs in de spiegel der geschiedenis,* p. 90).

17. Knippenberg, *Deelname aan het lager onderwijs,* pp. 51–52, 134; P. Th. F. M. Boekhout and E. P. de Booy, *Geschiedenis van de school in Nederland* (Assen: Van Gorcum, 1987), p. 156; Meijsen, *Lager onderwijs in de spiegel der geschiedenis,* p. 84. See also Corstius and Hollema, *De Kunst van het Moederschap,* pp. 54–55.

18. W. H. M. Werker, "De Vrouw in de Onderwijsherziening van Lijdelijkheid tot Daad," in *De vrouw, de vrouwenbeweging en het vrouwenvraagstuk,* vol. 2, ed. C. M. Werker-Beaujon, Clara Wichmann, and W. H. M. Werker (Amsterdam: Elsevier, 1914), p. 90; Inge de Wilde, "249 Vrouwen na Aletta Jacobs: Vrouwelijke gepromoveerden aan de Rijksuniversiteit Groningen, 1879–1987," Rijksuniversiteit Groningen, 1987, p. 7.

19. Boekhout and de Booy, *Geschiedenis van de school in Nederland,* pp. 191–92. Marianne Beelaerts, "De problemen van de jonge, intelligente vrouw," *Tijdschrift voor vrouwenstudies* 8, no. 2 (1987): 170.

20. *Reports of the Immigration Commission: The Children of Immigrants in Schools,* vol. 1, pp. 22–23.

21. For one example of European curriculum and levels see De Jong, *From Strength to Strength.* Jacob van Hinte provides a (clearly biased) overview of the elementary school situation in *Netherlanders in America,* pp. 870–76.

22. 1910 Public Use Sample. The sample for this data included not only children born in the Netherlands but also those born to a Dutch-born parent or parents, or those for whom one or both of the parents spoke Dutch. The rates for fourteen- and fifteen-year-olds in school were nearly double those for children this age out of school. Further, there was a substantial minority of girls aged sixteen and seventeen attending school.

23. Van Hinte, *Netherlanders in America,* p. 873.

24. This might have been in order to learn Dutch, but more likely it was the result of families who wanted Christian education for their children. See the case of Hendrika Rientjes-Berendschot of Holland, Mich., tape 1008, born in Nijverdal, migrated in 1920, PJM.

25. "Who Is Who in the Brat(t) Relation," p. 25.

26. Van Hinte, *Netherlanders in America,* p. 870.

27. I figured this data using SPSS on the 1910 Public Use Sample.

28. "Early History of the Derk Bruins Family to 1890," p. 112.

29. *Reports of the Immigration Commission: The Children of Immigrants in Schools,* vol. 1, p. 57.

30. Cornelis Kooiman, Hawarden, Iowa, to Aunt [Betje Kooiman], 17 Jan. 1910; "Oude brieven uit Amerika," p. 19.

31. Lubbigje Schaapman, Salida, Calif., to Willamientje Beltman, 19 Mar. 1911, HH, their translation.

32. Tape 1020, woman born in Noord Beveland in 1877, migrated with parents and eventually settled in Holland, Mich., PJM. The story concerns life on a farm around Noordelos, Mich., in 1882.

33. "Diary of Mrs. Gezina Visscher," p. 73.

34. De Jong, *From Strength to Strength,* p. 23.

35. *Reports of the Immigration Commission: The Children of Immigrants in Schools,* vol. 1, pp. 157–58.

36. See Solomon, *In the Company of Educated Women.*

37. "Editorial," *The Anchor* 14 (Jan. 1900), p. 76.

38. On this concept see Joy Lintelman, *The Go-Betweens: The Lives of Immigrant Children* (Minneapolis: University Art Museum, University of Minnesota, 1986).

39. See, for example, Susan Gal, *Language Shift* (New York: Academic Press, 1979); Pauline Burton, Ketaki Kushari Dyson, and Shirley Ardener, eds., *Bilingual Women* (Oxford: Berg, 1994); and Kulick, *Language Shift and Cultural Reproduction.* For U.S. immigrants one of the key works is Joshua Fishman et al., *Language Loyalty in the United States* (The Hague: Mouton, 1966), though gender is not a major component of this work.

40. See Kira Hall and Mary Bucholtz, eds., *Gender Articulated: Language and the Socially Constructed Self* (London: Routledge, 1995); and Micaela di Leonardo, ed., *Gender at the Crossroads of Knowledge: Feminist Anthropology in the Postmodern Era* (Berkeley: University of California Press, 1991).

41. For some insight on language study related to gender and history, see Joan W. Scott, "On Language, Gender, and Working-Class History," *International Labor and Working-Class History* 31 (Spring 1987): 1–13. Some historians have combined research on personal correspondence and U.S. ethnic perceptions effectively, and in these studies issues of language figure heavily. For an overview of this material see David A. Gerber, "The Immigrant Letter between Positivism and Populism: the Uses of Immigrant Personal Correspondence in Twentieth-Century American Scholarship," *Journal of American Ethnic History* 16 (Summer 1997): 3–34. Among historians combining the study of language and gender, there are at least two main theoretical directions. Virginia Yans McLaughlin exemplifies one, using anthropological techniques in combining gender and ethnic studies, focusing on oral histories; see "Metaphors of Self in History: Subjectivity, Oral Narrative, and Immigration Studies," in *Immigration Reconsidered: History, Sociology, and Politics,* ed. Yans-McLaughlin (New York: Oxford, 1990), pp. 254–90. A second approach derives from linguistics. Betty Bergland, for example, utilizes study of discourse to evaluate immigrant women's autobiographies; see "Ideology, Ethnicity, and the Gendered Subject: Reading Immigrant Women's Autobiographies," in *Seeking Common Ground,* ed. Donna Gabaccia (Westport, Conn.: Greenwood Press, 1992), pp. 101–21.

42. There are numerous studies of Dutch language use in the United States in the twentieth century. See especially Caroline Smits, *Disintegration of Inflection: The Case of Iowa Dutch* (Proefschrift, Vrije Universiteit te Amsterdam, 1996); Philip Webber, *Pella Dutch: The Portrait of a Language and Its Use in One of Iowa's Ethnic Communities* (Ames: Iowa State University Press, 1988); Daan, *"Ik was te bissie . . .";* and Jaap van Marle and Caroline Smits, "American Dutch: General Trends in Its Development," in *Language Contact across the North Atlantic,* ed. P. Sture Ureland and Iain Clarkson (Tübingen: Max Niemeyer Verlag, 1996). With the exception of Webber these studies are based on research carried out under the auspices of the P. J. Meertens Institute, including one extensive body of interviews done in the 1960s.

43. On this see Cliff Goddard and Anna Wierzbicka, "Discourse and Culture," in *Discourse as Social Interaction,* ed. Teun A. van Dijk (London: Sage Publications, 1997), p. 232. They adopt Dell Hymes's phrase "communicative competence" to describe the ways in which a speaker must use not only appropriate grammar and vocabulary but also style which fits the language and the setting (Hymes, "The Ethnography of Speaking," reprinted in *Readings in the Sociology of Language,* ed. Joshua Fishman [The Hague: Mouton, 1968], pp. 99–138).

44. This contrasts somewhat with the more elaborate model of "domains" of speech which Fishman and others utilize.

45. Goddard and Wierzbicka note that age and gender are "near-universal" in requiring different discourse styles. Other factors which can determine speech categories they describe as being much more culturally bound, including things such as kinship, clan, ethnicity, caste, or rank ("Discourse and Culture").

46. O. Vandeputte, P. Vincent, T. Hermans, *Dutch* (Lauwe: Stichting Ons Erfdeel, 1986), pp. 55–56. See also Vakgroep Neerlandistiek, Universiteit Wenen, "Dialecten," <http://www.ned.univie.ac.at/ publicaties/taalgeschiedenis/nl/dialecten.htm>, 14 May 1998.

47. Smits, *Disintegration of Inflection*, pp. 15–17.

48. This, I would argue, helps answer Gerber's question about what one German immigrant woman gained by experimenting with English ("'You See I Speak Wery Well Englisch,'" p. 62).

49. Studies of linguistic differentiation of African American servants from their employers, for example, illustrate how some Americans sought to impose these distinctions. Likewise, British English managed to incorporate class into vocabulary, accent, and linguistic mannerism. See Judith Rollins, *Between Women: Domestics and Their Employers* (Philadelphia: Temple University Press, 1985), chap. 5; and Peter Burke, "Introduction," in *The Social History of Language,* ed. Burke and Roy Porter (Cambridge: Cambridge University Press, 1987), pp. 1–20.

50. This is a crucial point. See Joan W. Scott's "On Language, Gender, and Working-Class History," in which she critiques Gareth Stedman Jones on specifically this point. Compare Gareth Stedman Jones, *Languages of Class: Studies in English Working Class History, 1832–1982* (Cambridge: Cambridge University Press, 1983).

51. On this see Van Marle and Smits, "American Dutch," p. 439.

52. On this see, for example, Kroes, *Persistence of Ethnicity,* pp. 90–93.

53. Lucy Fitch Perkins, *Cornelia: The Story of a Benevolent Despot* (Boston: Houghton Mifflin, 1919), p. 2.

54. See Susan Gal, "Between Speech and Silence: The Problematics of Research on Language and Gender," in *Gender at the Crossroads of Knowledge: Feminist Anthropology in the Postmodern Era,* ed. Micaela di Leonardo (Berkeley: University of California Press, 1991), pp. 182–83.

55. For an overview of this work see Susan Gal, "Language, Gender, and Power," in *Gender Articulated: Language and the Socially Constructed Self,* ed. Kira Hall and Mary Bucholtz (London: Routledge, 1995) pp. 172–73.

56. Jo Daan, "Problems of Code Switching: Dialect Loss of Immigrants of Dutch Descent," in *Papers from the Third Interdisciplinary Conference on Netherlandic Studies,* ed. Ton J. Broos (Boston: University Press, 1988), p. 151.

57. *Reports of the Immigration Commission: Abstracts of Reports of the Immigration Commission,* vol. 1, Senate doc. 747, 61st Congress, 3d session, 1911, "Per cent of Foreign-Born Employees Who Speak English, by Sex, Age at Time of Coming to the United States, and Race," p. 481, and "Per cent of Foreign-Born Employees Who Speak English by Sex and Race," p. 474.

58. Petronella M. de Boer van Pernis migrated from Rotterdam to Holland, Mich., in 1908 at the age of twenty-two (tape 1004, PJM).

59. De Vries, *Up from the Cellar,* p. 9.

60. Translation of:

In Nederland ben ik opgevoed
In Nederland leerde 'k spreken
Ik zal voor die taal steeds in 't gemoed
dezellefde liefde kweken
Niet dat ik op 't vreemde smaal
Ik let alles in z'n waarde
Maar ik zeg, voor mij is hollands taal,
de schoonste taal op aarde
(tape 1035, woman born in Ooltgensplaat in 1893, emigrated with parents [and seven siblings and an aunt] in 1908 and settled in Grand Rapids, Mich., PJM).

61. See, for example, the case of Ulbe Eringa. For information on this individual see also Brian W. Beltman, *Dutch Farmer in the Missouri Valley: The Life and Letters of Ulbe Eringa, 1866–1950* (Urbana: University of Illinois Press, 1996).

62. Bernardus de Beij, Chicago, to Pieter A. Lanting, Winsum, Groningen, 1 Apr. 1870, HH.

63. Van Hinte, *Netherlanders in America*, p. 1009.

64. "Holland Notes," *The Banner*, 25 Jan. 1917, p. 64.

65. "Lynden—A Home Far Away from Home," *Proceedings of the Association for the Advancement of Dutch American Studies Conference* (Orange City, Iowa: Northwestern College, 1985), p. 98.

66. On domains see Fishman, *Language Loyalty*.

67. See Fishman, *Language Loyalty*, p. 36. One of the striking features of mother-tongue figures was the rise in Dutch speakers between 1940 and 1960, in part created by a new wave of migration but at least partly the result of heavy maintenance efforts.

68. Tape 1004, woman born in Rotterdam in 1886, migrated with parents in 1908 and settled in Holland, Mich., PJM.

69. This parallels several aspects of Sydney Stahl Weinberg's findings on Jewish immigrant women in *The World of Our Mothers*.

70. For example, a domestic in Kralingen wrote to her sister in Beaverdam, Michigan: "Here everything goes on as always. *Mijnheer* [master, male equivalent for mevrouw] has been at home for some time. . . . *Mevrouw* still suffers from nerves . . . they both send their greetings" (Lucie, Kralingen, to Sister [Susan D. Langreis], 1 June 1895, HH [my translation]).

71. Posthumus–van der Goot and de Waal, *Van Moeder op Dochter*, p. 221.

72. I did a study of obituaries from *De Hope. Weekblad in het Belang can Maatschappij, School en Kerk* from the years 1880, 1898, and 1919. This newspaper, published from Hope College in Holland, Michigan, enjoyed a circulation not only in the area but also among Reformed Church members in various parts of the country. On the paper see Van Hinte, *Netherlanders in America*, p. 456.

73. HUBA, Board minutes, 1 Sept. 1898, p. 209.

74. The paper was published in Kalamazoo, Michigan, and was conservative and Republican in orientation. It appeared three times a week in 1919 but switched to twice a week in 1920. I went through all classified advertisements in the two-year period and then selected ten issues at random for systematic examination of all name listings found on the final page, which gave local news not only for Kalamazoo but also sporadically for various other locations, particularly in Michigan, Iowa, Wisconsin, and Minnesota. This page included all birth and

death notices, information on accidents, upcoming church events, engagements, anniversaries, a few reports of people visiting (mainly ministers and returning soldiers), and classified advertising for jobs, services, sale items, and spouses.

75. For example, the black-rimmed notice of the death of Abraham Treur sent in by his wife which included the names of several living relatives. She listed herself as Marie Treur-Hoogstraten and all other women were also listed with married name before hyphen. Two of the siblings were listed as still living in the Netherlands (*De Hollandsche Amerikaan*, 12 Apr. 1920, p. 4).

76. There were two exceptions to this rule. One was in referring to ministers, who were always male and listed as Ds. for dominie. The other was in relatively rare references to women in the Netherlands, when appropriate Dutch abbreviations would be used.

77. The paper was edited by ministers, and most of the correspondents were male. Women missionaries, as well as women mission board executives, however, also contributed. The latter group often wrote in English and someone translated their articles for the paper. This is based on a study of all issues from 1896 (when the paper began) to 1903.

78. This is based on a comparison of issues from three time periods, 1880–82, 1898, and 1919.

79. *De Wachter* 52, no. 52 (21 Jan. 1920): 15.

80. Cornelia De Groot, "Nine Farmerettes—They Prove Woman Is not Weak," article from unknown journal, date estimated at 1906, reprinted in the supplement to *When I Was a Girl in Holland*.

81. This is a form of passing according to some studies; compare Mary Bucholtz, "From Mulatta to Mestiza: Passing, and the Linguistic Reshaping of Ethnic Identity," in *Gender Articulated: Language and the Socially Constructed Self*, ed. Kira Hall and Mary Bucholtz (London: Routledge, 1995), pp. 354–61.

82. The exception was in speeches, where *"Dames en Heren"* (ladies and gentlemen) remained a standard form of greeting.

83. "Advertising Our Women's Societies," *The Banner*, 29 Apr. 1915, p. 264.

84. "Advertising Our Women's Societies," p. 264.

85. Academics disagree as to what exactly should be included as "Yankee Dutch." In popular parlance any mixture of Dutch and English qualifies, and I use that definition here. Dirk Nieland and John Lieuwen published several humorous books in this dialect. On the phenomenon see Walter Lagerwey, ed., *Neen Nederland, 'k vergeet u niet: Een beeld van het immigrantenleven in Amerika tussen 1846 en 1945 in verhalen, schetsen en gedichten* (Baarn: Bosch & Keuning, 1982), pp. 121ff.

86. Van Hinte, *Netherlanders in America*, p. 951.

87. Van Hinte, *Netherlanders in America*, p. 952.

88. Nieland, *'n fonnie bisnis*, p. 47.

89. Frederick Ten Hoor, "Preface," *'n fonnie bisnis*, p. 14.

90. *De Hollandsche Amerikaan*, 29 July 1920, p. 4.

91. *De Hollandsche Amerikaan*, 16 July 1920, p. 4. The person placed both the English and Dutch language ads in *De Volksvriend* as well.

92. Tape 1031, man born in Krabbendijke in 1883, migrated with parents in 1900 and settled in Holland, Mich., PJM.

93. Edward Bok, *The Americanization of Edward Bok: The Autobiography of a Dutch Boy Fifty Years After* (New York: Charles Scribner's Sons, 1922); De Groot, *When I Was a Girl in Holland*.

94. See Van Hinte, *Netherlanders in America*, pp. 948–50.

95. See Nella Kennedy, "The Man from Helmus: Dr. A. F. H. de l'Espinasse," in *A Century of Midwestern Dutch-American Manners and Mores—and More* (Orange City: Northwestern College, 1995), pp. 1–9.

96. See, for example, chap. 6 in Harzig, *Familie, Arbeit und weibliche Öffentlichkeit in einer Einwanderungstadt;* see also articles on various ethnic women's papers (Jewish, Finnish, Polish) in Christiane Harzig and Dirk Hoerder, eds., *The Press of Labor Migrants in Europe and North America, 1880s to 1930s* (Bremen: Publications of the Labor Newspaper Preservation Project, 1985).

97. Van Hinte confirmed this trend. He contacted several Dutch publishers in 1917, and found, for example, that there were eighty subscriptions to *Bildtsche Courant* (from the emigration hub of 't Bildt) going to America (*Netherlanders in America*, p. 1002).

98. The concept of worldview imbuing words, ideas, and language more generally with meaning is by no means limited to Dutch American Protestants, though they adhere to the concept. Mikhail M. Bakhtin offered a similar interpretation concerning what he termed belief or conceptual system (in Russian, *krugozor*); see *The Dialogic Imagination: Four Essays by M. M. Bakhtin*, ed. Michael Holquist, trans. Caryl Emerson and Michael Holquist (Austin: University of Texas Press, 1981), p. 425.

99. Using the phraseology of Bakhtin, these immigrants shifted out of the everyday genre and moved into another voice. See "Discourse in the Novel," in *Dialogic Imagination*, p. 358–549.

100. Martje Smit to Mother and brother, [14] May 1881, HH.

101. Aaltje, Sibley, to Uncle, 6 June 1907, HH.

102. I am indebted to Klaas van der Sanden, one of my Dutch instructors, for first drawing my attention to the distinction. Turn-of-the-century Dutch by persons of the class that migrated to America frequently reads like a stream of consciousness diary. In the midst of this often-rambling style, peppered with dialect and with Americanisms and often totally lacking in spelling conventions, come these ritualized phrases. Once you start looking for them they strike you continually in Protestant letters.

103. Herm. Hasselma, Paterson, N.J., to "Brothers, Sister, John, Herbert, Wil," 29 Dec. 1908, RL.

104. Jacoba Akkerman (Molenaar), Roseland, Ill., to Sister, 2 Jan. 1881, HH, their translation.

105. Johanna Heinen, Gibbsville, Wis., to friends, brothers and sisters and children, [Aalten, Gelderland], 22 Jan. 1892, HH.

106. Griet Bieleveld, Kolham, Groningen, to Brother, Sister and Children, 1909, HH.

107. Hendriene Mensink Bos, St. Anne, Ill., to Friends, Sister, Brothers, Nieces and Nephews, Sept. [1909], HH.

108. Willem and Jane Walvoord, Holland, Nebr., to Sister and Children, 28 Sept. 1909, HH.

109. Etje Houwerzijl, Walker, Mich., to Family, 29 Dec. 1917, HH.

110. On the infra- and supralapsarianism controversy see Bratt, *Dutch Calvinism in Modern America*, pp. 46–47.

111. Johanna Heinen, Gibbsville, Wis., to Friends, Brothers, Sisters, and Children, Aalten, Gelderland, 22 Jan. 1892, HH.

112. Etje Houwerzijl, Walker, Mich., to Mother, 29 Dec. 1917, HH.

113. When Edward Bok wrote his *Americanization of Edward Bok*, he used as his model the autobiography of Henry Adams. It was ignored by most Dutch Americans or, in the case of

some Christian Reformed publications, derided as Americanization propaganda. See Johannes Leendert Krabbendam, "The Model Man: A Life of Edward W. Bok, 1863–1930" (Ph.D. dissertation, Rijksuniversiteit Leiden, 1995), chap. 6.
114. "Diary of Mrs. Gezina Visscher."

Chapter 6: Our Father, Who Art Everywhere

Much of the information in the section "Women and Church Discipline" appeared originally in Suzanne M. Sinke, "Give Us This Day: Dutch Immigrant Women in Two Protestant Denominations," *Amerikastudien* 38, no. 3 (1993): 423–39.

1. Robert Swierenga stresses the continuity of the Dutch Calvinists as a group compared to integration of Dutch Jews and Catholics into the American scene in "Religion and Immigration Behavior: The Dutch Experience," in *Belief and Behavior,* ed. Philip R. Vandermeer and Robert P. Swierenga (New Brunswick: Rutgers University Press, 1991), pp. 164–88. It is also one of the main points in Kroes, *Persistence of Ethnicity.*
2. See Robert P. Swierenga and Harry S. Stout, "Dutch Immigration in the Nineteenth Century, 1820–1877: A Quantitative Overview," *Indiana Social Studies Quarterly* 28 (Autumn 1975). See also Pieter Stokvis, *De Nederlandse Trek Naar Amerika, 1846–1847* (Leiden: Universitaire Pers, 1977).
3. For an more detailed description of the theoretical issues involved see Bratt, *Dutch Calvinism in Modern America,* pp. 37–43. See also Peter De Klerk and Richard R. De Ridder, eds., *Perspectives on the Christian Reformed Church* (Grand Rapids: Baker Book House, 1983), particularly the articles by Doede Nauta ("The Gereformeerde Kerken in Nederland and the Christian Reformed Church") and Willem van 't Spijker ("The Christian Reformed Church and the Christelijke Gereformeerde Kerken in Nederland").
4. Lubbigje Schaapman, Salida, Calif., to Willamientje Beltman, 19 Mar. 1911, HH, their translation.
5. Religious publications often wrote on how home devotions should be organized. The article "Het Huisgezin en de Huiselijke Dienst" in *De Gereformeerde Amerikaan,* for example, noted that prayers before the family should not be too long, thoughtful, and spoken rather than recited formally (P. Jonker, Apr. 1907, pp. 145–50).
6. Tape 1092, PJM.
7. "Diary of Mrs. Gezina Visscher," p. 68.
8. Etje Houwerzijl, Byron Center, Mich., to Mother, 13 Apr. 1923, HH.
9. In *The Banner,* 19 Mar. 1914, the church news section included a list of persons ill or families who had lost a loved one, followed by "Let our prayers ascend for all those bereaved and afflicted. May the chastening rod be sanctified to our hearts and removed in God's favor" (p. 199).
10. Anja Kuijt, Chicago, to Gerrit [Kuijt] and Letha [Retel], Aug. 1908, HH.
11. Tape 1035, PJM.
12. Geertje Ruisch, Alton, Iowa, to friend, 19 Apr. 1885, HH. See also Geertje Schuiling, [Manhattan, Mont.], to brother and sister, [10 Feb. 1901, 22 June 1902, 24 June 1908], Hoogland Collection, RL. Each time she mentions it is Sunday.
13. Anje Nieveen Mulder, in a letter to her uncle and family written from Stuttgart, Kans., in Mar. 1889, wrote: "We live 5 miles from the Dutch church where Ds. Scholten is . . . Father and Mother are 36 miles from the station and we are only 5 that makes quite a difference especially when one is alone" (HH).

14. Trijntje Kooiman, Orange City, Iowa, to Anna de Vries, 16 Jan. 1910, HH.

15. Rubingh collection. Letter from Wildervank, 24 Mar. 1898, HH.

16. Tape 1018, PJM.

17. Dina Maria Oggel, Pella, Iowa, to brother and sister, 17 Dec. 1894, HH.

18. Tape 1008, PJM.

19. Maartje Lautenbach [Zondervan], Paterson, N.J., to brother and sister, Tzummarum, Friesland, 19 Dec. 1909, in Brinks, *Dutch American Voices*, p. 301.

20. "Douglas Park News," *The Banner*, 6 Apr. 1916, p. 229.

21. "De Westfield Zendingsfeest," *De Hope*, 22 July 1919, p. 8.

22. An editorial in the denominational press noted that in 1915 there were about two hundred Ladies' Aids or Dorcas Societies in the Christian Reformed Church (*The Banner*, 29 Apr. 1915, p. 264). The reports from various churches in *The Banner* continued to note men appearing at the groups, in particular men serving to lead women's bible studies. For example, see 4 Feb. 1915 "Holland Notes": "The Young Ladies' Sewing Circle of the 9th St. church held its annual social meeting upon the evening of Jan. 14. The pastor was the only gentleman present." Later in the article there is a report of three men giving speeches at the twentieth anniversary of the Ladies' Aid.

23. He and others in this endeavor saw their work as creating a new "city on a hill," and the similarities to early Puritan migration to America were generally striking. Within four years of initial settlement, Van Raalte pushed his Holland, Michigan, congregation to pledge 15 percent of church revenue for foreign missions and 50 percent for domestic missions. In the late 1860s, Van Raalte took his family and began an (unsuccessful) mission in Amelia County, Virginia (Samuel M. Zwemer, *The Ship That Sailed and the Keel That Never Kissed the Sea* [n.p.: Board of Domestic Missions, RCA (1947)], p. 12).

24. Christine van Raalte Gilmore, Amelia, Va., to Ben and D. B. K. (Brothers), 31 May 1869, Christine van Raalte Gilmore Collection (hereafter CvRG Collection), JAH.

25. Christine van Raalte Gilmore does not appear in VandenBerge's *Historical Directory of the Reformed Church in America*. Most personal information about her appears in materials about her father rather than in her own manuscript collection at the Joint Archives of Holland.

26. C. van Raalte Gilmore (in English), to Rev. P. Moerdyke, 11 July 1887, CvRG Collection, JAH.

27. Phelps was himself a missionary pastor to the English-speaking Hope Reformed Church congregation in Holland (Elton J. Bruins, "The Classis of Holland: A Brief History," in *In Christ's Service: The Classis of Holland and Its Congregations 1847–1997* [Holland, Mich.: Classis of Holland Reformed Church in America, 1997], p. 4).

28. "Frances Phelps Otte Writes of Her Life," *Alumni Magazine* (Hope College), Oct. 1950, p. 3.

29. Frances Phelps married John Otte, a doctor who went as a medical missionary to China. They traveled to the Netherlands to drum up financial support for their mission on their way to Amoy in 1887 (Frances Phelps Otte Manuscript Collection, JAH).

30. Speech of Cornelius Vander Meulen to Century Club, 4 Oct. 1965, quoted in Holm, "Biography," CvRG Collection.

31. "Our Lady Principal," *The Anchor*, 14 Jan. 1901 (women's edition), pp. 79–80.

32. Mrs. C. V. R. Gilmore, "The Elizabeth R. Voorhees Dormitory," *The Anchor*, 10 May 1907, p. 29.

33. Eloise Van Heest, "Women's Societies in Holland Classis," in *In Christ's Service: The*

Classis of Holland and Its Congregations 1847–1997 (Holland, Mich.: Classis of Holland Reformed Church in America, 1997), p. 6.

34. CvRG Collection, JAH. See also pamphlet, "The Federation of Women's Societies of the Churches of Holland, Michigan," Board of World Missions Manuscript Collection, folder "Federation of Women's Societies of the Churches of Holland, Michigan, and Vicinity," JAH.

35. *Seventh Annual Report of the Woman's Executive Committee of Domestic Missions of the Reformed Church in America for the Year Ending April 30th, 1890.* (New York: Nathan Brothers, 1890), p. 10.

36. Edith H. Allen, "A Tribute to Mrs. C. V. R. Gilmore," *Golden Years in Miniature: A History of the Women's Board of Domestic Missions of the Reformed Church in America from the time of its Organization in 1882* (n.p.: Women's Board of Domestic Missions of the Reformed Church in America, 1882–1932), p. 22a, JAH.

37. Allen, "Tribute," p. 22b. A report of the Particular Synod of Chicago in 1906 underscored the need for both languages; at that time in this synod two congregations used English exclusively, three had one English service each Sunday (of two or three services), six had one English service monthly, five had English services occasionally, and six used Dutch exclusively (Bruins, "Classis of Holland," p. 4).

38. The annual reports of the Women's Executive Committee give information on their "girl students" regularly from 1897. *Mission Field,* one of the English-language publications, dedicated its May 1899 issue to "girl student work" at Hope College, including a picture of all the female students as well as their principal, Van Raalte Gilmore.

39. See pamphlet, "Federation of Women's Societies of the Churches of Holland, Michigan."

40. Speech of Cornelius Vander Meulen to Century Club, 4 Oct. 1965, quoted in Holm, "Biography," CvRG Collection.

41. Note, for example, the picture accompanying "A Tribute to Mrs. C. V. R. Gilmore" p. 23 of Women's Board of Domestic Missions of the Reformed Church in America, *Golden Years in Miniature.*

42. Obituary of Van Raalte Gilmore, *The Leader* 26 (19 Apr. 1933), in CvRG Collection, JAH.

43. Kate B. Horton, "Zendingswerk door de Vrouwen," *De Hope,* 11 Jan. 1899, p. 1. The series appeared once a month until May, and then Horton continued to publish periodically in the paper.

44. This was comparable to mission publications for other groups which appeared at the same time, with the notable exception that women were neither the publishers nor major authors. See for comparison Lois A. Boyd and R. Douglas Brackenridge, "*Home Mission Monthly* and *Woman's Work for Woman,*" *American Presbyterians* 66 (1988): 273–76.

45. Mrs. L. P. Brink, mission wife for decades, found it difficult to speak to a public audience even in 1946. Only because her husband was dead and hence could not provide the story of the early years himself was she willing to say anything in public at all (Mrs. L. P. Brink, "Memories," in *Navaho and Zuni for Christ: Fifty Years of Indian Missions,* ed., John C. De Korne [Grand Rapids: Christian Reformed Board of Missions, 1947] p. 191).

46. See, for example, *Fifth Annual Report of the Woman's Executive Committee of Domestic Missions of the Reformed Church in America for the Year Ending April 30th, 1888* (New York: Nathan Brothers, 1888), pp. 23, 75.

47. *Eleventh Annual Report of the Woman's Executive Committee of the Board of Domestic Missions of the Reformed Church in America for the Year Ending April 30th, 1894* (New York: Lotus Press, 1894), pp. 13, 14; "Indian Missions," *Golden Years in Miniature,* pp. 50–51.

48. "Indian Missions," *Golden Years in Miniature,* pp. 49–60. Other Dutch American women served shorter terms (less than five years) at the missions. For example, Cornelia F. Bedell in *Fifty Years with America's First Families: A Brief History of the Indian Work of the Women's Board of Domestic Missions of the Reformed Church in America,* pamphlet (n.d., WBDMRCA) noted the presence of Nellie Rylaarsdan of Grand Rapids at the Comanche Mission, assisting Jennie Dubbink (p. 12).

49. While the Dutch-descended were also active in the mission to Kentucky hill people, this gained somewhat less public attention. Church women's mission groups also tended to give more to the Indian category; see *Thirty-First Annual Report of the Women's Board of Domestic Missions of the Reformed Church in America for the Year Ending April 30th, 1914* ([New York]: Reformed Press, 1914); and *Thirty-Fourth Annual Report of the Women's Board of Domestic Missions of the Reformed Church in America for the Year Ending April thirtieth 1917* ([New York]: Reformed Press, 1917).

50. The Dutch as well as the American flag flew at Women's Board of Domestic Missions (RCA) annual meetings for several years. See, for example, *Eleventh Annual Report of the Woman's Executive Committee of the Board of Domestic Missions of the Reformed Church in America for the Year Ending April 30th, 1894* (New York: Lotus Press, 1894), p. 5, when they report the American flag at the pulpit and the Dutch flag across the gallery, along with an orange streamer; and *Twenty-Sixth Annual Report of the Women's Executive Committee of the Board of Domestic Missions of the Reformed Church in America for the Year Ending April Thirtieth, 1909* (New York: Reformed Church in America, 1909), p. 8, when both flags were flown on one pole with the Dutch one below. The presence of the flags counterbalanced other aspects of the conventions. In 1894, Rev. Henry Dubois Mulford gave a speech entitled "The Hollander as an American Christian," noting that the colonial Dutch had taken much too long to switch languages and that this new immigrant group should not repeat the mistake. The following address by Rev. William Elliot Griffis, "The Hollander as Citizen," noted generally positive characteristics associated with the colonial Dutch which still held true—"firm and staunch, but conservative. . . . Tolerance had always been one of their virtues" (p. 7).

51. Rev. J[ohn] Dolfin, *Bringing the Gospel in Hogan and Pueblo* (Grand Rapids: Van Noord Book and Publishing Co., 1921), pp. 30–31.

52. "Zending onder de Indianen," *De Heidenwereld* 1 (Jan. 1897), p. 45.

53. Dick Halsema describes the early phases as (1) special committee, (2) classical responsibility with denominational supervision, and (3) independent classical work with minimal denominational supervision (Dick Lucas Van Halsema, "The Rise of Home Missions in the Christian Reformed Church, 1857 to the Present" [S.T.M. thesis, Union Theological Seminary, 1953]). Notably, neither Halsema nor Scott Hoezee and Christopher H. Meehan in *Flourishing in the Land: A Hundred-Year History of Christian Reformed Missions in North America* (Grand Rapids: Eerdmans, 1996) discuss any women's mission organizations, though individual church histories and Dutch American papers indicated there were some.

54. "The Indian Missions Committee," *The Banner,* 15 Feb. 1917.

55. "Diary of Mrs. Gezina Visscher."

56. Annual reports from the various women's auxiliaries appeared at times in the annual reports of the Women's Executive Board of Domestic Missions of the RCA. In 1890 the Ladies Prayer Meeting of the First Reformed of Grand Rapids, Michigan, reported "We now follow largely the programmes given in the *Mission Field.* The ladies engage freely in prayer and in conversation during the bible readings, and we greatly prize the opportunity we have there for prayer and conference" (*Seventh Annual Report of the Woman's Executive Commit-*

tee of Domestic Missions of the Reformed Church in America for the Year Ending April 30th 1890 [New York: Nathan Brothers, 1890], pp. 47, 54).

57. Records of the Women's Missionary Society, First Reformed Church, Holland, Mich., Manuscript Collection, JAH.

58. "Notulen Boek der Vrouwen Zendings Vereeniging van de Gereformeerde Gemeente te Ebenezer," [1904–9], JAH.

59. See Hill, *World Their Household*, p. 94.

60. Mr. C. Dosker, *Mothers and Missions* (Detroit: Friesema Bros., 1911), p. 2.

61. Dosker, *Mothers and Missions*, p. 13.

62. Dosker, *Mothers and Missions*, p. 8.

63. The examples of the sufferings of women in foreign lands (foot binding, child marriage, suttee, etc.) followed the pattern described as "evangelical ethnologies" by Brumberg in "Zenanas and Girlless Villages."

64. See, for example, the discussion of the biblical story of Lydia in the "Notulen Boek . . . Ebenezer," 1909.

65. Reports of mission festivals were regular fare in the church news section of *De Hope* in the late 1910s. In the 1890s many societies reported to the Women's Executive Board of *paas* (Easter) festivals used for mission fund-raising whereas later they generally used the title *Zendingsfeest* (mission festival). On the *paas* festivals see, for example, *Fifteenth Annual Report of the Women's Executive Committee of the Board of Domestic Missions of the Reformed Church in America for the Year Ending April Thirtieth, 1898* (New York: Press of E. Scott, 1898).

66. "Op 's Werelds Tooneel," *De Gereformeerde Amerikaan*, Mar. 1907, pp. 108–9.

67. See "The Church Census of 1906," *The Banner*, 9 Sept. 1909, pp. 588–89.

68. Editorial, *The Banner*, 3 Oct. 1918, p. 708. The Christian Reformed writer noted that this balance was encouraging "in view of the common complaint that women predominate in our American church life."

69. For such articles, see, for example, "The Men and Religion Movement," *The Banner*, 3 Nov. 1910, pp. 692–93, or "Men in the Church," *The Banner*, 16 July 1914, pp. 457–58.

70. Nieland, *'n fonnie bisnis*, p. 111.

71. Klaaske Noorda Heller, Oak Harbor, Wash., to Noorda Family, Ulrum, Groningen, 1909, in Brinks, *Dutch American Voices*, p. 171.

72. The church charged deacons not only with looking after basic physical needs of parishioners but also with assisting them emotionally. For an example of this charge see Henry Beets, "The Diaconate," manuscript, 1933, Henry Beets Collection, HH. Beets was the author of the most definitive work on the Christian Reformed Church in the early twentieth century, *De Christelijke Gereformeerde Kerk in Noord Amerika: Zestig Jaren van Strijd en Zegen* (Grand Rapids: Grand Rapids Printing Co., 1918).

73. "Heritage of Faithfulness," p. 14.

74. The Synod of Dordrecht (1607) initially laid out these steps for discipline.

75. One such letter read: "To the . . . Church at . . . Dear Brethren: This certifies that . . . , wife of . . . , is a member in full communion of the . . . Church of . . . in good and regular standing; as such she is, at her own request, dismissed for the purpose of connecting herself with our sister Church in . . . , to whose Christian fellowship and confidence she is hereby affectionately commended; and when received by you, her particular relation to this Church shall cease [Place, Date, Signature on behalf of Consistory]" (New Jersey Church, 1885, HH).

76. An 1888 case from a Wisconsin Reformed Church is particularly insightful. A young widow confessed to the consistory that she had not lived "Christian" in her marriage. The

consistory asked her to make this confession before the congregation, but she refused. The consistory reflected on this and agreed to let her join without public confession (HH).

77. One condition of access was anonymity. All but one of the consistories kept minutes in Dutch; one other switched to English very late in the period. The records are found at Heritage Hall, Calvin College, and the Joint Archives of Holland [Michigan].

78. In one Michigan church the consistory tried to wrest a confession out of a couple whose child was "a few days" early. The couple refused, and the consistory let the matter drop (HH).

79. For an overview on "American" attitudes see D'Emilio and Freedman *Intimate Matters,* especially the chapter "Within the Family." For an example of Dutch American attitudes see "Lust Not," *The Banner of Truth,* Mar. 1886, pp. 133–36, which stresses this is a problem for both men and women.

80. Christian Reformed Church, HH.

81. "Op 's Werelds Tooneel," *De Gereformeerde Amerikaan,* Mar. 1911, p. 140.

82. Gerhardus Rosenboom, Grand Rapids, Mich., to Jacobus Schoonbeek, Oude Pekela [Groningen], 21 Feb. 1888, HH, their translation. Also printed in Brinks, *Dutch American Voices,* pp. 278–79.

83. Brinks (editor of the letter collection) speculated that the lack of assistance from the most "pious" members of the family, particularly in taking care of the mentally impaired sibling, led one of Pul's children to distance himself both from the family and from any ethnic connections (*Dutch American Voices,* p. 254).

84. One case which appeared in the records of the Holland Home, which also looked into the background of its residents, indicated that a Mr. B had been censured by his church for beating his wife and "disorderly family life" and when he persisted in this behavior he was excommunicated (HUBA, Board minutes, 3 Sept. 1896, p. 33).

85. This stands in sharp contrast to the type of alliance between mothers and social workers which Linda Gordon portrays in *Heroes of Their Own Lives: The Politics and History of Family Violence* (New York: Viking, 1988).

86. Christian Reformed congregation, HH.

87. Several of the consistories were obsessed with Sunday observance, reprimanding people for almost any activity aside from going to church, even if this was done between church services: visiting someone at the hospital, playing outside, cooking, or mowing the lawn.

88. A Michigan consistory sharply upbraided Mrs. N for living apart from her husband or, as the case was, refusing to go back to him after he got out of prison. She made her living working in a hotel three days a week, including Sunday. The consistory frowned upon her doing this work at all, but especially on Sunday. They reported "nothing good can come of the children," and sent Mrs. N's case to Classis as a step toward excommunication (Christian Reformed congregation, case from 1903; HH).

89. Christian Reformed congregation, HH.

90. For information on the social hygiene movement, which fought venereal disease, see D'Emilio and Freedman, *Intimate Matters,* pp. 204–8.

91. HH.

92. Christian Reformed congregation in Michigan, 1902, HH.

93. In both Reformed and Christian Reformed cases, consistories asked Classis for advice concerning matters of importance, though they defined what was important differently. The major distinction was that in the Reformed Church Classis often reported back that they should not be bothered with that issue, which belonged at the congregation level. When women got the vote in one Reformed Church congregation in 1915, Classis wrote that the

matter "may and ought to be left to the Consistory and Church" (*Minutes of the Classis of Wisconsin*, Apr. 1915).

94. *Minutes of the Classis of Wisconsin*, Apr. 1909. A similar case occurred in an Illinois Reformed church, where the consistory admitted a man into membership in 1893 despite his marital separation. His wife refused to leave the Netherlands with him, and hence she received all blame and was charged with desertion (JAH).

95. *Acts and Proceedings of the General Synod of the Reformed Church in America*, vol. 20, June 1906.

96. West Michigan consistory notes, copied in minister's personal papers, HH. It is impossible from this to determine whether the woman was using a "romantic" turn-of-the-century argument about love in a marriage or whether she was referring to "Christian love for one another," to which consistories exhorted abusive husbands.

97. For example, an article in *De Grondwet*, "Echtscheiding."

98. This article refers to a meeting in Leeuwarden, Friesland (Netherlands). Most of the examples below refer to the Synod within the United States.

99. *The Banner*, 8 July 1920, pp. 422–23.

100. I did not find this trend in Reformed Church records. There the change may have occurred somewhat earlier, since divorce cases appear more often at an earlier date.

101. In terms of information, for example, *De Gereformeerde Amerikaan* warned women against the thoughts of Emma Goldman (Dec. 1914, p. 557) and Mary Baker Eddy (Dec. 1910, p. 611).

102. Cases from an Illinois and a Michigan Christian Reformed church, HH; Reformed Church congregation in Illinois, JAH.

103. For a discussion of mother's pensions see Ladd-Taylor, *Mother Work*, chap. 5. See also Theda Skocpol, *Protecting Soldiers and Mothers: The Politics of Social Provision in the United States, 1870s-1920s* (Cambridge: Harvard University Press, 1992).

104. Etje Houwerzijl, Byron Center, Mich., to family, 3 June 1923. Other information from letters in Houwerzijl collection, HH.

105. See, for example, "De Predikantsvrouw," *De Gereformeerde Amerikaan*, July 1908, p. 437.

106. This was the case in a fictional account of Cornelia De Bey's life, in which the character Cornelia explained why she couldn't go to the deacons in her church when she saw a family without coal for the night: "They'd have to have a meeting, and then they'd have to investigate, and they'd talk for a month!" (Perkins, *Cornelia*, p. 48).

107. HH, JAH; examples taken from Michigan, Illinois, and Wisconsin churches.

108. HH, JAH; examples from New Jersey, Michigan, Illinois, and Iowa.

109. After considerable haggling, a western Michigan consistory agreed to pay tuition for the children of Widow K to go to an English-language Christian school, HH.

110. "Notulen der Commissie der Kas tot ondersteuning van Emeriti Predikanten en Predikantsweduwen en weezen van de H. C. G. Kerk in N. Amerika," pp. 75–76, HH. For an overview of the organization see "Brief History of the Ministers' Pension Fund, 1869–1978," manuscript, HH.

111. Christian Reformed church in Michigan, HH.

112. One example of a general view of poverty appears in "Van 't een op 't ander," *De Gereformeerde Amerikaan*, Mar. 1907, p. 138: "Be careful not to lay the blame for your poverty on something or someone else. Because: 1. God did not create any poor people; 2. There may be no poor among his people; 3. Poverty comes through sin and thus is our own fault."

113. I draw this conclusion on the basis of the frequency with which widows and their children receive visits to check their conduct in comparison with others. Whether the over-representation of widows' children among those who went "wrong" is due to this scrutiny or due to the vicissitudes of living without a father in a highly patriarchal culture remains unclear.

114. Thus, using the terminology of Sara Evans and Harry Boyte, the Reformed Church provided more "free spaces" for women to develop their abilities (*Free Spaces: The Sources of Democratic Change in America* [New York: Harper & Row, 1986]).

115. See, for example, P. Jonker, "Co-education," *De Gereformeerde Amerikaan*, Aug. 1911, sec. Gemeenschapsleven, pp. 376–84.

116. See Gabaccia, *From the Other Side*, p. 83.

Conclusion

1. Donna Gabaccia illustrated that in the titles of two of her works: "Immigrant Women: Nowhere at Home," and her subsequent essay collection *Seeking Common Ground.*

2. See in particular Christiane Harzig, "The Ethnic Female Public Sphere: German-American Women in Turn-of-the-Century Chicago," in *Midwestern Women: Work, Community, and Leadership at the Crossroads,* ed. Lucy Eldersveld Murphy and Wendy Hamand Vent (Bloomington: Indiana University Press, 1997), p. 142.

3. See Gjerde, *Minds of the West,* part 3.

4. See Salamon, *Prairie Patrimony.* The pattern she describes as typically German would also apply for the most part to the Dutch.

5. On the role of strong versus weak state models and its importance for women's activism in the Progressive era see Sklar, "Historical Foundations of Women's Power in the Creation of the American Welfare State."

6. As land in the United States became scarcer and more expensive, increasing numbers of Dutch migrants opted for Canada. This was especially the case after World War I, when quota legislation went into effect in the United States. While migration generally was going down, this still resulted over time in a Dutch North American community which spanned the northern border of the United States.

7. Such adaptation in this period was common for other groups in the Midwest as well, for example, the need for newcomers to learn Norwegian in order to live and do business in part of rural Wisconsin discussed in Pederson, *Between Memory and Reality,* p. 37.

8. Walter Kamphoefner used this phrase in his comments on a related paper at the Social Science History Association meeting, Washington, D.C., 1997. This evaluation was one I knew well from my Dutch American relatives in the late twentieth century.

9. Brinks, "Impressions of the 'Old' World."

Index

SUZANNE M. SINKE has roots in the Dutch provinces of Zeeland and Friesland. She is an associate professor of history at Florida State University and the co-editor of *A Century of European Migrations, 1830–1930*. She is also the author of numerous articles on immigrant women.

Statue of Liberty–Ellis Island Centennial Series

The University of Illinois Press
is a founding member of the
Association of American University Presses.

Composed in 10.5/12.5 Minion
with Fenice display
by Jim Proefrock
at the University of Illinois Press
Manufactured by Thomson-Shore, Inc.

University of Illinois Press
1325 South Oak Street
Champaign, IL 61820-6903
www.press.uillinois.edu